Attempting to Bring the Gospel Home

Attempting to Bring the Gospel Home

Scottish Missions to Palestine, 1839-1917

Michael Marten

Tauris Academic Studies
LONDON • NEW YORK

Published in 2006 by Tauris Academic Studies.
An imprint of I.B. Tauris & Co Ltd
6 Salem Road, London W2 4BU
175 Fifth Avenue, New York NY 10010
www.ibtauris.com

In the United States of America and Canada distributed by
Palgrave Macmillan a division of St. Martin's Press
175 Fifth Avenue, New York NY 10010

ISBN 1 85043 983 4
EAN 978 1 85043 983 7

A full CIP record for this book is available from the British Library
A full CIP record is available from the Library of Congress

Library of Congress Catalog Card Number: available

Printed and bound in Great Britain by TJ International Ltd, Padstow, Cornwall from
camera-ready copy edited and supplied by the author

Contents

Figures

Referencing and Abbreviations

Scottish ecclesiastical sources

References are generally in two parts: a source identifier, and a date. If no date is available an estimation based on the previous and subsequent items is given.

CS-Accounts yyyy: pp	Church of Scotland General Assembly accounts
CS-GA yyyy: pp	Church of Scotland General Assembly minutes/proceedings
CS-GA-JMC yyyy: pp	Church of Scotland General Assembly Jewish Mission Committee report
CS-JMC dd.mm.yyyy	Church of Scotland Jewish Mission Committee minutes
CS-LW mm.yyyy: pp	Church of Scotland *Life and Work* (magazine)
CS-WAJM dd.mm.yyyy	Church of Scotland Women's Association for Jewish Mission minutes
FC-GA yyyy: pp	Free Church of Scotland General Assembly minutes/proceedings
FC-GA-JMC yyyy	Free Church of Scotland General Assembly Jewish Mission Committee report
FC-GA-WJMA yyyy: pp	Free Church of Scotland General Assembly Women's Jewish Missionary Association report
FC-JMC dd.mm.yyyy	Free Church of Scotland Jewish Mission Committee minutes
FC-MMR mm.yyyy: pp	Free Church of Scotland *Monthly and Missionary Record* (magazine)
FC-WJMA dd.mm.yyyy	Free Church of Scotland Women's Jewish Missions Association minutes
UFC-CCJ dd.mm.yyyy	United Free Church of Scotland Colonial, Continental and Jewish Committee minutes
UFC-GA yyyy: pp	United Free Church of Scotland General Assembly proceedings
UFC-JMC dd.mm.yyyy	United Free Church of Scotland Jewish Mission Committee Minutes
UFC-MR mm.yyyy: pp	United Free Church of Scotland *Missionary Record* (magazine)
UFC-WJMA dd.mm.yyyy	United Free Church of Scotland Women's Jewish Missionary Association minutes
UPC-GMBM dd.mm.yyyy	United Presbyterian Church General Minute Book – Missions
UPC-Synod yyyy: pp	United Presbyterian Church Synod proceedings

Jewish Mission Committee minutes are referenced as Church of Scotland minutes until 31.5.1843 and from then as Church of Scotland or Free Church of Scotland minutes. From 1900, when the Free Church of Scotland and United Presbyterian Church united, the minutes are referred to as the United Free Church of Scotland minutes.

National Library of Scotland, Edinburgh, Scotland (manuscript sources)
Manuscripts sourced from the NLS are identified with NLS. Examples:
NLS Acc 10139(i) or NLS Acc 4499(9): Paterson diary 20.10.1900

Biblical references
Biblical references or quotations, unless reproduced from other sources, are from the New
Revised Standard Version published by Collins, London, 1989 (abbreviated as NRSV).
Abbreviations of biblical books follow generally accepted norms.

Abbreviations

AIU	Alliance Israélite Universelle
CCJ	Colonial, Continental and Jewish Committee
CS	Church of Scotland (also known as the Auld Kirk)
EMMS	Edinburgh Medical Missionary Society
FC	Free Church of Scotland (also known as the Free Kirk)
FMC	Foreign Missions Committee
GA	General Assembly
JMC	Jewish Mission Committee
LJS	London Jews Society (London Society for the Conversion of the Jews)
LW	Life and Work (Church of Scotland magazine)
MMR	Monthly and Missionary Record of the Free Church of Scotland
MR	Missionary Record of the United Free Church of Scotland
PCI	Presbyterian Church of Ireland
SSCI	Scottish Society for the Conversion of Israel
UFC	United Free Church of Scotland (also known as the United Free Kirk)
UPC	United Presbyterian Church of Scotland

Note that Jewish Mission Committees were sometimes described in other terms, such as
the 'Committee for Conversion of the Jews'. For simplicity, 'Jewish Mission Committee'
is always used here except for the period 1910-1913, when the United Free Church
amalgamated it with the Colonial and Continental Committees.

Names; transliteration; population statistics; money
Names of individuals commonly found in western literature appear in their familiar Latin
form, where applicable using the form most often used by the individuals themselves;
sometimes this will result in more than one form of a name being used for the same
person when referring to different sources. Place names follow two patterns: when
using names quoted in source documents that are obvious even if the spelling is not in
use today (such as Beyrout), no further explanation is given, but when a place name is
not immediately apparent because the name now in use is different or the name used is
perhaps slightly obscure, I have tried, where possible, to provide a modern equivalent (e.g.
Smyrna/Izmir). The use of a particular name or spelling does not convey any political

meaning related to contemporary conflicts in the Middle East. This applies in particular to the use of the term 'Israel' which when used in the 19th century missionary context was always a descriptor for Jews and was not used to denote a political or geographic entity; equally, 'Israelite' is used as it usually is in Christian Biblical studies, to refer to the 'people of the kingdom of Israel' or 'Jews', as given in various English translations of the Biblical texts. For place names, where relevant, I have generally used the transliterations in Khalidi's survey of destroyed Palestinian towns and villages.[1]

For transliteration of other Arabic names or words, I have used a simplified system based upon that of the *International Journal of Middle East Studies*. Arabic and other foreign language terms in common use for which no translation is necessary in this context are italicised (e.g. *tanzimat*).

Referring to churches, the term 'Eastern' is used to refer to all ancient Chalcedonian and non-Chalcedonian churches of the Middle East. The missionaries themselves usually omitted to define which ecclesiastical group they were writing about, regularly using generic terms such as 'Eastern churches'. Although it may occasionally be possible to work out the grouping being discussed on the basis of traditions or geography, on the whole, for the purposes of analysis of the missionaries' work, it is not necessary to pursue this. Indeed, their generalisations about 'Eastern churches' say much about their understanding of the context they were in, a topic that is developed further in the text.

Population statistics for the 19th century Ottoman Empire are notoriously difficult to ascertain with any degree of certainty. In many regions regular statistics were not kept, estimates from foreigners often varied widely rendering most of them of limited use, and figures given by religious communities were anything but unbiased: many groups would have sought to give as high or low a figure for their population grouping as they thought would suit their purposes. I have tended to rely mostly, but not exclusively, on Courbage and Fargues' work.[2]

The money used in the Levant varied from one region to the next, as well as changing over various periods. The British pound, by far the most important international currency in the 19th century, is used where possible.[3] Denominations used in the region included British pounds, American dollars, French Napoleons, Turkish gold pounds etc., as well as various more local currencies. Where possible and/or desirable, I have attempted to provide a conversion into sterling, though the fluctuating values of the various denominations at times enables (at best) only a very rough approximation; where a conversion is given in the primary source material, it is quoted in the assumption that it will be reasonably accurate. The changes in the value of sterling itself over time are only relevant, as far as this text is concerned, to an understanding of the relative fall in donations: Max Warren gives an indication that 'what would have cost £1 in 1815, 1840, 1880 and 1910 would cost about £3. 5s. 8d., £4. 1s. 6d., £4. 19s. 5d. and £5 8s. 7d. respectively today [i.e. 1967]' though he also notes that consumer prices generally fell between 1815 and 1910.[4] There have been a number of attempts made to work through the multitudinous difficulties in using varied currencies and establishing comparisons and calculations, of which I have found the work by Şevket Pamuk,[5] particularly helpful. Issawi gives a general valuation of one pound for 5 dollars, 10 gold rubles, 20 marks, or 25 francs throughout the period 1800-1914,[6] and for the purposes of this work, that serves as a useful measure.

Confusion can arise over the use of descriptors for missions: the book describes mostly 'Jewish missions', which were distinct from 'foreign missions'. I have followed the convention prevalent in Scotland during the period under discussion. When reference is made to 'foreign missions', non-Jewish overseas missions are meant, whilst 'Jewish missions' could be overseas or 'at home'. General discussion of the 'missionary movement' etc., encompasses Jewish and foreign missions, unless otherwise noted.

In referring to the Bible, I have tended to use the dominant Christian term 'Old Testament' rather than 'Hebrew Bible', if for no other reason than that the missionaries themselves tended to use this term. This use signifies no theological or ideological position in terms of Christian-Jewish relations.

[1] Walid Khalidi (ed.), (1992) *All That Remains: The Palestinian Villages Occupied and Depopulated by Israel in 1948*, Washington

[2] Youssef Courbage/Philippe Fargues, (1997) *Christians and Jews under Islam*, London

[3] Appendix 7.2 rounds each amount *down* to the nearest £, though shillings, pennies and farthings are referred to in the text (1 pound consisted of 20 shillings, 1 shilling of 12 pennies, 1 penny of 4 farthings, denoted as £, s, d, f).

[4] Max Warren, (1967) *Social History and Christian Mission*, London: 175

[5] Şevket Pamuk, (1994) 'Money in the Ottoman Empire, 1326-1914' in *An Economic and Social History of the Ottoman Empire, Vol 2: 1600-1914* ed. Halil İnalcik with Donald Quataert, Cambridge, 945-985

[6] Charles Issawi, (1988) *The Fertile Crescent 1800-1914: A Documentary Economic History*, New York, Oxford: viii

Acknowledgements

For financial support at various times in the course of writing this text, I would like to thank the Carnegie Trust of Scotland, the Church of Scotland Israel Centres Committee, my parents William and Gunhild Cummings, the Miss Elizabeth Drummond Trust, the Hope Trust, the North Atlantic Missiology Project, the Spalding Trust, the United Reformed Church Committee for Inter-Faith Relations (Jewish Fund), and the University of Edinburgh's Faculty of Arts.

For help with documentation, I am grateful to the following: Eileen Dickson and her colleagues at New College Library, and Margaret Acton at the Centre for the Study of Christianity in the Non-Western World, both in Edinburgh, who assisted in locating various relatively obscure documents and volumes; Dr Louise Yeoman and her colleagues in the Manuscripts Department of the National Library of Scotland, and the Trustees of the National Library of Scotland for permission to reproduce portions of text; in Israel/Palestine, the Church of Scotland staff, particularly Emma Given, Rev Fred Hibbert, Chris Mottershead and Rev Clarence Musgrave were helpful in tracing certain items and in discussing some of the issues. For assistance in locating certain hard-to-find items, I would like to thank my old friend Dr Guy Marcel Clicqué.

There are a number of people who kindly allowed me to interview them, including descendants of some of the protagonists of this book, as well as others who knew them or have other connections to the missions. I wish to record here my gratitude to these people in allowing me an insight into their lives and their relationships with the people concerned. I have been privileged to be in contact with Dr Peter Green, the late Dr Emrys Thomas, and Mary Torrance, and have had written contact with David Byrne, a grandson of David Torrance. Particular reference must be made to Lydia Dorward – David Torrance's granddaughter – and her husband, Morrison, for their support and helpfulness. The willingness to spend many hours sharing childhood memories and their openness about their family history beyond anything a stranger has any right to expect or ask for, has been very much appreciated.

I am grateful to many people for their help, support and encouragement in my writing of this book. Rev Robin Ross is probably unaware of the great influence his work and thinking had on the early stages of my involvement in the Middle East, but without him, it is unlikely I would ever have considered addressing the topic presented here. The following, all of whom have played a role in one way or another in assisting my work, also deserve particular mention: Alison and David Anderson, the late Professor Alex Carmel, Dr John Chalcraft, my parents, Professor Carole Hillenbrand, David Kerry, Rev John McMahon, Dr Andrew Newman, Dr Anthony O'Mahony, Dr Inger Marie Okkenhaug, Sarah Ridout, Alex Ritchie, Dr Andrew Ross, and Dr Gavin White. Dr Runa Mackay helped, amongst other things, with medical terminology, Dr Andrew Wines (perhaps inadvertently!) encouraged an alternative approach to the issue of narrative, whilst a week working with Peggy Owens on contemporary conflict resolution helped develop thinking on the confrontational model of interaction. Dr Paul Lalor's unrelenting intellectual rigour in offering critiques and suggestions has been much appreciated. Jean Oliver proof-read the text and Julian Hosie prepared it for publication. Alex Wright and Elizabeth Munns of I.B. Tauris have been consistently helpful as the book has moved towards publication. Finally, a rural idyll was offered by Jo Richards towards the end of the writing process when it was most needed.

Above all, my wife, Sigrid, and son, Lennart, deserve my appreciation and thanks: for putting up with the protracted absences: overseas, in libraries, or in my study. Sigrid has seen the book go through a considerable number of permutations, whilst keeping her own demanding work going and providing the family income. She probably knows more than most ministers – even those of the Church of Scotland! – would, should, need or want to know about Scottish missions to the Middle East, having imbibed the themes and thinking that have at times dominated our life together for the last few years. Lennart deserves a special thanks for keeping me firmly rooted in contemporary reality by demanding I play trains, pirates and wizards etc. – this maintains a sense of perspective on real life when 'writing a big book,' as he once described it. This 'big book' is dedicated to Lennart, in the hope that he will grow up approaching all those he encounters with openness coupled with a readiness to understand, appreciate and treasure alternative ways of thinking about and living life.

London, September 2005

1

INTRODUCTION

This book describes the involvement of the Scottish churches in missionary activity to Jews in Palestine between 1839 and 1917, seeking to portray the Scots' understandings of their own role and of the effects of their work.[1] To this end, the sources employed are primarily Scottish. There are limitations involved in using only Scottish sources in that very few 'personal' sources such as letters or diaries remain, the majority of the material being of an 'official' nature, for example, minute books, formal correspondence and reports etc.[2] For the purpose of analysing Scottish perspectives on the work, the views of the receptors, with one or two notable exceptions, are not analysed. Charles Taber clearly states that 'there is often a considerable discrepancy between what missionaries intend to do, think they are doing, and report that they have done, and what actually takes place on the field as understood by the missionaries' audiences' and that 'the methods of missionaries and the content of their message were understood quite differently by missionaries and their audiences, and different implications were drawn from them'.[3] The aim here is to examine primarily the intentions, the actions and the reporting of the missionaries' activity, and from that try to form a picture of their perception of their thinking and actions. This is by no means to deny agency on the part of the receptors: far from it, as a description of such agency is an essential part of the history of a mission. However, in attempting to understand what the Scots were trying to do, the focus is on their perspectives, and to that end, their descriptions of their work, the reports they gave, and the understandings of their work in Scotland are accorded priority here. These are the parameters I will be using in the description and analysis of this aspect of Scottish mission history.[4]

In terms of their work in the region, it can be characterised in a number of ways. Most prominently, the main aspects I will focus on in presenting this under-researched area of Scottish mission history include competition and co-operation with other agencies, an inability to comprehend or empathise with understandings not their own, and perseverance in the face of apparent failure.

Very little has been written on Scottish missions in 19th and 20th century Palestine: publications by the churches from the early 20th century were intended to raise funds for existing work – and are therefore of dubious value for presenting a historical record that can be analysed and understood in a meaningful way today – and occasional items that are more recent tend to suffer from a lack of a sound historical basis, oversimplification or sweeping generalisations.[5] As work on the Anglican church and missions prior to the Mandate era is beginning to grow in volume,[6] so it is hoped that this book represents the emergence of similar work on Scottish involvement in Palestine.

Missions and mission history

Scottish missionaries' efforts directed to the Jews of Palestine generally came under the auspices of Jewish Mission Committees (JMC). Missions to Jews has been an extremely delicate topic, particularly since the Second World War and the recognition by most Western Christian churches of a level of complicity (or worse) in the Nazi Holocaust, and prior to that, the persecution of Jews over many centuries, particularly in Europe. Prosecuting such missions is now generally frowned upon by most major denominations, such activity as there is being carried out mostly by those on the fringes of the right/evangelical wing of Protestantism.[7] The criticism of contemporary Jewish missions has also been a factor in historical missions to Jews only being addressed in a more systematic and thorough way in recent years, barely being included in the general study of missionary activity. Even now, the discussion of historical missions to the Jews can still be extremely problematic for both Jews and Christians – whether in the West or in the Middle East – given the wider context of a complex and difficult relationship between the two traditions that shows no sign of easing as long as the ongoing political conflict over land in Israel/Palestine continues.[8] In this context, the model for engaging in historical research of missions suggested by Andreas Feldtkeller is helpful: mission activity may be a taboo, but mission history is not.[9] He seeks to uncover the multi-facetted nature of mission history, seeing it as an effort to seek justice/righteousness (*Gerechtigkeit*) in a specific political and cultural context: mission history, then, is a very human history of administration and communication, of concerns about finance, buildings, human and material resources, and quantifiable successes and failures. Mission history needs to be a dialectic: whilst the missionaries may have had, in their own perspective, altruistic or 'heavenly' aims, their actions were very much 'earthly' ones, intrinsically connected to the world around them: the world they came from (in the case of this study, a major imperial power) and the world they were going to (here: Palestine, an Ottoman-controlled territory). This study therefore attempts to portray and understand the missionaries' motivations within their own (colonial) framework, judging them by their own criteria for success, whilst seeking to place this narrative within the wider discourse of nineteenth century missionary activity and late Ottoman Palestine.

The Scottish churches and missionary activity

All but one of the missions in the Levant that emanated from the Scottish churches were directed at converting Jews; this book addresses these Jewish missions. Missionary motivation in Scotland and specifically the motivation for Jewish missionary activity need to be understood before examining the missionaries' activities.

The nineteenth century, imperialism, and missionary motivation

The nineteenth century is often seen as the great era of Western missionary motivation. There are a number of factors that led to this, and although the development of missions in Scotland began slightly later than those in England, enthusiasm for missions quickly took hold and defined several generations of Scottish church members, particularly in the Presbyterian churches that this book is examining. The wider context for the Scottish missionary effort was the general Western, and particularly the British, approach to mission activity.

British and Western missions in the nineteenth century

Stephen Neill states that although Christianity had spread beyond Europe, in 1800 it was not certain that Christianity would become a world religion.[10] The overwhelming incursion of North America by mostly European immigrants and the decimation of the Native American population meant that Christianity's place as the dominant religious system was assured there. In South America, Christianity's place was also secure due to the ruling classes' dominance of political, social and religious life, even if the penetration of the European religious system was not as deep as that of the North. However, in other regions of the world, such dominance was not assured: countries in the Far East had succeeded in either persecuting or evicting any who came as missionaries, India's ruling caste was largely untouched by Christian thought, there had been no significant conversion of Muslims anywhere, and in Africa, the tropical climate mitigated against anything more than symbolic European settlements in coastal areas. Although missions had existed, their ineffectiveness is ascribed by Neill to the relative weakness of Europe as a whole. With 'the age of revolution',[11] changes began that led to the possibility of European dominance throughout the world. The advent of European colonialism, heralded by Joseph François Dupleix and first translated into reality by the British in India, coupled with improvements in communications and transportation in the course of the industrial revolution (rail, post, telegraph etc.), led to the possibility of exploiting natural resources in a way previously not imagined ('the age of capital'). Controlling the sources of natural riches led to what Hobsbawm describes as 'areas of "dependent economy"' which served the 'world economy of the European maritime states'.[12] Maintaining the supply of raw materials that enabled industrialists to increase their profits by creating demand for items previously not thought of as necessary, items affordable by a greater proportion of the population than had hitherto been able to acquire such possessions, was part of the support the state needed to provide in order to maintain economic, and therefore political, pre-eminence in a European (and global) context.[13] Furthermore, domination over countries and territories abroad was seen by many not only as economically necessary, but as morally correct: communicating the values and norms of western 'Christian' society became an imperative of the new middle-classes ('the age of empire').[14] Jongeneel's *chronologia missionaria* describes this pre-imperial to imperial change as 'the recognition of the difference between mission from a minority position (no political power) and mission from a majority position (confusion of throne and altar)'.[15]

This came about not least through the parallel religious awakening in most denominations. The Evangelical Revival of the Protestant churches across Europe, whether in Germany, Scandinavia, or Britain, led to an unprecedented level of missionary fervour.[16] Personal conversion and holiness were coupled with an intense sense of civic responsibility, and this manifested itself in social concern (e.g. the anti-slavery movement) and missionary zeal. The appearance of non-denominational missionary societies across Europe was a new phenomenon, and this activity led to the unprecedented expansion of missionary influence around the globe, the fast new communications systems and existing or developing colonial structures facilitating such movements and their support.[17]

The Scottish ecclesial context and missionary endeavour

In the Scottish context, as noted above, the impetus for missionary activity did not come about quite as smoothly as in England.[18] Indeed, 1796 saw a motion in the Church of Scotland General Assembly for missionary work overseas defeated.[19] This might surprise, given that the preamble to the 1560 Scots Confession,[20] still an articulate expression of belief at this time,[21] demanded the preaching of the Gospel throughout the world, and article XVI even stated that,

> Out of the quhilk Kirk, there is nouther lyfe, nor eternall felicitie. And therefore we utterly abhorre the blasphemie of them that affirme, that men quhilk live according to equitie and justice, sal be saved, quhat Religioun that ever they have professed. For as without *Christ Jesus* there is nouther life nor salvation; so sal there nane be participant thereof, bok sik as the Father hes given unto his Sonne *Christ Jesus*, and they that in time cum unto him, avowe his doctrine, and beleeve into him, we comprehend the children with the faithful parentes.[22]

This clear statement of the power to exclude those of differing beliefs from the 'lyfe ... [and] eternall felicitie' to be found in the church implies the need to bring others into that circle. Although it derives its position from John Calvin's deeply Christocentric theology, the Confession as a whole went further than Calvin in its exclusiveness, who apparently found its biblical harshness unsettling.[23]

However, the Presbyterian churches in Scotland had been through a period of monumental change and upheaval in the eighteenth century, and this situation helps to explain the outcome of this vote against missions. In 1700, Scotland was extremely poor, with virtually no external trade markets.[24] Travel beyond the central region between Glasgow, Edinburgh and the Tay River was arduous and roads existed mostly as tracks (even the Edinburgh to London journey was regarded as being fraught with difficulty). Goods, ideas and education travelled slowly or not at all beyond this area. Crops were destroyed on at least four occasions in the eighteenth century, with consequent hunger in this mostly agricultural setting (in 1800, only 17% of the population of Scotland lived in urban centres of more than 10,000 people[25]). The single most significant event that helped to bring about change was the 1707 union between Scotland and England. With this move, a market for Scotland opened, and trade across the border brought increasing wealth and prosperity, even to the northern areas of Scotland.[26] The industrial era was one in which Scotland could participate fully, exploiting the large-scale industrialisation that the Victorian era brought with it: the natural resources required (principally coal and iron) were plentiful, there were two estuaries – the Forth facing Europe and the Clyde facing America – that were easily connected by rail and water, and the development of rail networks between England and Scotland made the transport of goods and services much more straightforward.[27] Changes in population patterns, with many moving to the new urban centres (partly willingly, partly out of economic necessity), played a substantial role in this economic revival, with a dramatic loss of inhabitants particularly in the Highlands.

This economic change helps explain the church's situation in the eighteenth and nineteenth centuries. The established Church of Scotland was Presbyterian, which in the Scottish context meant that individual parishes elected lay elders and a minister (the chairperson or moderator) to act as the kirk session – the church's governing body. This then sent ministers and representative elders to the local presbytery, which supervised clergy and was the first court of appeal beyond the congregation; it also dealt with local issues that went beyond the parish boundaries of individual congregations. Each presbytery (and until 1925 royal burghs) would send, from its own ranks, ministers and elders to the highest court of the Church, the General Assembly, which met annually, usually in Edinburgh in May, and in smaller 'commission' form at other times. All levels above local church level had, as far as possible, equal numbers of ministers and elders who had equal speaking and decision-making rights (though in the time period covered by this book, they were, of course, all male). This, and the fact that the Moderator of the presbyteries and the General Assembly was only held by any one individual for a year, was intended to ensure openness to change and protest.[28] The Assembly appointed committees to oversee the work of the wider church. Membership of the committees consisted partly of representatives from the individual presbyteries, and partly of people chosen by the Assembly. These committees were answerable to the Assembly, although in practice had considerable leeway to take decisions themselves. This was particularly the case if they were under the influence of strong conveners – who were not subject to the rule regarding one year terms of office, often making them very influential individuals. The committees produced reports on their work for the Assembly; these formed the basis of discussions at the Assembly. Although the Assembly could circumscribe a committee's work, the tenor of a committee's report could, of course, determine the Assembly's decision on an issue. Many perceived this structure to make for a relatively democratic form of church organisation.

Two tendencies dominated the eighteenth century church, the 'Moderate' and the 'Evangelical'. The Moderates, in the ascendant in the early decades of the eighteenth century, in part as a reaction to the bitter feuding and bloodletting of the previous century's religious and political strife, gradually lost ground to the Evangelicals, whose vibrant message of a personal gospel of salvation was more readily received than the steadfastness of the Moderates' message of the importance of reason and sagacity in religion. The Moderates' understanding was part of a long and distinguished line of Scottish belief and philosophy, one that incorporated liberalism and quality education, a relaxation of strict ecclesiastical regimentation, and increased tolerance within a context of established virtues, rather than fanatically held beliefs acerbically expressed. However, this liberalism in thought was coupled to an adherence to conservative and reactionary ecclesiastical politics. The Evangelical movement, on the other hand, criticised the Moderates for diminishing the spiritual life, and whilst not returning to the level of explosiveness in the pulpit or the narrow legalism of the previous century, stressed the need for 'enthusiasm' and a personal salvation, which found a resonance with many people facing social challenges in their new urban centres that their rural backgrounds had not equipped them to deal with. The 'aim, manner, and content of their preaching'[29] was what differentiated them from the Moderates, with the emphasis on the great Christian doctrines of sin, grace and redemption;[30] Evangelicals were correspondingly supportive of missions (reconciling this with the theological issue of predestination – which formed the backbone of the Westminster Confession – was shown to be possible by Chalmers, the leader of the Evangelical wing at the time of the Disruption[31]).

This division in mentality and attitude lay behind the 1796 opposition to the missionary vote at the General Assembly referred to above. Although the likes of John Wesley had preached in Scotland to little effect in terms of creating support for Methodism, he had succeeded in creating a strong interest in the idea that the salvation of individual souls was something all should be concerned about, and indeed, 1796 saw the creation of the Scottish Missionary Society and the Glasgow Missionary Society. Disagreement with the need for missionary activity stemmed mostly from the belief (widely held since the Reformation) that the command of Christ to 'Go ... and make disciples of all nations'[32] was directed only at the Apostles, and although others in the New Testament preached and taught, missionary activity was not seen as something to be engaged in by the contemporary church; the doctrine of predestination or election, referred to above, was also a factor. A new gift of the Holy Spirit and of 'tongues' was thought to be required for such activity.[33] This, combined with a fear of what might happen if missionary societies (which were not necessarily institutionally linked to a denomination) were to be given free rein, and warnings about the hostilities missionaries would face from fellow missionaries once abroad, served to defeat the motion to support missions. However, significantly, the defeat allowed for a review, since supporting missions was regarded only as 'highly inexpedient' and not as theologically incorrect.

In the meantime, missionary societies flourished without the support of the General Assembly. The Church of Scotland, ever more aware that it was losing ground to such societies, eventually passed (in 1824) a motion supporting the idea that missionary work should be carried out under the control of the Church; the first missionaries, Evangelicals Alexander Duff and John Wilson, went to India.[34] By this time, the Evangelical wing of the Church was in the ascendant, and there were many candidates for the ministry, enthused by the evangelical preaching of various charismatic ministers. The divisions between the Moderates and the Evangelicals had become more acute, and from the early 1830s, the so-called Ten Years Conflict over issues of Church-State relations and particularly patronage consumed enormous energies at all levels of society, from the remotest parishes through to the Edinburgh Court of Session and the House of Lords in Westminster. It was in 1834 that the Evangelicals first had a majority in the General Assembly, and this served simply to exacerbate the divisions, as right up until the Disruption which brought about the Free Church of Scotland, the Evangelicals tended to overestimate their level of support, whilst the Moderates underestimated it.[35] The Disruption and its effect on Jewish missions is addressed in Chapter 2.

Thomas Chalmers, since 1831 the undisputed leader of the Evangelicals and a prominent instigator of the Disruption, died in 1847, shortly after the Free Church was founded. Chalmers had had an inclusive view of the Christian commonweal of the people as a whole,[36] but his absence contributed to the increasingly middle-class nature of the Free Kirk, which by the 1860s was clearly the defining mark of its membership.[37] In this, it was no different to the Auld Kirk – both had lost touch with the newly emergent working-class over the course of the Victorian century.[38] Analyses of this trend indicate that despite strenuous efforts, both churches found it difficult to identify appropriate methods of engagement, with smaller groupings on the margins of Scottish ecclesiastical society (e.g. Baptists and various non-denominational organisations, including temperance groups and Freemasons) locating what little interest in religion there was. Despite this, the middle-classes, broadly Evangelical, engaged in a massive programme of church building (particularly between 1850-1880; this was a pattern repeated across Britain): part of their attempts to engage with the urban social problems around them. Numerous societies and organisations were also founded to deal with these issues, which were seen as 'interrelated products of spiritual failure of the individual': the 'list and variety of organisations was seemingly endless, providing the working classes with an inescapable onslaught of evangelical religion'.[39]

Although the middle-classes responded to social need with action, evangelicalism was above all a source of identity that differentiated them from the landed élite and the working-class.[40] Their social commitments, of course, played a role in the outward manifestation of this identity, and overseas mission work was a substantial part of this, although it was almost always just a minority who were involved in missionary work.[41] This was coupled with the change in the general sense of Scottish identity particularly in the second-half of the nineteenth and the early twentieth centuries (when most of the work described in this book took place), marked by seeing themselves as an integral part of the British Empire (in some ways more so than the English, it would seem).[42] Foreign missions were a substantial part of this element of identity creation, so as well as being a link between the churches and imperial ambition, 'missions re-cemented a sense of Britishness in the face of other cultures, and bound Scots for another century or so to a British identity'.[43] Linda Colley argues that apart from war, religion proved to be one of the single most unifying factors in the sense of Britishness, with the British seeing themselves as

> a distinct and chosen people ... [For] most Victorians, the massive overseas empire which was the fruit of so much successful warfare represented final and conclusive proof of Great Britain's providential destiny. God had entrusted Britons with empire, they believed, so as to further the worldwide spread of the Gospel and as a testimony to their status as the Protestant Israel.[44]

This sense of being British did not conflict with a sense of being Scottish, rather it acted as another layer of identity:

> For many poorer and less literate Britons, Scotland, Wales and England remained more potent rallying calls than Great Britain, except in times of danger from abroad. And even among the politically educated, it was common to think in terms of dual nationalities, not a single national identity.[45]

Colley's descriptions of the sense of connection to the Bible and the idea of Britain as being the new Israel, as developed over the period her book examines (1707-1837) shows development of a belief or myth that sustained and encouraged people.[46] Although a Scottish particularism existed in that more of the male population had fought overseas,[47] it did not make them 'better Europeans'.[48] Indeed, although the influence of Scottish Presbyterianism's emphasis on predestination and the salvation of the 'elect' (simplistically stated, individuals that God had already chosen to be saved; all others faced eternal damnation) can be difficult to ascertain in the Victorian era, it may be 'that success in business would engender confidence in one's status with God, thus generating further success in a cumulative way';[49] success in empire-building could clearly lead to very similar conclusions, fostering a sense of a special relationship with the deity. The Evangelical belief that God was still manifestly involved in the world, ready to intervene in response to 'contrition and prayer to mitigate the consequences of individual and personal stupidity and selfishness'[50] meant that even if human failings were evident, any negative situation could be turned around by God if the subject's prayers were of sufficient sincerity and their contrition at their supposed failings manifested itself in greater commitment.[51] As will be seen, apparent missionary failure in securing converts was often regarded as something that could be overcome, with numerous references to God's potential working on the 'hearts of the people' if only there was more fervent prayer on the part of all involved, increased generosity by donors, and, often, a more substantial workload on the part of the missionaries.

It would be inappropriate to conclude here without noting that the perhaps relatively benign impression given so far of the motivation for missions is not a complete picture. The results of conversion are essentially destructive, even if perceived as altruistic by the 19th century Scots. Destructiveness was inherent in their actions: it was, one might argue, a central and explicit part of their purpose, since they sought to destroy existing belief structures and create for their targets a plausible new belief system. Couching this in theological paradigms of *metanoia* or conversion might have served to obscure their purposes, but seeking change of belief as they wanted it, which in their view had to include a rejection of previously held beliefs, was clearly a destructive aim. Confluence with a colonial mentality and imperial framework of western behaviour and thought is clearly evident, as the only agency of others that is granted validity is that which accepts the missionaries' belief system.

In this context, the place of Jewish missions is a quite particular one, and comes within this setting of the Scottish church and its general motivation for missionary work.

Scottish motivation for Jewish missions

The motivation for missionary activity directed towards Jews is a part of the wider missionary motivation outlined above, but additional elements feature. Since most of the missionary activity to the Jews that this book is concerned with came from the Free and United Free Church of Scotland, that is the primary focus of the analysis offered below. This is also useful since although all three denominations operated Jewish missions in the Levant, the Free/United Free Church views were more pronounced than those of the Church of Scotland or the United Presbyterian Church and serve more readily as points of reference. The motivation for Jewish mission will be presented in three parts, reflecting changes in emphasis over time: firstly, the place of Jews and Palestine in Scottish thought will be portrayed, followed by more reflective theological analysis as biblical criticism developed in Scotland, closing with a pragmatic view of Jewish missions.

> There's no absence, if there remains even the memory of absence. Memory dies unless it's given a use. Or as Athos might have said: If one no longer has land, but has the memory of land, then one can make a map.[52]

Making a map, as described in Anne Michaels' novel, can be used to explain Scottish motivation for their concern for Jews,[53] this concern manifesting itself in a desire to convert them (their agency was not considered): offering, from the Scottish perspective, the benefit of their own experience of religion. Palestine was seen as the natural home of 'the Jews', and the terms were at times almost used interchangeably in Scottish discourse. Furthermore, Palestine was felt to be known in some intimate way to believers in the Christian gospel: this imaginary map was felt to be both real and realistic, shaped by Biblical and by fictional narratives,[54] e.g. the *Arabian Nights*.[55] As Victorian Britain saw itself in some way as the 'Protestant Israel', there was felt to be a deep connection to – and fascination with – the land of Palestine and Jews throughout Britain.[56] In the Scottish church, this was partly linked to the Evangelical movement's Biblical interpretation:

The church was of divine origin, with Christ as its head. The Bible was the inspired word of God, the foundation of all Christian belief: it was not to be questioned, but was to be accepted as the literal truth ... In broad terms the old ideas on these matters of doctrine, though called into question, survived in Scotland almost intact until industrial maturity, down to the 1870s and 80s.[57]

The Bible was read in such a way that the expectation of a 'new Israel', the manifold prophecies of the Old Testament, the belief that God would act in relation to what was perceived to be the 'chosen people' all received prominence – and all played a role in the Scottish mentality towards Jews and Palestine. For many who were aware of political events across Europe in connection with Jews, it seemed 'to be prophecy which blended with politics and common humanity to fuel the motor of Protestant evangelism'.[58]

In fact, Scottish contact with the Levant had been fairly minimal immediately prior to the 19th century. The last great movement of Scots to the Levant, and to Palestine in particular, took place within the context of the Crusades. Indeed, although the existence and location of Scotland would have been barely known to 12th century Arab geographers,[59] there appears to have been a Scottish pilgrim's hostel in Jerusalem in the 1160s, along with hostels from many other nations.[60] Although the Scottish contribution to the Crusades had been relatively small, and at times reluctant,[61] the lingering sense of connection to the 'Holy Land' remained. This can be located in folklore and fiction, with descriptions of Scottish Crusader exploits in Palestine recurring in various settings.[62] Pilgrimages, once the major Crusades were over, became peaceful rather than belligerent, with considerable numbers of Scots travelling to Palestine in the 15th and 16th centuries, and though this travel later declined, the idea of Palestine remained important:[63]

In oral tradition, in factual participation, in propaganda, in diplomacy, in the writing of history, in generosity to institutions, in the survival and influence of these institutions, the crusading movement ... had a significant impact in Scotland, which did not begin to decline until the sixteenth century ... The Crusades can be said to have had a significant part in bringing remote little Scotland 'beyond which there is no dwelling place at all' into the fold of unified western Christendom, and thereafter the movement had a long history, some remnants of which are still with us today.[64]

There are few recorded views of Scottish influence distinct from Western influence on the Near East through the Crusades. Whilst Hillenbrand has examined the Crusades from a Muslim perspective,[65] there is relatively little western literature referring to Scots, or going much beyond vague assertions presenting a 'battle won, war lost' image of the Crusades from the Arab perspective: 'Aprés, le centre du monde se déplace résolument vers l'ouest'.[66] This image of the 'fault' or 'break' between the 'two worlds' ('la cassure entre ces deux mondes'[67]) as dating from the Crusades would have found echoes in Scotland, with the perception of the (Muslim) East.

It was in the 19th century, with the beginning of missionary work overseas, that the interest in Palestine and in those who were, by dint of theological intuition and imagination on the part of Scottish theologians, deemed to be the 'natural' inhabitants of the land, 'the Jews', took hold again. This is evidenced not least by the fact that all the mission stations bar one that the Scots operated in the Levant were directed to the conversion of Jews. Jewish missions originating in Scotland existed in central and western Europe as well, though the missions in the eastern Mediterranean, and Palestine in particular, drew the most attention and interest of the churches and their membership. Jews in this context were seen as a nation, a people defined by clear characteristics that in and of themselves formed a national identity, an ahistorical, socio-ontological collective, to borrow Wehler's description of traditional models of national identity.[68]

The understanding of the place of 'the Jews' in nineteenth century Scottish thought becomes clearer by examining the participants of the first official church delegation to Palestine (c.f. Chapter 2). Black was a professor of Divinity, and Keith had written on 'the evidence of fulfilled prophecy',[69] indeed Keith was known as 'Prophecy Keith' in wide circles, particularly after the publication of his work *Evidence of the Truth of the Christian Religion from the Fulfilment of Prophecy* in 1823, 'designed as a refutation of the views of David Hume'[70] (a classic example of the Evangelical rejection of Scottish liberalism). Although the originality of some of these works on prophecy has been questioned,[71] his interest in the subject matter is undisputed. Bonar and McCheyne, the other two members of the party, were prominent in the broadly post-millenarian Evangelical wing of the church (Chalmers' position), but were convinced pre-millennialists, the view that would come to dominate Evangelicalism over the course of the 19th century.[72] In later years, Bonar published on a variety of themes, including a description of the geography of *Palestine for the Young*; this volume indicates much of the thinking behind the Evangelical understanding of the place of Jews and Palestine, and is worth closer examination in elucidating the prevalent perception of Jews and the Old Testament at the time.[73]

The chapter headings give the tone of the book: geographic areas are described using the names of Biblical tribes (e.g. after chapters on 'the mountains and hills' and 'the rivers and lakes' etc., the first of the tribe-based chapters is entitled: 'The Tribe of Judah'). The book, based on literal understandings of biblical texts, relates Old Testament 'prophecies' to contemporary affairs. For example, his perception of contemporary Palestine is related to the biblical text as he understood it:

> The land is not now what it was. On the contrary it is plainly written that because Israel "trangressed the laws, changed the ordinance, and broke the everlasting covenant," therefore "hath the curse devoured the land" (Isa. xxiv.5,6). See what sin works![74]

Every event in the land happened in order to fulfil prophecies, to enable God to make things happen, or to show the magnificence and extent of divine power. Lester Vogel identifies this divine connection to the land as 'geopiety': 'the expression of dutiful devotion and habitual reverence for a territory, land or space'.[75] This is a useful concept as it provides 'a way of examining the largely religious concept of the "Holy Land" in a secular context while gauging the weight and extent of its symbolic export'.[76] Geopious sentiment in relation to the Levant can be found throughout the west at this time, and dominated Scottish understandings of Palestine in the period addressed here. Bonar, like many others, was unable to see the land without reference to his faith: for example, his appendix 'Nations and Divisions of the Land' describes inhabitants of various eras. In the section 'before Joshua's day', there is a note of the

> *Anakim*, "Sons of the long-neck," referring to their stature. They were of the giant race that, beyond all doubt, were in possession of Palestine, as if to make Jehovah's promise to Abraham a thing altogether and in every way impossible ...
> What a land! such inhabitants! giants everywhere. Yet the Lord told Abraham that in this very land he would give peace by the Seed in whom all nations should be blessed. For what are obstacles to God?[77]

Clearly, if God had wrought devastation on the land in response to the transgressions of 'the chosen people' of the Old Testament, 'Israel' – i.e. Jews – and there were no obstacles that could impede the will of that same God, who had, according to the Scots' own understanding, said he would redeem his 'chosen people', then utmost confidence in the success of this redemptive venture could be had. Biblical studies as practised in Scotland served to confirm these perspectives rather than question them, as the Evangelical wing of the Church tried to stifle new continental, and especially German, methods of Biblical interpretation.[78] These might have led to a more differentiated understanding of the texts, but it was only late in the nineteenth century that such thinking began to take greater hold in Free Kirk circles, leading to the second, more theological, motivational factor in concern for Jews.

The move from the literal reading of the Bible exemplified by Bonar's *Palestine for the Young* to a more critical reading that enabled a differentiated theology of Jewish evangelism to grow was prompted in part by the notorious case of William Robertson Smith (1846-94), who, from November 1870, taught at Aberdeen's Free Church College. He engaged critically but openly with modern German methods of biblical criticism in various articles he wrote for the *Encyclopedia Britannica*, in particular one on the 'Bible'.[79] He brought biblical criticism to a wider audience than occasional academic papers in the past had done, and the depth of feeling against such methodology became very apparent. Questioning the translation and interpretation of biblical texts questioned the institutional churches' power to maintain authority over their theology, structures and membership, as well as their ability to exercise religio-political power within the broader context of society.[80] The result of the case was not only a re-affirmation of the importance of the Old Testament to the Scottish church but a developing understanding of biblical texts, so that the 'Church [eventually] found herself in an entirely new situation [in which] those appointed to train her students must have a measure of liberty'[81] and the ultra-strict Calvinism that had brought about the 1843 Disruption was replaced 'by a theological liberalism based on Biblical Criticism and by an evangelicalism like that of Moody and Sankey, two worlds of thought not always in harmony'.[82] Dwight L Moody and Ira

David Sankey had brought a new kind of revivalism to Scotland in 1873-4, involving 'preaching, singing and uplift, together with happy conversion',[83] heralding a religious populism that tried to appeal to a broad swathe of society, undermining somewhat the harshness of Calvinism.[84] It is unlikely that Smith would have been prosecuted in the United Presbyterian Church and almost certain that this would not have happened in the Auld Kirk, but the Free Kirk wrestled with this case as part of the process it went through to bring its dogmatic principles into the contemporary world. The challenge that Smith represented (particularly in the context of archaeology's increasingly vocal claims for evolution rather than creation) addressed the core of Evangelical belief in the literal revealed truth of biblical texts long seen as essential to Jewish evangelism.[85]

By the beginning of the twentieth century, with the changes that had taken place in the understanding of biblical texts, the understanding of the place of Jews in the religious world-view of the Scottish church had changed. This had an attendant effect on the motivation for missionary work, which can be illuminated by examining a volume published in 1903 written by Andrew Bruce Davidson, a professor of Hebrew at New College,[86] probably the most prestigious and influential of the (by this time, United) Free Kirk's colleges. Davidson was amongst the foremost scholars of his day, his works widely read in academic and non-academic contexts, reflecting many generally held views of the time.[87] His chapters are devoted to various aspects of prophecy, the last being 'The Restoration of the Jews'.[88] It provides a rationale for engaging in missionary work among Jews that illuminates the thinking of the time, as well as pointing to attitudes to Jews and the land. Although it becomes clear by the end of the chapter that Davidson did not see 'restoration' as a physical restoration to the land, universalising the divine promises made until they apply to the Church as a whole – i.e. the whole believing community – the methodology he takes to reach this position is worth following.

Early in the chapter, Davidson notes that in

> our day millenarian views usually accompany belief in the restoration of the Jews to Canaan; but in the early Church, which was, in general, millenarian, belief in the restoration of the Jews to their own land does not seem to have been at all prevalent. Indeed, it seems hardly to have been known.[89]

Canaan, the biblical term for the land attributed in the Old Testament to the Israelites, was still regarded as somehow belonging to 'the Jews',[90] and 'millenarians' (actually, pre-millenarians) who held that 'the real second coming of the Lord precedes the millennium' i.e. the period of 'the highest condition of the Church's prosperity',[91] were attached to the idea of a 'restoration of the Jews'. The early Church saw no further role for Jews in the divine economy, unlike the church of Davidson's time:

> In those early times what was most prominent was the unbelief and intractableness of the Jews; the Church had not before it what is now to us so imposing and wonderful,

and suggestive of a deep providential design with them, their continued severance from, and refusal to amalgamate with, other nations of the earth, as Balaam foretold ... [c.f. Num 23:9] ... Such a history could not yet present itself to their minds ... this singular fact has greatly influenced modern speculations regarding the Jews, and helped interpreters in many cases to reach meanings they might not otherwise have reached.[92]

Secular history and contemporary affairs could, then, be used to understand the biblical prophecies regarding Jews' position in the cosmos, and this enabled the Church to reach its turn of the century understanding, summarised by Davidson:

Now, the Church does not ... believe in the pre-millennial advent, nor does it ... believe in the restoration; but while in the ancient Church most believed in the pre-millennial advent who did not believe or dream of the territorial restoration, many now hold the restoration who deny the pre-millennial coming; while, of course, the majority, or perhaps all, of those who are millenarians are also restorationists.[93]

Davidson proceeds to describe four views which fall into these categories:

- There will be no national conversion of 'the Jews', rather individuals (who may make up the nation) will be converted: God deals with individuals, not nations.
- Whilst there will be a conversion of all Jews (or so many that it can be regarded as a 'national conversion'), there will be not be, or need be, a restoration as an integral part of the conversion. Movement and migrations cannot be predicted or denied, these 'events ... are part of the providence of God like other national movements, and are no essential elements in the development of Christianity, and therefore find no place in prophecy'.[94]
- Conversion and restoration will take place as one event, this on the basis of Gen 17, when the covenant with God and the promise of the land were linked. This view adds to the second the notion of 'the permanent heritage'.[95]
- The fourth view incorporates the third, but adds that the place of the restored Jews will be of greater glory than of other peoples; they will act as interlocutors with God (Is 61:5-7) and the city and temple rites will be re-established. If restoration is a part of God's redemptive work, then this position logically follows, for some function for the restored people must be found in the providential plan: and 'thus the supremacy which many advocate over the other peoples is naturally arrived at'.[96] Davidson notes this is not an easy position to maintain.

In outlining his own view, Davidson argues that although the Old Testament speaks of the redemption of the people and the restoration to the land together, Scripture's concern is with people and not with lands, making these texts difficult to understand. This is particularly so in the light of Rom 11, which he sees in terms of non-Jews coming to a position of belief, though this is not necessarily the *means* for this to happen.[97] Jealousy on the part of Jews will enable their redemption to take place, which will only happen once the entire world believes the Christian gospel: 'therefore to preach this conversion [of the Jews] is most of all to preach the gospel to the weary world'.[98] However, this is a gradual process, and can begin before the world in its entirety is Christian, justifying missions to Jews at the present time:

> The Jew is provoked to jealousy by them that were not a people, but whom he now sees to be the people of God. The sight disquiets him, and awakens memories within him. It fills his mind with the profoundest emotions, with regrets that cannot be stifled, and a longing that he cannot repress, with a sorrow over lost advantages and over a life thrown away, and with the thought of a blessedness lost to him, and now enjoyed by others. This is the jealousy which the sight of Gentile faith shall awaken.[99]

On the same page he explains that it is the 'superficiality and insincerity' of contemporary Christianity that puts Jews off, since no 'real godliness' can be found in it.[100] Davidson proceeds to describe a restoration that will encompass the 'Gentiles... [as] fellow-heirs with Israel, and of the same body; but they do not thrust out Israel'[101] since although in 'Jesus Christ there is neither Jew nor Greek; but there are both Jews and Greeks,— Jews first, and also Greeks'.[102] The restoration will be to Canaan but Davidson universalises this, as well as making it something not contained within earthly time and space:

> Canaan was the heritage of God to man, but over this heritage there pass such changes as necessarily accompany the changes in man's spiritual relations. This heritage is transfigured and expanded; it becomes the world to come, the country which the patriarchs sought, the heavenly Jerusalem, the 'all things' which, according to Ps. 8, are destined to become subject to man, the kingdom that cannot be shaken,— whatever eternal realities remain, after the things that can be shaken have passed away.[103]

In terms of missions, then, it is clear that Davidson sees missions to Jews as having two aspects: firstly, it is a part of the world's conversion process and the move towards bringing Christianity to all people everywhere, and secondly, it is part of the promise of the 'end-times' and is necessary for the restoration to Canaan, though the physical restoration is not an important feature of the work. One of the primary hindrances for success in mission work is the lack of 'godliness' in the contemporary Christian churches. These attitudes, as will be shown, are reflected in the mindset of most of the Jewish missionaries in the Levant.

Finally, a third motivational factor for Jewish missions can be identified, developed mostly towards the beginning of the First World War. By Davidson's time, though still present, the romantic attachment to the region itself as a motivator for mission activity had diminished somewhat, and the notion of missions to Jews had become much more integrated into a vision that encompassed the conversion of all peoples; increased links to other Jewish missions encouraged exchange among practitioners and additional, pragmatic, reasons for missions developed. A volume by John Hall entitled *Israel in Europe* (issued in 1914 'by Authority of the Jewish Committee' of the United Free Church[104]) has a concluding chapter arguing the case for Jewish missions; the very first sentence of this defence clearly states that 'The Jew has rights in the Gospel equally with every other creature under heaven'.[105] That 'the Jew' played a 'tragic part ... in the purposes of the grace of God' does not mean Jews are to be excluded from the perceived benefits of the Christian message, but rather, it 'ought to constitute an appeal of a peculiarly touching kind, and to fortify immeasurably the claim which he shares with the rest of humanity',[106] even though the task might appear difficult. Christianity has a deep affinity with Jews: it is founded on a person who came as a Jew, and the immediate converts were Jews, furthermore, much of Christian heritage is Jewish (referring specifically to the Old Testament): 'We have literally come into the heritage of the Jew'.[107] Christian hostility to Jews is seen by Hall as another reason for missionary activity: having condemned Jews and persecuted them over many centuries, Christians owe them the best they have to offer: belief in the (of course, Evangelical) Christian faith.[108] The prospects for conversion are seen to be good, since their 'spiritual qualities' mark them out and make them more receptive to the Christian message; recognition of Jesus' importance is increasing amongst educated and informed Jews, so that the 'Jew is becoming Christian at a much quicker rate than is the heathen, and the future is great with expectancy'.[109] That, allied with the 'quality' of many of the converts[110] make for an incentive to continue and expand the missions' work, for 'one can see in imagination what a testimony to the power of Jesus Christ such a Hebrew Church would be, and what an effective instrument would lie to hand for the winning of the whole world to Christ'.[111]

Hall therefore presents largely pragmatic reasons for Jewish missions, an addition to Davidson's theological arguments and general geopiety.

Jews as Jews – the link between theology and imperialism

What is clear from the analysis offered above, regardless of the supposed place of people of Jewish faith in the divine economy, is the refusal of theologians in Scotland (in common, it should be pointed out, with most other western theological scholars of the time) to see Jews as anything other than their own construct of what Jews should be. This fits a pattern, described in broad terms by Robert Carroll:

> Where Christians had power Jews suffered, where Christians were powerless Jews were better off ... There were many campaigns to convert them to Christian belief and practice, often involving enforced conversion, but even the converted Jews remained second-class citizens. Throughout its history Christian ideology could never tolerate the Jew *as* Jew. The roots of that intolerance are ... in the New Testament and especially in the Fourth Gospel's formulation of the problem.[112]

Proceeding to enumerate his reasoning for this, Carroll summarises what many other authors have already demonstrated about the inherent anti-Judaism of the Greek New

Testament, and especially the gospel texts.[113] This has obvious consequences for a theology that for centuries understood the biblical texts to be its foundation stone:

> The Jews in the [passion] story may be ciphers created by Christian communities as the necessary foil to their claims about Jesus. However, the common term shared by 'the Jews' of the Gospels and the real members of the Jewish people – namely the description 'Jew' – has throughout history been sufficient identification for the vast majority of Christian readers of the Gospels. For them there has been a clear common identity between Jews and 'the Jews', and they have held *all* Jews responsible for the murder of Christ. No amount of sophisticated modern readings will persuade them otherwise. Not even the rise of critical theology has changed that attitude to reading the Gospels.[114]

Carroll elaborates on the impossibility of using the biblical texts for historical purposes due to the lack of 'referentiality *outside* themselves'[115] – note that all the missionaries did precisely this, e.g. in relation to ruined Palestinian villages.[116] The image of 'the Jews' was intrinsically connected to their image of themselves as Christians, and existed and was imbued with meaning only when viewed from this perspective. If Europe's image of other lands at this time can be described as 'an amplifier, or a long shadow, making their own sensations more audible or visible to them ... [with] room for all kinds of fantasy, credulity, deception and self-deception, and the development of stock responses',[117] then the image Scottish missionaries had of 'the Jews' can be seen as part of this kind of imperialistic discourse – self-definition by 'the Jews' (individually and collectively) was not seen as necessary (or desirable). This fits Saidian Orientalist imagery: 'secondhand abstractions'[118] of groups that might have wishes and desires, but do not have the power or authority to bring these to fruition.[119] Said, interestingly in the context of this book, uses the language of conversion:

> all cultures impose corrections upon raw reality, changing it from free-floating objects into units of knowledge. The problem is not that conversion takes place ... To the Westerner, however, the Oriental was always *like* some aspect of the West ... the Orientalist makes it his work to be always converting the Orient from something into something else: he does this for himself, for the sake of his culture, in some cases for what he believes is the sake of the Oriental.[120]

The Jews of Palestine, and in so far as they were acknowledged by the Scottish missionaries, the Muslim and Christian populations, were seen as 'member[s] of a subject race and not exclusively ... inhabitant[s] of a geographical area'.[121] During the 19th century Palestinian Jews were not under direct political control of the West – though this was certainly developing: Britain had claimed for itself the 'defence' of the Jews in the Ottoman Empire with the appointment of its first Consul in Jerusalem[122] – but in the thinking of the church, Jews were already subjects, in Gikandi's phrase, Jews were

a part of the 'grand narrative against which to read the imperial experience':[123] these
Scots had given Jews a place in the imperial centre. 'The Jews' had killed Jesus, 'the
Jews' had rejected the Christian Christ as their messiah since the resurrection, 'the Jews'
(in Palestine) were lazy and covetous and dependent on outsiders,[124] and 'the Jews' (in
Palestine) were now to be offered (another) conversion at the hands of missionaries from
the 'Protestant Israel'. 'The Jews' were subjects of the missionaries' own world-view
and in this context were in need of conversion to Christianity, or to put it another way,
needed to be converted to Christianity in order to fulfil the Scots' own perceptions of
the place of 'the Jews' in the divine economy, thus removing from 'the Jews' any identity
they might wish to define for themselves – in Said's terms, they had been 'converted'
to perform a function for the Western missionaries, and were then ready to undergo
a conversion to Christianity. The Evangelical Scots' own knowledge of conversion,
faith and the gospel was above all a subjective knowledge (to use Søren Kierkegaard's
language[125]) and they perceived themselves as offering 'the Jews' the benefits of this
knowledge and faith. In other words, their perception of themselves was not only
that they were fulfilling what they understood to be biblical imperatives, but that they
were being altruistic in their desire to share what they felt had benefited them.[126] Their
complicity in the imperialistic framework, intellectual, theological and practical,[127] was
not something that they considered, indeed, it is doubtful their world-view could have
accommodated such a position.

However, that the Jewish population of Palestine was under imperial control from
Constantinople was roundly condemned by the missionaries on numerous occasions
(suffering the abuse of 'the Turk' – another Orientalist construct), and with increasing
urgency once the possibility of change became more apparent with British military
advances during WWI. The status of Jews in Palestine changed with British military
victory over Ottoman forces, though they remained imperial subjects unable to exercise
their own wishes and desires for governance; of course, the same can be said of Muslims
and Christians in Palestine. On a political level this is most clearly exemplified in relation
to both Jews and Arabs in the differing promises of the Balfour Declaration, the Husayn-
McMahon Correspondence and the Sykes-Picot Pact; and though these are not all dealt
with in detail in this book, the missionaries' reactions to these and the developing situation
in the inter-war years has been described elsewhere.[128]

Having examined the Scottish context in the period this book covers, a brief outline
of the political and religious landscape of the Middle East in this period is called for.

The Levant, 1838-1917

There is little point in reproducing here a history of the Middle East for the time
span covered by this book – such a history can be found in numerous texts by authors
far more qualified to offer a general history.[129] Instead, this section is an attempt to
portray the religio-political situation the missionaries found themselves in, providing a
background for understanding their actions.

As Philippe Fargues points out, the Ottomans, until their conquest of Syria and Egypt, controlled a mostly European and Christian empire, and devised a system of governance that took the religious characteristics of their populations into account. This was the *millet* system, which allocated control for a number of civil functions (marriage, inheritance, education etc.) to a subjects' religious authority, which was recognised by the Sublime Porte.[130] A *millet* could only be created by the Sultan, and until it was, a religious grouping, a *dhimmi*,[131] had to work through existing *millets* – so, for example, initially, all Christians in the Empire came under the Orthodox *millet*, though other *millets* were soon created, and over time, as churches underwent division and schism, further *millets* were recognised.[132] Catholics (Latins) were not recognised as a *millet*, not being seen by the Porte as a local community, but did have a special status that allowed them to function within the Empire. Protestants were granted *millet* status in 1850, but without special jurisdiction over their affairs.[133] Movement between the *millets* themselves as well as to or from Islam declined as religious communities tended to live in the same locales resulting, for example, in relatively few mixed marriages.[134] The Christian population flourished in some parts of the Ottoman Empire, notably in Greater Syria, and occasional conversions took place, including from Islam to Christianity.[135] However, largely the communities developed separately, with different demographic patterns: in particular, it seems that Christians had a longer life-expectancy than Muslims, which accounts, in part at least, for the increased proportion of Christians in certain areas.[136] Because co-religionists were under the same religious authority regardless of where they lived in the Empire, migration within the Empire was straightforward for *dhimmis*,[137] a factor that is noticeable in terms of the occasional converts described in this book who could move quite freely from one administrative area to another.

Whilst the *millet* system can be seen as strengthening the minority communities from the inside, the Capitulations 'enticed them to the outside'.[138] The first Capitulation agreement (named after the *capita*, or headings) was between France and the Porte, allowing trading privileges to French merchants, these later being extended to include commercial, civil and penal matters in order to guarantee the interests of the traders. Over time France extended the reach of the Capitulations agreements to include those of similar belief, i.e. Maronites and Catholics. Britain, Austria and Prussia followed the French lead, 'protecting' particular population groupings – of particular note here is that the British 'protected' Jews. As the Ottoman Empire appeared increasingly frail to the western powers, there was a keen sense of a need to maintain existing positions of strength in the region ('the Eastern Question'[139]). With the western interest in the eastern Mediterranean increasing in the 19th century, in part due to easier travel to the region, the western powers opened consulates in Palestine to safeguard their interests and 'protect' 'their' populations: the British in 1838, the French, Prussians and Sardinians in 1843, the Americans the following year, and the Austrians (replacing the Sardinians) in 1849, with Russia being represented by an agent connected to their Beirut-based Consul General (opened in 1839). Churches and religious orders linked to these national representatives founded numerous institutions across Greater Syria, the Catholics, Anglicans and

Prussians (Protestant, and some Catholic[140]) being especially strongly represented.[141] Muhammad Ali's conquest of Palestine and his subsequent retreat became a factor in the move to change the administrative arrangements for Greater Syria in the course of the *tanzimat* reform, Jerusalem increasing in importance not least because the religious leaders based in the city had jurisdiction over the whole of Palestine.[142] However, it is worth noting that 'much of the northern region [of Palestine] has to be seen as subject to economic and political forces deriving not from Jerusalem, but from its provincial capital, Beirut'.[143]

Although trade within the 19th century Ottoman Mediterranean was high, trade with Europe was not, and was clearly an area of potential growth.[144] With the increasing interest from the west, but a certain reluctance to trade directly in the interior of the country, especially in Ottoman Asia (as opposed to Egypt), opportunities arose for the Christian and Jewish minorities, encouraged to look beyond their own context by the involvement of the west through the Capitulations and later the consuls, to develop a role as intermediaries in European-Ottoman trade.[145] This resulted in further openness to all things European, as well as greater economic wealth for these groups and concomitant poverty for some Muslim entrepreneurs as European products replaced indigenous materials, whilst the *tanzimat* reform also brought with it a measure of political equality (though with unexpected side-effects[146]). Cultural relations developed too, particularly with the growth of missionary schools throughout the Empire, bringing about

> a change in customs, in particular practices that would reduce the mortality rate ... inequalities in education quickly became apparent between regions and, within regions, between religions. Everywhere the Christians moved considerably ahead of the Muslims ... Jews ... received less schooling than the average in the *vilayet* where instruction was widespread ... but were at the head in the most backward *vilayet*.[147]

The Levantine Jewish community, the primary target of Scottish attempts at evangelisation in the Ottoman Empire during the 19th and early 20th centuries, had undergone a period of decline during the 17th and 18th centuries, but with the advent of the *tanzimat* reforms, new avenues for the community's revival emerged. As the Porte encouraged foreign investment in the Empire, western Jewish financiers became involved in industry, construction and banking, where possible using local Jews as agents. This enabled the latter to re-engage in the Ottoman economy, paralleling developments that Armenians and Greeks had undergone in the previous two centuries through their contact with western Christian traders. Jewish merchants not only utilised connections to western finance, but also attempted to identify gaps in the market that their Christian neighbours ignored, and in certain parts of the Empire the Jewish community prospered financially,[148] though this was not a uniform development, impacting less on Greater Syria than Anatolia, for example.[149] In terms of language usage, most Ottoman Jews could not read Hebrew with any degree of fluency, but tended towards Judeo-Spanish (and to some extent French). This was encouraged by newspapers and publishers, who often translated material from Hebrew; much of the newspaper production was centred on Anatolia, with more limited efforts in Egypt, Palestine and Rumania.[150] Violence against Jews did occur, most notably centred on accusations of ritual murder/the historical blood-libel, of which the 1840 'Damascus Affair' is amongst the most prominent;[151] retaliatory violence also featured at times,[152] but stability and a measure of protection was offered in connection with the Capitulations, and repeated affirmations of the equality of religions from the Sublime Porte also played a role in minimising further attacks.

In Palestine itself, the Sephardic Jews resident over centuries were firmly established subjects of the Ottoman Empire. The influx of Ashkenazi Jews, who from 1877 outnumbered the Sephardic community,[153] generally shared European prejudices against the Empire (and to some extent against the Sephardic Jews), and refused to integrate as Ottoman subjects.[154] With regard to Zionism, Sultan Abdülhamid II recognised the potential danger of the incipient nationalist movement as a hindrance to his ideal of Islam as a unifying force for his Empire; consequently he sought to limit immigration by various means, but with little success.[155] Actual population figures are disputed (and contentious, given the contemporary political context), as the scholars utilised here show, McCarthy's first figures being based on Ottoman, the second on Zionist statistics:

	McCarthy (Ottoman)	McCarthy (Zionist)	Shaw	Courbage & Fargues
1850	13,000			
1856		10,490		
1860	13,000			
1880	14,460			
1882			24,000	27,382
1890	17,614		47,000	
1895		43,790		
1900	22,905			
1908			80,000	
1910	31,778			
1914		73,100	85,000	58,644

Figure 1-1 McCarthy, Shaw, Courbage/Fargues: Jewish population statistics[156]

Whilst it would serve no useful purpose to attempt to reconcile these figures here, reached from a variety of sources, they clearly point to the marked increase that came about from the 1880s, with many new arrivals clustered in cities and new agricultural settlements[157] (the Jerusalem and Acre *sanjaks*, which included Hebron, and Tiberias and Safad respectively, the primary areas of Scottish missionary engagement, show corresponding increases[158]). The missionaries were clearly engaging in Palestine at a time of considerable change and ferment in the situation of their primary target.

Scottish attitudes to Jews have already been described above, but in terms of the Christian and Muslim populations it is notable that in general the missionaries had no real appreciation of the complexity of the ecclesial context they were in, only rarely differentiating between the various Christian denominations they encountered. Even the differences between Chalcedonian and non-Chalcedonian churches seem to have been irrelevant for most of them, with general references to the 'churches of the East' etc. being used when describing these churches. Similar patterns of ignorance can be identified in relation to Islam.[159]

Courbage and Fargues close their chapter on the position of Christians and Jews under Islam during the Ottoman period noting that:

> The economic and demographic recovery of the Eastern Christians took place in a singular international context which ended with the First World War. The colonial and expansionist West had established its hegemony while proclaiming its Christianity. Economic and missionary victory went hand in hand.[160]

It is to the exploration of the Scottish missionary aspect of this 'economic and missionary victory' that this book now turns, Chapter 2 exploring how the missions began and looking at the early attempts at missionary work in Greater Syria, before moving on in Chapter 3 to give an account of the larger scale missions in Palestine, particularly in Galilee and Hebron. The missionaries' context and background is examined in Chapter 4, whilst Chapter 5 analyses the missionaries' methods and their interaction with the local population. Concluding observations and remarks on this putative 'missionary victory' constitute Chapter 6, showing how, as part of the imperial project, the missionaries failed to deal with the dialectic of identity and difference they were faced with, this symbolising the failure of the imperial ambition as expressed in the desire for religious conversion.

PART I:
THE MISSIONS

2
THE BEGINNINGS
Exploration, and the first missions in the Levant

The deputation to Palestine and Lebanon and its immediate consequences
The Scottish Presbyterian involvement in Palestine began with the Church of Scotland General Assembly in 1838; prior to this there had been limited interest in Jewish mission, but 'the subject of the Jews had ... recently begun to awaken attention among the faithful servants of God in the Church of Scotland'.[1] It was suggested that the recently-formed Committee for the Conversion of the Jews,

> collect information respecting the Jews, their numbers, condition, and character, -- what means have hitherto been employed by the Christian Church for their spiritual good, and with what success, -- ... [what openings there might be] for a mission to their nation, and where these are most promising, -- and generally ... to take all prudent measures, ... at home and abroad, for the advancement of the cause, and report to next General Assembly.[2]

To pursue this, it was resolved to send a deputation to Palestine and other countries where Jews lived. The group consisted of four individuals: Dr Black, a Professor of Divinity in Aberdeen, Dr Alexander Keith,[3] a minister, Rev Robert McCheyne, a minister in Dundee, and Rev Andrew Bonar,[4] an assistant minister in Perthshire. The definitive account of the journey was written by Bonar and McCheyne (who were only in their late twenties when they undertook their journey) and republished many times.[5] Bonar was the main author of the text,[6] and since McCheyne died in 1843 as the third edition was going to the printers, subsequent propagation of it would have been primarily in Bonar's hands.[7] Although the deputation were to assess the situation of Jews in all the countries they visited, Palestine was the main focus and will be addressed here.

The group left Dover on 12.4.1839 having received letters of support from governmental officials and met with members of the London Jewish Society (LJS) (who had already been engaged in mission to Jews for some time). They arrived in Gaza, having come from Egypt, at the beginning of June. As they travelled, they analysed the situation they found using the Biblical tools they had, apparently in the expectation, initially at least, that the country would be as described in the Bible, despite the centuries that had past. When this was not the case, their Biblical analysis helped them out. For example, they recalled Biblical curses and prophecies of doom when they encountered 'damage': on the way northwards to Jerusalem, they saw many small villages, leading them to reflect on the great change since 'Judah and Israel used to be "many as the sand which is by the sea in multitude'"[8] – but now the towns were desolate: 'And the fulfilment is all the more striking, when the traveller remembers that in these ruined cities and villages not one of even the few inhabitants is a Jew'.[9] They believed the land in general to be under a curse because of the supposed rejection by Jews of the Christian messiah. This curse was referred to, for example, as they travelled through the 'Pass of Latroon':

> The sight of the terraced hills, with their bright verdure, lighted up by the brilliant beams of the morning sun, made us think how lovely this spot must have been in the days of David and Solomon, when its luxuriance was yet unblighted by the curse of Israel's God.[10]

They felt they recognised the divine promises in what they saw: on learning of Shiloh being in ruins, they wrote that 'The words of the prophet are still full of meaning; "Go ye now into my place which was in Shiloh, where I set my name at the first, and see what I did to it for the wickedness of my people Israel."'[11] An attempt was made to correlate every geographical location with its Biblical counterpart and the party often reflected on Jesus' itinerant lifestyle as they travelled, with comments such as: 'This road must have been often traversed by our Lord in going from Jerusalem to Sychar and Galilee.'[12]An extensive knowledge of Old Testament prophetic texts is apparent in all that they wrote, underpinning a pervading geopious sentiment.

The group met British consular officials and Europeans already working with Jews. They spent longer in Jerusalem than in any other single location during their time in Palestine: almost two weeks.[13] They had frequent contact with John Nicolayson, a Dane who had originally come to Jerusalem in 1826,[14] and although he appears to have had difficulty settling at first,[15] not least due to having to leave for Malta in 1828 on the advice of the British Consul for fear of war, he returned to the Levant in 1831 travelling between Jerusalem, Beirut and Constantinople, albeit with no apparent successes in terms of converts. In 1833 Nicolayson settled in Jerusalem along with two other missionaries. Their ambition was to set up 'an English church' with 'episcopal authority'. Nicolayson wanted a press similar to that of the Americans but with Hebrew characters in order to print and distribute literature. In the meantime, they organised services (daily in Hebrew, weekly in English, Arabic and German). In 1838, Nicolayson bought a plot of land for the eventual erection of a church on behalf of the LJS, a complex transaction as he wanted to hide his ultimate purpose.[16] In 1839 Nicolayson, writing for the LJS journal, stated that a number of 'native Christians', Latin and Greek, were wanting to join the English church. He had succeeded in temporarily putting them off (the original aim of the LJS – to convert Jews – was clearly not being fulfilled[17]) – this marks the beginning of difficulties that were to emerge with the local churches over the admission to membership of 'outside' churches.[18] It was at this time that the deputation arrived in Jerusalem.

Their other contact was with the British Vice-Consul, William Young, the first foreign consul to be appointed to Jerusalem. This had been facilitated by a joint effort on the part of the Consul-General in Alexandria, Patrick Campbell, liasing with Muhammad Ali, and the Ambassador in Constantinople, Ponsonby, liasing with the Sublime Porte. It was July 1838 before Ponsonby had obtained the necessary *firman*, and Young only arrived in Jerusalem in the autumn. He gave the Scots estimates for the numbers of Jews in Palestine, as did (separately) Nicolayson:[19]

	Young	Nicolayson
Jerusalem	5,000 or 6,000	6,000 or 7,000
Nablus	150 or 200	200
Hebron	700 or 800	700 or 800
Tiberius	600 or 700	1,200
Safad	1,500 or 2,000	
Haifa	150 or 200	150 or 200
Sidon	250 or 300	300
Tyre	130 or 150	150
Jaffa	60	60
Acre	200	200
Villages of Galilee	400 or 580	400 or 500

Figure 2-1 Young and Nicolayson: population estimates

Young estimated approximately 10,000 Jews in Palestine at the time, but noted the difficulty of obtaining accurate figures.[20] Their status, he thought, was generally poor, and that although their lot had been better under Muhammad Ali, 'the common people hate them, and they are exposed to continual wrongs'.[21] Greek, Armenian and Roman Catholic Christians supposedly treated Jews worse than their Muslim counterparts did, although Palestinian Jews were becoming attached to British Christians, and

> the fact of a British Consul being stationed here on their account has greatly contributed to this effect. How wonderful that a British Consul should be sent to the Holy Land, with special instructions to interest himself in behalf of the Jews, and having for his district the very region formerly allotted to the twelve tribes of Israel! And how much more wonderful still, that our first Consul in Jerusalem should be one actuated by a deep and enlightened attachment to the cause of God's ancient people! At present, however, the Jews make less use of his influence than they might do...'[22]

Of course, in how far the influence (potential or actual) of the Consul is accurately assessed is open to question, since this assessment appears to have been based largely on Young's own statements, hardly an impartial commentator. Some of Bonar and McCheyne's statements, at times expressed openly to Jews, did little to endear them to the local populace, and might for some of their listeners merely have been more of the 'continual wrongs' mentioned earlier, for example, when they go to the Mount of Olives and see the Jewish graves, they opine:

> They expect to arise from these tombs at the resurrection, and see Messiah among the first. How awful their disappointment when they find that they die only to pass forthwith into consuming terrors, and that they arise only to the resurrection of damnation! Disappointed hope will aggravate the woe of a poor lost man of Israel, – he thought he was at the gate of heaven, and finds himself in the porch of hell![23]

Whilst not necessarily overtly hostile, their encounters with Jews cannot be described as unequivocally positive, as this account of McCheyne meeting a Sidon Jew who had invited him to his house shows:

> After some preliminary questions, the Hebrew Bible was produced, and the first part of Ezekiel xxxvii. read, from which Mr M. shewed him his state by nature. He seemed a little offended, yet not wanting to shew it in his own house, tried to change the subject of discourse, and offered coffee.[24]

On another occasion, in Sūr (Tyre, as the Scots called it, ignoring its local contemporary name in favour of its Biblical name), they engaged in discussions with a local rabbi, and later met with other Jews at their *khan* and discussed further: 'One, as he departed, cried, "Come away from that Epicurus." Some were a little angry, but most were kind and good-natured.'[25] Some of Moses Montefiore's companions, who were travelling through Palestine at the same time as Bonar and McCheyne's group, are recorded as having told some local Jews that the Scots 'were come for the purpose of making them Christians, and had been warned to enter into no discussions', which was their explanation for being 'looked suspiciously upon' when trying to speak to Jews in a synagogue.[26] However, whether locals were 'a little offended', 'a little angry', 'kind and good-natured' or suspicious, no success in terms of conversion was recorded.

During their time in Jerusalem, they discussed with Nicolayson a list of questions that the Church had given them.[27] They asked about the numbers of Jews in Palestine, and here record 7,000 in Jerusalem and 12,000 in all of Palestine,[28] a figure that in recent years had remained largely static as the numbers moving to Palestine (largely from Central and Eastern Europe, it is implied) did not exceed the numbers who died there.[29] The delegation asked about the feelings of Palestinian Jews towards Christianity and about the success so far in gaining converts. Nicolayson mentioned some who had converted, although numbers were minimal; some, from further afield, had sought out Nicolayson, but 'the first native Jew awakened at Jerusalem was Rabbi Joseph, in September 1838',[30] who had been forced to leave for Constantinople due to difficulties with the city's Jews: a '*herem* or ban of excommunication was pronounced in the synagogues against the Missionaries, and all who should have dealings with them'.[31] However, when a medical missionary then arrived in the region, this was ignored, and although another ban was pronounced, it proved to be difficult to stop people from using the medical facility: 'This interesting fact shews the immense value of the medical missionary'.[32] He claimed there were three more making enquiries of him about Christianity. Although converts had been few, there were other successes Nicolayson drew their attention to: he claimed the distinction between true and false Christianity had been clearly drawn,[33] the study of the Old Testament had become obligatory[34] and the 'word of God has become more and more the only ground of controversy. The authority of the Talmud is now not appealed to; the only dispute about it being whether it is to be referred to at all, or what is its real value?'[35] Nicolayson felt that the main difficulties lay in the ongoing support of those that had converted; a proposal had been made for a printing press and medical facilities, although the creation of a hospital was underway.[36] From the Scots' questioning, it became clear that the main method employed by Nicolayson lay in personal contact, the selling of Hebrew Bibles (he claims to have sold 5,000), and the gift of New Testaments to those he felt he could trust with it. The chief characteristic of Palestinian Jews was felt to be that they were 'strict Rabbinists' and 'superstitious in the extreme', noting that 'their real characteristic may be inferred from the fact, that those who come are the *élite* of the devotional and strictly religious Jews of other countries. They have so little trade that their covetousness and cheating are turned upon one another'.[37] This pointed to the oft-noted comment that Palestinian Jews were essentially lazy, relying on the charitable support of Jews from elsewhere.[38] The Scots also make very practical enquiries about the health situation, the cost of living in Jerusalem and related matters. Before leaving, they summarise their assessment of the qualifications needed by a missionary to the Jews in Palestine. Although lengthy, it is worth citing extended parts as it gives an indication of the size of the task they felt they were asking others to do:

Hebrew is the most necessary language ... and ... is spoken chiefly in the Spanish way. A Missionary should study ... Arabic in his own country, and the more thoroughly he is master of these the better, but the true pronunciation can only be acquired on the spot. Yet Arabic is not so absolutely necessary as Hebrew. Spanish, too, is useful, and also German, and he must know Italian, for the purpose of holding intercourse with Europeans in general. Judeo-Spanish is the language of the Sephardim, and Judeo-Polish of the Ashkenazim (i.e. Jews from Europe). All of them know a little Italian. All Jews in Palestine speak Hebrew, but ... it is absolutely necessary to know the vernacular tongue, in order to be sure that you and they understand the same thing by the words employed. A Missionary ought to be well grounded in prophecy, and he should be one who fully and thoroughly adopts the principles of literal interpretation, both in order to give him hope and perseverance, and in order to fit him for reasoning with the Jews. It is not so much preaching talents as controversial that are required; yet it is to be hoped that both may soon be needed. He ought to have an acquaintance with Hebrew literature to the extent of understanding the Talmud, so as to be able to set aside its opinions. Acquaintance, too, with the Cabbala is necessary, in order to know the sources of Jewish ideas, and how scriptural arguments are likely to affect their minds ... A knowledge of Chaldee and Syriac would also be very useful ... there ought to be both Jewish and Gentile labourers; the Gentile to form the nucleus, the other to be the effective labourers ... a converted Jew ... [if educated and ordained] would combine the advantages of both; still a Gentile fellow-labourer would always be desirable. Faith and perseverance are the grand requisites in a missionary to Israel. He should never abandon a station unless in the case of absolute necessity. He may make occasional tours in the country round about, but he must have a centre of influence. It is of the highest importance to retain his converts beside him, and form them into a church; for two reasons:- 1. Little is done if a man is only convinced or even converted, unless he is also trained up in the ways of the Gospel. 2. The influence of sincere converts belonging to a mission is very great. It commends the cause of Christ to others. At the same time it ought, if possible, to be made a rule to give no support to converts, except in return for labour, either literary or agricultural.[39]

There are a number of noteworthy points here, amongst others:

1)   the relative lack of importance in knowing Arabic (and therefore in communicating to non-Jews);[40] unlike in other mission fields where the work was directed to any who would listen, the authors here were interested in only one distinct segment of the population;[41]

2)   the rejection of any (at the time) modern methods of biblical interpretation. The literal understanding underpinning the communication of their beliefs was believed to be the most effective method for converting others. Exhibiting doubt in scriptural texts, which is what many English-speaking missionaries thought the continental interpretational methods amounted to, would counteract the certainty of salvation they were offering their non-Christian listeners.[42] The emphasis on 'controversial' skills instead of preaching is also noteworthy – Jews needed to be convinced of Christianity before they could benefit from preaching;

3)   the importance of creating and maintaining a community for those who had been converted for purposes of support and further evangelisation; it is not mentioned, but this would also serve as a useful promotional tool in pursuing financial support in Scotland. The envisioned ongoing centrality of the overseas missionary, which can be equated with a lack of willingness to allow any new churches to become independent, was to become less fashionable in later years, although circumstances might on occasion make a European essential;

4)   the reluctance to support financially any converts unless they provide work for the mission. This has parallels to missionary thought elsewhere, and is not just to be taken as a reference to the *halukah*.[43]

Later, they met with a former rabbi from Yarmouth, George Wilden Pieritz, who had been converted to Christianity and was working in Palestine on behalf of the LJS[44] along with two other converted Jews, a Mr Levi and a Dr Gerstmann (a medical missionary in Jerusalem[45]); Pieritz regarded himself as the successor to Joseph Wolff.[46] Their encounter with Pieritz is of interest since he expounds further on a variety of issues including the suitability of Palestine (and other localities) as mission fields.[47] Pieritz gave them the lowest estimate for numbers of Jews in Palestine;[48] the Sephardic community was described as lacking in morals and tending much more towards 'Pharisaism' than foreign Jews, with e.g. polygamy being permitted, although not among the Ashkenazim.[49] Hebron was regarded as the most 'moral' city as far as Jews are concerned, followed by Jerusalem and Safad, with poverty prevalent in all areas. This poverty, however, made them more open to the missionaries, because 'in other lands, where they are involved in business, or rich and comfortable, they will not attend to the missionary'[50] – the missionaries did not think it a problem to use others' poverty in this way; in how far it is an accurate methodological assessment is open to question. Pieritz argued that 'Talmudic logic' is far superior when confronting Jews than 'the power of the syllogism' so that 'Talmudic knowledge' should be a necessary requirement for a missionary – one advantage being that 'it enables the person to argue by Talmudical logic, which is much shorter and more striking than scientific logic.'[51] How Pieritz, himself a converted Jew, envisaged missionaries who were not converts from Judaism acquiring this knowledge is not elaborated upon.[52]

The Scots proceeded to travel to Beirut (by sea), and then to Galilee. After their visit to Safad, and after they left the Levant, they decided that this would be the most suitable place for a Scottish mission to be based.[53] They gave a number of reasons for this:[54]

1) the climate was favourable: missionaries could spend winters in Tiberias and summers in Safad, benefiting from the best of the climate in both areas;[55]

2) there was no missionary presence at the time, although missionaries from Jerusalem occasionally travelled to Galilee;

3) the Jews in Safad appeared to have good communications with Jews elsewhere in the country, enabling news about missions to be spread more easily;

4) there was virtually no employment so Jews have 'abundant leisure to read and discuss';[56]

5) the Jews there were 'in deep affliction… a state of mind more favourable than carnal ease for affording opportunity to press upon them the truths of the gospel.';[57]

6) were employment to be sought for converts, the area was suited to agricultural enterprise, and this would enable converts to be independent of the missionaries for their material well-being;

7) Safad, as one of the four cities in Palestine described as holy to Jews, was held in especial affection by them, and they expected the Messiah to come first to Galilee;[58]

8) since Jesus came to Galilee (they refer to Mt 4,13), 'who can tell whether he may not choose the same favoured spot to make light spring up again…?'[59]

9) equating Safad with the city on the hill,[60] they suggest that it would become a centre

from which missionary activity would reach those around it, and even 'the whole Jewish world'.[61]

10) as the LJS was based in Jerusalem and the south of the country, it would not be appropriate to initiate a mission in that area, but the north, containing nearly half the Jews in Palestine, 'still represents and open and uncultivated field';[62]

11) Safad was in relatively close proximity to a number of other cities with important Jewish populations (they list Tyre (Sūr), Sidon, Acre, Haifa, Beirut and Damascus).

Bonar and McCheyne do acknowledge difficulties, focusing on the transfer of power in Syria from Muhammad Ali to 'the feeble grasp of the Sultan',[63] resulting in the entire region being politically unstable. However, were this to change, the locality would be very attractive as a centre for missionary work.

Following this extensive trip – they wrote that they had 'visited every city and village in Palestine where Jews are to be found (with the exception of Jaffa, and two small villages on Mount Naphtali)'[64] – they produced a report for the 1840 General Assembly which concluded with an immediate reaction to the situation in Damascus,[65] and enthusiastic meetings took place in what appear to be a considerable number of parishes on the subject of missions to the Jews.[66] However, other events conspired to thwart any attempt by the Church of Scotland to put the recommendations to pursue work in Palestine into practice. A mission was started in Hungary arising out of the contacts made during the visit by Keith and Black, with the sending out of Rev Daniel Edward to Jassy in Moldavia,[67] followed shortly afterwards by John Duncan, William Owen Allan and Robert Smith who all went to Pesth. Palestine itself, however, was to remain untouched by the Scottish churches for another four decades. With the Disruption, the Church of Scotland was too busy trying to salvage the remains of its tattered structure and possessions to expend energy on overseas work. The Free Kirk, meanwhile, which all four missionaries in Hungary had joined (and all foreign missionaries but one had joined as well), dealt with a report on Jewish missions as one of its very first items at the 1843 General Assembly, and it continued to pursue mission work among Jews. Other mission stations were founded (indeed, a few years later, Bonar's presbytery of Perth was requested by the 1846 Free Kirk General Assembly to give him leave to work in Constantinople as a missionary to the Jews for three years[68]), but generally without the obvious successes in terms of baptisms that were hoped for.[69]

One other immediate result worth noting was that in July 1840, McCheyne travelled to the Presbyterian Church of Ireland (PCI) and spoke in both Dublin and Belfast, following which the Irish passed a resolution at their 1841 General Assembly initiating their mission to the Jews, work which directly impacted on the Scots with the creation of the Damascus mission. McCheyne died unexpectedly a few years later; Bonar lived to see the Sea of Galilee mission grow and flourish, the Free Kirk JMC recording an extended obituary minute when he died, acknowledging his significant role in their history:

He was one of the saintliest of men. For nearly sixty years he has been before the Church occupying an ever increasingly prominent position ... As a preacher he was intensely ... evangelical, while to the interpretation of Scripture he brought ... a scholarship which enabled him to weigh the original text, a spiritual insight which opened up meanings to him which were hidden from others, and a sanctified genius which made many passages brighten as under an almost heavenly light ... What moves the Jewish Committee specially to cherish his memory is the circumstance that he was the author of that 'Narrative of a Mission to the Jews' which describes the beginning of the enterprise which it is now its business to superintend. That Mission is a never-to-be-forgotten one, and in the removal of the last representative the Committee would hear a call to recognise the singular goodness of God in connection with their work hitherto and to increased earnestness in the continued prosecution of it.[70]

By this time, he was the last surviving member of the original deputation, having continually supported Jewish missions through his publications and public life.

Early plans; the temporary abandonment of plans for a mission in Palestine

Following the return of the deputation, indeed during the deputation's travels, the JMC discussed a variety of possible locations for missions to convert Jews.

In April or May of 1839, the JMC began deliberating the possibility of a mission in Aden, reckoning there to be about 200,000 Jews in the interior, this being 'the most interesting population of Aden'[71] but although this was discussed for over a year, a grant being made for this purpose[72] and the government agreeing to protect such a mission,[73] it was decided that nothing should be done about this until after a mission had been established in Palestine.[74] The Committee, in August 1840, together with the recently returned deputation from Palestine, discussed what their next step should be 'respecting the first station to be chosen for the settlement of a Missionary to the Jews.' Protracted discussion with the deputation resulted in the following resolution:

1. That Palestine, and particularly Galilee must ultimately become a most important station for our missionary operations and ought to be occupied ... as soon as circumstances render it advisable.
2. That however ... the unsettled state of that country seems to make it inexpedient if not impossible at present to attempt there any missionary work.
3. Given the political circumstances ... beginning a mission in Europe would be more desirable ...
4. That while in Palestine two missionaries at least would be required, even to commence the work, in Europe it might be commenced by a singe labourer with an assistant, who might also be preparing for Palestine – a consideration which the difficulty of procuring Missionaries renders important.[75]

The JMC later agreed to make representations to Lord Palmerston in order to ensure that the British government acted in such a way with regard to 'the East' that 'care should be taken to secure free access for Missionary operations' – clearly they were guarding their own future freedom to act.[76] No response from Palmerston is recorded.

On 2.6.1841, a search for suitable missionaries for Palestine was initiated,[77] and later that month it was decided to instruct an existing missionary (Dr Duncan in Hungary) to prepare himself for a trip to Palestine in order to assess the political situation for the JMC.[78] However, Keith, not Duncan, was called upon at a meeting held a short time later when the JMC,

> conversed over the subject of the Mission to Palestine and feeling the importance of having one established efficiently in that country as soon as possible, they ... [decided] to communicate with Dr Keith and ascertain whether he would be ... disposed to return to Palestine with some companion and establish a Mission there; and also to see whether he could suggest any qualified person to accompany him, and in the meantime recommend the [committee] Members ... to endeavour to hear of some properly qualified person for that important field of labour.[79]

It is noteworthy that Keith, one of the original members of the deputation, was suggested as the JMC's emissary; having brought back glowing reports the first time, possibly similar was expected were he to return. However, Keith preferred to go to Pesth to help Duncan's successors there should he, Duncan, be sent to Palestine, which was agreed upon by the JMC.[80] Subsequent meetings discussed the detail of an exploratory trip, and the JMC also wrote to Lord Palmerston regarding the government's opinion on the safety of a mission in Safad. One of Palmerston's subordinates replied on the 9.8.1841:

> Viscount Palmerston directs me to acquaint you ... that he apprehends that there is nothing in the State of Syria which could render it dangerous for such a Mission to establish itself at Safed, but he will ... make enquiry ... of the Officer in Command of the British detachment in Syria. If however the Society should ... send such a Mission out, His Lordship would recommend that it should go in the first instance to Beyrout: and his Lordship will give ... letters of recommendation to Her Majesty's Consul at Beyrout, instructing him to obtain ... all the information and every facility ... [the missionaries] may need and to afford them all the protection which they may require.[81]

The JMC resolved to thank Palmerston (no further communication from his office is recorded), and to proceed as quickly as possible with setting up a Palestine mission, waiting only for the return of a missionary at that time working in Jamaica, who could lead the work. This is one of the first examples of the church using the imperial element of British political power in seeking to intervene on their own behalf in internal Ottoman affairs.

However, the Foreign Office letter, containing from the perspective of the JMC an authoritative opinion, appears to have led to a change in emphasis which would take many years to change. No decision on this is in evidence, but Palestine virtually disappeared from the JMC minutes, and attention was turned to Beirut. Indeed, when discussion with the Irish equivalent of the JMC regarding a Mission in this region took place just a few months later, they quickly resolved to send someone to Beirut, not Palestine (see below). Of course, Palmerston was by no means suggesting that the Church should not proceed to Safad, merely that they should make contact with the British Consul in Beirut before proceeding to Safad. The joint mission with the Irish to Beirut which ended up in Damascus is the only brief involvement the Auld Kirk or Free Kirk had with the Levant in the intervening years. It is unclear why they did not plan to go to Palestine, but whatever the grounds for this, very little serious reflection on sending a missionary to Palestine occurred in the JMC's minutes for many years.[82]

The Free Kirk, to which all the Jewish missionaries, and virtually all the funds and properties went following the Disruption of 1843, prosecuted missions in various locations across Europe and Constantinople over the next decades. Although Palestine occurred in occasional minutes, it remained as an aim, a goal to be achieved, but no substantial movement occurred in this direction. Meanwhile, the work that was carried out covered specific areas: based in one central location, travel in the surrounding area was accepted as the norm, following the pattern of contemporary missions elsewhere in the world.

Damascus

As already noted above, the mission in Damascus, the city so closely connected to the conversion of Paul (Acts 9) was the only foray by the Free Church into the Levant until the latter decades of the 19th century. The Damascus mission was conducted in conjunction with the PCI, a denomination with which the Free Church would have felt broad sympathy theologically – this interest on the part of the Irish was inspired by McCheyne's visit there in 1840.

Co-operation with the Presbyterian Church of Ireland

A November 1841 meeting of the Free Kirk JMC noted Irish plans for a mission to Syria, and decided that 'steps should be taken ... that the two Missions acted in co-operation with one another'.[83] It was discussed further the following month: the Irish had reported that they would soon be in a position to send someone and enquired of the Scots their missionaries' salary level.[84] The Scots decided to offer to send someone to accompany an Irish missionary; a March 1842 meeting confirmed the interest but noted that although contact with the Irish church was ongoing, no appointment had yet been made.[85] This meeting also discussed the possible appointment of Pieritz, encountered by the original deputation in Palestine. He had left the LJS (due to 'some difference of opinions regarding the management of the Mission at Jerusalem') and had offered his services to the Scots; they contacted the LJS about him, eventually deciding that it would not be 'expedient' to employ him at that time.[86]

At this stage, the Committee appears to have become concerned at the demands being placed upon it by the rapid expansion in mission stations and the lack of suitable personnel (the work was expanding in Central Europe, though not, at this time, in the Levant). This resulted in existing commitments being reviewed and arrangements for the coming year decided upon (the year ran from one General Assembly – held in May – to the next):

> considering the small number of Missionaries they still had and that there was no prospect of assistance from Ireland, Mr Hamilton ... having written that unexpected difficulties had arisen in their way ..., that ... it would be inexpedient to think of occupying Palestine at present; and while keeping the Station prominently before them, ... the following arrangements should be made for the ensuing year, viz – that Dr. Duncan should be stationed in Holland and ... Mr Pieritz should be sent there ... with him, if he was employed by the Committee [which as already pointed out, did not then happen], that Mr Smith & Mr Allan should be stationed at Pesth and Mr Edwards and Mr Phillips remain ... at Jassy.[87]

It can be regarded as no mean achievement that in a little over three years the Committee had five staff working in a mission field that until that time had been completely new to Scottish church life, although the Committee was clearly struggling to maintain the work.

The mention of Irish 'difficulties' is slightly odd (it is not clear what is being referred to) because by July the PCI had found a suitable candidate and were seeking advice from the Scots about their candidate. The Irishman was to be Professor Hart, a Belfast professor of Hebrew – although he quickly withdrew and was replaced by a William Graham, who is not described in any detail in Scottish sources.[88] The Scots decided Allan, at that time destined for Pesth, should accompany Hart/Graham, and recalled him for ordination. Dr. Wilson, a Scottish missionary in India imminently on his way back to Scotland via Syria, was requested to assist in establishing a mission there. It was decided that the mission 'should be at Jerusalem if the country at Saffit was not settled and this notwithstanding the establishment of the London Society's Mission there' – this is notable for the conscious decision to enter into a possible conflict with the LJS.[89]

Subsequent meetings ironed out the detail of the proposed co-operation: each missionary was to be answerable to their own church, although they would work together on the ground and the committees would exchange copies of their instructions to their missionaries so that they could be kept informed of the overall picture. It was initially suggested that Graham and Allan travel to Egypt to meet Wilson, but this was then altered to Beirut, where it was also decided the mission should be opened – although they do leave this open to wherever should be appropriate according to their assessment once in the region.[90] As already noted, the idea of creating a mission in Palestine, either in Safad or in Jerusalem, was dropped, although the minutes give no indication of why this might be.

By November the Committee had met both Allan and Graham (at meetings in October), Allan had been ordained by Hamilton Presbytery and was to be married before leaving Scotland, Graham was already on his way, and Allan was then sent via, among other places, Constantinople. This was so that he would have the opportunity of meeting an experienced missionary there, William Gottlieb Schauffler,[91] contingent upon his still being able to reach Beirut in time to meet Wilson. Allan's salary was set at £300 a year plus a contribution for rent, which the Committee decided upon since 'owing to the disturbed state of Syria, [rent] was very high' in Beirut.[92]

By this time, Syria was not in as much of a 'disturbed state' as the Scots thought. Greater Syria at that time had been restored to Ottoman control, Muhammad Ali having signed the Treaty of London in 1841 which compelled him to withdraw from all the territories he had occupied except Sudan. The Hatt-i Sharif of Gulhane, a statement of royal intent issued in 1839, proclaimed that it was deemed appropriate 'to seek by new institutions to procure for the provinces which make up the Ottoman Empire the benefit of a good administration',[93] and under the terms of Gulhane, Muslims, Jews and Christians were to be treated equally in the creation of new laws;[94] missionaries would have seen this as a positive move to enabling their ambitions. Having had control of the country since 1833 with his son, Ibrahim Pasha, as governor, Muhammad Ali had forced through a number of domestic administrative changes similar to those successfully implemented in Egypt, including monopolisation of important trade (which damaged local craft industries) as well as legislation which also created equality, including conscription for all regardless of religious affiliation.[95] The trade implications of Muhammad Ali's actions led to Britain persuading the Ottoman government in 1838 to sign the Treaty of Balta Liman, which provided for the abolition of all trade monopolies within the empire and granted foreign goods entry at a tariff of only 3%;[96] other European powers followed with similar agreements, and this, together with strict enforcement of the Capitulations eventually ensured that Egyptian influence, economic independence and development was severely curtailed. Conscription caused more severe problems, however, with Bashir II (1788-1841), a Shihab Maronite Christian ruler, co-operating with the Egyptians and thereby increasing the sectarian divide, particularly on Mount Lebanon. He had helped Egypt with taxation and arms acquirement. The Druze, who were subject to conscription, resented Bashir II's role in relation to the Egyptians, even though he had persuaded the Egyptians to halve their initial request for conscripts. Difficulties increased when Bashir II (albeit reluctantly) agreed to disarm the Druze altogether because they (and the remainder of the population of Lebanon) had supposedly resisted conscription. Renewed conscription orders were issued, but a major insurrection arose against this in 1838: Bashir II's son and 4,000 Christians helped the Damascene governor and Ibrahim Pasha crush the rebels. This fed into an emerging pattern of distrust between Maronite and Druze communities: the former had appeared to benefit more from the Egyptian occupation, whereas the Druze had felt this had happened at the expense of their own status. 1838 marked the beginning of lasting and pervasive hostility, and even though the Christians sided with the Druze against the Egyptians in a rebellion in 1840 (which, with Bashir II helping the Egyptians, was again crushed), a reconciliation between the sects was not going to be possible. The 1840 war marked the beginning of the end of Egyptian involvement in Syria, as western powers – Austria, Britain, Prussia and Russia – intervened to prevent, as they saw it, the break-up of the Ottoman empire, and to re-establish control of Syria by the Porte; after such tensions as had arisen, it was not possible to revert to previous patterns of administration, however, and from 1843 the mountain was divided into *kaymakamates* or administrative areas, one for Druzes and one for Maronites, which met with limited success (in part because of poor or impossible planning, for example, the Druze *kaymakamate* contained mostly Maronites).[97] However, at the time that the Free Kirk wanted to enter the region relative stability existed, coupled with ever increasing European control over the eastern Mediterranean.[98] The 'high rent' in Beirut was therefore unlikely to have come from the 'disturbed state of Syria,' but from the increasing prominence of the city port as international trade, particularly with France, grew.[99]

Having earlier decided that they would be happy to work in the same location as the LJS, the Committee now encountered problems with this: the PCI had asked for tracts for their missionary in Beirut from the LJS; these had been refused on the basis that the LJS already had a missionary in Beirut. It was resolved that the Scots could try and acquire tracts from them; a few weeks later the Committee spent time resolving how to get tracts to Syria, although whether these were from London is not clear.[100]

The last meeting of the Committee in the undivided Church took place on 5.4.1843 and noted a singular turn of events. Allan, on arrival in Constantinople, had found that the LJS missionary there, a Mr Schwartz, was about to leave and abandon two flourishing schools – the minutes indicate no reason behind this – and that he, Allan, felt this was an opportunity not to be missed. Wilson later met Schwartz, and had a 'high opinion of… [him] as a Missionary'.[101] He was employed by the Committee,[102] and Allan took over the running of the schools.[103] The Committee, presented with a missionary several thousand kilometres away not carrying out the instructions they had given him, no doubt felt they had no choice but to acquiesce with Allan's decision, somewhat lamely noting that 'plague' in Beirut appeared to be bad and that Allan should stay in Constantinople for the time being, the agreement with the PCI still being binding and expecting Allan to maintain contact with Graham; meanwhile sending £50 to help with the running of the schools.

Excursus: The Disruption

The Disruption of 1843 has already been referred to in Chapter 1. In summary, the conflict centred around the rejection of state patronage of the Church of Scotland, resulting in members of the General Assembly of that year forming what became the Free Church of Scotland.[104] The self-perception of the Free Church was not of being a 'breakaway' church but rather of being the 'true' church. The Church of Scotland found itself being abused as the 'residuary establishment' and it took some time for it to recover its energy following the departure of approximately 38% of its ministers, 40% of its membership, and a still higher percentage of its elders,[105] leading 'within a short time ... [to] around 800 [Free Kirk] congregations'.[106] Some of the most able students also left for the Free Kirk.[107] In very broad terms, the upper and lower-classes (such as there were within the church) remained within the Auld Kirk, whilst the middle-classes went over to the Free Kirk.[108] This pattern is of particular relevance when considering missions, since the middle-classes had become ever more confident following the 1832 Reform Act (which gave much of the middle-class the vote[109]). They pressed for being able to choose their own ministers (the Veto Act, which gave congregations the power to veto a patron's choice of minister, did not go far enough for the likes of Thomas Chalmers and other evangelicals), and this social grouping were among those who most readily volunteered for missionary service.[110] In addition, many of the ministers who left were from the younger generation, those ordained after 1830 (over half of these left the Auld Kirk).[111] These factors help to explain the energy and enthusiasm for missions (in general) to be found in the Free Kirk, and go some way to explaining the struggle the Auld Kirk had in regaining its missionary involvement.[112]

The JMC's invitation to its missionaries makes for a clear understanding of the issues, and follows a complete record of the 'Protest' made at the General Assembly:

> The Committee directed a formal communication to be made immediately to all the Missionaries of the late Committee, informing them that the Assembly of the Free Protesting Church cordially invited them to adhere to that Church, and had resolved to maintain the Mission to the Jews, and anxiously desired the benefit of their services in connection with it; and that the Church had little doubt that they would be able to maintain this Mission as efficiently, if not more so than ever, and that the Salaries and Allowances of the Missionaries would they trusted be at the same rate and on the same footing as formerly.[113]

The Disruption was seen as being a firm break: for example, Chalmers, in a House of Commons report of 1847 on sites for churches replied that a reunion was impossible: only a 'restoration', meaning the Auld Kirk moving to the Free Kirk position, could result in a united church.[114] There can be no doubt that the Committees of the two churches needed to make a fresh start or re-establish their authority over the area they were responsible for – explaining the Free Kirk's clear position with regard to its missionaries.

This bore fruit for the Free Kirk, for by September the last of the JMC missionaries had written back to inform the Committee that they were going over to the Free Kirk.[115] The Free Kirk saw it 'as a point of honour' to maintain and extend the 'schemes' of the Auld Kirk, including the 'Jewish Scheme', and so 'it was not surprising that the six missionaries in the field adhered to the cause of the part that believed most strongly in the conversion of Israel.[116] This no doubt strengthened the hand of the Free Kirk JMC, which since its meeting on 23.6.1843 had been negotiating the fair division of resources with the Auld Kirk. It can be assumed that the Free Kirk took a reasonably hard line on this matter, since at that June meeting they decided that the funds in hand really belonged to them, especially so if all the missionaries went with the Free Kirk: this was decided on the basis that the money had been given for the specific purpose of working with Jews, and only they would be able to do that since the missionaries were with them.[117]

With this, the consequences of the Disruption were completed for the Free Kirk; the Auld Kirk valiantly struggled on in the face of adversity: the 1843 JMC General Assembly report, given just days after Chalmers and his supporters had walked out, is couched in pained terms:

> Dr. Hill stated verbally, that, though there were abundant materials for a Report, yet, from circumstances well known to those present, no detailed Report could at present be given. The General Assembly again appointed a Committee for this object, and nominated the Rev John Hunter to be its Convener.[118]

The subsequent year's accounts show no payments to active missionaries (the £226 10s 4d shown are presumably made to the Free Kirk for their missionaries, since in the following year over seven times that amount is shown as expenditure for missionaries),[119] though over time a commitment 'to Jewish missions... [was] revived in the post-Disruption Kirk',[120] with missions in Europe and the Levant.

The development of the mission

Whilst the JMC clarified arrangements following the Disruption, it continued its work. Communications with the PCI continued,[121] as did the exploratory work Wilson and others were charged with. Wilson wrote to the Committee early in August from Constantinople, 'stating the reasons which had induced him and Mr Graham to advise that the joint Presbyterian Mission in Syria should be stationed at Damascus and not at Beyrout, as intended, – which arrangements the Committee approved of'.[122] Unfortunately for contemporary readers, the reasons are not elaborated upon or even hinted at. The PCI appear to have approved of this change of heart as well, since that is where the Mission, originally destined for Palestine and then for Beirut, was eventually founded. The only further comment came in a subsequent meeting when Wilson 'at the request of the Committee made a statement of the condition of the Jews in Arabia and Syria',[123] but again, no further detail is given. The only information available is from the Assembly reports, when Wilson explains why he and Graham preferred it to Jerusalem: 'solely because, at the latter place, there is already an efficient mission in operation'.[124] Either the Committee had had a change of heart over its readiness to go to Jerusalem despite the presence of the LJS, or Wilson, an experienced missionary, had made this decision and then communicated it to the Committee – this latter would seem more probable.

No difficulties are mentioned in founding the mission, and at the beginning of the following year, Wilson is found addressing the Committee, pleading for a library for the missionaries – Allan in the meantime having joined Graham. This library was to contain 'Arabic Books & Books on the Jewish Controversy and School Books'; Wilson was prepared to go to London to arrange for their transfer to Beirut. Duncan, who in the meantime had been recalled to Scotland as Professor of Oriental Languages at the Free Church college, lent his support to this undertaking.[125] The Committee assented, and allocated £100 to be split between the three categories Wilson had outlined: £50 for books on the 'Jewish Controversy', and £25 for Arabic and £25 for school books; the Irish Committee was to be informed of this.[126] This allocation clearly illustrates the Committee's priorities, and their belief that disputation and well-founded argument would prove to be the most effective means of gaining Jewish converts; the conditions and contexts under which Jews might have been able to access these materials is not elaborated upon.[127]

At this same meeting, Wilson urged the Committee to make moves towards having a 'medical person attached to the Mission at Damascus... [since] nothing could be more attractive to the Jews'. Wilson's recognition at this stage of the importance of medical mission as a means of outreach is illuminating.[128] Medicine had only just begun to be thought of as a part of the missionary endeavour and many were sceptical of such moves (the Edinburgh Medical Missionary Society (EMMS), which also worked in the Levant, was only founded in 1841 and represented the first major breakthrough in the use of medical missionaries[129]). Scotland, more so than England, was probably more open to the possibility of a medical contribution to mission at this time.[130] At this stage, the medical profession was still regarded with scepticism by missionaries and churches, full professionalisation only coming about with the 1858 Medical Act.[131] In later years, the acceptance of medical missionary work grew, and particularly in Scotland, represented an increasing concern to relate Christianity and civilisation, which 'became more convincing as an imperialistic cast of mind became dominant'.[132] Medical missions proved to be a useful tool of missionary organisations in 'Islamic' contexts,[133] although whether Wilson had this in mind is doubtful: although only a small percentage of the population in Damascus was Jewish, with the majority being Muslim, and he would only really have been interested in the Jewish population. However, despite the foresight shown by Wilson in suggesting this possibility (he even suggested a possible candidate – the son of Dr. Keith), there is no further reference to this topic in the Committee's minutes. It is worth noting, however, that it was agreed to appoint a medic and to open a medical dispensary in Constantinople in 1844, indicating that it was not the idea itself that put the Committee off starting something along these lines in Damascus.[134]

At this stage, the individual who became Allan's successor, Daniel, came to the attention of the Committee: Wilson had met him, and together with Duncan suggested that he go to Damascus to work as a teacher under the two missionaries already there.[135] The Committee must have been convinced of sufficient progress in Damascus to move so quickly at increasing their numbers, but this is not recorded in detail: Allan is noted as requesting Bibles for which 'there was a great demand ... on the part of the Jews';[136] the Committee agreed to approach the LJS about procuring copies, but not much more appears on this topic at this stage. The Committee's secretary wrote to Damascus to enquire about whether such a position would be useful to them; at a meeting several weeks later the Committee arranged for further training of Daniel, presumably having received an affirmative reply from Damascus.[137]

The beginning of the end of Scottish involvement

In what appears at first to be a contradictory move, the Committee then initiated steps to reduce their level of involvement in Damascus: it decided that Allan should be sent from Damascus to Constantinople (the Irish were also invited to send someone to join him there), since a Mr Robson, an appointee of the PCI,[138] was to join Graham at Damascus. The Irish were to be consulted on this move, but the only other condition, made very clear, was that this should not 'interfere with… [the Damascus Mission's] efficiency or prospects in the slightest Degree'.[139] Daniel was to be on his way to Damascus, but in terms of importance, there can be no question that an ordained missionary was ranked more highly than a teacher – and in any case, it was to be the following year before Daniel actually went.[140] How the Committee could envisage that withdrawing one of the founders of the mission less than a year after he had arrived would not affect the operations 'in the slightest Degree' is somewhat hard to imagine: it can hardly be that they felt Allan had been ineffective, or they would not have wanted to send Daniel out to work with him and Graham, and in any case, requests for literature and Bibles had been noted and attempts made to procure such items: there was clearly a willingness to invest in the mission. On the other hand, Allan bemoans his struggle with the language, so that the General Assembly is told that,

> while the Word may thus [through literature] be silently working its way, there is also a disposition, not indeed to inquire, but to converse; so that Mr Allan, in his letter of last month, writes, "we have still to lament rather over our inability to speak, than our want of opportunities."[141]

It may be that the Committee felt that a missionary who had so far distributed literature but could not engage in serious discussion with the readers could easily be moved to another location without great loss. What still remains confusing about this situation is that there appears to have been no intention to replace Allan, relying on Robson to take on his work, and wanting themselves only to send a teacher.

The apparent contradictions in the Committee's decisions lay not in Damascus, but in Constantinople, the topic of much concern for the JMC over the previous months. Allan's work in Constantinople, brief though it had been, appears to have made enough of an impact for him to be sent back there, and the demands of the work there had given the JMC so much to consider and discuss that they probably felt this was the simplest way to proceed. They record that

> in scarcely any other city in the world – perhaps in none – are the Jews more numerous than in Constantinople, being estimated at 80, 000 … That station has occupied much

of the attention of the Committee during the past year. In addition to the school, a dispensary and institution have been established ... It hence became necessary that Mr Allan should remove from Damascus to that city, when his presence at the former could be more easily dispensed with, on the arrival of another missionary at that station from the Presbyterian Church of Ireland.[142]

Damascus, meanwhile, had become such a low priority, that apart from the above note and other similar mentions,[143] it did not even feature as a full item in that year's General Assembly proceedings. Indeed, in April 1846, the Committee wondered whether they had expanded too quickly into too many fields, leaving themselves vulnerable to weaknesses in the various mission stations. The discussion concluded that this was indeed the case, and that an appeal should be made within the Church for men of experience (no mention of women) to come forward and work for the Committee.[144]

The final stages

The September meeting recorded a letter from Daniel in Damascus (but no indication as to the contents); at this meeting the Secretary was directed to communicate with the PCI to confirm that if Graham (in Damascus) were to pay Daniel from his Church's funds, the Scots would refund the amounts drawn; an enigmatic instruction to the Secretary to write to Graham in Damascus 'about Daniel' closes the meeting – presumably this refers to the salary issue.[145] Clearly, the interest in Damascus was waning, and only pecuniary support was on offer. The management of Daniel had been left to the PCI (the 1846 General Assembly records that he 'went from us to be an assistant to them'[146]), and apart from a vague expression of hope for results, no further report was given. The minutes of the JMC record increasing questions around his continued employment in Damascus (in July 1847 it was discussed, without a conclusion being reached, whether Daniel should be sent to Constantinople, 'as it seemed doubtful if it was expedient that he should remain at Damascus'[147]). This issue was possibly cast further into question by undefined issues around his behaviour arising out of correspondence with the Irish missionaries and their superiors in Belfast.[148] In May 1848 the Committee found itself discussing a complaint from Americans in Syria about Daniel's comments on one of their employees,[149] – whether this was the same issue as the Irish were referring to is not clear.

Daniel was clearly becoming more of a problem for the Committee in Scotland. The issue of his continued employment came to a head, however, in June 1848 when the Committee was requested to sanction his marriage and assure him of the permanence of his post with them after receiving a letter from him,

intimating his intention to marry and wishing to know if the Committee would say whether he was to be kept there permanently; – the Committee were of opinion ... that it would not be advisable to retain Mr Daniel at Damascus, – and considering his anomalous position, the late misunderstanding with the Irish Missionaries, – and the difficulty of receiving reports concerning his efficiency, – they thought it would be necessary to have the report of parties, upon whom the Committee could depend as to his whole qualifications for being in the employment of the Committee, and in what capacity; – and therefore resolved that he should be directed to proceed to Constantinople to be under the Missionaries there ... and until their Report, the Committee deferred saying whether he might be permanently continued in their service; and considering the salary of the Labourers there of equal standing with his, they resolved that his salary should be reduced to £100 after leaving Damascus; and in these circumstances, they could give no sanction to his marriage.[150]

Daniel's reaction to this meeting's conclusions, which clearly doubted his ongoing viability as their employee, is not known. Financial difficulties that the Committee were experiencing in any case would not have made them any more open to continuing with his employment if his 'effectiveness' was in doubt (that same meeting also discussed the Committee's financial problems), and three weeks later the Committee resolved to end his employment with them, not even sending him to Constantinople:

the Committee ... could give no sanction to ... [his marriage], as it depended on his being permanently in their employment; ... [but] as Mr Daniel was not under the authority of any of the Committee's Missionaries at Damascus, and as there had been some complaints against his conduct there, it was not expedient to continue him at that station; and ... they did not think he could be sent to any other station; ... therefore, they thought it would be best to discontinue Mr Daniels connection with the Committee, and they directed him to be informed of this, and that they would pay the reasonable expense of his return to this country, or to any other place in Europe he thought more for his advantage, and allow £100, as one years salary – as a gratuity to maintain him after his arrival in Europe, until he got other employment.[151]

Subsequent queries around Daniel's expenses occupied the JMC's further meetings, as did his search for other employment: the Committee produced a nondescript reference for him to the LJS, explaining they had had little opportunity of assessing his work since there had been no ordained Scottish missionary in Damascus. However, he had been found to be 'uniformly obliging and attentive' and that the reasons for their ceasing their employment of him were due to having no ordained missionary of their own in Damascus and a 'desire to discontinue the Station' there – they do not appear to have mentioned that it was they who withdrew the one ordained missionary they had had there. Further queries from the LJS as to 'whether the want of energy or zeal formed any ground of disqualification' were rebutted with the explanation that 'they did not know where to employ him in the capacity in which he had been previously engaged'.[152]

Thus ended the association of the Auld and Free Kirks with Damascus. Although the Irish continued the mission in Damascus, the joint element of it had failed, not in the first instance from lack of progress, but primarily due to the demands of other locations and lack of suitable staff to supply the perceived needs (Allan being sent to Constantinople) – as the members of the Committee had themselves realised, they had expanded too quickly without the material resources to back up their commitments. Replacing Allan with Daniel, in the Committee's eyes an inferior employee because not ordained, did not serve to stabilise or increase their commitment to the mission station. In fact, rumours, substantiated or otherwise, about Daniel's behaviour only led to a decreasing sense of commitment. When he finally forced the Committee to make a clear decision about his long-term future with them by requesting security in the context of his planned marriage, they quickly withdrew their support. Allan's sojourn in Constantinople prior to his arrival in Damascus may have attracted him to that city more than to staying in Damascus, but the Committee also appears to have been more assured of his work being a 'success' in the Ottoman capital than in Syria – the criteria for this measure of success not being explicitly stated, but existing schools which only needed maintenance and/or extension were doubtlessly preferable to the founding of completely new institutions for a Committee with finite resources. Allan's limited Arabic will have contributed to this, but it is not known how proficient he was in any other languages which may have assisted him in Constantinople.

It was to be many years before the Free Kirk ventured into Syria/Palestine again. The crisis of 1860 did not move the Auld Kirk or Free Kirk as such to any great activity in the region, although other religious organisations did take up work there as a result of the war, such as Bowen Thompson's schools network, the EMMS, and the Lebanon Schools Association. The JMC's ventures in Palestine in the latter part of the century were not in partnership with other bodies: as mission work developed during the 19th century, sending bodies were able to draw on increased resources and were less reliant on working in partnership. Although this might have made some of the management issues clearer, it created other problems, the Near East providing an example of the negative implications of such individual activity, as countless organisations worked alongside each other, often in competition and seeing each other as rivals (c.f. Richter's famous analysis of 'the waste of energy that results from the dividing of the missionary undertaking in Syria among so many small, independent missions'[153]).

Aleppo

The United Presbyterian Church, formed in 1847 by a union,[154] was smaller than either the Free Kirk (with which it eventually united in 1900 to form the United Free Kirk) or the Auld Kirk. However, interest in Jews and missions to Jews also existed, and although some work had been initiated (for example in Hamburg), this took a more prominent place in the life of the church when the Scottish Society for the Conversion of Israel (SSCI) transferred their work to the United Presbyterian Church in 1857.[155] The transfer was linked with an overture to the United Presbyterian Church's Synod of that year from Kilmarnock Presbytery, which acknowledged the existing work of the Church overseas, pointed out that there were 'very many of the seed of Abraham according to the flesh in various parts of Africa' and suggested that 'the Synod should forthwith resolve to add a Jewish branch to their present missionary operation'.[156] The SSCI, a body deriving most of its support from members of the United Presbyterian Church, offered, with particular reference to the Kilmarnock overture, to transfer its work to the Church; this was accepted, leaving it to the Mission Board to 'consummate the necessary arrangements, preserving as far as possible the spirit of catholicity in this movement, so as to retain the contributions of Christian brethren of other denominations'.[157] The desire for secure financial arrangements was clearly expressed, and any ideological or theological problems the United Presbyterian Church may have encountered with non-United Presbyterian Church support for the SSCI were overlooked in favour of the purpose of bringing about conversion of Jews.

When the SSCI was transferred to the United Presbyterian Church, one of the employees who was subject to that transfer was Rev R Grant Brown, at that time stationed in Alexandria, working alongside an ordained doctor, Hermann Philip. Their respective salaries were at that time £200 and £250, with Philip receiving a further £42 in benefits.

Aleppo is suggested as a mission station

Brown had not fared well in Alexandria and had been forced to leave, citing ill health (Philip likewise departed shortly thereafter and the mission was passed over to the Auld Kirk).[158] However, Brown was keen to remain in the region, and one of the early meetings of the United Presbyterian Church's Mission Committee following the transfer of the SSCI work noted that he was to 'visit Syria and the Holy Land – that he was instructed to look out for a suitable place where he might labour among the Jews', that he had considered Gibraltar, Algiers, Joppa, Jerusalem, Damascus, Beirut, Safad and Aleppo, but considered the latter to represent the most promising opportunities.[159] He gave a number of reasons for this:

> 1. There are six or seven thousand Jews without any Missionary 2 The field was recommended by several American Missionaries who had laboured there among the Armenians. 3 The climate is dry and seems to suit his constitution 4 The Jews speak Arabic which he has learned. and 5 There is a small Protestant Church there over which a Medical Missionary was about to be placed, which would give him the benefit of Christian fellowship.[160]

He added that Aleppo would be a good centre for wider work, and gave a description of Aleppo's demographic mix that showed Jews forming approximately 6% of the population (100,000 inhabitants consisting of 60,000 Muslims, 6,000 or 7,000 Jews 'and the rest [a third of the population!] various sects'[161]). Courbage and Fargues indicate a Jewish population in Syria, Lebanon and Palestine of 27,382 (1.3%) in 1882[162] with the vilayet of Aleppo in 1914 with 10,046 Jews of a total population of 331,024, i.e. 3%.[163] The estimates regarding the numbers of Jews may therefore have been reasonably accurate, but that of the overall population appears to have been quite wrong (even though the city itself was only part of the *vilayet*).[164]

The fact that there 'was a desire expressed by some members of the Church to commence a Mission to the Turkish empire' and the general hopefulness communicated by Brown, along with his offer to himself go and start the Mission, led the Committee to agree to his proposals, 'with the assurance that should the way forward be found open, they will be ready to reinforce the Mission by a second and even by a third labourer'.[165] Brown accepted the offer on 23.8.1857,

> expressing his hearty acceptance of the call of the Committee ... believing that it is the will of his Lord and Master Jesus Christ, and trusting that in answer to the prayers of his people, by whose gifts he is supported, the Lord will go with him and exhibit the riches of his grace in the conversion of Jews and Gentiles.[166]

The early development of the mission

On this positive note, Brown is despatched to Aleppo, presumably leaving sometime after mid-September.[167] At first there is no record of his activity in the city, indeed no mention of him in the minutes at all until June 1859 based on a letter he wrote at the end of April[168] – presuming a departure of September 1857 this is 19 months after his departure. It is inconceivable that there had been no communication from him prior to this, but no records exist. His April 1859 letter and the committee's discussions centre on his salary level, which he had found to be too low, given the 'high prices of provisions, servants wages and other items' so that despite 'the utmost economy' he had spent more than £250 a year and was forced to seek a raise.[169] This was not necessarily a surprise: Europe experienced a recession in 1857/8 which tightened credit for business elsewhere, including in the Levant, and a poor cereal harvest in 1858 in the region coupled with a general decline in purchasing power resulting in part in increased nomadic raiding meant that the economic situation in Syria on Brown's arrival was not good.[170] Aleppo may have been more expensive than usual as much traffic from Baghdad changed course to Aleppo rather than Damascus following a substantial plundering of one particular caravan in 1857.[171] It is, of course, difficult to estimate the effect of this on Brown's own finances, particularly with regard to his and his family's expectations, but the Committee instructed its Secretary to 'request special information with regard to the present state and prospects of the Mission and the scale of prices and wages'.[172]

The subsequent meeting of the Committee sheds interesting light on the servant issue – it appears Brown had brought from England a servant, Mary Hersack, had despatched her by steamship back to England in the autumn of 1858, but had failed to cover her fare – the captain of the ship in question had then requested the fare from the Committee. The Committee sought information from Brown before agreeing to the captain's demands (although this topic does not reappear in the minutes). What is noteworthy is not that Brown had servants, but that he even brought these with him from Britain, an unusual move, since most missionaries would have had servants from the country they were in.[173]

Brown's response to the request for specific information on his expenses and the mission's chances took some time to deal with, as the Committee was not satisfied by his first attempt, and was only prepared to give consideration to a one-off increase for the current year following his second letter.[174] An issue of some importance for the future of the mission was also examined at this time, as Brown had made contact with the British Consul in Aleppo, James Henry Skene, who had apparently been elected the emir of 'the Arabs of the desert'.[175] Skene had persuaded these Arabs to settle two hours from 'the Jewish town of Jadif', seven hours from Aleppo, and was reportedly anxious to promote their religious education. For the estimated four million Arabs (Brown's figures) 'in this country bounded by the great curves formed by the cities of Bagdad, Mosul, Diarbeker, Oorfa ... Aleppos, Damascus and Jerusalem' there was no Christian involvement and Skene had invited Brown to become involved, suggesting that he go to Jadif and from there preach as often as he could to the Arabs. Brown appeared happy to involve himself with this project created by a British imperial representative, and asked two explicit questions of the Committee: 'Am I sanctioned in attempting to commence the work near Jadif till others are prepared for it? and Would the United Presbyterian Church be willing to occupy this new field as a permanent part of their missionary operations?'[176]

The Committee agreed that the first question could be answered in the affirmative; the answer to the second would depend upon the results of his work there. They gave his attempt financial support: a meeting in February authorised rental of a house in Jadif as well as purchase of a horse, at the Church's expense; his salary for 1860 was also set at £250.[177] However, there is no further mention of this scheme in the minutes of the Committee, and it is not even clear if Brown rented the house or purchased the horse; as mentioned, Skene's scheme failed, though it is not clear at what stage this happened.

That meeting also recorded receipt of two long and disheartened letters from Brown, complaining of an apparent lack of success, the cost of living,[178] and renewed estimates of the numbers (6,000 Jews, '30,000 nominal Christians who acknowledge the authority of the Pope' and 70,000 to 80,000 Muslims) and the fact that he was the only 'Evangelical Christian Teacher' there (but he did not specifically ask for a colleague[179]). He had employed a colporteur who spoke Arabic, Turkish and English and was a 'sincere Protestant' – a move the Committee approved of, reiterating their belief that they regarded 'the field as very important and deserving of an earnest trial ... they encourage Mr Brown to persevere in the work'. He expressed gratitude for the extra income the Committee had assured him of, which noted that 'the wages of servants and the modes of living shew that ... necessities ... are ... dearer than in this country, and that a European family ... must experience difficulty ... in getting on with any degree of comfort on ... less ... than £250 a Year'.[180]

The work is expanded

Brown's future colleague, John Wortabet, wrote to the Committee on 2.4.1860, applying for a position as a Jewish missionary in Syria, enclosing background information of his career to that point. Wortabet, a Syrian whose father was an Armenian priest,[181] had been ordained by the American Beirut mission in 1853 but had left them, according to his letter, because he wanted to visit Britain and he was unhappy at the 'peculiar relation, implying missionary supervision, in which the native ordained minister stood to the Missionaries of the Board'.[182] Being a doctor as well as a minister, he was offering his services in both capacities; the Committee gave an initial positive reaction and agreed to meet with him.

The May meeting recorded a meeting with Wortabet on 10.4., and found that he agreed with the Committee on substantial points of doctrine, that he was a member and minister of the Syrian church, and that he had not seen the United Presbyterian Church's Basis of Union nor their formula for ordination. These latter two documents were given to him, and he later gave written assent to their contents, agreeing to becoming a member and minister of the Church should his offer of service be accepted. Robson, the PCI missionary in Damascus (c.f. p42), vouched for Wortabet, as did at least one other individual known to the Committee. Wortabet clarified two conditions under which he would work for the Church:

> 1st That he be equal to a European Colleague in standing and office, there being no supervision of one over the other, and 2nd that he be equal with him in the matter of salary, being sensitive to this point as he considers that inferiority of salary implies inferiority of position or qualification on the score of nationality, but at the same time that he would not make perfect equality of stipend a necessary or indispensable condition.[183]

The Committee would likely initially, at least, have been astounded by Wortabet's demands. Other United Presbyterian missions would have employed native agents, and generally none of these would have been employed under similar conditions or pay to the Scottish/western missionaries. This was the position of all missionary organisations at the time: the 1860 Liverpool missionary conference clearly maintained that native agents should not be paid the same amount as a western missionary, in fact quite the contrary, they were urged 'by Western missionaries to make every effort to identify as fully as possible with their native brethren in the material-social sphere, since to do otherwise would seriously diminish their effectiveness'.[184] Although no record of such a meeting exists, it is fair to assume that Wortabet had met with Brown or had at least corresponded with him and that he was clear about the pay scales involved: Brown's extra £50 a year may be what Wortabet was referring to when he qualified his demand for equality by stating that it need not be 'perfect' – equally, one might argue that the Committee had only granted Brown a salary of £250 in February 1860,[185] and this may well have been after the probable contact Wortabet had had with him. Once appointed,

Rufus Anderson, the Secretary of the American Board of Commissioners for Foreign Missions, Wortabet's former employer, communicated in strong terms his disapproval of the United Presbyterian's level of salary and position for Wortabet, arguing amongst other things that their native agents would become disillusioned with the level of pay on offer if they heard about Wortabet, and being placated only after assurances that the Scottish mission was sufficiently distant from the Americans that no interference would result.[186]

Wortabet was accepted, the Church acceding to his conditions by making him equal in status to Brown and paying him the standard £200 for a Jewish missionary, acknowledging that since Brown had found this to be too little, Wortabet might also need more. Wortabet was therefore sent to Syria 'to labour in Aleppo and its vicinity, as a Missionary especially to the Jews', as his letter of appointment put it.[187]

Prior to Wortabet's departure for Aleppo, he spoke at the annual 'Missionary Meeting' that formed a part of each year's Synod, his topic being 'The present Aspects of Christianity in relation to the Mahomedans in Turkey' – there is no record of his speech.[188] He left with an outfit and medication paid for by the Committee to enable him to practice medicine on arrival, the Treasurer expecting fees to be collected for medical treatment and these to be clearly accounted for.[189]

Wortabet intended to travel via Beirut to Aleppo, in order to visit relatives in Beirut. The timing of his departure coincided with the time that the war on Mount Lebanon was spreading inland to Damascus:[190] Zahleh, the most significant town on the Mountain, was taken by Druze in a well-executed plan on 18.6.1860 resulting in numerous casualties,[191] this in turn gave rise to the fear of increased violence further inland.[192] In the end, Aleppo was spared substantial levels of fighting,[193] evidenced in part by the sudden increase (by 50% to 6,000) in silk-weaving factories in Aleppo after the destruction of competing factories in Damascus in that year – the supply being intended for the Egyptian market.[194] Brown, reportedly on the advice of the British Consul, 'in consequence of the excitement caused by the intelligence of the massacres in the Lebanon and at Damascus... [took] his family first to Biliss and then to Leradia'.[195] This appears to be based on a letter written by Brown on 26.7.; the same meeting records that he wrote again on 1.9. and the Committee minutes note, presumably based on the September letter, 'that the way now seems open to return to Aleppo but that he [Brown] was labouring a very severe attack of Ophthalmia' (i.e. conjunctivitis). The Committee approved of Brown's actions, and (perhaps somewhat naïvely) 'expressed a hope that the dreadful scenes which had occurred in Syria and the vigorous measures that have been taken to punish the perpetrators will turn out for the furtherance of the Gospel'.[196] Wortabet needed to travel through precisely the areas facing such 'dreadful scenes,' and reported in two letters written in August (and read at the October meeting) that 'he had been detained in Beyrout by the disturbed state of Syria' but that he had preached for the Americans and had worked with sick refugees, carefully noting that the medicines he had used belonged to the American mission and requesting 'whether or not in the terrible emergency' he found himself in he would be allowed to use the medicines paid for by the Scots – to which request he received no explicit answer, although the Committee recorded its approval of his actions, requesting him to proceed to Aleppo as soon as it appeared 'to be open and safe'.

By 30.10.1860, Wortabet had settled in Aleppo and wrote to the Committee requesting a salary increase,

> owing to the dearth of things in Aleppo, which led Mr Brown to ask for a grant, as well as to my losses in Hasbeiya, which leave me quite unprovided for in the matter of furniture against the coming winter, I am sorry that I have to make the same application. I had intended to have done without it; but I find this quite incompatible with our comfort and I need hardly urge the favourable consideration of my application to the Committee.[197]

The more sceptical reader might wonder in how far Wortabet could know that he would need more funds having been in Aleppo for at most two months when it had taken Brown almost 1½ years to establish this; although the massacre at Hasbeiya was undoubtedly 'one of... [the] darkest moments' of the civil war with about a thousand people being killed and only 40 or 50 men escaping[198] and Wortabet's belongings almost certainly did not survive (he, of course, had only just left Scotland in early June when the fighting took place), it does seem very early in his employment to be considering such a move. Be that as it may, no doubts appear in the minutes and his request was later approved.[199]

Something that may have played a role in this decision was the apparent success of the mission. The same meeting of the Committee discussed a proposal formulated jointly by Brown and Wortabet on 13.11.1860 that they obtain a place for public worship and open a 'superior' school for boys and one for girls, this communication being one of the few references to their work together. They calculated a budget

> for the first year including £30 for pews for Chapel and Desks for Schools, £173, and annually £143, namely Rent of suitable buildings for Chapel and Schools £30; Salaries for male and female head Teachers £70 Salary of Assistant Teacher for Boys School £27 and Incidental Expenses £16.[200]

The teaching staff were to come from Beirut. With what appears to be minimal discussion, the Committee agreed to these proposals 'provided that the expenses do not exceed what is stated and that the buildings be rented only'.[201]

Wortabet wrote again in early August, giving an account of the first examination of the schools by the British Consul, James Skene, and his wife, which seems to have been a success. He urged the Committee to write to Skene and thank him 'for his and his Ladys interest in the Mission, and friendship to ourselves. They have been very kind' – a request to which the Committee readily acceded.[202]

Misunderstandings arise – Brown departs

Brown left Aleppo the following year, 1863. This came about essentially from misunderstandings and offences taken that could perhaps have been avoided, given a more careful and sensitive approach to their employees' state of mind by the Committee, and more patience by Brown.

The first meeting of the full Committee that year,[203] on 27.1., discussed Wortabet's application for a salary increase to £250, which was agreed to, although the Committee did request 'a joint statement… from him and Mr Brown whether a less Salary than £250 a Year may not be sufficient in Aleppo.'

Brown had previously indicated doubts about the viability of the mission, but the Committee had then sent him a colleague and his disenchantment had been relieved. The setting up of the schools seems to have lifted his spirits. But at the end of 1862, he appeared to be approaching disillusionment once more, writing in a letter on 28.11. that the house he was in was to be let to another tenant from March and that he wished to make a visit home in the spring. He gave three reasons:

> that he may consult with the Committee and other friends whether it is not the Lord will, that he should find another field of labour, since on the one hand the Mission has now an excellent staff and machinery which can go on very well without him and on the other as no visible blessing has been given to his labours during the first five years; that if they continue in the East they may be invigorated by a temperate summer … specifying the cases of Mrs Brown, his eldest girl and himself "who suffered all last summer … which materially incapacitated him for work:" and that he may make arrangements for his revered father living with him during the rest of his life which he wishes to do.[204]

The claim that the Mission was on a solid footing was indeed true, at least financially and in terms of staffing: not only were there the two missionaries appointed from Edinburgh, but another letter of the same date indicates 'seven Teachers and Evangelists employed in Aleppo, Killis and Idlib … whose salaries amounted to £204.15.6 a Year' (the emphasis is Brown's) – this was noted immediately after Brown's request had been described.[205] Another letter, also written on 28.11., requested permission to print material at the Beirut missionary press for their work: this was approved after the discussion on the request to visit Britain. These factors would have clearly indicated to the Committee that the mission was growing in size, costs, and therefore, so it would have appeared, in potential. Brown's personal request was dismissed in curt terms:

> the Committee state that they regret that Mr Brown has hinted the idea of leaving the Mission, which has been but recently organised and which has not yet had an adequate trial – that they consider the reasons stated as quite insufficient to warrant so important a step; and that if any members of the Family require for the sake of

health to be sent to this country, they will on obtaining medical testimony to that effect, be prepared to favourably view the matter.[206]

Whilst doubtlessly correct in terms of the requirement for a medical certificate (and Brown would have been aware of this requirement, common among missionary organisations of the day), the Committee appear to have ignored the plea for reassurance and support that Brown's communication appeared to contain. The letter of the Secretary outlining this position was plainly offensive to Brown – he makes this clear to the Committee at a later stage – and although no copy of it exists, it was probably formulated in very similar terms to the minute.

Perhaps waiting for the Committee's response,[207] Brown wrote on 5.3. requesting a married couple who had trained as teachers and who would be willing to work in the boys' and girls' schools he and Wortabet had created. This request was read at the Committee's June meeting, and was immediately followed by the report of a letter Brown wrote on the 14.5. 'resigning his position in Aleppo and his connexion with the Mission', which itself was followed by the reporting of yet another letter written on the 13.5. informing the Committee that for health reasons he was 'on account of the advanced state of summer, immediately to leave Aleppo and come home with his family' – a medical certificate signed by Wortabet and a Dr Theodore Besedoff (of whom nothing is known[208]) was enclosed. The 13.5. letter stated that 'a visit home would likely be for the benefit of his eyes and that this visit should be made in the summer and autumn months'.[209] In the light of Brown's resignation, the letter about the teachers was not mentioned further at this meeting.

Brown's reasons for resigning should have come as no surprise to the Committee – he had, after all, expressed similar views on at least two occasions in the past:

> The reasons ... are, that after five Years labour none has appeared to receive his testimony concerning Christ – that it is the duty of Christs servants to depart from places where they are not received – that he cannot reconcile his mind to receiving the money of the church, whilst no fruits are produced and that all the agencies established in the Mission can go on without him.[210]

Brown presented his resignation in theological and honourable terms, both for himself and for his Church. In Mk 6:11 Jesus tells his disciples that 'if any place will not welcome you and they refuse to hear you, as you leave, shake off the dust that is on your feet as a testimony against them'. Brown obviously felt that five years with no baptisms represented a lack of success; at least no baptisms are recorded and when four do eventually occur, they are minuted in Edinburgh, implying such an unusual event that it is inconceivable earlier baptisms would not have been recorded in this way.[211] Mk 6, with its account of Jesus unable to work in his home town due to the lack of faith he found followed by the admonition to his disciples, is clearly being referred to in Brown's resignation letter. He presents himself as honourable in not wanting to take more of the church's money for a Jewish mission that had produced no Jewish converts; this does not appear to have led the Committee to reflect on the validity of their mission at all.

This may have been because on 14.5., the day Brown wrote his resignation letter, Wortabet also wrote to the Committee, 'intimating that he entertains views different from Mr Brown regarding the state and prospects of the Mission'. The Committee agreed to accept Brown's resignation (they clearly had little choice about this – he had probably already left Aleppo by the time the Committee was having its meeting) and regarded it

> as the resignation at once of his position in Aleppo and of his connexion with the Committee and that they at the same time state that they do not consider the reasons ... as being satisfactory, and that they regret that he did not communicate his decision in time to allow the Committee to express an opinion on it, or to consider what measures ... to take in consequence of it, before he left.[212]

It was further agreed to request further information from Wortabet on what they should do now Brown had left the mission.

Brown's resignation appears to have been carefully thought through, although the timing of the letter about taking leave and the resignation letter appear to contradict this. However, it could be reasonably surmised that Brown formulated the letter about taking leave on 13.5., perhaps with a particular event occurring or affliction worsening (either his own or of his family) prompting him the next day to put in writing what he had been reflecting on for some time. Clearly his letter of 28.11.1862 stating that he wished to consult as to 'whether it is not the Lord will' that he should work elsewhere is a precursor to the resignation letter of 14.5.1863, which states in more detail why he doubts the effectiveness of his labours.

A few months later, Brown addressed the Committee. The minutes convey the pain he felt at his treatment:

> Mr Brown, specifying his reasons for resignation, said that he was influenced by the ... Minute of this Committee of date 28th January 1863, and especially the letter of the Secretary communicating that Minute, as a refusal to allow him and his Family to come home even for the sake of health, and as conveying "a stern rebuke" for his proposing to do so.[213]

The Committee then attempted to explain the issues involved from their perspective and an apparently amicable resolution was reached:

> The letter of Mr Brown of 28th November 1862, the Minute of the Committee, the letter of the Secretary and Mr Browns letter of 16th April 1863 were read; when, after some conversation, Mr Brown declared that he was quite satisfied on the one hand that in his letter of 28th November he had inadequately stated his wishes to the Committee and on the other that he was mistaken in thinking that the Committee

refused in their minute of 28th January 1863 to grant either him or his family liberty
to come home for the sake of health, provided that Medical testimony should be
afforded shewing that such a step was necessary as well as in looking upon the letter
of the Secretary as administering to him a rebuke.'[214]

This is the end of Brown's involvement in Aleppo and the Committee's minutes record
no further discussion on the matter. It is unclear why Brown was 'quite satisfied' with
the Committee's conduct when it had led him to resign. Had he been unclear about
the matters raised he could have written to ask further details – the time that elapsed
would have allowed this to take place. Had he been convinced of the future of the
mission, then he may have taken these steps, but the response to his November letter,
being based on mission rules rather than an understanding of Brown's doubts, may have
convinced him that his personal future did not lie with the Committee. The Committee
and the Secretary, through a lack of sensitivity to his needs for reassurance (it could
even be regarded as quite courageous of Brown to express doubts so explicitly with his
employers) helped to turn Brown further away from the purpose of the mission, and
left him feeling he had no choice but to resign.

The last years of the mission

Wortabet, for whom Brown's resignation was perhaps not an encouraging sign (there
is no indication of any personal animosity between the two), became responsible for the
mission himself. He made it clear in his response (written on 6.7.1863) to the Secretary's
letter mentioned above that a colleague 'who can speak the Arabic language' was desirable,
and that 'with the abatement of his medical services [he will] carry out the objectives of
the Mission' in the meantime. He suggested someone already in employment in the Near
East, Rev John Hogg, at that time serving in Alexandria, although this came to nothing.[215]
Of Aleppo, Wortabet (conveniently? since it was clearly not proving successful in terms
of converts) ignored the mission's original target group, the Jews of the city:

> there is in Aleppo an Arab-speaking Christian population of 17000 "destitute of
> anything like direct Missionary labour." [the minutes quote Wortabet's letter] – that
> the American Mission deals with those only who speak ... Turkish ... – that he does not
> think the work there more difficult or unpromising than ... [elsewhere] in Syria – that
> they have been able to accomplish both in the matters of preaching and of Schools,
> as much as could reasonably have been anticipated, and that he does not think that
> the present state of the Mission would warrant it being broken up.[216]

The lack of reference to the Jews Wortabet was employed to convert was overlooked
by the Committee. This could well be due to another letter of Wortabet's which he wrote
on 1.9. and which was also read to the Committee. In this he informed the Committee
that not only had he admitted four adults to the communion, but that one of them
'was an ex-Bishop of the Armenian Church, and [he] had thus laid the foundation of

a United Presbyterian Congregation in Aleppo'. The Committee, which several years before had censured Benjamin Weiss for forming French-speaking congregations in Algiers,[217] appears to have made no comment on the notion that United Presbyterian congregations might be formed in Aleppo, though perhaps this was because it would not be a European-language congregation. This is certainly a different view to that of the Americans working e.g. on Mount Lebanon, who wanted to form an indigenous church, rather than a copy of their own denomination (even if this did take time, it was a clear and explicit intention).[218] It is not clear who the 'ex-Bishop' was, or if the other adults brought into the communion were related to him. At a subsequent meeting the Committee also discussed Wortabet's salary again, and agreed that it should be £250 a year from then on – they had in fact granted him the extra £50 every year until then.[219]

Brown's request for teachers, presented to the Committee simultaneously with his resignation letters and therefore receiving scant attention at the time, was referred to again over a year later, when in October 1864 the Committee 'called attention to the request which was made a considerable time ago ... for a Teacher to be sent from this country for the Female School.'[220] 'The propriety of finding one or two Female Teachers for the Girls School at Aleppo' had recently been discussed.[221] The October minute notes that there were 'two Ladies in this town [who were] studying Arabic with a view to the Mission field', one or both of whom might be sent to Aleppo. The Committee felt that Wortabet should be consulted on this matter; his response, recorded in a subsequent minute, shows signs that he too may have been becoming disillusioned with the work in Aleppo, for he wrote (the minute quotes his letter) that 'after a long consideration ... it seems to me that unless you send out another Missionary and are willing to raise the expense and the efficiency of the Mission, the present state of our work does not call for a female Teacher from Scotland'.[222] Nothing further comes of this discussion, and the matter is not raised again – in any case, the cholera outbreak that occurred in Aleppo later that year overshadowed all plans for development that there may have been.

Finance appears to have dominated Wortabet's communications with the Committee, or at least, these are the matters that are minuted, and an interesting issue in connection with finance arose at this time, reflecting again on Wortabet's sense of self-worth in relation to western missionaries and local staff.[223] In August 1864 (and discussed at a meeting in September) Wortabet wrote requesting a grant for one of his catechists and teachers based in Killis, one Denour Abdie, of £10 in order to assist him with debts 'incurred partly on account of the insufficiency of the school fees and partly because he had to pay 500 piastres urgently when he became a Protestant'.[224] Granted by the Committee on that occasion, a further application for an identical amount was made for the same individual the following year, although no reason for the grant was given second time around. What is interesting to note is that the grant should be made, 'as for reasons which he [Wortabet] does not state he does not wish to raise the Salary'[225] – the salary had not changed from the previous year's £27. It may seem odd at first that Wortabet, a Syrian by birth and on a salary almost ten times greater than that of his assistant, a fellow Syrian, should refuse to countenance an increase of such a relatively small amount.

Although Wortabet's income had been set to be the same as Brown's and he appears to have succeeded in spending it, the determination to keep his assistant's salary so low (going so far as refusing to give reasons for this) indicates something of Wortabet's attitude: his desire to be treated as a European given his educational background and status meant that he was unable to implement the material-social identification that might have been expected.[226] The Committee was not happy with this secrecy and made this clear to Wortabet – but approved the second grant.

Although 'Asiatic cholera'[227] had existed in the Ottoman Empire since 1821, the 1865 outbreak was particularly severe (Wortabet's account was 'very affecting' and described how it 'literally decimated the inhabitants, carrying off ... the writing master of the Boys School and his wife, one of the members, his wife and all his children except one'[228]). The Hijaz and the cities of Mecca and Medina with their large visiting populations formed centres for the disease, with an estimated 30,000 pilgrims dying that year. Increasingly rigorous quarantine restrictions had only begun to be imposed from the 1850s, but despite this 1865, 1893 and 1902 saw further serious outbreaks across the Empire.[229] With the Near East being one of the most urbanised regions in the world in 1800 (almost 15% of the population lived in towns of 10,000 or more inhabitants) and this urbanisation increasing in the 19th century, it is easy to appreciate how quickly such a disease could spread if unchecked.[230]

It might be assumed that Wortabet, employed as a medical and not simply an ordained missionary, would find such a crisis giving him ample opportunity for work. However, in a letter of 10.11.1865 he informed the Committee that he had left the city, saying that

> It was my intention to have stayed ... and to have done my best for the sick and the dying; but ...[due to] my ill health ... brought on by the fatigues of the summer season, and a return of the fever and the great prostration which followed it, I found it my painful duty to leave the city and seek the high mountain air. I left with my family (and Isa of Idleb) along with Mr and Mrs Skene for the mountains of Kissab where we stayed nine weeks.[231]

This was the first time that Wortabet's health had come as an issue before the Committee – it is fair to assume that had there been serious problems in the past, the Committee would have known about them (as happened with Brown). The Committee's Secretary replied in a letter of 29.12.1865 in no uncertain terms to Wortabet, an extract from his letter being quoted in the minutes immediately after Wortabet's letter:

> I regret extremely that your state of health made it necessary for you to remove from Aleppo during the ... Cholera. I abstain from pronouncing any opinion farther than an expression of regret. I have hesitated to submit your letter to the Church. It is the only instance of the kind that has occurred in any of our Mission Stations; and I am afraid that the Church would regard in an unfavorable light the fact that at such a time a Medical Missionary left the field.[232]

Wortabet's expression of remorse at having to leave ('It was my intention to have stayed... my painful duty...') was obviously not nearly strong enough for the Edinburgh office, a fact recognised by Wortabet, for he responded with another letter on 30.1.1866 in response to the Secretary's communication 'in which at considerable length he assigns the reasons which induced him to leave Aleppo'. He said that he deplored the fact of his departure as much as anyone, was not prepared 'either to deny or to extenuate his leaving,' and had received criticism from several quarters for his action (although this is entirely plausible, if not even likely, Wortabet does not substantiate this, and may have thought that such a statement would have spoken for him with the Church), but,

> that the question is, not so much how far injurious was his withdrawment from the city during the Cholera, as how far he was justified in doing so, when ... he was too unwell to attend to those duties which the Epidemic brought with it – and then he ... saw the first two cases and felt unequal for these duties – that he had lost all appetite for food and was extremely feeble – while the fever threatened to return every day and did return after he had left – that he long hesitated, and that it was only when he had scarcely strength to walk that the conviction forced itself upon him that out of regard to his health and probably his life, it was his duty to withdraw with his family who were all more or less in feeble health.[233]

After protracted discussion, the Committee formulated a resolution based on their rules, expressing regret for Wortabet's action and criticising him for not obtaining a medical certificate attesting his unfitness for work in the city; that any medics in the city might have been more interested in treating cholera patients than in supplying medical certificates to western-appointed missionary staff did not appear to occur to the Committee. Another communication from Wortabet was discussed, regarding a further £50 to be paid on top of his salary (already at £250) so that his two eldest boys could receive further education, the only Protestant seminaries (this did not necessarily refer to theological training establishments – c.f. the American 'seminary' in Abeih) available being in Constantinople and Beirut, both of which were very expensive. He had applied to a fund for aiding missionaries' children to receive an education in Edinburgh, but this application had been denied 'on the grounds that Syria is his native country, whereas the Scheme is intended for those Missionaries who are labouring in a foreign land'.[234]

It appears as if doubts about the future of the mission were beginning to emerge on the Committee's part and to have an impact on their decision-making, for although they had invested relatively large sums over the course of eight years, they decided to defer judgement on their employee's request until they had received the annual report from Aleppo. Wortabet's departure from the city during the cholera outbreak would, of course, have done little to encourage the Committee's positive assessment of him.

The report, written on 6.3., arrived in time for the subsequent meeting, held in June, and was read along with a letter of 12.3. from Wortabet. His letter is remarkable for some of its similarity to Brown's prior to his, Wortabet's, appointment:

I cannot conceal the fact that I am disheartened and discouraged, and that the hopes I had formed all along as to the prospective results of the Mission are beginning to fail. As a Jewish Mission I have already written to you, our work is a complete failure so far, our various Agencies if turned to the Jews would not work at all. We turned our efforts to the nominally Christian Churches because to them alone was there any door of access. The work among them is not so hopeful as you or I could wish; and it is possible the question of the continuance of the Mission may be once more taken up by the Board. If the Committee are satisfied with what is being done, and are willing to continue the Mission with the hope that the future may yet see the results of that measure of outlay of labour and expenditure which has been incurred. – I have an earnest request to make. It is that a colleague to myself be sent out. I cannot bear any more alone the burden of responsibility and labour and discouragement.[235]

Another letter, written at the end of April, repeats the sentiments about a colleague, and adds the telling remark that 'the shaken confidence in me implied in your last letters makes me more unwilling than ever to bear the responsibility of carrying on ... alone'.[236] The Committee faced a difficult decision: Brown had become despondent and Wortabet had been sent to work with him; however, Brown had left a few years later. Now Wortabet had expressed similar doubts and made a similar request: should the Committee heed his call for an additional missionary (with high immediate and long-term costs) or should it simply close the mission altogether?

A long minute recounting the history of the mission precedes the answer to this question, stated with absolute clarity for the first time by the Committee, despite Brown and Wortabet's previous statements explaining exactly the same notions:

1. That as a Mission to the Jews ... [of] Aleppo [it] had after eight Years trial completely failed.
2. That in its secondary aspect as a Mission to ... nominal Christians ... it has also failed.
3. That looking at these results which they very deeply deplore, the Committee feel that they would not be authorised to continue the Mission longer than the close of the present Year. And
4. That this Minute be communicated to Dr Wortabet, in whom the Committee have unabated confidence and that he be requested to state what are his views and wishes for the future.

They stated that they 'specially regret the failure ... on account of its being a Mission to the Jews' and would have continued had there been any prospect of success – presumably measured in terms of numbers of baptisms – but they did not turn from Wortabet, asking him if he knew of other locations 'where as a Missionary for the Jews his services may usefully be employed'.[237]

Wortabet replied shortly afterwards, apparently having either foreseen the Committee's decision to close the mission station or having decided to go anyway, stating that whilst he was glad to have retained their confidence, he had been offered and had conditionally accepted an invitation to a medical chair at the Syrian Protestant College at £250 a year. Regarding the continued offer of employment as a missionary to the Jews if only a suitable place could be found, he stated that he did 'not know of any such place, as the Jewish field seems to be the least promising, all the stations with the exception of Jerusalem having been practically given up'.[238] He suggested the Aleppo station might be handed over to 'the United Presbyterian Church of America or the Turkish Aid Society – who have missions in that region,'[239] and indeed, it was handed on (to the Reformed Presbyterian Church of America).[240]

Apart from clarifying some outstanding financial matters, this represented the end of the Aleppo mission. Lasting less than ten years, it was the only United Presbyterian Church mission in Syria. There were missions also in Algiers, Alexandria and in Hamburg, but these were generally not large, and met with mixed results: Algiers (where Hermann Philip had worked[241]) was passed on to the Union of Free Evangelical Churches in France in 1863. Philip had been ordained in Edinburgh in 1850 for the mission in Algiers, and went to Alexandria when a substitute, Benjamin Weiss, arrived (ordained in Glasgow for the Algiers mission in 1852). Weiss essentially created French-speaking congregations with converts from Catholicism, and the United Presbyterian Church felt this did not serve the purposes of a Jewish mission and withdrew.[242] Alexandria ceased to be a United Presbyterian mission in 1858, after first Brown, who moved on to Aleppo, and then Philip, resigned for health reasons. The station was passed on to the Auld Kirk. The Hamburg mission, founded in 1847, resulted in a small number of converts, but by 1862 was passed on to the PCI, who ran it for many years.[243]

In summary, the United Presbyterian Church expressed a strong desire and eagerness to be involved in mission among the Jews, and indeed, was one of the first Scottish churches to found a Jewish mission station after the creation of the mission in Hungary. However, several factors conspired against the Church achieving any notable successes: the apparent inability of the Committee to respond helpfully to doubts on the part of its missionaries and to reflect on what this might mean for the mission; the relatively small size of the Church and therefore of its recruitment possibilities; the apparently unfortunate choices in terms of staffing occasionally made (such as Weiss); and the inability to recruit additional staff when those employed were unable or unwilling to carry on (as in Aleppo). These factors combined meant that sustaining these relatively small mission stations over any length of time proved to be very difficult. The Aleppo mission, rather than being known for its Jewish converts, is today perhaps mostly remembered, if at all, as an early employer of John Wortabet, known for his descriptive work on religious traditions in Syria[244] and the Arabic dictionaries that bear his name.

Conclusion

Missions to Jews from Scotland began with a theological position arising from the perceived place of Jews in Scottish Reformed theology. This bore little relation to the actual situation of Jews in Europe or Palestine, but was based on a particular way of reading and understanding biblical texts, as outlined in the Introduction. From this came the 'Mission of Inquiry' to research the situation of European, and especially Palestinian Jews. Wide dissemination of the experiences and findings of the travellers in Scotland and beyond broadened support for the work that the JMC proposed to undertake, but moves to initiate a mission in Palestine were slower than the travellers and their readership might initially have expected, due in part to 'the unsettled state of that country'[245] during and after 1840. In the meantime, work was begun in Central Europe, Constantinople, and Damascus. The Disruption of 1843 was less of a traumatic experience for the mission work than might be expected, because all the missionaries went over to the new church and high levels of energy and enthusiasm meant that basic financial commitments could initially be sustained. However, as the mission station in Damascus shows, the failure of the Free Kirk to commit meaningful levels of resources and personnel left the Committee feeling somewhat detached and with less of a sense of responsibility for the development of the mission. The co-operation with the PCI was undoubtedly welcomed, not least since it would have spread the costs and responsibilities, but it also led to a lack of clarity about who would be responsible for less senior staff members like Daniel. More important than all of this, however, is the interest in Constantinople, which was fast developing into an important mission station for the Scots, and would continue to be such well into the 20th century: it appears that in these early years the Committee overstretched itself in terms of its commitments and found itself unable to sustain as much interest or support in the Damascus mission as in the Constantinople mission. The PCI prosecuted and developed the mission with additional staff and resources over the years.

Aleppo represents a different scenario. The United Presbyterian Church, which eventually united with the Free Church in 1900, was a considerably smaller body than the Free Church, but had taken over work from the SSCI and employed missionaries who already knew the region: Brown (who had worked in Egypt) and Wortabet, himself a Syrian. It appears that Brown's language skills were reasonably developed, and with his past experience one might assume a measure of success, particularly since he was not working alone but with a Syrian who had already undergone religious conversion to Protestantism (albeit not from Judaism: his father had been an Armenian priest). However, where opportunities appeared to present themselves, the Committee was unwilling or unable to grant the support that their missionaries wanted, resulting, from the missionaries' perspectives, in slim chances for a successful prosecution of the work. This, combined with protracted family health problems, led Brown to give up work, followed a few years later by Wortabet, both in disappointment at the lack of conversions.

There are some tentative conclusions one might draw from the running of these two mission stations, since although every situation is unique, there are some common factors.

Firstly, they were both initiated in towns that were selected by the missionary once he had been appointed and sent, and minimal, if any, consultation with other members of the church who had been in these towns took place. In this context, appointing a missionary, and then seeking possibilities for him to work, might have impinged on the level of support that could be offered, with total dependency on the portrayal of the situation by the missionary himself (one thinks, perhaps, of the assessments Brown made of the perceived possibilities for conversion in Aleppo). Secondly, both churches ran other missions which appeared, for a variety of reasons, to be producing more tangible results. This came about partly through the employment of more staff and resources, but also, perhaps, because they were located in cities where there was already a Protestant mission presence, for example, Hamburg and Constantinople. Ample records exist suggesting that western missionaries had at the very least reasonable contact to each other in such contexts, and this would have resulted in mutual support for the missionaries on the ground, and/or direct competition with which they could measure their achievements and which might stimulate further developments of the mission station.

The extent to which these factors played a role in subsequent mission work is a complex matter. Although the following chapter picks up the thread of missions in Palestine in the 1880s, there had, of course, been missions elsewhere in the meantime. However, it is notable that more care was taken over the choice of locales when this was available to the mission committees (especially Tiberias and Safad; there was less of a choice in Hebron and none in Jaffa, though these latter two were already established missions by the time the Scots became involved). Furthermore, more comprehensive staffing arrangements were put into place within a relatively short space of time, and cooperation and contact with other missions was actively pursued. It would be difficult to imagine that the mission committees had not 'learnt' from the experiences of their predecessors, though in how far institutional memory would cover some of these matters is difficult to determine precisely. More likely, one can see the missions in the latter part of the 19th century as fitting into methodological contexts of widespread missionary activity of the time, a context that included failures and successes in the past, of which the Damascus and Aleppo missions were but one part, and a relatively small and insignificant one at that.

THE LATER MISSIONS
Establishing a long-term presence

The intervening years

After the withdrawal from Damascus and Aleppo, Scottish missionary engagement in the Levant decreased. The United Presbyterian Church withdrew after Aleppo, becoming involved again only as part of the United Free Church with the Hebron mission. The Free Kirk and Auld Kirk both operated a number of missions in central and eastern Europe, and around parts of the Mediterranean, but nothing in Palestine. The existing stations produced regular financial difficulties for their committees, generally with little to show, numerically at least, in terms of converts.[1] Despite this, expansion in the Levant was discussed. In the Free Kirk, for example, the topic came up in 1851 but was then not explored further.[2] In 1875 a medical mission in Palestine was briefly considered, and consultations with the PCI ensued,[3] who rebuffed them, arguing 'there was no place for a Medical Missionary, the ground already being occupied' and suggesting they give their money to the Lebanon Schools;[4] this they did not do as the funds they had intended to use were part of a legacy for 'a Missionary to Jews in Palestine'.[5] The JMC supported other organisations, but always ensured Jews were the recipients of the work: several annual donations were made to 'Mrs Mott's School for Jewish girls at Beyrout',[6] but a request from the British Syrian Schools was refused as there was 'no evidence of Jewish children'.[7] A school for Jews in Damascus was considered, but financial constraints prevented the JMC pursuing such a venture.[8]

The Sea of Galilee: Tiberias and Safad

The Free Church mission in Tiberias is synonymous with the name of David Watt Torrance (1862-1923), the founder and longest-serving member of the mission. Torrance spent all his adult life in Palestine from the mid-1880s, apart from a short break forced upon him by the 1914-1918 war. Tiberias, with its satellite mission station in Safad, became perhaps the most significant Scottish mission in the Levant, not least in terms of the geopious attraction of Palestine and the Sea of Galilee.

A vacancy for a medical missionary without a mission

It is unclear where the impetus for starting work in the Levant again appears to have come from: there is nothing to indicate that it was a result of a particular event or a process of consultation. A minute early in 1883, under the heading of 'medical missionary', notes an advertisement for a position and a recommendation – not taken up as a Scot was preferred – of a German Jewish doctor.[9] It is not even clear this vacancy is for Palestine – that can only be deduced from subsequent minutes. Torrance was mentioned at the subsequent meeting as one who had nearly completed his medical studies and was considering the possibility of working as a medical missionary, but given his circumstances, they simply noted his interest.[10] In any case, there was as yet no mission station for him to go to. A 'Sub-Committee on Medical Missions' was asked to look into the possibilities in Galata and Safad.

There was already a medic with Scottish connections working in the Galilee region: Dr Kaloost Vartan, an Armenian married to a Scot who had qualified in Edinburgh before going to Nazareth in 1861 and starting a dispensary there; from 1.1.1866 he worked for the EMMS. A hospital with eighteen beds was formally opened in 1871. By the early 1880s he was building on 35 acres which he had purchased for a hospital, but ownership of the land was disputed so no *firman* was granted and the building was never completed; it was 1903 before a renewed search for a suitable site began (Vartan died five years later). Vartan's work influenced all other medical missions in the area.[11] The Free Kirk JMC naturally turned to him for advice on their project in mid-1883.

His reply, reported in October, confirmed Safad as a possibility, and so a sub-committee was formed to examine the financial viability of a medical mission.[12] A few months later Vartan confirmed that 'a Medical Missionary would be welcomed by many of the Jews in this town'.[13] Consequently, it was decided to open a mission in Safad, and for a sub-committee to meet with Torrance about this. It was also decided that the Vice-Convener should communicate the essence of the proposed mission to the LJS, who had already initiated a mission in Safad.

The next four weeks were busy: Torrance was appointed to Safad and 'studies in Theology, German, and special medical branches, including hygiene' were arranged for the spring and summer so that he could leave for Palestine in the autumn. The contact with the LJS had been less straightforward: it was reported that a statement had been prepared 'setting forth at length ... [our] position ... with a view of inducing them ... to leave the field open to us'. On the Friday before the JMC meeting, the LJS had 'appointed a Medical Missionary to Safed, and [they] would be glad if we occupied Hebron'.[14] When the Committee met again in February, the LJS had two agents going to Safad. The JMC would not have wanted to 'intrude' on geographic territory that another Protestant society had already claimed as 'theirs'[15] and this explains their decision not to go directly to Safad, but for Torrance to be accompanied by a Committee member, Dr James Wells, in order to 'examine the whole field with a view of finding the best available sphere for a medical mission'.[16] Wells had received permission from his congregation, Pollokshields West in Glasgow, to go, and Torrance had the previous day resigned his position as surgeon. Travelling expenses – £100 each – and Torrance's first salary were arranged; Wells would have been in receipt of a stipend from his congregation.

There is virtually no information available about this trip: the brief chapter by Wells in a book on the Sea of Galilee Mission published by the JMC in 1895 does not actually cover the trip in any detail.[17] Wells mentions that they travelled with the superintendent of the Glasgow Medical Mission, one Dr Laidlaw, and Vartan. They recommended Tiberias as suitable for a medical mission. Surprisingly, Wells noted that

> Though we did not know it at the time, we were substantially repeating the recommendation made by McCheyne and Andrew Bonar ... in 1839. In their famous "Narrative of a Mission of Inquiry to the Jews" (30th thousand, p.284) they say: "... We could not help desiring that the time would come when our beloved church should be permitted to establish a mission here..."[18]

Wells himself noted that the book was famous (citing a page from the '30th thousand') but appears not to have been aware of the conclusions Bonar and McCheyne reached. It seems almost impossible that the 1884 travellers would not have read the 'Narrative' before travelling, or would not at least have been aware of its conclusions, but this appears to be the case, if Wells, writing ten years after the trip, is to be believed.

Wells' chapter elaborates on the 'power of medical mission in that land,'[19] citing two examples of the warm welcome foreign medics received from the people and the reverence with which they were treated, the latter example coming from another trip Wells made to Palestine in 1891 and having nothing to do with the 1884 trip. Comparisons with records of Jesus' healing in the gospels abound, and the superiority of the westerners is made clear: 'my comrades were giving these bigoted Galileans the only exhibition of Christ's gospel which as yet they either care for or can comprehend'. [20]

The recommendation for Tiberias was approved in April 1884.[21] The remainder of the summer was taken up with making arrangements and preparing Torrance for departure, who was formally appointed by the Committee on 17.6.1884. The terms of his appointment were typical of other JMC missionaries: a £250 a year salary, outward travel and accommodation to be provided, £30 allowed for 'outfit', the initial term to be for five years with six months notice on either side, the Committee to pay his return fare if he stayed the full term, '[m]edicine and instruments to be provided, and a native assistant appointed to be ready if possible on his arrival' – this latter appointment was to be made with the help of Dr Carslaw of the Free Kirk's Lebanon mission. He was to obtain a certificate of good health, and was to travel via Constantinople in order to obtain a 'Turkish diploma', allowing him to practice medicine in the Empire. On arrival he was to spend some time with Vartan; he was also supported in his suggestion that he receive special instruction at 'Fever Hospitals', any such training to be completed by the end of October to allow him to proceed as soon as possible thereafter to Palestine (it is not known whether he actually did pursue this, nor where he might have had such training). A 'document ... in favour of Dr Torrance' was to be obtained from the Ambassador in Britain – it is not clear if this materialised. 'Instructions' for Torrance were also to be drawn up, and a group was appointed to develop these (reproduced in the Appendix).[22]

Valedictory services were held in Anderston Church in Glasgow and Barclay Church in Edinburgh in November, and Torrance sailed on 2.12.1884, as reported at the December meeting, when the sub-committee appointed to formulate instructions to him reported back; Torrance's acceptance of these is recorded a few months later.[23]

The Committee attached a great deal of importance to the success of Torrance's mission, the importance of which is reflected not least in that most meetings in these early years have as the first substantial business item the Sea of Galilee Mission. This happened even when there was precious little of any significance to report.

Upon arrival in Palestine, Torrance proceeded to Nazareth, where he worked with Vartan and began learning Arabic.[24] By March, he had visited Tiberias and reported that 'the people [were] eager for his medical services', and recommended the acquisition of a site (as yet undetermined), which was promptly approved by the Committee.[25] Torrance also drew attention to Vartan's concerns about the threat to his work from the Ottoman authorities. The Committee was aware that the EMMS was trying to meet the Foreign Minister Earl Granville, in order to seek support from the British government in exerting pressure on Constantinople to desist from (as they saw it) interference in missionary activity and property. This would affect the Free Kirk too, and they immediately arranged for a small group to participate in the EMMS lobby efforts with the imperial power; there is no record in subsequent JMC minutes as to whether a meeting at the Foreign Office did actually take place. What is known is that Vartan faced the loss of the premises he had purchased and begun to build on.

It is worth adding a note at this stage about the population mix in the region; some mention of this has already been made in Chapter 1 above. Statistics for the Galilee as such are not available, but Courbage and Fargues note that whilst in 1852 only 4% of the population of Palestine was Jewish (13,000), these were located in the districts of Jerusalem, Acre and Nablus.[26] Population growth within the Jewish community rose dramatically, from 7.4% in 1860, to 21.1% by 1882, and 32.6% in 1895.[27] Immigration played the substantive role in this: between 1850 and 1914, 84,300 Jews moved to Palestine, 44,000 of them after 1897.[28] Whilst many moved on, the JMC were clearly establishing their presence in Palestine at a time that would see a substantial increase in their target group.

The establishment of the Tiberias and Safad missions

By September 1885 Torrance had hired premises in Tiberias from the chief rabbi, apparently with the help of Vartan,[29] with the intention of beginning work in November; it is known that he was in place by the end of the year. Medicines and equipment totalling almost £150 were sent from Scotland, in March 1886.[30] Prior to their arrival, Torrance reported that 'he ... [had] been in great request for his medical services, and that he ... [had] been doing all he could in the absence of the medicines'. Conscious of the ultimate purpose of their work, and not just the desire to provide medical services, a supply of bibles and tracts in various languages was arranged for Torrance's use.[31] The moves towards establishing a firmer foothold came with a proposal from the Glasgow Jewish Ladies' Association to establish a school in Tiberias, a proposal that the Committee welcomed.[32]

The Association and corresponding organisations in other urban centres in Scotland represented one of the few ways in which Scottish women could support missionary work, since all other committees were male, whether ordained or lay. The first such Association (for foreign missions) was established in 1837 in Edinburgh when 22 women formed a committee (with male office-bearers) for raising funds, procuring information, forming further branches and securing the services of well qualified teachers for service in India; a Glasgow equivalent opened shortly afterwards.[33] Jewish missionary work attracted a similar interest, though for many years the Jewish Associations played a minimal role in the management of missions, concentrating primarily on the promotion of the work. Within the Free Kirk, it was only when the various local Jewish women's associations united to form the Women's Jewish Missionary Association (WJMA) in 1895 that records of their meetings began to be kept together with those of the JMC itself.[34]

The women acted more quickly than the JMC perhaps expected: by May they had identified a possible teacher and requested agreement from the JMC regarding a suitable property for a school and accommodation for the teacher. Torrance welcomed their involvement,[35] but though he had secured premises for five years,[36] this would have been for his medical practice and/or his own accommodation needs. The requests from the Ladies' Association were put on hold whilst the JMC enquired of Torrance regarding the cost and availability of property.[37] By September Helen Fenton of Blairgowrie[38] had sailed for Palestine, along with Torrance's sister.[39] Fenton was 'a trained missionary teacher with experience in Turkey',[40] though it is not clear when or on whose behalf she was there. Torrance's sister went as 'a voluntary worker among the girls',[41] though she may also have gone in order to assist Torrance with his domestic affairs, and does not appear to have had a formal role in the mission.[42]

Torrance was at this time responsible for the medical and the 'spiritual' element of the work in Tiberias. This was not entirely to his liking, preferring medical work. He was keen to have an ordained colleague, a matter helped along by a donation of £200 gifted for the express purpose of helping appoint an ordained missionary.[43] William Ewing, a Glasgow theology student, was appointed in February 1887 for five years, beginning from his ordination.[44] On completing his studies he was sent to Leipzig to study at the Institutum Judaicum. In consultation with Torrance, his stay in Leipzig, intended to last only for the summer, continued until the end of the year, his ordination taking place in Glasgow on 10.1.1888.[45]

The Institutum Judaicum in Leipzig had been founded in 1871, based on the similarly named institute in Halle founded in 1728, which had closed on the verge of bankruptcy in 1791/2. The Halle institution arose from the German pietist movement, its closure coming as a result of a fall in donations as pietism became less mainstream. The Leipzig body initially failed, but was revived in 1886 following a lecture by one of Franz Delitzsch's (1813-1890) students, Wilhelm Faber, who had worked hard at creating a student environment amenable to academic study connected to the practice of mission. The Institutum was part, not of the university, but of the missionary arm of the Lutheran Church; despite this, it generally did not engage directly in missionary activity, seeking rather to equip missionaries with the tools to do the job. The ultimate aim was to convert Jews, the study of Judaism being the means for achieving this. Delitzsch, a convinced Lutheran despite his pietistic tendencies, was a noted Hebraist and publicist,[46] and probably had more of an influence on British and American theology than any other German theologian of the time.[47] He was head of the new institute, which after his death became known as the Institutum Judaicum Delitzschianum.[48] Apart from its purpose, it was also notable for the fact that Jews as well as Christians taught there – one could imagine that this may have been one of Ewing's first encounters with Jews.

With the limited sources available, much of the Tiberias-Safad mission appears to be a continual series of property renting or acquisition proposals followed by renovation and building proposals on the one hand, and a continual series of requests for further staffing and material resources on the other (one might wonder, particularly in later years, in how far the concentration on these issues detracted from the low number of converts the mission could claim). In the early days, of course, there was clearly a need for property – Torrance and his colleagues at the very least needed somewhere to live and work. Having secured this basic minimum in the spring of 1886, he made a number of suggestions for property purchase, none of which were followed up.[49]

Shortly before Ewing's arrival in Tiberias, a proposal 'for purchase of land on the shore of the Lake which he [Torrance] considered suitable as a site for a school, dispensary, and teachers' and missionary's dwelling' came to the JMC;[50] it was explicitly minuted that unless the matter was urgent, i.e. the property would no longer be available, it would be desirable to await Ewing's arrival and opinion. Whether Ewing would be able to form a useful opinion quickly enough (Torrance had after all been living in Tiberias for some time) did not appear to be a consideration. Two meetings later, it was noted that Torrance had written and telegraphed and that £300 had been sent to him. He had already paid the first instalment towards the purchase of this plot, in the north-eastern part of the town. The Committee simply noted their approval. This plot is almost certainly the land that the hospital was later built on.

Ewing and his wife arrived in April 1888. There were now five Scots: Torrance, his sister, Fenton, Ewing and his wife. Fenton and Torrance had secured the assistance of at least one local individual each for their spheres of work, though the Committee tended to view these assistants almost as personal employees of the Scottish staff – they were never consulted about matters pertaining to the mission, were paid from funds held in Palestine and not in Scotland, and were only exceptionally referred to by name in formal JMC documents; only rarely is it clear exactly what they did. To all intents and purposes, they were invisible to people in Scotland.

Shortly after Ewing's arrival he told the JMC that Safad 'should be occupied permanently'.[51] This, the Committee was aware, brought the possibility of conflict with the LJS a step closer – a while after the initial JMC-LJS communications, the LJS had written to confirm that they had no intention of giving up their work in Safad, but were instead opening schools in the town.[52] Ewing would almost certainly have been aware of the background situation. The JMC reacted cautiously, not rejecting Ewing's proposal outright, but consulting with Torrance and seeking his involvement in plans for such a step, 'taking in view the need of economy and that no legitimate ground of offence should be given' to the LJS.[53] Safad had been regarded as the 'summer station' for the Tiberias staff, but was not, at this stage, a full mission station.

Caution in relation to the LJS was warranted: the October meeting records a letter from the LJS taking exception to the mention of Safad as a 'summer station', never mind a full mission station. In the course of the recorded discussion justifying Safad, an interesting note about the target group is made:

> Tiberias, is during five months of the year unsafe for a European to live or work in ... [so] a summer retreat must be found; and ... Safed ... [is] the only suitable place. The presence of the Free Church ... however, does not mean rivalry. On the contrary ... harmonious co-operation, and mutual help – medically or otherwise [is desired]. The ... Free Church Mission ... is wider than that of the London Society, as it embraces Muslims and Christians, of which there are considerable numbers ... in need of all that a Christian Medical Mission can do for them. Besides, the field is so large and so very necessitous that there is ample room for ... two friendly Missions without danger of collision. The Committee earnestly hope the foregoing explanation and assurance will convince the London Society that their fears of future trouble are groundless.[54]

Comity, the delineation of territory between missionary organisations,[55] was clearly not a problem for these Scots, particularly as they claimed to target Muslims, Christians and Jews, unlike the LJS. However, this was not entirely true: their intention was to reach Jews; Christian and Muslim contact was a by-product, and at no other point is there an explicit statement that the mission directed its efforts deliberately to non-Jews: indeed, Jews are clearly favoured (for example in terms of school fees, which were lower or not payable at all for Jews). However, this communication appears to have been successful in persuading the LJS at the time that 'their fears of future trouble ... [were] groundless' since subsequent meetings approve proposals for a permanent mission in Safad, with 'an assistant Doctor, two Scripture Readers, a Colporteur, a Dispenser, a dispensary attendant, and a female teacher ... total estimated annual expenditure ... about £540' whereby salaries came to £320.[56] Shortly after this, in February 1889, Torrance and Ewing requested a male teacher for Safad.[57]

The mission work develops and expands on all fronts

The Committee responded appointing William Christie, a teacher, for five years in the first instance. He had already indicated an interest in Jewish mission work, and was to go to Palestine after a period of study at the Institutum Judaicum.[58]

A proposal from Ewing was also discussed on the basis of 'a deputation of native Christians ... requesting that a boy's school should be set up in Tiberias': the missionaries had approved of this idea and wanted to recruit a teacher from Beirut.[59] This meeting also granted Torrance home leave, appointed Dr Selim Daoud to act as his locum at

£100 a year; they clearly felt Ewing knew enough to be able to run the mission on his own.[60] Meanwhile, Fenton had opened a girls' school

> with a large attendance of Jewish girls ... [but] Khērems were sent down from Jerusalem banning those who countenanced the institution, and all the Jewesses vanished, leaving only a few Moslems and Christians. Miss Fenton was not dismayed, it was no new experience to her; but the Doctor felt keenly the averted looks and distant demeanour of the townspeople who had hitherto been so friendly.[61]

The medical work provided inroads around the hostility the missionaries felt, and with Ewing in place to take on some of the direct evangelistic work, and with the acquisition of a boat in 1888, the formal acquisition of property title deeds,[62] and the ongoing expansion noted above, the mission was clearly well on the way to being firmly established, as Torrance conveyed when he attended the JMC that summer. Unfortunately, Selim Daoud drowned in a boating accident on the lake.[63] Although a replacement was found in Dr Khaleel Saadi, recommended by the Beirut missionaries, Torrance returned home earlier than planned, in October, having been ordained, along with Christie, as an elder of the church. Christie, having returned from Leipzig, had married and was on his way to Tiberias via Beirut, where he was to learn Arabic.[64]

A new house in Tiberias was agreed to by the JMC at a cost not to exceed £1,350,[65] and this, as well as other property issues, turned out to be one of the causes for serious disagreement between the missionaries, important because it heralded a significant organisational development. The minutes note that

> a serious difference had arisen ... at Tiberias. Mr Ewing was dissatisfied with the return of Dr Torrance sooner than he had expected. They differ in regard to the buildings, especially as to the house for Miss Fenton, and also as to the location of the doctors for the winter, Mr Ewing wishing Dr Torrance to go to Safed, while the Dr prefers to remain at Tiberias.[66]

No recorded disagreements between Ewing and Torrance prior to this exist, and one might wonder as to the nature of Ewing's dissatisfaction with Torrance's early return. Various communications aimed at resolving the matter ensued, including clear instructions affirming Torrance's views on where he should be working, the configuration of available housing, and warnings of public perception:

> The eyes of the Church and of a far wider circle have been fixed on this Mission; the interest felt in it is alone of its kind; and it would be nothing short of a public calamity, where no matter of principle is concerned, if there should be anything like divided counsels and permanent estrangement.[67]

Ewing announced his resignation, but left it to the Committee to decide on whether he should go or not,[68] then stated he wanted a clear separation of work from Torrance. The Committee was left confused, and said it 'deeply deplore[d] the attitude Mr Ewing has taken up, the reason for which they cannot from his letters understand',[69] but offered pastoral and theological advice, noting they were not in a position to prevent him leaving if he wanted to do so.

It would seem that Ewing had reached some kind of crisis point, though even for the Committee at the time, far less for historians many years later, the reasons for all this are unclear. Personal issues may have been a factor, but by April 1890 Christie (who had been in Beirut for much of this period), Ewing and Torrance had written to indicate 'a revival of brotherly feeling and mutual confidence' and the resignation had clearly been withdrawn.[70] Certainly in Ewing's own account of the mission, published many years later, no mention of this episode occurs.[71]

This conflict presaged one of the most important developments in the structural organisation of the mission: the creation of the Sea of Galilee Mission Council. Indeed, the Committee's pleasure at the resumption of good relations between Ewing and Torrance formed the first paragraph in the minute that resulted in creation of the Council.[72] The Council, in theory at least, allowed for the devolution of day-to-day decisions, with regular reporting to the JMC of the work of the mission station as a whole, rather than relying simply on individual missionaries' reports (which, needless to say, were still expected). All decisions related to formal matters on the ground were left to the Council: dealing with the 'Turkish Government', purchasing land, and purchasing and maintaining buildings and boats, though of course, in all matters the Council would be 'subject to the Committee at home'. Most notably, of course, budgetary restrictions meant that the Council was far from free to do as it pleased.[73] The Council was to consist only of male European missionaries: women (or at the time, the woman, in the person of the teacher[74]) were only to be involved in discussions, not decisions, if some aspect directly relating to their work materialised. Torrance and Ewing were to alternate in the chair, with Christie functioning as Secretary (the text of the minute establishing the Mission Council is reproduced in the Appendix below).[75]

This having been arranged, Torrance was already making plans to return to Britain, having had his leave cut short the previous year through Selim Daoud's untimely death, and a new locum was appointed, one Dr Faris Sahyun, who had previously worked for the LJS.[76] Once in Scotland, Torrance made further representations to the JMC about the mission at the same meeting as Ewing's withdrawal of his resignation was announced, though Ewing's letter also stated 'that it is impossible for him to contemplate a renewal of his engagement when this term of five years expires'.[77] This was left more open after further contact, including via a member of the JMC, Mr Macphail, who had travelled to Palestine and met Ewing.[78] Meanwhile, Torrance negotiated further capital expenditure, partly for a permanent house for himself, and partly for sanitation and medical equipment. It was agreed that on his way home to Tiberias, he should travel via Constantinople and apply for a *firman* for building a dispensary and hospital.[79]

Further meetings of the JMC resulted in much deliberation of Mission Council decisions with regard to buildings – throughout the year, buildings were discussed, with the missionaries always keen to press on, partly no doubt, simply for practical reasons – whilst the JMC, tempered by financial realities, constantly urged restraint and delay.

Travel to the region had been perceived to be a difficult, expensive and arduous process, and one that most people would never have contemplated undertaking for pleasure. However, Thomas Cook had begun to offer tours in the Middle East, and gradually Committee members began to visit their mission stations overseas, though generally as a part of a private trip they were making anyway. Reference has already been made to a visit by one Macphail, and at the first meeting in 1891, the Convener, James Wells, who had originally travelled to Palestine with Torrance in 1884, announced his intention to use an extended holiday in order to visit 'Egypt, Palestine, and other countries, and hoped at the same time to visit our various mission stations'.[80] The JMC were clear about the benefits of this trip, on the one hand bringing 'the missionaries more into touch with the Committee', whilst on the other hand he would also be able 'to obtain as full information as possible regarding the different spheres of work and the operations carried on'. The minutes elaborate on the former purpose in more detail: 'they expect that he will also be able to inform the Missionaries of the views of the Committee on various questions, and they trust that he may be enabled to advise and encourage the missionaries and other workers in their labours for Israel'.[81] Communicating the Committee's views clearly took precedence over finding out what the Missionaries might be experiencing on the ground, at least as expressed in the formal records of the JMC. The Vice-Convener, Rev J G Cunningham, chaired meetings until Wells' return in the autumn.

The Committee agreed to proceed with the construction of Torrance's house and send money for this. This contrasted with their reluctance to engage a few months later with Christie's house, which was 'not watertight, and ... he had been forced to leave it and go to Tiberias ... [the Mission Council] earnestly recommending that a new house be built'.[82] Despite the obvious urgency for their missionary, and the fact that he was now no longer in Safad, where he worked, a decision was postponed until the Convener's return. The September 1892 meeting records the JMC's 'gratitude to God for the restoration of the Convener, whom they thanked for his services on behalf of the Mission during his tour'.[83] His report at the next meeting, is, unfortunately for historians, not recorded in detail:

> The Convener made a brief statement of the impressions he had derived from his recent visit to the Stations – (1) We have excellent Missionaries, (2) Our Missions are well equipped, (3) There is an element of uncertainty from the age of some missionaries, (4) The work is very difficult, and (5) Nobler life at home is indispensable if we are to do good.

It is not entirely clear what the fifth statement means, whether it refers to Scotland ('home') or to the missionaries' living arrangements.

Until this time, the JMC Secretary had been a volunteer, but the JMC was at this time participating in a discussion with the Colonial and Continental Committees (responsible for overseeing Free Church congregations in these territories) as to the possibility of sharing a Secretary. This was eventually agreed to, with a salary set at £300 a year to be divided equally between the three committees. Although the JMC recommended their existing Secretary, Rev William Affleck, the General Assembly appointed George Milne Rae; Affleck became Vice-Convener.[84] This brought institutional and personal contact with someone used to dealing in an imperial context a little closer to the JMC.

Building the hospital and consolidation of other work

The early 1890s marked the beginning of a period of relative stability for the mission following the establishment of all three branches of work[85] and the initial organisational teething problems culminating in the creation of the Mission Council. Torrance proposed building a hospital for £2,500,[86] a plan that became reality partly perhaps because he moved very quickly in purchasing land, as notified a month after his proposal:

> Mr Ewing and Dr Torrance ... have purchased a suitable site for a hospital adjoining the mission houses, for £100. The Committee in the special circumstances sanctioned the purchase, but agreed to draw attention to a previous communication against borrowing. Dr Torrance ... had to pay £50 to the local authorities for a favourable report regarding the proposed hospital. The Committee agreed to remit £150 in payment ... but direct that the erection of the hospital not be begun without the sanction of the Committee.[87]

Torrance was perhaps manipulating the committee in purchasing the land so quickly (one might wonder in how far the procrastination around Christie's dilapidated living quarters might have encouraged this), but the plans were already under discussion, and a site next to the mission houses was obviously ideal.

At the same time as approving the hospital, one of the core purposes of the Tiberias mission, Ewing was rebuffed in his proposal to 'get leave of absence to visit the Bedouin Tribes beyond Jordan', being told instead to concentrate on the existing work.[88] The numbers, as recorded in Ewing's book of 1914, showed that in terms of the Jewish aspects of the mission's work, there were plenty of Jews to whom he might (more profitably, no doubt, in the eyes of the Committee) direct his attention: in 'Tiberias there are certainly more than 5000, but probably not quite 6000 souls. Of these, something over 3500 are Jews, about 150 Moslems, and 300 or 400 are United Greek and Orthodox Greek Christians.'[89]

Recording the tedious minutiae of planning and progress for the hospital would not serve any great purpose here,[90] but some salient details are worth noting. Torrance had applied for a *firman* for the plans he had submitted, for which a Scottish architect, Campbell Douglas, apparently known to the Convener, volunteered his services. The building proceeded before receipt of the *firman*, though it was thought best 'to erect not more than half of the Hospital at first, if practicable';[91] the issue of *firmans* for the Sea of Galilee and Constantinople missions (particularly for schools, but also for medical facilities) occupied much time. Concerted pressure, mainly through the involvement of the British Embassy in Constantinople, with the most senior JMC missionary there, Dr Hannington, dealing with many of the communications for the JMC, generally produced results.[92] Building work proceeded with a dispensary and what was termed the 'out-door portion',[93] based on the architect's detailed plans that had been sent to Torrance.[94] By September 1892, the first mention of an appeal Torrance had initiated for subscriptions towards beds appeared, with two beds being sponsored for £20 each;[95] earlier in the year, one of Torrance's twins had died, and he and his wife had agreed to 'provide a cot in the new hospital as a memorial of him'.[96] Between November 1892 and November 1893 much of the building was complete[97] and the JMC was in a position to consider the total cost of the completed building (estimated by Torrance at £3,241 by the time various additional work had been completed) and address the annual running costs.[98] Donations, both small and large (e.g. a legacy of £1,000 for a ward), were forthcoming, as the hospital by the lake where Jesus is reported to have carried out much of his healing ministry clearly caught the imagination of people in Scotland.[99]

Meanwhile, as the hospital was being built, the work of the rest of the mission continued. For Torrance in particular, the building of the hospital was in all likelihood a great strain on his energy, given that he was also expected to continue his usual duties. Whilst exact figures for the number of patients etc. are difficult to ascertain, Ewing records that in the first nine months of the new hospital's existence, there were 12,956 out-patient attendances, with Torrance himself performing 184 operations; these figures indicate perhaps the high level of demand prior to the opening of the hospital as well.[100]

Figure 3-1 Hospital and mission buildings as seen from lake[101]

Staffing issues took up a considerable amount of the Committee's time, with offers of service from both Scots and others (for example, a Canadian woman applied to work for the Committee, though the offer was not taken up[102]), the need to replace staff either because of death (such as the 'Arabic Scripture Reader, Assad El Hus'n'[103] – his position was not immediately filled) or because they moved on, or the appointment of 'native assistants' (e.g. Torrance appointed a Dr Nakhli Rubaig for six months at a cost of 50 Napoleons/£40 plus board and lodging[104]). Local staff were not paid at Scottish rates, but long service was recognised, e.g. for Saadeh, who was granted a salary increase (from £100 to £120) in recognition of 'three years in the service of the Mission, ... [having given] the Missionaries great satisfaction'.[105] Occasionally individuals from Scotland offered their services gratis to the mission; if the role of the individual fitted the Committee's perception of the needs of the mission, they tended to be accepted.

However, by far the most time-consuming staffing issue in this period was Ewing's position. After the earlier conflict between Ewing and Torrance, Ewing agreed to stay until the end of his term. A year before he was due to leave, he made it clear that he was not prepared to extend; his wife's health given as the reason.[106] The Committee accepted his resignation with regret, as did Torrance, urging a successor to be appointed (perhaps wary of being left to deal with Ewing's responsibilities as he had done prior to Ewing's appointment[107]). Suggestions of candidates were noted, but not immediately acted upon.[108] These moves took a considerable time. In January 1893 the Convener noted Mrs Ewing's death, and the Committee

> instruct[ed] the Secretary to convey to Mr Ewing ... [their] warmest sympathy and further to ask Mr Ewing whether, in the new circumstances in which he was providentially placed it would seem to him to be his duty to recall his resignation and to devote himself afresh to the work of the mission in Palestine.[109]

It is perhaps doubtful that Ewing experienced his wife's death as being quite as 'providential' as the Committee saw it; in any case, he did not change his mind. The next meeting recorded a suggestion by Ewing for a successor (Dr Gustaf Dalman from Leipzig[110]) whilst by March, he is recorded as having written to the Convener on 30.1.1893 stating that he would probably be leaving Tiberias at the end of March, would not return and the JMC should not delay appointing a successor. The JMC hoped he would reconsider, and did not act[111] until the May meeting, when Ewing was present and made it clear yet again that he 'could not see his way to return'. The Committee bowed to the inevitable, 'recorded this decision with regret, and resolved to advertise ... for a successor'.[112] Torrance's request for a replacement was finally underway.

The advertisement was repeated, indicating that no suitable candidates had been forthcoming[113] (though the previous meeting had turned down Rev Nathaniel Zerbeck from Leipzig: 'it is desirable to appoint a Scottish minister'[114]). Torrance was not entirely without support from Scottish colleagues, since a volunteer had come for a year as his assistant in the form of one Dr George Wilson, the Committee paying local wages

(£100/year) and travel: Torrance had asked for a volunteer to help him with the work, and had been made aware of Wilson's offer.[115]

The successful candidate was John Soutar, a theology student, appointed in September for an initial five years, approximately six months after Ewing had left Tiberias and 17 months after his intention to leave had first been received by the JMC.[116] Allowances and expenses were provided for, and the Presbytery of Arbroath was asked to ordain him before he left for Palestine; this happened on 9.11.1893 at Carnoustie.[117]

One might wonder at the time the JMC took over this appointment: perhaps the only plausible explanation for the delays being the events during the Torrance-Ewing dispute, and Ewing's consequent threat to resign. Perhaps the JMC felt he might be persuaded to change his mind again. The Committee's apparent insensitivity regarding his wife's death probably had little influence on Ewing's decision: having decided a year before his term of office was due to expire that he wanted to leave, it is likely that this was not only because of his wife's ill-health (in that case he might have argued for an earlier return to Scotland). Whatever the reasoning, Ewing retained an affection for the JMC which was clearly mutual, as he later became its convener and authored a volume describing the Committee's efforts which was published under their auspices.[118] Unsurprisingly, Ewing's own account of the mission's work mentions none of this: indeed his own role in the mission's work is barely mentioned.[119]

In terms of conversions, little is reported, indicating that little was happening. One of the few accounts is about

> a Jewish Youth of 15 at Safed [who] has been under instruction ... and wishes to become a Christian, but that his father has absolute power over him till 18, and that his life is not safe, and steps must be taken for his speedy removal. The Committee, disapproving of the proposed step, ... [draw] Mr Ewing's attention ... to the fact that it will never do to interfere with the legal rights of Jewish parents.[120]

This incident resulted in the brief imprisonment of one of the local mission teachers[121] and a letter by Christie in a British newspaper (for which he was reprimanded by the Convener).[122] It was later reported that

> since the release of the teacher and the young Jew, the Government are very anxious that the whole affair should be forgotten, but that the Governor does all he can to annoy the missionaries. The young Jew remains firm. He [Christie] further states that in spite of the bitter opposition the schools progress, and that he is on the best of terms with the Missionaries of the London Society in Safed.[123]

In the same minute, Torrance urged the JMC to appoint an additional teacher in Safad, 'owing to the severe competition of Baron Rothschild's School, which has a large staff of teachers' – Rothschild's Jewish school being one of the first signs of Jewish competition to the Scots' mission. This pre-dates concerns about efforts on the part of the Alliance Israélite Universelle (AIU)[124] to provide education to Jews in Palestine, though competition between the various foreign agencies was clearly an issue, as the LJS/Safad example showed. This was a recurring theme, so that the uncertainty over the buildings in Safad meant dealing with Christie's leaking house was left until the missionaries took matters into their own hands: the Committee having delayed action repeatedly, Ewing eventually told them that another house had been rented for him. The Committee somewhat lamely 'Resolved to sanction the amount required'.[125]

The hospital opens; the growing dominance of finance

The hospital's opening in 1894, attended by local notables of various religious persuasions,[126] marked a turning point in the JMC's work, financially, and in terms of the quality of the work that was carried out. Here, an overview of the financial situation will be given, followed by looking at the changing pattern of work through the hospital.

Towards the end of the building works, Torrance had estimated the annual running cost of the hospital at £740. Most of this was additional to existing commitments. Torrance wanted the money to provide

(a) salaries of assistant-surgeon, head nurse, second nurse, two native nurses, cook, cleaner, washer-woman, out-door man-servant and boy, dispenser, & attendant (b) house-keeping for resident officials and twenty-four patients (c) medicines and apparatus.[127]

For the first year the JMC wanted this sum reduced to £500, 'to be derived, if possible, from special donations, and any deficiency to be made up from the Foreign Jewish Allocation.' The subsequent item indicates why the Committee began to place a higher emphasis on the financial situation:

steps should be taken ... to prevent the recurrence – as has been the case for the last five years – of a deficit in the General Fund, either by obtaining an increase of income, or relinquishing some of the work. In particular ... the Convener should be requested to make in the February ... *Monthly* an appeal for special donations towards the up-keep of the Hospital.[128]

The threat of giving up work that the Committee was involved in would have been worrying to all the JMC's staff except perhaps those at the Tiberias hospital – that was less likely to be given up having just been built at great expense. However, this indicates one of the dominant priorities for the JMC over the coming years. JMC members were now to receive printed minutes and financial statements prior to each meeting, rather than relying on a hand-written minute book. Financial difficulties existed for all the mainstream churches from the 1890s. Although this was not yet the onset of large-scale secularisation in Scotland which decimated the churches in the 20th century, the proliferation of societies catering to specific needs (c.f. Chapter 1) was linked in part to the success of many of the smaller churches at the expense of the mainstream churches. Whilst Callum Brown maintains that 'the growth of popularity of the independent evangelical sector was an addition, not an alternative, to attendance' in the mainstream churches,[129] Michael Lynch points out that the alienation of the urban working-classes and the poor had already changed the membership of the mainstream churches to such a degree that when the 'orthodox churches were forced to compete along the same lines [as the smaller churches or evangelical societies, they usually met] ... with much less success'.[130] The significant role of the women's movement, although partly ignored by scholars such as Brown and Lynch, also played a part in the decreasing commitment to the churches, as Lesley Macdonald points out:

> For numerous women of all classes, church worship and church-based organisations had for long provided the only significant community beyond the domestic domain. That was no longer true: organised religion would now have to compete for the time, talents and means of some of that erstwhile silent majority which it had invariably taken for granted.[131]

The dismantling of certain social strictures, the possibility of women being admitted to universities, and the 'general growth of the movement for women's rights – in property, law, education and professions, and politics' – was important in women's decreasing support of the mainstream churches.[132]

The Committee was not without resources: it had over £27,000 in investments, though it was only allowed to use the interest from this for its ongoing work.[133] There was, however, external support, including a United Presbyterian Church offer of £250 annually to support the work in Galilee; it was decided this would form the basis of Soutar's salary, and the Convener and Secretary of the United Presbyterian mission committee were invited to join the JMC as a result of their contribution.[134] Budgets and accounts were soon also expected from the Mission Council, with strict instructions that 'no payments in excess of the budget ... shall be made without the special approval' of the JMC; the accounts were to include 'a detailed statement of all sums expended ... these accounts must be considered and passed by the Mission Council before they are sent home'.[135] Decisions about larger sums were mostly passed to the Finance Sub-Committee, now a permanent feature of the JMC (it would appear that sums of more than about £25-£30 were often dealt with in this way).

The JMC were fully aware of the extent of their financial problems: at the May 1894 General Assembly, a few months after the opening of the Tiberias hospital, it reported that they were 'getting into a chronic state of deficit, owing to the growth of the work, and especially to the rapid development of the Palestine Mission ... the committee needed about £600 a year in addition to what the Church had been ... giving them'.[136] Outlining the ideals and practices of the work pointed also to its rationale: whilst there might have been little to show in terms of baptised Jews (there had been none since the founding of the mission[137]), those who knew the work best were well aware that that was no test. Much of the fruit could not be shown or tabulated ... A process of permeation was going on. The patient loving labour was not and could not be in vain. Other missions, too, reaped sometimes what the Jewish Mission had sown, and they looked with firm confidence for a great ingathering in God's time. (Applause.)[138]

The hospital work, of medical treatment and evangelism, was outlined by Torrance:

during January and February ... 35 Jews, 13 Moslems, and 13 Christians were admitted ... and that during that time 31 operations (exclusive of a great many minor operations) were performed without any deaths ...
A short service, with an address and prayer, is held by the medical missionary in the waiting-room each dispensary day before the medical work is commenced, and also on Sunday an Arabic service is held by the doctor, which is attended by the hospital workers, patients, and others. Herr Goldenberg, the Scripture reader, attends to the outdoor waiting-room, and converses and reads with the patients as they wait ... [for] the doctor. He also visits the wards, and being a Hebrew Christian, and well up in the objections of Jews to Christianity, he is often able to entirely remove their difficulties.
[There are Biblical texts in several languages in each ward, but] All our agents ... try to be living Gospels, using all suitable occasions in conversation with individuals to minister to the soul, and it is in connection with this personal dealing that we look for most fruit.[139]

This pattern of activity was bearing fruits, since 'relief to the suffering sick' was increasing, and, from the missionary perspective, more importantly,

Prejudice against Christianity is being broken down ... wherever our work is known. The sore feelings of Jews against Christians on account of ancient and modern persecutions is meeting with an antidote, though infinitesimal compared with what they have suffered ...
That we are making some impression on the Jews is shown by their leaders being more alarmed, more watchful and strict, and preventing as much as they can their people from coming under our influence.[140]

Clearly, in the eyes of the Scots, the hospital was having its desired effect:

Our Tiberias hospital is a wonder and a joy to the Galileans when in sickness. In contrast with their squalid huts and tents, its sweetness and cleanness, its pervading atmosphere of Christian love in that loveless land, its power to bless, and its abundance, seem to them scarcely to belong to this world. Under its roof they feel as if they were in the Paradise of God. To them it is a real Bethel.[141]

The mission hospital, according to the missionaries, affected Christians and Muslims too. Muslims, apparently, were 'willing listeners ... and very frequently assent to a clear and simple statement of the gospel plan of salvation, their own ruin, Christ's righteousness, and restoration through his blood'. It is only the threat of 'death at the hands of their co-religionists and the Government' that prevents public profession of faith.[142] For Christians, Torrance saw the mission as providing something completely new to the region, going so far as to state that the

> ears of the people are opened and opportunities are had of preaching the gospel of Christ, which for hundreds of years was never heard by the inhabitants around these sacred shores, or the regions around, until the establishment of our medical mission. The native *Christians* are reforming, reading the Scriptures, and all – beginning with their priests – trying to live lives more in accordance with the precepts of Scripture than hitherto.[143]

In other words, not only was Torrance claiming for the Scots the offering of charity to the sick, but also claiming for themselves alone the correct interpretation of Biblical truths and an evangelistic mandate, which the Christian institutions already there had not carried out 'for hundreds of years'; a clear statement of power.

Figure 3-2 Tiberias: the mission is to the left, north of the town[144]

It is worthwhile elaborating in this detail on this first report to the full Church of the JMC's new hospital, since the principles outlined here set the pattern for subsequent decades. In 1895 Wilson records the 'methods of work' along these lines, and there is no indication that practices changed significantly over the next years. He closes his chapter giving thanks: 'There is great reason for thankfulness and encouragement in the work at Tiberias. The members of the mission have to a large extent won the affections of the people'. Thus the hospital, which had been founded in order to find a way of reaching the people of the Galilee (c.f. p65 above), clearly appeared to be serving its purpose, according to the missionaries.

What is most interesting in all this is the lack of recognition of local agency: people were clearly utilising the education and medicine, but were avoiding conversion. The missionaries did not recognise this, and thought that local use of the services represented a first step towards conversion. Despite years of work following similar patterns, it does not seem to have occurred to them that the locals were getting what they wanted from the missionaries, but were very clear that they did not want to embark on the process of conversion.

A few months after the opening of the hospital Torrance's wife, Lydia Huber, who had grown up in Palestine the daughter of a missionary, died in childbirth; the baby girl died shortly thereafter.[145] Their first pregnancy had resulted in twins, but these had both died within a year of birth, so that the only surviving child was Herbert, born in 1892, who many years later succeeded his father at the hospital, working there throughout the Mandate years.[146] Huber's sister had worked in Tiberias at the mission, and had died shortly before her sister.

At this stage, Torrance had been ordained an elder, but was reluctant to be ordained a minister, eventually letting himself be persuaded by the JMC and being ordained in Anderston Free Kirk on 15.9.1895,[147] where five years earlier he had married Huber. Torrance wrote to the JMC prior to his ordination clearly outlining his doubts, but also expresses his willingness to accept the JMC's wishes, recognising the ordination as an honour:

> When the proposal was made to me two years ago, I refused ... on the ground that I considered the needs of our Mission in Palestine demanded, not one missionary with what might be called a *double* qualification, but two men with *separate* qualifications.
> In the past, as well as attending to the bodily wants of the people, I have tried ... to commend the Gospel ... This has been the crowning joy of my labours, and I trust will continue to be, and I do not consider that were I ordained my influence ... would ... be increased among the people.
> I am still of opinion that the medical wants of the people of Galilee and the prejudices of the Jews, justify me in labouring as a *medical* missionary, and I feel so clearly that my talent and call are those of the medical missionary, pure and simple, that I would only agree to the proposal of the Committee ... on the distinct understanding that I continue to labour as I have done hitherto, and that only in case of emergency would I be called upon to preach and teach, or to exercise the special functions of the Ministry.[148]

His statement about the 'emergency' role perhaps reflects not only his concern that his own perception of his role might change, but that the JMC might feel they could dispense with an ordained missionary if Torrance was there as a medic and a minister.

Evangelisation; education; the Women's Jewish Missionary Association

The Sea of Galilee mission is usually thought of as a medical mission, though this was only one aspect of its work, albeit the major aspect. There was also a medic in Safad (for many years Dr Khalil Saadeh, who had trained at the Syrian Protestant College; as a non-European, he did not have a role in the Mission Council[149]), as well as schools in both towns, and means for direct evangelism. Thus were found all three of the main methods employed in Jewish mission stations outlined in Chapter 5. In both towns the role of the WJMA, barely touched on so far, was significant.

The establishment of the WJMA has already been outlined briefly. That the various localised women's associations came together in 1895, with the Tiberias hospital open, education and evangelism in Safad and Tiberias well underway, and above all, the finances of the JMC in poor shape, is no great surprise. The new WJMA defined its purpose as: 'to undertake ... the management and financial responsibility of all the work among women at the various stations maintained' by the JMC.[150]

This move is also an indication of the increasingly independent role of women within Scottish society and the churches.[151] The WJMA, similar to its Foreign Missions Committee (FMC) counterpart, was made up of women, but the Secretary was male, being also the Secretary to the JMC. The Ladies' Associations had for many years given money and support for the work of women in JMC stations but the WJMA brought the potential strength of women's involvement in the work in Scotland into an institutional framework. Of course, the WJMA supported all the missions of the JMC, and not merely the Palestine missions. In terms of finances, the WJMA reported in 1896 that it had collected about £675, and presuming a £400 contribution from the JMC, found itself only £300 short of the total expenditure for their area of concern, and, provided the JMC amount was to be forthcoming, committed itself to raising the additional £300 in the future.[152] These substantial sums, and the intention of raising more, would have been gladly received, even if the JMC was initially perhaps hesitant about the devolution of areas of responsibility. But tapping into the potential for increased publicity and therefore income, with the result that lower financial commitments were expected of the JMC, was certainly welcomed.[153]

The educational work, supported by the late 1890s by the WJMA and previously by the various Ladies' Associations sending funds directly to the JMC (and receiving some feedback and influence on this basis), had resulted in boys' and girls' schools in Tiberias and Safad.

The Safad mission had suffered from the inability of the JMC to make firm decisions in the light of the LJS mission presence. For a number of years, the LJS was used as a reason (excuse?) for not pursuing the expansion of the work, particularly in terms of property, as the example of Christie's leaking house shows. By 1895, this had changed slightly: 'Ground has recently been purchased at Safed, and the committee contemplate an extension of the mission there as soon as funds are supplied'.[154] At one stage it appeared as if the Free Kirk was prepared to forgo control of (part of) the mission station in Safad: lengthy and complicated deliberations starting in 1892 with the Convener of the

Foreign Missions Committee (Western Division) of the Presbyterian Church in Canada, Hamilton Cassels, regarding the appointment of one Rev Charles A Webster, B.A., M.D. as a missionary to Palestine, eventually led to the JMC concluding that,

> In the altered circumstances at Safed, consequent on ... Dr Webster ... [settling] there and ... [co-operating with the Free Kirk Mission], resolved that it is desirable that the Presbyterian Church in Canada should assume charge of the station, and that their representative there should have control of the Mission, receiving such aid from this Committee as may be mutually agreed on.[155]

The 'altered circumstances' were related to both Christie and Saadeh's positions, and are described in the same minute: Saadeh had renewed a previous request for a period of leave, prompting the JMC to ask the Mission Council 'for their opinion regarding the further employment of Dr Khalil Saadeh'; Christie's position was also in question. The JMC had appointed a sub-committee to 'consider certain matters of grave importance in connection with the present condition of the Mission Station of Safed',[156] which reported back:

> The subject remitted to them ... did not involve any charge against Mr Christie's moral character, which was without reproach, but had to do with circumstances affecting his usefulness as a Christian missionary at Safed, and made it needful to consider whether, now that his five years' engagement had come to an end, it was desirable it should be renewed. The Convener ... stated the result of the sub-Committee's conference with Mr Christie ... and also of his own interview with him ... After deliberation it was resolved to call in Mr Christie, who ... said that on looking back he saw not a little to regret, but gave the assurance that if the Committee should see their way to send him again to Safed, there would be nothing wanting on his part to secure and maintain satisfactory relations with the members of his own family circle as well as with the agents of the Mission. Resolved that Mr Christie may on the expiry of his furlough be sent back to Safed for a year on probation, provided the Committee are satisfied that a complete reconciliation has been effected between him and his relatives, that needful readjustments in the staff at Safed have been made, and that Mr Christie's health has been completely restored.[157]

There is no concrete indication of what might have been wrong: whether the relatives mentioned were his family in Palestine[158] or in Scotland, which of his colleagues he might have had disagreements with, nor what other circumstances might have affected his 'usefulness as a Christian missionary'. All official accounts of his work appear to be without comment on these issues; once again, as with the Ewing-Torrance conflict, the lack of any personal correspondence or writings preserved from this period means that it is impossible to ascertain exactly what this was about. Christie returned to Safad in the autumn (accompanied by Soutar's bride) to have his infant son die shortly after,[159] whilst Torrance asked for Saadeh's resignation, to take effect from July.[160] Webster had meanwhile been in Haifa, recovering from illness, and he decided to stay there for the time being, later informing the JMC that he would not be leaving at all.[161]

To return to the property purchase in Safad mentioned above: this was bought early in 1895, through much work by Soutar.[162] Difficulties quickly arose since the LJS claimed it had the right of first refusal on property purchases, and a sub-committee of the JMC was created to deal with this issue.[163] It was resolved to send a delegation to London to meet with LJS representatives;[164] this happened on 4.7.1895, with the Convener, another JMC member, and Torrance (in Scotland on furlough leave) representing the Free Kirk. The JMC later noted that in the dispute about the claimed pre-emptive right of the LJS on property purchases, the LJS agent had taken the issue through the local courts, although the Free Kirk had wanted the matter resolved through the British Consul-General in Beirut, the normal method of resolving such issues under the Capitulations system prevailing in the Ottoman Empire at that time. The JMC, in a classic example of colonial attitude, recorded 'how deeply this Committee deplores that one Christian Mission should have sued another in a non-Christian Court', and sought to eliminate the problem by, as they saw it, the LJS re-taking control over the actions of their agents in Safad.[165] It was eventually recorded that, quoting the LJS letter, the Londoners had 'direct[ed] him [Mr Friedman, their agent] to discontinue further controversy on the spot, and to obtain no more legal opinions'.[166] Whilst not all the issues were totally clarified at this time, the way was now open for the Scots to pursue building work and expansion.

Christie, meanwhile, had been the subject of a communication from the Presbyterian Church of England, who had asked the JMC whether they would object to him being invited to apply for a post with them. The JMC had no objections, not a great surprise given the reluctance they had shown in giving him a firm renewal of his contract, and in May the JMC was informed that he had accepted an appointment as a Jewish missionary in Aleppo and would be leaving the Free Kirk mission in September; it is almost certain that this was the mission in Aleppo that had originally been founded by Scots.[167] A new candidate for the Safad mission was appointed, Rev J E H Thomson, a licentiate from the United Presbyterians, who was subsequently ordained by his denomination; his wife was appointed by the Glasgow Ladies' Association to replace Fenton at the Girls' School.[168] This appointment was just one example of increasing co-operation between the United Presbyterians and the Free Kirk prior to the 1900 union, and the consideration of Webster (even though this appointment never materialised), indicates openness to engage with other denominations as well. A Head Nurse for the hospital was appointed in July 1895, one Eleanor Adamson Dowrie, and Torrance was asked to identify another suitable candidate who could be appointed as a second nurse.[169] George Wilson, who had been in Tiberias on a local wage for a considerable period, applied and was appointed as a medical missionary to Safad.[170] Meanwhile, Soutar, by December 1896, appeared to have mastered sufficient Arabic 'to address the patients who assemble for treatment at the Hospital or Dispensary'.[171]

Six months after Dowrie's appointment, Torrance sent a telegram[172] (and a letter two days later), 'intimating a purpose of marriage between himself and Miss Dowrie, asking whether Miss Dowrie might resign, and proposing a substitute for her. Resolved to telegraph – "Dowrie permitted resign, substitute accepted;"'.[173] Requiring a female missionary to resign upon marriage was normal, as Macdonald explains: 'Those who succumbed to matrimony were automatically deemed to have resigned, though most married other missionaries and in fact continued their labours unpaid'.[174] A successor to Dowrie, Miss List, was quickly identified, and sailed to Tiberias on 15.10.1896.[175]

Figure 3-3 The Safad mission properties [176]

With the buildings situation in Safad clarified, the Secretary submitted plans, presumably agreed by the Sea of Galilee Mission Council, for proposed buildings: '(1) a House for Dr Wilson, (2) House for Summer Quarters for the Tiberias Missionaries, (3) a Dispensary and School.' The first and third items were approved, whilst the consideration of the second was postponed – presumably on the basis that the other buildings were more essential to the core purpose of the mission.[177] The total cost for Wilson's house, estimated at £1561 16s, was approved and the building work, due to be completed in November, began.[178] Further building work took place in Safad over the next years – the first time that the Safad mission had been granted the possibility of meaningful investment in property, as even the JMC realised in a minute of 1898.[179]

The work at Safad developed in a similar way to that in Tiberias – the medical facility was, not, of course, on the same scale as the Tiberias hospital (the EMMS hospitals in Nazareth and Damascus were probably the only institutions in the area to rival that), but the schools developed and grew, and possibilities for increasing work amongst adults were taken up. There were not only addresses to patients attending the clinic, but biblical and theological texts were disseminated (this with the financial support of the National Bible Society of Scotland),[180] and services were held. The schools consisted, in e.g. 1899, of an 'Arabic Boys' School' (with 33 names on the roll), a 'School for Jewish Lads' (41 pupils), both run by the JMC,[181] and Jewish and Muslim girls' schools (with 23 and 120 pupils respectively at the end of the year, though in the latter only about 80 attended regularly) run by the WJMA.[182] The Muslim girls, it was reported,

> can repeat texts, hymns and Bible stories, *ad libitum* ... It is very pretty to see our little ones repeating texts, some barely able to pronounce the words. We have a larger number of older Moslem girls here than in Tiberias, and they come to us to learn sewing and lace work and we give always the Scriptures. As a rule they are quiet, gentle and devoted to their teacher.[183]

The Jewish girls apparently appreciated their school too, and the staff felt 'very hopeful' about it, with 'the children coming to us ... [being] a nice age, and very quiet and regular and attentive'.[184] However, the Christian element could cause problems:

> When School began again in October, some of our big Moslem girls did not return, and ... we learned they had been heard singing a Christian hymn by the Qadi (or Judge), and forbidden to attend our School. We hope to see them soon in School, for they love to come.[185]

In 1897 Soutar reported similarly, the JMC minutes quoting in part from one of his letters:

> both schools are suffering ... from Government opposition; that all the Moslem children had been withdrawn, that a new Moslem school for girls had been started by the Government, and new teachers had been secured for the old-fashioned boys' school ... A determined effort is now being made throughout the country to withdraw all Moslem children from Christian schools. In the Irish Presbyterian Mission at Damascus several schools have been closed.[186]

Jewish leaders also opposed the schools, usually by means of a *cherem*, or ban. However, the effect of these bans did not usually last long,[187] and so whilst there may temporarily have been fewer pupils, the numbers soon recovered. The missionaries tended to see this as a triumph for their work and the effect this was having on the local population. In March 1894 the JMC minuted another letter from Christie:

> stating that on his return from Tiberias ... he found that a severe *Cherem* had been pronounced against him, and the thirty-six young Jews who had been for some time in the habit of attending at his house for instruction; and that circumstances like this were a strong plea for an Industrial College.

This points to a significant area of the missions work, the so-called 'Industrial Mission' – significant although it was never implemented.

The 'Industrial Mission' – the project that never happened

The first baptism of a Jew was to turn out to be a very productive one for the Mission.[188] James Cohen was baptised on 10.2.1895, as reported by Soutar to the JMC, who instructed 'the Secretary to send ... a suitable message to Mr Cohen'.[189] That the Secretary could find the time to do this is in itself an indication that this was a rare event. Cohen, born in Russia, was taken to Safad at 13, initially attending Rothschild's school, becoming a gardener in a 'Jewish colony' for 2½ years prior to his conversion. He then attended the Syrian Protestant College before becoming an evangelist in Tiberias; he was ordained in 1912 by the Presbytery of Sidon, at the JMC's request.[190] The JMC missionaries regarded him as a model of what Jews could become once they converted: not only in terms of the enlightenment they found in Christianity, but also, as a converted Jew himself, as the best type of missionary for work amongst Jews.

However, Jews (and indeed Muslims) who converted to Christianity faced ostracisation (or worse) from their family and home communities. The missionaries repeatedly argued that some form of employment was needed to give potential converts the means to earn a living, as well as being able to form social relationships with other converts.[191] The missionaries could be blunt: 'If we cannot give a Jew work ... in asking him to become a Christian we are asking him to starve' (Soutar).[192] The missionaries argued that this represented a significant barrier to conversion for many and that such material factors should not be allowed to prevent a potential conversion. Sending converts to work at other mission stations or even to Scotland was strongly discouraged, and rarely sanctioned by the JMC.[193] Given that this was not a realistic option, the obvious solution seemed to be a local facility, either an 'industrial school' where converts, especially the younger ones, might learn a trade, or an 'industrial mission' where converts could earn a living, perhaps, though not necessarily, in their own trade. Elsewhere, such a scheme was often seen to encourage (western) civilisation – to use missionaries' language – in those contexts that were perceived to need it.[194] What Torrance and others were suggesting did not have 'civilising' as its primary motive (that is not to say it was not part of the motive); rather they hoped the method might help achieve their primary purpose of conversion.[195] As Jewish colonies increased in number, the missionaries also suggested agricultural work; elements of competition are apparent.

In 1898 Soutar reported that, 'by means of a special donation', he had been able to send a pupil to the 'Industrial School of the American Mission at Sidon'; although intended only for their own pupils, the Americans had allowed this 'to show that the American Mission was one with the Scotch', as Soutar put it. The minutes 'record[ed] the pleasure with which the Committee had heard this announcement'.[196] What would have given the Galilee missionaries greater pleasure would have been a JMC commitment to initiate a similar scheme. Instead, when it was next raised, on this occasion in connection with a possible property purchase (having already been mentioned several times with no results), the JMC stated their view that 'buying land was only a part ... of providing industrial work for Jewish enquirers or converts, and that they could not recommend any action ... in the meantime', rather, the standing sub-committee was asked to enquire and report.[197] The United Presbyterian/Free Kirk union in 1900 might have been a factor in further procrastination,[198] and further delay occurred when the sub-committee's convener moved to England – Ewing, formerly of Tiberias, took over.[199]

A plot of land was offered for use as a 'Hebrew Christian Colony', but it was not acted upon.[200] However, the JMC's new 'Industrial Mission sub-committee' later noted that the FMC was also planning an industrial mission, and the JMC hoped 'it may be possible to regard the [Jewish] needs ... and to entertain some well-considered plans for meeting them'.[201] A company had been formed, and the Mission Council wrote to the JMC noting

> that the Scottish Mission Industries Company was now constituted, and would be prepared to consider any practicable scheme for industrial work among Jews – that the Council can suggest industrial work ... such as tanning, saddlery, fish-curing, etc., but ... do not consider themselves qualified to draft a scheme for ... such work, and urge that an expert may be sent to investigate ... and report.[202]

Given that the missionaries had long been arguing for such a company, this must have seemed a very positive move.[203] However, their suggestions for possible work were regarded as somewhat vague, and the Company directors responded saying that without a 'practical suggestion, they did not "consider that it opened out any immediate prospect of their entering into any undertaking in Palestine," but they ... would be glad to receive ... any [further] information or proposals' – they were clearly unwilling to send an 'expert'.[204] The missionaries reacted promptly, Torrance proposing purchasing a plot 'very fertile and well fitted ... [for] Industrial Mission work';[205] he was told it would be considered and a few months later the JMC welcomed two company representatives, who described plans to purchase a substantial site in the Plain of Gennesaret[206] – the site Torrance had mentioned. The JMC warmly welcomed all this, promising no financial support, but co-operation and promotion of the project, having 'long felt the absolute necessity of a scheme of this kind in order to conserve the result of their Mission work ... and create a Christian community'.[207] The scheme appeared to be progressing, since a minute records that 'land on the Plain of Gennesaret, previously negotiated for, is likely to be purchased soon, on behalf of the ... Church ... by a Company to be formed for this purpose',[208] but the project is not mentioned again, and nothing more was done. It is interesting to note that at no point do local people appear to have been consulted.

Although no reason for the demise of the scheme is apparent from the minutes, Livingstone presents a description of the circumstances indicating the project essentially ran out of time. Franciscans offered a higher price for the land than the Scots, who were unable to raise additional funds in time. The 'Church crisis' occupied the attention of many,[209] and the Franciscans completed the purchase. In classic Evangelical anti-Catholicism,[210] Livingstone noted bitterly: 'the territory had passed ... [to] the Roman Catholics. They sold it later to the Jews for three times the amount, and it is now ... a flourishing colony, and one of the most valuable sections of land in Galilee'.[211]

A similar opportunity did not arise again. The attempts to appropriate a model designed for a 'primitive' context (using the missionaries' language), into the more 'civilised' context of the Levant did not appear to fail because this appropriation was faulty, but for simple human and practical reasons. The obvious parallels to the Zionists' 'Jewish colonies' are not mentioned by the missionaries, though an Industrial Mission would obviously have been another imperial-style enterprise competing for local resources.

The mission in the years up to 1914

The work in Tiberias and Safad in the years before 1914 are marked by a period of relative stability, but limited growth, as financial restrictions made expansion largely impossible. For example, in 1904 Wilson requested a relatively small amount in order to increase by 4 or 6 the beds he had in Safad, at a cost of 'sevenpence per patient per day ... Wilson had 12 in-patients in the Dispensary rooms (6 Jews, 3 Moslems, and 3 Roman Catholics), and he had hitherto obtained from friends privately the money required for this purpose'. The request was rejected.[212]

In an attempt to reduce costs the United Free Church amalgamated the JMC and the Colonial and Continental Committees, despite JMC resistance. After the 1910 General Assembly the three committees addressed all business together, breaking down each meeting into three main parts. Interestingly, the new committee's name dropped the 'mission' element – an unconscious acknowledgement that conversions were few? – and became the Colonial, Continental and Jewish Committee (CCJ). This did not last: the 1913 Assembly recreated the JMC, separating it off from the Colonial and Continental Committee; it is difficult to ascertain whether combining the three committees reduced costs. However, it is certain, judging by the amount of business carried out, that the meetings must have been interminably long, and more importantly, the numbers participating in the work, even just through being a part of the committee, would have been reduced (the membership of the new committee was not the combined membership of the three previous ones). Reducing the ownership of the work therefore came at a time when ever more funds were required in order to expand and develop the work, particularly, but not exclusively, with regard to the hospital.[213]

Missionaries on furlough leave were expected to play their part in encouraging support for the work, in part through travelling and speaking to congregations. For example, it was announced in October 1904 that Soutar, on furlough leave, had speaking engagements every Sunday until the following May. He told the JMC he had 'met with much encouragement'.[214] A sub-committee was created to examine opportunities for further promotion of the JMC's work[215] which proceeded to produce promotional material (for example, early in 1905, 20,000 copies of a promotional booklet were printed, followed by another 10,000 soon afterwards[216]), develop preaching opportunities, and similar such work. The JMC published missionaries' reports, and on at least one occasion published details of promotional work carried out in Scotland. In 1907, a temporary appointment was made of someone who could promote the JMC's work in Scotland; it was really only in the war years, when the missionaries had been recalled to Scotland, that this idea was developed more fully.[217]

Figure 3-4 Torrance walking 'where the 5000 are supposed to have been fed' [218]

In 1904 Torrance warned that he did not want to renew his contract, due to his pay and conditions of service, which he felt necessitated higher recognition; this caused the JMC considerable concern. A request for an extra £100 'to go towards the expense of board and education of his family' in Scotland was rejected but he also requested:

> (1) permission to come home every alternate summer to visit his children, and (2) the guarantee of a retiring allowance in the event of his being unable through ill-health or old age to carry on active work. He further "most reluctantly" proposed "as an alternative" that he might have leave to supplement his present salary by fees from foreign travellers and the richer natives.[219]

Private practice was rejected outright, but the alternative options were addressed. However, other circumstances, particularly Soutar's unexpected death (see below), meant that this matter was postponed, though in the end, the JMC, despite their financial strictures, acceded to Torrance's requests, with effect from February 1907:

> sanction[ed] in the case of Dr Torrance, on the ground of exceptional service for ... more than twenty years, a personal grant of £100 a year, including children's allowances, over and above the salary of a married missionary, as provided by the rules, or a salary of £400 a year without the allowances mentioned.[220]

Whilst it might appear Torrance was trying to force the hand of the Committee (he undoubtedly knew they would have been very reluctant to lose him), his salary had remained static for two decades, whilst his expenses and the cost of living had risen. He had two (surviving) children, Herbert born in 1892 by Lydia Huber, and Marjorie born on 2.1.1898[221] by Eleanor Dowrie, who had died in December 1902, and since he was unmarried at the time of his salary increase application, his children would not have been with him, but in Scotland, either with other members of his family or in school; it was to be another few years before his marriage to Elizabeth Welch Curtiss. The JMC, in making it clear their grant was an exception based on Torrance's long service, was taking precautions against other staff requesting similar additions to their salaries.

Regarding other staff: Wilson had been in Palestine for a considerable number of years, but took the JMC's worsening finances as one of the reasons to resign, as well as 'his desire to seek another sphere of life and work', a move that was accepted by the JMC; he left in June 1905.[222] Soutar suggested James Cohen be appointed 'Native Pastor at Safad', a suggestion the JMC felt unable to decide upon without consulting the Mission Council. There was no response to this prior to a telegram from Torrance intimating Soutar's death: he had returned to Palestine in late October suffering from dysentery, and had died on 13.12.1905.[223] The JMC's minute records something of their impression of his character, aside from having been a most able student, his

> swift mastery of the Arabic language, his habits of close observation and calm reflection, his sobriety of judgement and wisdom in counsel, above all, his whole-hearted devotion to his high vocation made a great impression on ... [those] around him, while his kind yet manly nature won for him many friends. It is impossible as yet to estimate the full value of Mr Soutar's services; but, reflecting upon his quiet courage, his calm strength, his sanity of view, his clear mind and chivalrous heart, the Committee feel that, in the providence of God, a great influence for good has been removed from the Mission field.[224]

The JMC considered a letter from Soutar and recommendations from the Mission Council for two significant decisions: firstly, Cohen was transferred 'from Tiberias to Safed on a salary of £60 a year, with house rent-free, his duties being, besides the ordinary work of an evangelist, teaching Hebrew in the Girls' School and assisting in the Evening School', and secondly that Wilson was not to be replaced by a local doctor and the assistant dispenser was to be given one month's notice – i.e. their Safad clinic was to close. A proposal for a girls' boarding school was welcomed, but thought not financially possible, though it was decided to use the premises vacated by the medics for setting the schools on a firmer footing:

> the first floor of the Dispensary premises shall be used for the Girls' School; the second floor for the Boys' School; and the third floor for the dwelling-house of the headmaster of the Boys' School – Miss Jones and her teachers occupying the house formerly occupied by Dr Wilson.[225]

Soutar, who was buried in the mission burial ground at Tiberias, had worked at creating a Protestant community, as reported at the General Assembly on various occasions, and once he died and Torrance was left taking some of the responsibility for his work, it became apparent that some form of consolidation of the community was required. Torrance put it in terms of imminent needs: 'for the protection and well-being of the native Protestant Christians associated with the Mission, "the establishment of a new religious community in the district, and the appointment of a representative (*mukhtar*) in each place" might soon be needful'.[226] Under the *millet* system, each community within the Ottoman Empire had its own representative, and for a Protestant grouping not to be constituted as or associated with a distinct group would have brought with it civil and legal disadvantages. The obvious choice was to establish a connection with the American mission's church based in Lebanon. The Americans were happy to help out, suggesting that churches might be organised in Tiberias and Safad with each electing an elder who could attend Sidon Presbytery meetings.[227]

Soutar's successor was a difficult choice: the JMC had identified two suitable candidates, Thomas Steele of Glasgow's theological college, and S H Semple, a probationer. A majority preferred Steele,[228] and following the usual medical examination and ordination, he was sent to Leipzig for a period of training. However, he was not well, and informed the JMC that due to 'overwork for the last three years ... his medical adviser had enjoined absolute rest for some time' – a sign of problems to come. However, he left for Palestine as planned, accompanied by Torrance who was returning from furlough leave, on 20.1.1907.[229] Steele appeared to be settling in, though his health was poor, and by December, Torrance had telegraphed: 'Invalided Steele home, *phthisis pulmonalis* [i.e. TB[230]] – Scrimgeour, Torrance'.[231] He was medically examined and sent to a sanatorium in Kingussie, near Inverness, still being paid by the Committee who awaited further medical reports. A year later, the JMC medics found him to be in somewhat better health, but still unfit for a 'return to duty in the East', and he formally resigned his position, never fully recovered, and died on 19.12.1911.[232]

Torrance was keen to replace Steele as soon as possible – his workload would have increased – and the JMC decided to offer the job to Semple, who had been passed over in favour of Steele. By the time the JMC offered him the post he was in Lahore, working for the Colonial Committee. Both Semple and his employers were happy for him to move,[233] and following understandably careful examination of his medical certificate,[234] he was appointed, leaving Lahore in June and returning to Scotland; he was at the Committee's meeting on 27.7.1909, and arrived in Palestine by the end of October. Perhaps since he had already worked overseas, Semple appears to have moved into his job with relative ease. Apparently Torrance 'broke down' early in the year, but his spirits markedly improved with Semple's arrival.[235]

Figure 3-5 'Dr. Torrance in Arab Dress' [236]

Torrance had been in Palestine for 25 years, having spent more than half his life there (he was 47 in 1909). William Ewing and George Milne Rae, the Committee's Convener and Secretary, sent Torrance a letter produced on vellum marking the occasion. The themes of geopiety, assumptions about local responses, and future hope dominate:

> We are well aware that you count it a high and sacred privilege to have borne your testimony to the Master through all these years, amid the scenes consecrated by His earthly presence. We know, too, that, in the discharge of your onerous duties, you have not sought the praise of man. But we welcome the present as a fit opportunity to say … how greatly we have appreciated your unselfish devotion, and the fidelity and zeal with which you have pursued the end of our enterprise. We are deeply gratified by the success that has attended the exercise of your professional skill, which, together with your kindly interest in their welfare, has won for you a place of affection and honour in the hearts of a grateful people.
>
> It is to us a matter for gratitude to God that you have been able to maintain your position through all the changes that the years have brought, thus lending continuity and coherence to our Missionary efforts.
>
> It is our hope and prayer that, from the sowing of these years, a rich harvest may yet be gathered to the praise of the Messiah.
>
> We unite most heartily in the best of good wishes for you and yours, and earnestly trust that there still lie before you many years of happy and fruitful service.[237]

The occasion was also marked in Tiberias, where representatives from various communities addressed Torrance and his influence over quarter of a century of work:

Jews (Ashkenazi and Sephardic), Greek Catholics, Greek Orthodox, and Muslim. 'A member of the Young Turks Society ... [gave] a glowing speech in French, and a pastor of the German Catholic Mission at et-Tâbigha added to his eulogies'.[238] Gifts and speeches from the staff were also included in the celebration.

In the years that Torrance had been in Tiberias, he had seen the expansion of his own work from a simple house where he offered medical treatment to a substantial hospital treating hundreds of patients a year, and though he was ever keen to expand (a maternity department, a 'ward for sick tourists' and various other ideas were dominating his thinking at the time[239]), a great deal had already been achieved. Educational facilities had been created: schools teaching Muslim, Christian and Jewish children, and evening classes for adults, both of which appeared to continue relatively consistently despite occasional opposition from local Muslim and Jewish dignitaries. Dissemination of biblical texts and itinerant teaching and preaching had been firmly established, and regular services in various languages had been held for decades each week (those who happened to be patients in the hospital swelled the numbers – they tended to be taken to services). Whilst the Tiberias mission had medicine as its main focus, in Safad it was particularly the Girls' School that was developed to a high level, particularly after boarding became possible. This happened through a Girls' Home where up to six girls could stay, run by Lizzie Jones,[240] whilst the school was under the direction of Gwladys Jones (no relation). The 1910 Budget estimate showed seven local staff working under Gwladys Jones, and, in 1911, 110 pupils were recorded: 66 Muslims, 24 Jews, and 20 Christians. Of course, Torrance could not be credited for all of this,[241] and many others played a significant role in various aspects of the work, but the continuity of his long service, the commitment and dedication to the mission as a whole,[242] and his undoubted position as 'senior missionary', even if others were supposed to be appointed to equal positions, meant that he carried a great deal of responsibility, and consequently also deserves some of the credit, for enabling the work to develop in this way. The one area of obvious and near total failure was that of conversions, the stated core function of the mission. There were virtually no Jewish converts whilst the converts there were had largely been poached from other Christian denominations. Torrance failed to see that the locals were largely appropriating what they saw as desirable (education, medicine) but did not see these as part of the conversion process, unlike Torrance and his colleagues.

Ecumenism; Zionism; World War I

The first great ecumenical conference of the modern era was the 1910 World Missionary Conference, 'which inspired a new search for an ecumenical approach to mission throughout the world',[243] and to which the Convener, Vice-Convener and another member were appointed delegates,[244] but the influence of relations beyond the borders of Presbyterian Scotland upon the work of the CCJ made themselves felt before that. There had long been contacts with outside bodies, but these had been sporadic and/or related to a particular purpose, such as the appointment of an individual. Long-term connections had been few, the Institutum Judaicum and the American mission, e.g.

through Sidon Presbytery, being two of the most obvious exceptions.[245] But the 1910 Conference helped cement a number of further connections, for example, participation in the Continuation Committee of the 1910 Conference was invited, subscriptions were paid for membership of the International Jewish Missionary Conference, and delegates were sent to events such as the 'Conference of Representatives of Missionary Societies';[246] such contacts increasing as World War I approached. The Committee also addressed more events affecting Jews in parts of the world where they were not working, for example, in 1905 they recorded their abhorrence at

> the terrible tidings of horrible massacres and revolting cruelties recently inflicted on the Jewish people in many parts of Russia. They ... protest ... these brutal outrages, and express deepest sympathy with God's Ancient People ... The Committee are assured that this protest will command the sympathy and approval of the whole Church, as well as the entire Christian community.[247]

A grateful response from the 'Chief Rabbi of the United Congregations of the British Empire', to whom a copy of the minute had been sent, was received.[248]

A review of 'Jewish Mission Literature' prepared by the JMC in 1916 stated that the war could bring about positive opportunities for the churches, Jewish well-being in the JMC's eyes, needless to say, being connected to the presence of missionary activity:

> We are also led to the conclusion that, through the war, the Jewish world is being broken up to such a degree that ... [there is] a quite unparalleled opportunity in Jewish Mission work. While many cast hopeful eyes towards Mesopotamia and the Holy Land, the Russian Empire has now ... been opened to the Jews, and new migrations of great masses ... are already taking place. Severance with the old and dark Ghetto conditions proceeds apace and is likely to be still more thorough. Their settlement in regions where Missions are few or altogether non-existent may be regarded as certain. It will be impossible to establish sufficient new permanent stations. Accordingly, great expansion of the itinerant Mission will be wanted. As already stated the itinerant Mission depends largely on literature ... [and so] the provision of suitable literature to meet the coming needs will also be seen to demand special consideration as a specific part of the general question.[249]

This brings us to the missionaries' attitudes to Zionism. The Committee minutes record little of the missionaries' attitudes to Zionism or 'the Jewish question', though there is more during the war, but it was, as might be expected, the Balfour Declaration and General Allenby's capture of Jerusalem which elicited the most comprehensive reaction to the Jewish situation.

Figure 3-6 Torrance during World War I [250]

Immediately prior to the Declaration, the JMC, along with other British churches and missionary societies, had sought to impress upon Balfour the need, in the new political circumstances that were arising, of ensuring the ongoing independence and freedom to act of any British missionary and society in Palestine.[251] The achievements of the political and military powers were welcomed, and in 'the new situation created in Southern Palestine by the advance of our troops',[252] the possibility of Paterson returning to Hebron was referred to, as was Torrance's return: perhaps not directly to Tiberias, but initially to work for the Syria and Palestine Relief Fund (an ecumenical body to which the United Free Church had also contributed, and which was dealing with most of the British churches' efforts to provide relief in the region during the war), something that Torrance was by no means averse to. By the time the Committee next met, Allenby had taken Jerusalem:

> The Convener made reference to the Capture of Jerusalem by General Allenby and his troops as an event of momentous importance in the history of the world and of the Kingdom of God, and on his suggestion it was agreed to record the feeling of the Committee that, inasmuch as the Holy City had, after centuries of oppression by an infidel power, now come under Christian sway, no effort should be spared to uphold the freedom gained at so great cost of Christian effort and sacrifice.[253]

Connecting their own imperial authorities to the divine purpose was marked not only in the minutes, but in a 'United Service of Thanksgiving for the Delivery of Jerusalem' called by the JMCs of the two churches held on Sunday 16.12.1917.

The meeting also recorded a lengthy response to the Balfour Declaration, which had been prepared by a sub-committee and acknowledged that it showed the government was keen to 'find a settlement of the Jewish question'. It was sent to the Prime Minister, the Secretaries of State for Foreign Affairs and Scotland, the Archbishop of Canterbury, the President of the Free Church Council, societies and churches working in the region, and the press, seeing

in the advance of our gallant troops in Palestine, and more especially in the liberation of the Jews, largely through Christian sacrifice, an earnest of the final deliverance of the Holy Land from the oppressive rule of the Turk, and ... [thanking God] for the success which has attended the effort and sacrifice of His Majesty's Forces...

[Reminding the government of the] deep and long-continued interest which the Christian Churches of this country have had in the Holy Land, and of ... [their work] for the material, moral and religious welfare of the peoples resident there ... [they urge the government] in any future determination of policy ... [to] consult the Christian Churches...

[They note that the Balfour Declaration] fails to take account of the formation of fresh non-Jewish Communities, and, in particular, of members of the Jewish race becoming Christians, ... [and are convinced that] desirable or just ... [governance in Palestine requires:]

(*a*) Generally, the fullest civil and religious freedom for the adherents of all faiths equally;

(*b*) Specifically, the same equal rights and liberties for Christian Jews as for non-Christian Jews; and

(*c*) Particularly, that the Christian Churches be no less free than under Turkish rule to continue their Missionary enterprise.[254]

The 'Christian sacrifice' for the Jews (the 'sacrifice' was not for Muslims or Christians!) required at the very minimum the freedoms that the missionaries had had under Ottoman rule. Locals were ignored – it was above all necessary to consult the western churches about Palestine's future. Britain might have understood itself to be a Christian nation, but the United Free Church clearly wanted to safeguard against the *realpolitik* that might have induced preservation of the status of existing religious groupings and prevented efforts at conversion. The Foreign Office responded, assuring the JMC that the 'Government are fully aware of the importance of the questions raised ... and will exert their influence to secure that the civil and religious rights of all non-Jewish communities and individuals in Palestine shall be effectively safeguarded'.[255]

The use of similar language to the Balfour Declaration may have done little to assuage the concerns of the JMC, but this is not commented on further. In general, the influx of Jews to Palestine was seen as an opportunity to be grasped, with neither the Committee nor any of the missionaries voicing concerns at the possible implications.

After the war, with the British in control of Palestine and later given the Mandate of the territory, Scottish missionaries developed varying positions on Zionism: this will not be developed further here.[256] However, prior to the war, it would be fair to say that the Sea of Galilee missionaries saw Zionism as unrealistic under the prevailing circumstances, or simply naïve. There are not many sources on this topic, and Livingstone's biography published after Torrance's death in 1923 is unreliable in this regard since the author writes in retrospect with knowledge of what has happened. He does, however, cite Torrance on some occasions (though it is not clear where from) and this offers an insight into his thinking. For example, in 1897, around the time of the Zionist Congress in Basle he states:[257]

> We do not think it likely that a Jewish kingdom will be established, but if present restrictions on the entrance of Jews and the purchase of land were removed, it would soon in larger measure be owned and occupied by this ancient race ... That this may occur is not at all unlikely, and thus Palestine may be looked upon strategically as an important field for mission work, far beyond what might be considered were the present Jewish population alone taken into account.[258]

Beyond this, there is relatively little, though Zionism exercised the minds of others in the churches; Chapter 4 below portrays an analysis of further statements on this topic.

The 1914 war itself led to the British staff in Galilee being withdrawn, as the September meeting noted; by the October meeting, Torrance and Semple were present, along with colleagues from Budapest and Constantinople.[259] Torrance reported that 'the native workers were in charge of the schools, and that Sister Frieda [Blaiker, who was Swiss[260]] was carrying on our patient work'. Torrance seemed sure that the Empire would join the British in the war and left most of his belongings in Tiberias, expecting to return shortly. He immediately began working at Glasgow's Western Infirmary, but joined the military as a Lieutenant, working at a war hospital in Glasgow when the Ottomans allied themselves with Germany.[261] Blaiker continued her work, though parts of the properties had been appropriated; an American missionary reported that the Tiberias and Safad missions had been taken over and were being used as schools.[262] Subsequent meetings recorded increasing destruction and removal of property from the missions' buildings. Blaiker was eventually forced to give up and returned to Europe;[263] Cohen fared less well. Exempted from military service as a minister, he tried to continue his evangelistic work, but difficulties in sending his pay into what the British government regarded as enemy territory meant that he began to supplement his income with passport photography. Accusations over a job led to his imprisonment and beatings; acquitted and released, he came under renewed suspicion and was arrested again. He went to Constantinople – why or how is not clear – where he died of typhus, leaving a widow and child in Safad.[264] It is noted below that Paterson served in the region during the war; similarly Gwladys Jones took up a post as YWCA Secretary in Cairo, with provision for a return to Safad secured.[265]

The Committee lodged, for all its mission stations in the Ottoman Empire, notices with the Foreign Office of buildings and valuables under control of opposing forces; it was the FO which first informed the JMC of the state of their property.[266] The notices were part of a wider claim that was to be made at the end of the war for British property damaged or destroyed by its enemies (the extent of success is not clear, though the reliance on the political authorities and link to imperial power obviously is). Fundraising continued apace, though since there were few expenses, this was geared towards generating monies for restarting the missions. Various missionaries, including Semple, but not, it appears Torrance, engaged in regular speaking engagements to raise funds. Few records of these exist, though ironically, perhaps, given his few engagements, a summary of one by Torrance can be found in the Church of Scotland magazine, in which he appears to have mostly spoken about the history of the mission, presenting it as 'an inspiring lesson as to what can be accomplished through patience, faith, and zeal'.[267]

The JMC participated in relief efforts, which given the geopious sentiment around the occupation of Palestine by Allenby and all that that might herald for Jews, seemed to raise substantial sums: Livingstone cites £25,600 being raised in the 'War Fund'.[268] Such activity was also supported on an ecumenical level, including the Syria and Palestine Relief Fund. Many of the pre-war staff returned to their posts after the war, or moved on to other organisations in the Levant;[269] Torrance succeeded in getting to Tiberias in 1919. He was then able to rebuild much of the work before he died in 1923, partly with his son Herbert who had joined him in 1921. Although he witnessed the beginnings of serious conflict between Palestinian Arabs and Jews, it was Herbert who became more deeply involved in attempts at reconciliation and advice to the Mandate government.[270]

Hebron

The Mildmay Mission in Hebron

Until 1900 the United Free Church had only one mission station in Palestine: at the Sea of Galilee. One of the other 'many small, independent missions'[271] in the region was the Mildmay Mission, which operated a hospital under Alexander Paterson in Hebron. Paterson was born in 1863 in India to a Scottish missionary doctor who later worked for the EMMS in Edinburgh before dying in 1871 aged 38. A Free Kirk member (and later ordained elder[272]), Paterson started his overseas career working in Aden (1888-1891)[273] three years after qualifying as a doctor. He had expressed a desire to work in Africa with Robert Laws, but this came to nothing: for various reasons he was unable to leave his post in London at that time. En route to Aden, he began to learn Arabic in Cairo, before taking over the development of the Aden mission after Ion Keith-Falconer's death. A trip to South Africa accompanying rescued slave children to Lovedale, a Scottish mission station, resulted in Paterson meeting his future wife who worked there, a Miss Muirhead, before moving to Cairo to start in private practice. He worked at various times for the Church Missionary Society (CMS) in Cairo, and received other offers of work, including one from the Church of Scotland, to work in Smyrna for the JMC. This came to nothing; theological musings in his diary revealed that the Disruption still played a role for him: 'Can I as a disestablisher accept service from them with a good conscience & if so will my freedom on this question be hampered?'[274] In April 1893 he was offered the post of medical missionary in Hebron by the Mildmay Mission, who had initiated work there six months earlier.

He travelled to Hebron via Constantinople in order to acquire Ottoman recognition of his medical qualifications, arriving in Hebron on 19.7.1893. Ewing's biography[275] describes the 'fanaticism' of Hebron in some detail,[276] though Paterson's colleagues, 'ladies by nature and breeding', were ideal for the town, in his words: 'Especially among eastern peoples, ... a gracious bearing and manner meeting their own oriental courtesies half way ... [is like] an open sesame. This is incomparably true with a wild and fanatical people like that of Hebron'.[277] Paterson proceeded to offer medical services in the largely Muslim town (for the mid-1880s Schmelz records 100 Christians and 600 Jews in the *kaza* of Hebron, compared to 40,800 Muslims[278]). He developed the clinic's services and established, according to Ewing's account, a reputation for his practice in much of the surrounding area. Conversions are not recorded, and indeed, records of explicit missionary activity (how, in what context, using what resources) are scarce, beyond mention of the work of the 'Mildmay ladies'.

Towards the end of the 19th century, the Mildmay Mission was seeking to dispose of the Hebron mission. Paterson had already taken up contact with the Free Kirk over the possibility of their involvement, though others were interested in acquiring his services: the LJS would have taken him for work in Jerusalem, but stipulated 'confirmation' (probably meaning confirmation into the Anglican Church, which Paterson was unwilling to consider); Bishop George Blyth had no such qualms, offering him work in Haifa and later Jerusalem.[279] However, Paterson appears to have preferred waiting for the Free Kirk response.

Paterson, through Anglican friends in Jerusalem, had met a Mr Martineau in the course of visits to friends in England, and Martineau had expressed a desire to 'spend part of his wealth on some worthy institution in Palestine'[280] – their mutual friends had recommended Paterson to him, and he offered £3,000 to help him build a hospital, the donation to be tied to Paterson, almost regardless of which institution took on the mission. It is not entirely clear at which point Paterson heard about this, but in October 1900 he and his wife were recalled to Britain to confer with the Mildmay Mission on the future of the mission, bearing in mind Martineau's gift. Paterson visited Martineau, who increased his offer to £5,300 and was happy to go with the United Free Church,[281] when the Mildmay Mission made it clear they did not wish to pursue the work.[282] Paterson took the offer to his church, hoping they would take it on.

The United Free Church takes over

The November meeting of the United Free Church JMC discussed the proposal, noting the £5,000 offer – Martineau intended the extra £300 to be '"at the special disposal of Dr. Paterson personally," to supply wants or defects which he judged to be essential or desirable'.[283] A sub-committee was asked to examine the issue, recommending on 18.12.1900 that the offer be accepted, eventually agreed to by the JMC on 26.3.1901, which noted that two more supporters were offering a total of £470 a year for several years.[284] As specified by the terms of Martineau's donation, Paterson was appointed to direct the work.

Details over residency for the last of the 'Mildmay ladies' and an annual budget – Paterson estimated an annual cost of £870 – were approved and it was also agreed that there should for the moment be no schools established in Hebron.[285] Martineau's donation was received, along with the extra £300 for Paterson; the joint conveners wrote to thank him. Martineau was never named in the Committee minutes, with communications generally going through Paterson, giving him a certain measure of influence. Paterson spoke at the General Assembly, his first address there, and crucial in encouraging support for the new United Free Church project. He stated that the mission

> had been carried on as a mixed mission, for Mohammedans as well as for Jews. When it was remembered how hard a soil each of these religions supplied, and that they lived in one of the most fanatical cities in the world, both as regarded Islam and Judaism, they would understand why he came to them with empty hands.[286]

This attempt at lowering expectations of success was based on his work there for the last few years, but he wisely noted future possibilities of success by setting the geopious and religious context, before outlining factors that should encourage faith in the project:

> Hebron was not only a city of great antiquity, but was regarded both by Jews and Moslems as a sacred city. Moslems ranked it with Mecca, Medina and Jerusalem; while Jews remembered it as one of the Cities of Refuge. Both claimed descent from the Patriarch Abraham – Israel through Isaac, Islam through Ishmael – and both revered his tomb ... [As known] the return of the Jew to Palestine was a historical fact; and if the immigration into Hebron had not gone on *pari passu* with ... [other areas], that was due to repressive legislation, and the terrorism exercised by the fanatical Moslem population. Yet even there the Jew was beginning to feel his way.[287]

This change was something that had been witnessed and was ongoing, meaning that the work should be supported for its potential:

> The Gospel was proclaimed in the dispensary, the Bible was read and explained ... it was wonderful to see how an entrance could be found into the heart of even a Mohammedan or a fanatical Jew, if only he were approached with a measure of tact and kindliness.[288]

He closed with a plea for support, and set sail for Palestine in June, arriving on 22.7.1901. He immediately set about expanding the work: initiating a house purchase, taking on staff, developing relations with the LJS in Hebron, and employing the 'native teacher' of the Berlin Lutheran Society. All was approved by the JMC, as was a payment to the Mildmay Mission for the mission property (nearly £300). Medicine purchases were also approved, enabling Paterson to continue the clinic. Shortly thereafter, Paterson employed the daughter of Kaloost Vartan, the founder of the EMMS hospital in Nazareth, as a nurse. He was also put in touch with the Constantinople missionaries, 'with the view of his obtaining a Jewish Evangelist, able to use Judæo-German and Judæo-Spanish';[289] it is not clear what became of this.

This points to an interesting issue about the motivation behind taking on the mission. Hebron was widely seen as one of the four holy cities of Judaism in Palestine,[290] but as Schmelz has shown, there were very few Jews living there. Figures for the mid-1880s are given above; his assessment of 1905 shows less than 100 Christians, 800 Jews, and 56,600 Muslims in the *kaza* of Hebron; whilst most of the Jews can be expected to have lived in the city itself, it still points to only a very small number. Ewing cites at most 2,000 Jews, 'a handful of Christians' and 20,000 Muslims in Hebron itself at the turn of the century.[291] Paterson had stated at the General Assembly that the mission was to both Muslims and Jews. And yet it was taken on by the *Jewish* Mission Committee – why? There are three main factors that can be readily identified: firstly, the proposal came to one of the first JMC meetings after the United Presbyterian/Free Church union in 1900, and the United Presbyterian members, having had no Jewish missions at the time of the union (these had been given up some time earlier) were here given the possibility of becoming involved in a new mission rather than just continuing the Free Church missions:[292] this would have given them greater opportunities for influence and responsibility than they might otherwise have had. Secondly, the geopious associations of the Abrahamic legacy were readily incorporated into the United Free Church's self-identity, as the 1901 General Assembly record shows: 'Hebron is a place dear to all Christians, not only ... [as] the oldest city in the world, but as containing within it the dust of the Patriarchs, whose names will be loved as long as God's Word is precious to the children of men'.[293] Thirdly, of course, the substantial donation by Martineau would have greatly eased financial worries that taking on such a responsibility entailed. Under these circumstances, if Muslims were converted as well as Jews, that would be all to the good.

The development of the mission and its hospital

Paterson succumbed to typhoid within a year of returning home to Hebron, but aided by Dr Wheeler, an Anglican medical friend in Jerusalem, he recovered, though later in the year, he returned to Britain for an operation – it is unclear what this was for.[294] Six months spent in Britain were used in convalescence, but he also attended meetings of the JMC, as did most of the missionaries if they were in Scotland at the time of meetings. Of particular significance is the agreement with the German mission, the Jerusalem Union, in Hebron, which Paterson was able to play a direct part in through his participation in meetings.[295] This agreement, approved by the JMC in October 1902 for five years in the first instance,[296] recorded that the JMC 'reserves to itself the Medical Mission work; while the Jerusalem Union undertakes the Clerical work'. The latter were to be responsible for the 'the forming and building up of an Arabic-speaking Congregation', whilst evangelisation would be carried out by both missions. Jewish converts would be free to join the Arabic congregation, and if they could not follow the Arabic, the United Free Church would provide alternative worship opportunities 'until such time as they are able to profit by the general service of the Church'. The Germans would be responsible for pastoral care, whilst both could operate schools, English and German being taught respectively.[297]

Figure 3-7 Paterson's original hospital[298]

Whilst education remained an option, this arrangement clearly relieved the Scots of anything more than medical work. Evangelisation in the course of such work was to be encouraged, of course, but the onus for creating and sustaining a local church had been passed on to another body. This focus on medical work became more important as the LJS, on hearing of the United Free Church's involvement, had withdrawn all its medical staff from Hebron: 'They heartily ... [wished] the prosperity of our work'.[299] By this time Paterson and his wife were back in Hebron, soon seeking a second nurse to help with the work, partly to replace the last of the Mildmay staff who had left, and partly perhaps, in anticipation of additional work with the departure of the LJS; a Mary Jane Bell was appointed.[300] Vartan had meanwhile been promoted from nurse to matron.[301] The Mission House was divided to form a male and a female ward, allowing the receipt of in-patients and full surgical work.[302] Only six beds were available, in contrast to what Paterson saw on a tour that included the EMMS hospitals in Nazareth and Damascus and the hospital in Tiberias.[303] Paterson continually sought to expand the work of the mission, wanting to employ a local evangelist at £40-£50 a year (request denied), another – a European – almost two years later at £200 (again denied),[304] start a girls' school (sent by the WJMA to the JMC 'for advice' and never appearing again in the minutes)[305] – as well as securing property and continuing his normal medical work.

The first dispute over Martineau's money came when Paterson initiated plans for a hospital. He appears to have assumed that the £1,100 he thought necessary would be available from general funds, leaving the £5,000 for the development of the work. The JMC made it clear that they saw the £5,000 as providing for the entire cost of the hospital including site procurement and development, a point that Paterson later acquiesced in.[306] He then requested that the JMC send £500 to a local bank so that he would have funds available if a suitable property became available; the JMC refused, arguing they could send the money by telegraph on receipt of a request.[307] If Paterson had assumed he would be relatively free to use Martineau's gift as he saw fit, the JMC were determined to ensure ultimate control remained with them as much as possible.

In 1906, Paterson's wife was unwell, with medical certification that she should spend time in Britain, and he applied for furlough leave a year early; it was granted him on condition that his next leave would be a year later.[308] This enabled Paterson to attend JMC meetings at a decisive time in the JMC's relations to Martineau. Pressure to act on the hospital plans grew, since Martineau wrote to the JMC asking for an explanation for the delay in the use of his donation; the Vice-Convener, Paterson and Torrance (also in Scotland at that time) were delegated to address this with him, but on account of his ill health he asked for views to be communicated only through Paterson, further strengthening the personal bond between them. The JMC agreed with the donor that 'if the first step of purchasing a site is not completed' by 31.12.1907, 'the building of the Hospital should be admitted to be impracticable, and should be abandoned'; he would then gift only a portion of the original sum in order to sustain for some years the existing work in Hebron.[309] On 22.10.1907, the JMC called on Torrance and Paterson – now back in Palestine – 'to use all diligence in quest of a site': Paterson replied on 21.11.1907 that he hoped to have secured a site by the end of the year.[310] The 28.1.1908 meeting heard that he had bought two lots for £320 and £240, given the urgency, money was sent immediately. Legal problems ensued, but Paterson succeeded in securing the site.[311]

Eighteen months later, Paterson described the development of the site, but required approval from the JMC for work to be done and was therefore asked for a detailed budget. A further illness on the part of Paterson, due to 'overwork and worry',[312] hindered the process, but it was agreed to proceed with some essential work without a budget.[313] Paterson then requested £100 to pay an instalment to his architect, which was refused – this was the first the JMC had heard of an architect being employed.[314] This individual was Archibald Dickie, someone who had spent some time in Palestine with the Palestine Exploration Fund[315] – perhaps Paterson had first met him in this context. The subsequent meeting examined Dickie's plans, who assured the JMC that £5,000 would cover the cost. The plans were circulated to various members of the Committee and others for comment.[316] It was decided to (re-)appoint Dickie as architect, specifying requirements and needs, and reducing costs to £4,000 (presumably to allow for furnishing the property), all plans to be approved by the JMC.[317] Ewing was full of praise for the design: 'racy of the soil, and apt to the canons and material resources of local building'[318] Dickie was eventually paid his £100 initial bill.[319]

Aside from the hospital building, one of the most significant appointments Paterson was able to make occurred as he and his wife were travelling through Switzerland on furlough in 1910. Visiting a Scottish minister and his family, Paterson entered into conversation with the daughter, Marian Wilson, 'a lady doctor, long approved of in theory but now first seen in the flesh', as Paterson put it. She readily agreed to work with Paterson, and did so as his Assistant until the war, relieving him of half his medical cases, particularly important with his oversight of the building works. Wilson was probably the most highly qualified female appointee in Scottish missions in Palestine, though her salary, cobbled together from various sources, did not match that of her male colleagues. Although Ewing reported 'prejudice' from the local population because of her gender, this 'was conquered by her skill'.[320]

Figure 3-8 Archibald Dickie's design for the Hebron hospital [321]

Much of Paterson's communication in the years preceding the war centred on the building process and continual requests for further funds to be sent, which, in the pattern set above, was done only when necessary. An attempt, initiated by Martineau and intimated by Mrs Paterson, to name the incomplete hospital the 'Queen Victoria Hospital' – according it the ultimate imperial descriptor – was unsuccessful: the Secretary of State for Scotland noted that 'it was not ... usual ... to associate the name of the Sovereign or his predecessors with an incomplete scheme', suggesting the matter be reconsidered once the hospital was open.[322] Martineau died on 10.12.1910, not living to see the hospital completed.[323]

In 1911 the Committee sent a deputation to visit its mission stations and report on the work being carried out.[324] The Convener, William Ewing, and Vice-Convener, W S Matheson, made the trip: Ewing's biography of Paterson records this as a positive event, the two being impressed with what the mission was achieving in the town, especially compared to 'Hebron in the dark old days when ... the Hospital was not'.[325] Several recommendations were forthcoming: (a) that the building of the hospital should be progressed as soon as possible, (b) that once the hospital was complete, educational facilities should be offered, (c) that a clerical missionary, perhaps a probationer, should be appointed who would ideally have teaching skills and be able to help with the schools plan.[326] These measures (and the financial implications for this and other mission stations) were agreed on 14.11.1911. Staffing and building requests continued much as before, and no noticeable change in pace of work or priorities is apparent from this time on. In any case, building work was dependent on a *firman* from the Sublime Porte, which was not immediately forthcoming. Sustained pressure from Paterson on the British Embassy in Constantinople and via the JMC on the Foreign Office (communications continued through into 1913) eventually produced his desired result and thanks were expressed directly to the late British Consul in Jerusalem for his help in the matter (witness here again the direct link between the imperial and religious authorities, the latter relying on the unequal power relationships created by the former in order to achieve its goals).[327]

Medical work continued and evangelisation efforts were sustained in the midst of the building and legal conflicts. Paterson requested 'Christian literature in Arabic' for use in the mission,[328] and staffing issues made for regular changes: most of the nurses appear to have moved on after a few years service. No mention is made again of the link to the German mission, the second five year term having been due to end in 1912. Whether this co-operation disintegrated prior to its formal end is not clear; perhaps that is the reason for the 1911 deputation recommending a clerical missionary, though it was not acted upon at the time; it has already been noted that the Jerusalem Union's work in Hebron was not regarded as a success.

World War I and its aftermath

The 1914-1918 war brought all work to a halt. The meeting on 15.9.1914 noted that all staff, including Paterson, had been instructed to leave, bringing all British staff back to Britain. Paterson did not do this, though he did not force his staff or his family to stay. The JMC proceeded to 'record their appreciation' of Paterson's remaining in post 'to care for the Christians in the place and to look after the property'.[329] This was not sustainable: the American consul who was trying to help British subjects leave did not know the whereabouts of Paterson, and it soon became apparent that the mission had ceased to function: the old and new hospitals had been officially sealed, as had eventually Paterson's house (after he had secured documents with the American Consul in Jerusalem[330]), and the last his wife had heard at the time of the December meeting, he was in Jerusalem.[331] Pressure through various channels (religious and political) was suggested a month later, to ensure that British missionaries could leave, and that local Christians would not be persecuted.[332] By the next meeting, 16.2.1915, Paterson was present, and whilst he spoke of the mission property (only two camels, used for building work, had been taken when he left), he does not appear to mention his own brief internment: this is only noted in a concise entry in his diary.[333] The JMC continued to pay salaries to its staff until such time as they were in other employment: Paterson was soon appointed a Lieutenant in the Royal Army Medical Corps and served in various localities in Britain before being sent to Egypt, and then on to Hebron, as Principal Medical Officer under the Occupied Enemy Territory Administration, but connected to the Syria and Palestine Relief Fund, an ecumenical church agency set up towards the beginning of the war.[334]

With the close of the war, Paterson continued in post in Hebron, though his last years working for the United Free Church were marked by dispute and discord, resulting in the mission being handed over shortly after the war to the CMS at great financial loss, with the hospital not yet complete, but functioning, and Paterson eventually leaving. Ewing, Paterson's friend and biographer, painted a picture of a hasty and ignorant group of investigators determined to close the mission down, come what may.[335]

Figure 3-9 The Hebron hospital after WWI, as handed over to the CMS [336]

Despite the bitterness of his last years working for his church, Paterson appears to have felt that his work in Hebron was a worth-while enterprise. A certain disregard for rules (exemplified by his consistent attempts to spend monies and bypass his Committee) combined with creativity, enthusiasm and energy (shown in his constant attempts to develop the work of the mission whilst himself doing several jobs at once: evangelist, medic, buildings and construction manager) make for a character perhaps best suited for a solitary mission – one might wonder how these characteristics would have served him in the wider context of the Sea of Galilee mission, for example, where the senior missionaries were more dependent on each other's decision-making occurring within the structures of the Mission Council. His apparent lack of concern at the failure to generate conversions from Judaism or Islam points to his greater interest in providing a social service which on the side offered the opportunity to evangelise, and he perhaps saw his medical services as less of a tool of conversion or means of access than was the case in Tiberias. In addition to this, he was quite adamant that although run by a Jewish mission committee, he was serving (and hoping to convert) Jews and Muslims, as he stated in his first General Assembly speech. Unfortunately, few records of his personal views on such topics are extant: Ewing's biography does not delve into such matters.

Figure 3-10 St. Luke's, Hebron – the hospital in the 1950s[337]

What has not been mentioned in any detail in this section is Paterson's attitude to the Mandate and to Zionism. Proctor covers this to some extent, noting that Paterson's views diverge from those of his fellow Scottish missionaries in his assessment of the political situation, but does not outline why this might be the case.[338] Most of the missionaries were happy with British rule, but Paterson criticised British officials 'for attempting "to foist their incongruous and incompatible nostrums as a panacea" on people whose "temperament and traditions" they did not understand'.[339] He felt the British clearly favoured the Zionists, 'ignoring peaceful appeals by the Arabs, and using excessive force against them'.[340] However, he also played a practical role in mediating between rulers and subjects in Hebron, for which he was praised by the British; Herbert Torrance and others did likewise, not necessarily an easy role in terms of their relations with the increasingly divided population groupings.[341]

One might look to the background of the missions in Palestine for an explanation of Paterson's different reaction to all the other Scottish missionaries to what was happening: all the Palestine missionaries *except* Paterson were appointed into their post by the JMC (including Jaffa, which was more or less reconstituted after the war). Paterson, in contrast, did not join the JMC with the express intention of seeking primarily the conversion of Jews in Hebron, rather, the JMC provided him with a suitable vehicle to further his own ambition of creating a medical service in Hebron where he already lived and worked – can a measure of self-aggrandisement perhaps be identified here? – and with the backing of a wealthy sponsor who attached his donation to the individual rather than the institution, he had, or thought he had, a certain measure of freedom to act as he chose. The German Lutherans having responsibility for non-medical parts of the work perhaps distanced him further from a more pro-Jewish standpoint; in any case, the clear connection to Jews does not seem to have been quite so strong for Paterson, who was more concerned at offering a service to those who most requested it (witness, for example, his request for Arabic language literature – in contrast to the Sea of Galilee mission, there is no record of Paterson seeking Hebrew literature). This more detached attitude to Jews in general, and their conversion in particular, perhaps goes some way to explaining his later concerns about Zionism, British bias, and its effects on the Arab population.

Jaffa

The Tabeetha school in Jaffa came into the hands of the institutional churches without their planning it, as a result of a bequest by the founder, Jane Walker-Arnott; it is doubtful whether the churches would have wanted to have much to do with it had they been given more of a choice. Here, the school's history until Walker-Arnott's death will be examined, followed by the churches' response to her bequest.

The Tabeetha School during Walker-Arnott's lifetime

Jane Walker-Arnott,[342] born near Kinross in 1834, first lived in Jaffa from 1858-1860, working for a CMS couple. With the 1860 war she was forced to move to Cairo, returning in 1863, by invitation of German friends who had initiated a small hospital in Jaffa, to found a school.[343] Starting with 14 pupils in rented accommodation on 16.3.1863 (moving to purpose-built accommodation on 1.11.1875[344]), and barely herself able to communicate adequately in Arabic, the numbers had risen to 50 by the summer, Christians, Jews and Muslims, though the numbers on the roll varied considerably over the years. She developed a 'Home School' where girls lived with her. The funding for the school came mostly from private subscriptions, and included prominent people such as Thomas Cook (who included her school on the itinerary for his tour groups, thereby no doubt increasing her support base), but also many ordinary people that Walker-Arnott recruited as supporters during visits to Britain, where she built a following as one of the 'ladies of culture' that ran similar private enterprises in various locales, with even a measure of direct congregational support, although no formal institutional connection existed.[345] By 1882 a small hospital had been founded in Jaffa, associated with the school, with staff funded by the Mildmay Mission. The schools taught in Arabic with some English for older girls, the emphasis being on 'domestic training to prepare the girls to make 'good' marriages and on encouraging the more capable girls to train as teachers in their turn',[346] beyond this, of course, the purpose was 'first and foremost, to teach the scholars to read the Bible, and to show them the love and grace of God in Jesus Christ our Lord';[347] after 1891 all the suitable girls were 'bound by contract to teach for a certain time in return for the education they had received'.[348] In the 1890s, an Industrial Mission was started in connection with the school, focusing on lace work, which was sold in Britain and America; by 1909, 500 people were working on this project.[349] At the turn of the century, the school's work was described in the following terms by two former pupils, Miriam Wahhab and Leah Wassermann:

... there were only three classes in which pupils remained for three years. The youngest pupil was six and the oldest eighteen. English, Arabic, Mathematics and Geography were taught as well as Religious Knowledge. In the afternoons ... the pupils did hand work and embroidery. Twice a week each class participated in musical drill and singing. On Friday evenings the pupils practised hymns for the Sunday service. On Saturdays many ... painted. Twice a week they were taken for a long walk – their only form of outdoor exercise. On special occasions they were allowed to play games. Normally they had to prepare their lessons or knit their stockings so there was not much time to play. Attendance at morning and evening prayers was compulsory ... Jews and Moslems attended as well as Christians.[350]

Christmas and Walker-Arnott's birthday on 1. June were celebrated, the former with games and singing, the latter by an excursion and picnic to Sarona, now a part of Tel Aviv serving as the headquarters of the Israeli army, then the location, amongst other things, of a German mission school.[351]

Towards the end of Walker-Arnott's life, the school's roll decreased, and Wahhab's impression of the school as a whole was of a 'somewhat sombre institution'.[352] Walker-Arnott died on 21.5.1911, her funeral bringing an estimated 3,000 Muslims, Jews and Christians together.

Walker-Arnott's gift and the churches' response

The Auld Kirk, as opposed to the Free Kirk, had no Palestine missions, although it operated Jewish mission stations in Beirut and Alexandria, as well as in other locales in Central Europe and the eastern Mediterranean. However, it was her own church, the Auld Kirk, that Walker-Arnott desired should operate her school (incorporating the school itself, two 'outside day-schools in the town and the Industrial Department ... with the lace workers'[353]), as noted in a letter later reproduced in the Church of Scotland General Assembly Report: she requested the Home Committee, which oversaw the work from Scotland and raised funds, to continue the work, and if they felt they could not, to offer it in turn to the Auld Kirk, the United Free Kirk, and the CMS (who already had a mission in Jaffa and would therefore 'perhaps have no difficulty in carrying on the work'[354]). The Home Committee sought Church of Scotland assistance in a lengthy letter within ten weeks of Walker-Arnott's death, although provisional arrangements to continue the work were made: since the school had no financial difficulties, it could continue for some time whilst the Church decided on its course of action.

The Auld Kirk, though keen,[355] in considering the financial implications, could not decide on the matter, and instead opted to bring the matter to the General Assembly and publish an article about the offer in the Church magazine, *Life and Work* (LW).[356] This article, under the sub-title 'In the Footsteps of Dorcas', a clear allusion to the New Testament origin of the name 'Tabeetha', included an obituary and a lengthy explanation of the position: the Home Committee had offered the school to the JMC, which noted the attendance of Jewish girls, the value of the property, and the funds and investments that supported it (the Industrial Mission was not to be passed on). The offer was welcomed for four reasons: (a) *'The Tabeetha Mission ... is in the Holy Land.* – It gathers round it a multitude of sacred associations, and appeals to a very natural and widespread sentiment', (b) the large numbers of Jews in the area and the numbers that pass through Jaffa made it 'difficult to find a better centre for Jewish work', (c) since the mission is already well-established, rivalry would not be a factor, and (d) *'The Mission is looked upon with favour by the whole community.* – ... [enjoying] a prestige which is entirely favourable to successful work'.[357] The appeal to geopious sentiment, the opportunities afforded by the numbers of Jews in the area and the perceived positive sentiments towards the mission, uncomplicated by rival western missions, made for a 'great opportunity'.[358] However, an estimated £500 to £600 would be needed annually to sustain the work, even if many of the present supporters continued their donations, and neither the JMC nor the WAJM felt able to take this on. Unwilling to dismiss the offer that 'to them [had] the appearance of a sacred trust', the matter was passed, in sentimental and geopious terms, to the General Assembly:

> Surely a mission in the Holy Land, offered to the Church in such touching circumstances, to benefit and bless the kinsmen of our Lord according to the flesh in "those holy fields" associated with Himself and the first days of His Church, will carry with it an irresistible appeal.[359]

If the Assembly could be persuaded to take on the Jaffa mission through its JMC, additional financial demands would be given increased legitimacy; existing supporters were requested to indicate their willingness to provide ongoing support, which, in the course of only ten days before the Assembly, sufficient numbers did: the JMC felt the promises of £120 a year for five years were worth building on.[360]

Prior to the Assembly, the JMC had intimated to the Home Committee its desire to seek to operate the Jaffa mission together with the United Free Kirk's JMC, a proposal 'entirely consistent with the views' of the Home Committee, which had United Free Kirk as well as Auld Kirk members,[361] resulting in a broad Assembly resolution that allowed the JMC to proceed as it saw fit:

> recognising the value of the Mission, and its special advantages as a sphere of operation among the Jews of Palestine, authorise the Jewish Committee to endeavour to obtain funds ... apart from the ordinary funds of the Committee.
> [The Assembly] ... further empower the Committee, if they see fit ... to consider favourably any proposal to conduct the Mission conjointly with the Jewish Mission Committee of the United Free Church.[362]

Any proposals were to be authorised at the next Assembly; the article noted that similar steps had been taken by the United Free Kirk Committee; meanwhile the Home Committee maintained the work.

During the negotiations, financial support grew, with the Auld Kirk side recording 'about £250' by November 1912,[363] and £530 by the same time the following year, realising the budgeted £200 a year to fund the mission for five years a few months later.[364] However, the process of reaching agreement was arduous, despite a firm proposal for sharing all responsibilities equally through a joint committee being drawn up at a meeting of the two churches' representatives on 27.2.1913,[365] primarily because the United Free Kirk was concerned at the financial implications of taking on the work. However, negotiations were resumed later in 1913.[366]

LW reports describe the gradual process of negotiation and fundraising, with a report of a meeting of Auld Kirk and United Free Kirk JMC representatives with the Home Committee receiving prominence. William Ewing, at this time United Free Kirk JMC convener, presided over the committee that was initiated to prosecute the negotiations and work. The only mention of the actual work in Jaffa is made indirectly by referring to the new edition of a 'little pamphlet describing the Mission'.[367]

The United Free Church JMC, on 17.3.1914, finally agreed to recommend proceeding with the joint operation to its General Assembly, appointing its representatives to the Joint Committee on 19.5. However, it was only with the outbreak of war that information from Tabeetha became more generally available to the membership of the two churches. An article describing the new administrative arrangements (consisting of a committee of 20, half to come from each church, with three from each church to be trustees of the property and funds, chaired by the convener of the Auld Kirk JMC Tabeetha sub-committee) also mentions for the first time Walker-Arnott's successor, Madeline G Stevens, appointed by the Home Committee soon after the founder's death, who had 'the advantage of close friendship with Miss Grierson' of the school.[368] However, 'the latest phase of events in the near East' – Britain had entered the war on 4.8.1914, the Ottoman Empire on 29.10.1914 when it bombed Russian ports in the Black Sea – were, in striking understatement, 'most unfavourable to the conduct of Mission work': the 'abrogation of capitulations, involving the loss of consular protection' made the missionaries' position 'intolerable and insecure', and some had already left. Although not explained further, the 'conditions of life at Jaffa ... are very serious'.[369]

So serious, indeed, that when 'it became inevitable that German influence would involve Turkey in the war' all the staff left (mid-September) and Church of Scotland members were told in March 1915 that 'the work has been entirely suspended', 'no communication is available with Jaffa', the mission buildings had been left in charge of 'trusted servants', and the American Consul in Jaffa was attending to the mission's interests', though at the time the status of the premises and staff was not known[370] – witness here the converging of religious interests with political and imperial interests in the comments about the Capitulations and the links to the American political establishment.

Therefore, although negotiations had been successfully concluded, and the Home Committee had handed over responsibility to the joint committee of the two churches, they were unable to take over the reopening of the school session in October. However, a plea for ongoing financial support was made (since no demand on the ordinary funds was to be allowed for the first five years of the churches' involvement, such support was very necessary), noting that 'exceptional' costs would be likely once the school reopened, which, the committee hoped, would be as soon as possible to allow 'the work ... [to] take its place in furtherance of the Kingdom of Christ in that land, which will ever be distinctively known as the Holy Land'.[371] The plea for financial aid recurs in a later article in LW, which closes noting the geopious context of the Tabeetha mission: 'Jaffa is the "Joppa" of ... Acts, where St. Peter raised to life the saintly woman from which this Mission takes its name, and where he was living when summoned to Caesarea by ... Cornelius'[372] – it can be safely assumed that this sentence, which appears without further contextual explanation at the end of the article explaining the present administrative arrangements, was intended to elicit generous donations.

Jaffa was bombed in November 1917 after the British occupied it, causing severe damage to the school's roof; internal furnishings had already suffered greatly. However, the buildings were used as headquarters by the British navy, before Stevens returned in June 1918, reopening the schools in October 1919.[373]

It can be seen that the church membership, unless supporting the mission during Walker-Arnott's lifetime, learnt virtually nothing about the ongoing work at Jaffa, almost all public information being directed to a description of the negotiating process; it was also not discussed at JMC meetings. By the time negotiations concluded, the war prevented any work from continuing, and so it was to be seven years from Walker-Arnott's death before church participation in the work had any meaningful effect. That the school was able to continue for three years (until the war) under direction of the Home Committee and its new head is perhaps a mark of the stability and strength of the institution on an organisational level.

Conclusion

The development of these three missions provides an interesting continuum from the missions in Chapter 2. Starting there with the primacy of direct proclamation of the gospel (termed 'confrontation' in Chapter 5), Tiberias and Hebron from the beginning sought to use medicine as a tool to access those Palestinians who might convert to Protestantism, whilst Jaffa used education in this way. 'Straightforward' confrontation was clearly seen as not being enough, since few converts were won. This change in methods is examined more fully in Chapter 5, but here it can already be noted that this represents not just a change in method, but a change in purpose to the mission, even if this was not explicitly recognised by the protagonists.

There are general features to these missions that are of particular note. In relation to Zionism and British governance, the Sea of Galilee missionaries' and Paterson's attitudes have already been addressed (p95 and p108 respectively), and more general attitudes will be examined below (p138), but it is also of interest to look at the role of geopiety. All three missions resorted to geopious sentiment in their fundraising and general propagation within their constituency in Scotland, but with Jaffa, it seems particularly pronounced.

Jaffa (Joppa) is not mentioned in the Old Testament or the gospels, unlike Hebron or the Sea of Galilee. A likely reason for the increased emphasis lies with the missions the Church of Scotland did *not* operate: although the JMC ran missions in Beirut and Alexandria, it controlled none in Palestine, which made it more attractive:

> The Committee anticipate much pleasure in conducting "the Tabeetha Mission" in conjunction with ... the United Free Church ... and feel gratified that it has been found possible to have a joint sphere of action in commending the Gospel ... to Jews in the Holy Land. Such united work they believe will react in benefit to the Churches themselves, and in stimulus to the whole work of Jewish Missions.[374]

That the Churches should 'benefit' from conducting a mission in a particular geographic space points to the significance of that space for the self-defined narrative of the Church. The United Free Church was markedly more reserved, in part, perhaps, because of doubts about its ability to sustain the work financially, but also, almost certainly, because it already had two missions in centres of great geopious significance: Hebron with its Abrahamic link that forms the original foundational myth of Judaism, Christianity and Islam, and the Sea of Galilee with its connection to Jesus, representative of the foundational myth of God's renewed involvement in human affairs. Compared to these, a connection with a miraculous act of an apostle after Jesus' resurrection might seem somewhat lame.

Of interest is also the almost complete absence of the local population in the missionary accounts. Only if employed by the mission is there a remote possibility of mention in the official records, and even then names are often omitted. During the negotiations for the Hebron and Jaffa missions, locals were neither consulted nor considered, and hardly mentioned – mission is something that is done *to* them, rather than something in which they might *participate*, and so the decisions about *how* it might be done are not theirs to influence or formulate (they were also excluded from the Mission Council). Local agency in reaction to the missionaries' intrusion is ignored or not understood, turning Palestinians in the Scottish accounts into invisible recipients of missionary munificence. This attitude to the local population also points to the Scots' lack of awareness of any influence on themselves through their encounters. These themes will be returned to in Chapters 5 and 6.

The frequent resort to colonial power structures invites comment. Making use of the powers offered by the Capitulatory agreements (and in the case of Jaffa, bemoaning when these no longer function) and turning to political authority whenever it was deemed appropriate or necessary marks out this later involvement of the churches. Less use was made of the political powers in the early missions, but as the idea of empire developed and grew in the second half of the 19th century, so the resort to such power as there was increased. Representatives of the colonial powers may or may not have had an interest in the success or failure of the missions in terms of converts, but any perceived opportunity to further influence and control segments of the political and economic sphere within the Ottoman realms was taken. Fear of deepening involvement by Russia and other western powers meant that British consular officials were generally prepared to act on behalf of the churches if asked to do so. That Britain was approaching a point of crisis in its financial circumstances, only able to support its burgeoning empire through ever more acquisitions,[375] was an incentive to greater influence, and in any case, Britain was still stronger politically and militarily than the Ottoman Empire, and often able to enforce its will upon the Porte, particularly where opportunities for freer trade might appear. In that sense, the missionaries' regular appeals to their political authorities served to further the influence and power of the western states in the context of the Ottoman Empire.

In Hebron, Paterson appears to have had little active interest in converting Jews, and one might wonder in how far his few pronouncements on this topic are to some extent, at least, lip service to the JMC and its needs. Certainly, with the shifting of responsibility for schools and a congregation to the German mission, he could concentrate his energies on the hospital – which he seems to have done, constantly prodding the JMC to allow further expansion and construction, without necessarily offering much of a rationale in terms of numbers of Jewish patients. He was, of course, in an unusual position due to the connection of substantial funding to his person, rather than the mission, which enabled him to act with a measure of independence of the JMC that they did not always approve of. For a period in the early years, one can see Paterson pushing at the limits of what the JMC would allow him to do with the money from Martineau: disagreements about where building funds should come from, and the confusion over the appointment of the architect serve as two examples of this. Beyond this, the Hebron mission is also notable for its appointment of the first woman doctor to one of the Scots' Palestinian mission stations. Here, again, Paterson's slightly removed attitude to the JMC is apparent: he offered her the post and only subsequently made the necessary arrangements with his employer to bring her to Palestine.

In the Sea of Galilee mission, the creation of the Mission Council, in part as a way of dealing with the personalities involved and in part a way of devolving certain areas of responsibility, meant that the entire structure was more formalised than in Hebron. Administrative negotiations over endless matters large and small, pressing and long-term, between the missionaries and the Mission Council on the one hand, and the JMC on the other, meant that reaction to events was sometimes substantially delayed, a prime example being Christie's leaking house. The extensive operation involving numerous staff in both towns meant that the ultimate purpose of the mission – Jewish conversion – could be pursued more actively than Paterson did in Hebron. However, few successes are reported, blamed by the missionaries in part on the failure to create the Industrial Mission. Given that this did not happen, the JMC's lack of provision for (potential) converts to leave the Galilee, perhaps going to another mission or to Scotland, was seen by the missionaries as yet another hurdle preventing conversion. At no point is there a reflection on the purpose of the mission and its effectiveness (not even when marking anniversaries such as Torrance's 25 years in Tiberias), with the missionaries, and to a lesser extent the JMC, always seeking to ensure the right circumstances or conditions for conversion – this is one way of interpreting the Industrial Mission. That the missionaries may have been offering something the local population did not want, alongside the education and medical care that they did, does not seem to have occurred to any of them. This will be examined further in Chapters 4 and 5.

PART 2
THE MISSIONARIES

4

THE MISSIONARIES' CONTEXT
AND BACKGROUND

This chapter will examine in more detail the missionaries' context and background. Describing firstly their ecclesial and social context, their relationship to their sending committees and employers will then be addressed, concluding with an examination of the relationship the missionaries had with the wider church constituency.

A 'small minority of congregations [containing] within them minority groups' – the recruiting grounds and support basis of the missions

Andrew Porter presents a positive image of the place of missionary giving in Britain in the early 20th century, 'In 1908, Britain contributed some £2.4 million to the support of Protestant missionary work, approximately 40 per cent of the world total, and exceeded within Britain as an object of charitable donations only by education and church-building.'[1]

This perspective is reflected in varying forms in other texts, the nineteenth century often being portrayed as an era of unsurpassed missionary interest and generosity to social and religious causes.[2]

However, although this high level of financial support would seem to indicate a broad basis of support for missions, Andrew Ross argues convincingly that this is only within limited confines, at least in Scotland. He examines support for a particular Church of Scotland mission in Africa, but the patterns he describes are relevant to other fields as well as to e.g. the Free Church. Writing about the period between 1874 and 1881, he notes that:

> A warning to the general assembly [of the Church of Scotland] of the possible need to close mission stations and discharge missionaries because of a lack of financial support, when added to the desperate lengths the [Foreign Missions] committee had been driven to in order to get any staff at all for Blantyre, makes nonsense of any claim that the Church of Scotland was on fire with concern for mission to Zambesia or for anywhere else overseas.[3]

Later periods suffered from a similar dearth of financial support: Ross notes that even though donations did periodically increase, these additional donations did not keep pace with the desired rate of growth, and many wealthy congregations failed to support the work in any meaningful way.[4] Even in the run-up to the First World War, although the FMC's debt had been covered, financial givings did not keep pace with the level of activity on the ground, or the proposed level of activity, 'In the first decade of the new century, although several plans for the extension of Blantyre's work ... were sent to Edinburgh, not one ever reached ... the FMC because of the nature of the financial situation.'[5]

Staffing issues were equally problematic, with few suitable candidates making themselves available for work in Malawi. A great number of vacancies was the result, with the FMC even seeking to recruit candidates from any other presbyterian churches in the world.[6] Ross concludes his essay by arguing that the integration of the missionary work into the church structures (in contrast to many other European missionary movements, for example), may not have helped the missionary movement in Scotland since a number of congregations and presbyteries showed outright hostility to supporting missionary work. There clearly were successes, but these need to be seen in a broader context that is not necessarily a positive one:

> The period ... [1874-1914] saw brilliant work done by Church of Scotland missionaries in many countries, but it was not a period in which there was any widespread concern in the Church for the work these men and women were sent to do. A small minority of congregations contained within them minority groups who supplied the support that allowed this work to go ahead.
> ... what has been seen as a time of supreme interest in the mission of the church overseas appeared very differently to the men concerned with carrying it out. Dull indifference was the mood of Scotland in their view.[7]

Ross explains the prominence of missions in church life and in national press by way of news and social factors: in the absence of cinema, and radio and television broadcasting, missionary news provided a space in which information about the expansion of the British empire could be heard (whether one supported such expansion or not[8]), and at a time when the 'church-going middle-class Scot would seem to have favoured neither the theatre nor the pub',[9] the social function of missionary meetings should not be ignored.

Ross shows that although his focus in this article is on the Blantyre mission of the Auld Kirk, the picture he presents is not 'a peculiar one' but applies to the church as a whole.[10] Even at the time this was identified as an issue: for example, an 1882 article in the Church of Scotland LW warned 'that missions were unpopular in the sense that every congregation had people who were not only indifferent, but hostile' quite aside from an issue of patience with the apparent slow progress of missions: 'What with our steam engines, our telegraphs, and our telephones, we are so accustomed to rapidity of movement and quick results that we lose patience with every undertaking that does not move to a speedy issue'.[11] The United Free Church JMC was clearly also aware of this, as the result of an analysis based on the public accounts for 1907 – the year before Porter's figures referred to above – showed:

> it appeared (*a*) that, of the 1656 congregations in the Church, 649, or 39 per cent.
> ..., gave no collection for the Jewish Fund; and (*b*) that ... £2413, received last year
> ... [from congregations], represents about *three farthings* in every pound raised by the
> Church for all purposes, exclusive of local Building Fund, Emergency Fund, and
> Dispossessed Congregations Fund. A detailed analysis ... of the givings of all the
> Presbyteries of the Church was appended. Resolved (1) to record ... thanks ... to Mr
> Matheson [who carried out the analysis]; (2) to print 1800 copies of his review of
> the Fund for circulation among the ministers of the Church.[12]

The Committee's conclusion as a result of this analysis was that further promotional work was urgently required, particularly in those presbyteries 'that call for special effort'. The three farthings in the pound, i.e. 0.3125% of total normal church income, even if it was coming from 61% of churches, was still a pitifully small proportion of the overall resources of the Church, even in financially difficult times. Distributing these details was one immediate way of trying to encourage more generosity from congregations.

It is into this context then, of minority groups in a minority of congregations being interested in and supporting missions, that the work of the Scottish churches in the Levant must be seen, although the JMC work had a demographic, not a geographic focus.[13] It is clear that the mission stations and missionaries in Part I generally fit into the pattern Ross describes. Even in terms of the Committee structure, it is the same small select group of individuals that support the work of the missions long-term, either through involvement in the relevant committee, personal financial commitment, financial and other support from their congregation, and more often than not, all three. Some financial trends are outlined here in the Appendix, though it should be clear from Part I that finances, or rather, lack of finances, often played a prominent role in decision-making processes. Equally, there were times when it proved exceedingly difficult to recruit appropriate personnel from these minority groups within a minority of congregations. The candidates that *were* appointed therefore become all the more interesting.

Educational and social background – the missionaries as products of a 19ᵗʰ century aspiring middle-class

The educational and social background of the missionaries can be assessed on a variety of levels. Before beginning on this, however, a differentiation must be made between male and female missionaries: most of the men in the more senior positions had some kind of university background, at times to a high level, whereas most of the women did not; of course, this difference was in part simply a reflection of the social reality in Scotland at the time, but it makes assumptions on the basis of educational background more complex when gender is taken into account. In general, there is more information available about the men, not least since certain aspects of the missionary work, particularly in later years, were passed from the JMC of the churches on to the Women's Associations and fewer of these records have been preserved. Whilst this can, of course, be problematic, the male missionaries will therefore be looked at first, with comments then being made on the differences for female missionaries.

In terms of educational background, several of the male candidates for the various missions applied directly from university whilst still engaged in their studies, or shortly thereafter.[14] Indeed, it seems that they were, in part at least, actively recruited from one of the four Scottish university divinity colleges; all candidates came from or had attended one of these colleges, with the exception, of course, of medical missionaries. That they were at university points to relatively high academic achievement, and often (where noted), good schooling. In biographies of missionaries published during or shortly after their own lifetimes, this was a recurrent theme.[15] It is clear from Bonar and McCheyne's assessment of the desired abilities for missionaries to the Jews that high qualifications were required, and the JMCs generally adhered to this pattern.

It is noteworthy that with the exception of medical missionaries, for a long period all male candidates had a divinity background: it was taken for granted that only a clerical missionary would be able to carry out the work required. However, it is clear that a degree in divinity was not in and of itself sufficient for work in the Levant, aside from the need to learn local languages. Many were required to engage in further training, most noticeably at the Institutum Judaicum Delitzchianum. Teachers and medics formed the exception to this rule: suitable experience or training was deemed more appropriate, but it is noticeable, for example, that teachers were not a part of the Tiberias Mission Council, the body that dealt with the day-to-day running of the missions in Tiberias and Safad. Instead, an ordained missionary without educational qualifications directed the schools' activities and the work of the teachers. The education of ordained clergy should not be underestimated, however: Bebbington cites a rural Aberdeenshire Free Kirk minister who in a 'single and far from exceptional year' purchased 518 volumes and 12 pamphlets, reading '58 books in their entirety, with much of several others and 17 pamphlets'.[16] This was not unusual behaviour, as reading the diaries of ministers of the time indicate.[17]

The women who applied were generally already past the educational stage of their careers: when recruited for teaching positions, they tended to be teachers in Britain, though they might find themselves in the field working under the direction of men who had come from a university background with perhaps only limited experience of working in Scotland. Missionary work appealed to women for various reasons, partly because they would be allowed to work in fields that would not be open to them at home, but 'not least because there were areas of the mission field open to them alone'[18] – whilst mission women in the Levant did not necessarily perform the pioneering role that occurred in some other places,[19] there were clearly areas of work that men were less ideally suited for, medical care of women being but one example (Paterson's use of Marian Wilson is notable here, though she had, of course, not trained in Scotland). With regard to Irish women missionaries in the late 19th and early 20th centuries – though the comments are equally applicable to Scottish women – Myrtle Hill argues that

It is clear that for many young women ... a combination of religious, cultural, and educational influences, strength of personality, and lack of challenges on the home front, made missionary work an attractive option. A professional female missionary body emerged which, in the context of limited career opportunities, enabled women to support themselves and to earn respect and authority as experts in mission affairs ... [quoting Janet Lee:] 'In essence, missionary work allowed women to stay within the confines of socially sanctioned notions of femininity, yet stretch these boundaries and experience opportunities normally reserved for men.'[20]

The women who went to work in mission fields would invariably be single: marriage (in the circumstances this was usually to another member of the mission staff) was generally deemed equivalent to resignation, even if they mostly continued labouring unpaid; this was particularly so in the early years. As Macdonald points out,

it was expected that male missionaries would enjoy the companionship and support of marriage, [but] females were required to repay their expenses if they married within five years of appointment. Thus at an early stage, the principle was established that those who were to teach heathen women about the blessings and family ideals of Christianity were themselves to be single and childless.[21]

Jonathon Bonk, in his study of LMS staff, shows that the missionaries who went to China were far better educated than those who went to Africa:

This was standard mission practice for the time, since it seemed obvious that the civilized and literate citizens of the Far East required a degree of refinement and formal training exceeding that of illiterate and primitive savages. In Central China, University graduates were more the rule than the exception; and virtually all missionaries were either ordained, university graduates, or medical specialists. Most of the early missionaries to Central Africa were artisans.[22]

The Scots who went to the Levant, men and women, clearly fall into the same category as the LMS missionaries to China. Although Levantine culture and heritage, particularly that which was identifiably Muslim rather than Jewish or Eastern Christian, was denigrated and condemned, there is a general recognition that the people of the Levant were not 'illiterate and primitive savages' – this being the dominant European image of much of Africa. Although in the missionaries' eyes the level of education and culture in the east was clearly not at the same level as the Christian (Protestant) west, there was an underlying recognition that this could be changed: after all, what was proposed for eastern Christians, at least in the early years was not that the religious tradition be abandoned, but that it be reformed.[23] Abandoning it would have indicated something of the worthlessness of what was there, reforming it meant that the foundations were regarded in some way as being acceptable, though clearly something had gone awry over the years to produce a manifestation of religion that repelled the missionaries. Only once it appeared that reformation was unlikely or impossible was abandonment promulgated – this, however, more for tactical than ideological reasons.[24] This being the case, a high level of educational achievement as well as devotion and commitment was required – the ability to argue and present a case in terms that the target audience would understand, the ability to learn and use vernacular languages in spoken and written form, and the ability to deal appropriately with local political and religious authorities, even if these latter contacts, especially, were often of a controversial nature.

The educational background of the missionaries can be used partly to deduce details of the social background of the missionaries: in the absence of public funding, it would likely be people from families that could afford a quality education that would receive it (though a considerable number also worked during their studies in order to pay their way). The differences can be illustrated by comparing the backgrounds of two of the most famous Scottish missionaries who started their life's work less than a decade apart, one being David Torrance, the other being Mary Slessor, who worked in West Africa (this marks a similar parallel to Bonk's China/Africa pattern).

Torrance, born 6.11.1862, came from a medic's family: his father was a doctor in Airdrie, a Justice of the Peace and for a time a town councillor and burgh treasurer. An enthusiastic Freemason, he was also an elder in the Auld Kirk (though his wife and children went to the Free Kirk). Torrance attended 'the Academy' and when his father died, his mother moved the family to Glasgow, where Torrance, aged 16, immediately started his medical training at the university, whilst working in the public dispensary with the purpose, according to his biographer, of relieving his family of the costs of his studies.[25] Torrance received an invitation to work for the Free Kirk JMC whilst sight-seeing in New York, and in February 1884 set off on his first exploratory trip to Palestine.[26] In contrast to this relatively privileged background, Mary Slessor, born 2.12.1848, had an alcoholic father who was a shoemaker and drove the family to penury through his drinking, resulting in both mother and daughter (and possibly other members of the family) working as weavers in a factory in Dundee. Slessor was 11 at this time, and initially worked half-days with the other half-day being given over to school attendance, and then, once she worked full time, attended school at night; the father died whilst Slessor was probably still in her teens. She attended the United Presbyterian Church and Sunday School and went to Old Calabar in August 1876, aged 28, having pursued what appears to have been a relatively limited education in Edinburgh once she had applied and been accepted for overseas work in May 1875.[27]

These two examples present a situation of clear opposites: even though Slessor would not have been in a position to pursue a medical career at the same level as Torrance because of her gender (though nursing might have been a possibility), it is clear that her economically and socially deprived background presented her with far fewer opportunities than Torrance's middle-class oriented, well-educated family background. Macdonald points out that

> had she remained in Scotland, her tremendous gifts and potential would surely have been frustrated, and perhaps entirely stifled, if channelled within the constraints of teaching or home mission work ... But in the life she developed for herself in West Africa, she demonstrated the truly liberating possibilities of foreign mission work for women.[28]

Though she was to become one of the most famous missionaries to Africa of the 19th century, Slessor's formal education was clearly not of the same calibre as Torrance's. In this instance, the gender issue is of limited relevance, since although women were unable to go to university until the passing of the 1889 Universities (Scotland) Act, her social background would have made such a move extremely unlikely, even after 1889. Although Torrance was an exceptional character in many ways, all the Scottish missionaries in the Levant demonstrated a high level of educational achievement,[29] either as ministers, teachers or medics, and their behaviour once in the Levant was clearly directed to the middle and upper classes.[30] This fits the above comparison between missionaries to the Levant and China, and those who went to environments perceived to be more primitive.

Beyond this, there is not a great deal of information about the missionaries' backgrounds available, but whether examining Torrance, Paterson, Semple, Gwladys Jones or almost any other member of the Scottish missionary staff in the region, the level of education and conduct once in the field (at the latest) points to a middle-class orientation for both men and women. It was only with the second extension of the franchise in 1867 that skilled artisans in Britain were given the vote[31] and regardless of the Auld Kirk and Free Kirk division in the aftermath of 1843, the churches as a whole were of the middle-classes, particularly the leaders of the churches, and generally the churches had great difficulty in reaching out to the unskilled working-classes.[32] When reflecting on the difficulties the missionaries encountered in relating their gospel message to the people of the Levant in order to achieve conversions – who had such a very different culture and background to their own – one might reflect on the fact that had the missionaries stayed in Scotland, many of them would perhaps have had similar problems in trying to relate to the working-classes, whose background was largely alien to that of the predominant culture within the churches. However, the general ease with which the churches in Scotland connected to the upper-classes in society, whether in government or landed wealth, can be coherently construed as an indicator for the aspirations of the middle-class church: its attention focusing on 'upwards' rather than 'downwards' within Scottish society, aspiring to something that was perhaps within their reach and apparently more attractive to the majority within the churches than making common cause with the working-classes. The upper-classes would have had, to some extent, a similar educational background, and the (seeming) ability of the higher classes within society to 'make things happen' would have appealed to missionaries and church leaders (including missionary committee conveners) keen to spread support for their cause as widely as possible. It is interesting in this context to note the appeals to secular authority figures in furthering the aims of missionary work: 'We cannot ignore the affinity between colonization and the making of – or desire for – middle-class sensibilities', as Gikandi puts it, this being an era when the dominant European narrative, incorporating the rest of the world, defined itself in terms of 'modernity and bourgeois identity'.[33] The missionaries can be seen in the context of this narrative, creating and being part of it.

In terms of support for the missions, the most ardent supporters were individual ministers (and some elders) who spent many years serving the committee, often coming from wealthy congregations: one of the most striking examples being that of James Wells of Pollokshields, whose church donated substantial sums to various parts of the Tiberias hospital as well as other causes, and who was freed to serve the Free Kirk's JMC on regular occasions. This obviously resulted in missionaries visiting these congregations when on furlough, thus further deepening the connection between these middle-class congregations and the missionaries. A consequence of this was that the missionaries therefore had less time to spend with such working-class congregations as there were,[34] and this perhaps prevented missions ever capturing the public imagination in the way and to the extent that would actually have served their purposes well (this would apply to both 'Jewish' and 'foreign' missions), in the way that Andrew Ross argues in his essay described above. This is most graphically illustrated by the singular failure to secure adequate and increasing funding, as described in the Appendix. The static income of the JMC is indicative of the Committee's difficulties in reaching out beyond their existing constituency for support, a reflection, perhaps, of their inability to enthuse more than just the pre-millenarian Evangelical middle-classes who were already convinced of the need to support the work.

From Edinburgh to the Middle East: relationships between the churches and the practitioners

How the Scottish committees maintained control of the missionaries

The general structure of 19th century Presbyterian churches in Scotland has already been outlined briefly above (all the churches had a more or less identical structure), but the practical working of this structure describes in large measure the relationship between the executive (the committee in Edinburgh) and the practitioners (the missionaries on the ground).

The committees had a secretary – at first a committee member, from 1892 (in the Free Kirk) an employee – who was responsible for day-to-day communication with the staff overseas. This person was answerable to his (all the secretaries were male) committee, and where there was a female branch of the work (e.g. the WAJM) he also served this grouping. Communications from missionary staff were also directed at times to the convener of the committee, who would usually, it seems (few records exist), respond in person, perhaps after consulting with the Secretary. Secretaries were often in place for many years (the first Free Kirk employee, George Milne Rae, died in post on 24.3.1917[35]) and this ensured a level of continuity, though also, perhaps, of stagnation. Conveners were also often in post for long periods, but committee membership changed more regularly (the annual General Assembly was a time when committee composition was amended), though here again, the most active members stayed on year after year and therefore had more knowledge of and greater influence on the work. But on the whole, the two key people in Edinburgh were secretaries and, to a lesser extent, the conveners, who usually came from Edinburgh.[36]

The missionaries were given a wide mandate to implement the committee's purpose. Only rarely was this elaborated on in any detail in written form, though historians are fortunate in having two relevant sets of instructions from the Free Kirk available: firstly to missionaries in Amsterdam (and elsewhere) in 1871[37], and secondly, the 'Instructions for Torrance on leaving for Tiberias', in 1884[38] (both are reproduced in the Appendix).

The Amsterdam instructions (in response to various difficulties which arose around the method and practice of the incumbent of the time) emphasise strongly the 'primary end of the Mission, viz, the conversion of Israel' and although activity amongst other groupings was not excluded, it was clearly not to be regarded as a priority. The emphasis is on direct, confrontational missionary activity.

Torrance's instructions are intriguing in that even though they come from a *Jewish* Mission Committee, Jews are not mentioned once: instead the themes are the patients, the local people, the neighbours around him – and the Committee would certainly have been aware that Tiberias was populated not only by Jews. He is urged to engage in speaking about the gospel at the earliest opportunity, with 'the acquisition of the native language' (unspecified) being a high priority in order to reduce the dependency on an interpreter. Regular reports to the Committee were requested, and he was to be guided by 'wisdom and experience' and trust in God to fulfil his mandate. With regard to the practical method of his work, the first paragraph instructed him to engage in biblical exposition with the patients each day before they were treated: beyond that, opening a hospital or clinic in whatever shape or form might be suitable was left entirely to him, obviously in negotiation with the Committee in terms of costs, staffing and other obligations that might be involved.

Both sets of instructions placed a high value on good relations with those in the immediate environment, regardless of the context, whether Amsterdam where there were many other Protestants who might have been sympathetic to the Scots' work, or the Levant, where hostility might be expected.

These instructions were, however, of necessity vague. It is unlikely that any of the committee members would have visited the countries and locales where the missionaries worked, and if a missionary was starting a new mission (such as Torrance was employed to do), then the committee would have had little choice but to trust in their missionaries' common sense – and the notion that what they were doing was fulfilling the will of God and would therefore be guided and blessed.

Since the missionaries were given relative freedom in the execution of their work, necessitated by the distances and the slow methods of communication involved, the question arises how the committees retained control over the work of their missionaries. Communications consisted essentially of telegrams, letters and meetings: telegrams were prohibitively expensive (so were only used for urgent and brief instructions), letters were relatively slow – it would not be unusual for the reply to a letter to take a month before reaching the original sender – and meetings generally only occurred when the missionaries returned to Scotland on furlough approximately every five years.

Missionaries in Scotland were regularly invited to attend meetings of their committee (it seems that those who had served for a number of years in particular were invited): for example, there are a number of meetings at various times which note that Alexander Paterson or David Torrance attended.[39] Apart from this, when returning from the Levant, missionaries seem to have met at least with the convener, and perhaps with a small group of people from their committee. These encounters, and the meetings in full committee, would generally be the most direct way for the committee members to find out about work being carried out on their behalf by their missionary.[40] These meetings did not necessarily involve discussions about policy, substantial expenditure items or other major issues: the missionaries' presence in Scotland was not connected to such issues, but to their furlough entitlement. This resulted in situations such as Torrance attending a meeting in September 1890 (which included a relatively straightforward discussion on a house for his use, at a cost of £1,350), and then a few months later submitting a proposal by letter from Tiberias for the building of a hospital at the substantially greater cost of £2,500.[41] On the whole, meetings with the committees seem to have been appreciated by committee members and missionaries alike.

When missionaries were in the field, letters did not form the only basis of direct involvement by Edinburgh since they were very slow, making reaction to events difficult and quick decisions impossible. Therefore, telegrams were regularly sent from the office in Edinburgh or from the missionaries, often in response to a request by letter, usually for urgent matters involving finance. This would often take the form of a brief confirmation to be followed by a letter: e.g., responding to a query regarding a property transaction, the committee sent a telegram stating: 'Ewing. Safed. Contract must not exceed thirteen fifty. Payments depend on progress of work. Letter follows. Wilson'.[42]

This points to the instrument of ultimate control: it was the Edinburgh-based committee that financed the missions and it was through the tool of financial control that the secretaries and committees influenced what was happening on the ground. Even when the Mission Council was created, this body had to send its accounts, budgets and minutes to Edinburgh, and decisions to spend significant sums or enter into major legally binding obligations were to be decided by the JMC.[43] When it did not comply with this expectation, this was made very clear; for example, what must have been one of the first Council meetings to be reported to the JMC elicited the following minute:

The Committee desire to inform the Council that it is their part to gather information and send it with their opinions to the Committee, and to act only on instructions received from them. Further, the Committee, as Trustees of the liberality of the people feel that no new expense should be incurred without the express sanction of the Committee.[44]

Until the creation of Mission Councils, and to some extent thereafter, this requirement to have expenditure approved applied to regular as well as unusual expenditure of small and large amounts. For example, in 1892, Torrance suggested purchasing medicines from Beirut instead of Scotland, having just had to buy £20 worth from there since a shipment from Scotland had been delayed due to customs problems: 'The Committee acquiesced, but on the understanding that every important order first obtain the Committee's sanction'. At the same meeting, the sum of £8 was approved for 'summer accommodation at Safed' for the Tiberias staff, and, £400 having been raised for teachers' housing in Safad by the Women's Association, further public appeals were approved. A few months later, a bill of £1 1s was approved for payment of tracts.[45]

These examples are cited as evidence of one committee's interest in the minutiae of financial control, but numerous other examples exist. At times missionaries seem to have ignored the limits on their spending powers, as did the Mission Council in the example above; serious infractions usually resulted in further reminders of the need to consult the committee,[46] though short of bringing them home or severing employment relationships the JMC could do little more than rebuke its staff. This did not happen with any of the missionaries in the Levant, though there is one instance of a JMC sacking an employee.[47]

This points to the limits of the control that the committees had over their employees.

The limits of control

Since financial control rested with the committees, and was on the whole largely respected by the missionaries, it might appear that this represented a high measure of control over the activities of the missionaries.

However, as has been pointed out, the guidelines or instructions to missionaries were so broad as to allow the missionaries relative freedom to act. Of course, this was not a freedom without limits – accountability for their actions and the need to prove some kind of results in order to ensure a continued supply of funding from Scotland would be the two most practical reasons for working within a clearly defined framework. Almost all missionary locations employed more than one Western missionary, and this would also have introduced an element of peer pressure and mutual critique: the Torrance-Ewing conflict would appear to indicate something of this nature. Furthermore, inaction or laziness would not be encouraged: these 19th century middle-class Scottish Presbyterians had a background that would tend to emphasise the need for hard work and would generally not look favourably on apparent idleness.[48] Finally, one of the main reasons for being in the region in the first place was a profoundly personal and religio-spiritual one, and this evangelical fervour would have motivated their work in ways that historians cannot easily measure, being restricted to examining the political and material consequences of how this motivation was put into practice, as this book seeks to do.

The Mission Council, made up of senior staff at a mission station, necessitated a level of formal accountability, but the JMC only intervened (or was asked to intervene) when the Council was unable to come to a clear decision, or the matter under discussion went beyond its remit. Although the JMC received Council minutes (there are several times when issues are raised at JMC meetings as a result of receiving the Council minutes[49]), it did not receive agendas: in other words, the JMC's relation to the Mission Council was essentially retrospective. Whilst missionaries undoubtedly incorporated items into the agendas of meetings at the request of the JMC,[50] the Council tended to act on the sentiment of the first paragraph of its constitution:

> The Mission Council is to be regarded as the local representative of the Jewish Mission Committee, and is responsible to the Committee for the whole Mission work done within the area under its charge, and for the economical expenditure of all the moneys, whether sent from home, or contributed locally, for carrying on the work.[51]

The JMC sometimes felt the need to ensure its primacy in addressing certain issues – a clear attempt at reasserting control. For example, in 1897 summer arrangements for Tiberias staff were discussed by the JMC, having been presented with the latest Mission Council minutes. The JMC minutes hint at dissatisfaction with the Council's deliberations, and the JMC's Finance Sub-Committee was asked to 'inquire into the responsibilities of the Committee … and … the whole question of summer arrangements, and … report'.[52]

Such examples indicate a difficulty for the committees in Scotland: the remote location of the work, the impracticality of frequent visits, the generally slow methods of written communication, and often a lack of background knowledge with regard to the social, historical, geographic and political context, combined to lead almost inevitably to a great deal of autonomy for the local missionaries, and a corresponding limit to the control of the central church in Scotland.

However, accountability to the church membership in Scotland who supported the missions financially, has already been mentioned, and this relationship warrants further examination.

From the Middle East to Scotland: communicating with church members

Of the main groups of people who travelled to the Levant, church missionaries had the most regular opportunities to offer direct feedback about their encounters to 'ordinary' people in Scotland: those engaged in business, diplomatic activity, or simply travelling for their own pleasure or edification could speak or write about their experiences, but missionaries had a wide constituency who would read their letters and articles, and turn out to hear them when they travelled around the country visiting churches during their periods of furlough leave. McAllister, noting that most nineteenth century British Christians had an 'idealist vision' of missionary work, goes so far as to say that

> The missionaries' knowledge of the cultures and languages of foreign people and their heroism as bearers of European civilization and the gospel to distant, remote lands gave to their narratives tremendous authority. Throughout the nineteenth century, the narratives of missionaries were the primary lens through which Western Evangelical Christians viewed the indigenous people of Asia, the Middle East, India, Africa, and the Carribean [sic] and South Sea Islands.[53]

Since those Christians in post-Disruption Scotland interested in missions were largely from the Evangelical wing of the churches, people who might never otherwise have heard about cultures and peoples beyond their own borders were given opportunities to hear at least the missionaries' interpretation of these.[54] This being the case, it follows that the images of the Levant that the missionaries encountered and described in their writings and speaking engagements would have had a profound influence on the way they were seen in the Scottish context. Books and journals are left for historians: whilst missionary meetings can sometimes be identified in terms of date and place, they were generally not recorded.

Books with religious themes issued by mainstream publishers represented the context for church publications, some of them drawing on missionary expertise, a prominent example being George Adam Smith's *Historical Geography of the Holy Land*.[55] Alexander Andrew's *My Visit to Palestine*,[56] a 'book for the young', is one of many texts with an educational aim.[57] Smith and Andrew spent time with the missionaries, indeed Smith explicitly thanked several Scottish missionaries in the Preface to the first edition,[58] whilst Andrew recounted travelling around Tiberias and Safad with missionaries.[59] Publications by the church JMCs that were designed to increase the support of the missions were competing with the likes of these volumes.

Missionary books

Few of the Free Kirk/United Free Kirk JMC missionaries did more than write articles for the church magazine, but the Committee itself published books (or sanctioned their publication). An important example is *The Sea of Galilee Mission of the Free Church of Scotland*, published in 1895 shortly after the hospital was opened. Additionally, there were two companion books published in 1914, issued 'by Authority of the Jewish Committee of the United Free Church of Scotland' under the heading *Our Jewish Missions*, the first, written by William Ewing, formerly of the Sea of Galilee mission, entitled *The Holy Land and Glasgow*, the second, *Israel in Europe*. This latter, written by John Hall, a member of the JMC, has already been referred to since it contains a rationale for Jewish missions (c.f. p16 above). These volumes also contain funding appeals, clearly indicating their promotional purpose.[60]

Geopiety forms a dominant theme, particularly in the Sea of Galilee volume, which consists of chapters written by a variety of people connected to the work. Beginning with an account of the origin of Scottish church interest in Jewish mission, the second chapter consists of 11 verses of a hymn text written by McCheyne 'at the Sea of Galilee on July 16, 1839':

> Fair are the lakes in the land I love,
> Where pine and heather grow;
> But thou [Sea of Galilee] hast loveliness far above
> What Nature can bestow.
>
> It is not that the wild gazelle
> Comes down to drink thy tide,
> But He that was pierced to save from hell
> Oft wandered by thy side.
>
> ...
>
> O Saviour! gone to God's right hand!
> Yet the same Saviour still,
> Graved on Thy heart is this lovely strand
> And every fragrant hill.[61]

Whilst the author loves his own country of Scotland ('pine and heather'), the immeasurable superiority of the Palestinian lake comes not from natural surroundings ('the wild gazelle') but from the deity incarnate, whose presence many centuries ago is brought into the present, and the emotions behind the hymn are validated and given meaning by presuming Jesus' fond memories of the area. Similar such sentiments are found when explaining the benefit the hospital brings. A reference to Bethel is discussed below (p156), but numerous other geopious connections exist, extending not only to the land itself, but also to the mission: 'Our Galilee Mission brings now, as in the days of Christ's flesh, "the double cure" within reach of the suffering thousands in Galilee, in Decapolis, and from beyond Jordan'.[62] The use of the Roman/Biblical name for the region to the east and north of the Jordan can only have been deliberate, with the intention of evoking an emotional response connected to church members' Biblical knowledge, and 'the double cure' – i.e. physical and spiritual – that the Scots were now able to provide was clearly linked to Jesus' own physical and spiritual ministry.

Aside from the historical account behind the founding and development of the mission, which is replete with geopious sentiment, there are also accounts of the mission's work. Statistical measures are notable by their absence, with accounts revolving around personal encounters and presented in a narrative style using the present tense, e.g.: 'In one of the beds opposite is a fair-haired, intelligent-looking Jew ... in delicate health ... but ... now gaining strength every day ... He brought ... with him a well-thumbed Torah ... [but this] was soon laid aside in favour of a copy of a Gospel in Hebrew'.[63]

Since conversions were few and far between, this kind of narrative presented an ideal opportunity to showcase Jewish interest in Christianity, thereby demonstrating the importance of supporting the mission.

It is not clear precisely how many copies of this volume were sold, though several thousand were printed. Likewise, the quantity of the 1914 volumes sold is not known.

Both the 1895 and the 1914 volumes contain a number of photographs. These range from images of Tiberias, Hebron etc. to portraits of a 'Tiberias Jewess'[64] and some of the missionaries, as well as to images of fishermen pulling nets ashore[65] – again, the link to the Biblical narratives is clear. Ewing's volume, including a chapter on the work of the Jewish mission in Glasgow written by Christie, who had moved from the Sea of Galilee to Aleppo and then to Glasgow, also recounts the early years of the church's interest, describing briefly the 1839 deputation. The exploratory trip by Wells and Torrance is described, along with the building of the hospital and a description of the work carried out by the mission. This is categorised into 'Healing, Evangelism, and Education'[66] – c.f. Chapter 5 below. Accounts of work are more general, and less dependent on individual cases of treatment than in the 1895 volume. The work in Safad is described, as is the work in Hebron, following a brief introduction into the work prior to the United Free Kirk's involvement. Quotations from the missionaries are used to explain the work, sometimes taken from printed reports, and sometimes direct speech. The local employees are more frequently named, and their names are given in a more nuanced transliteration, for example, the Safad boys' schoolteacher's name is given as Mu'allim Mas'ūd Qorbān.[67] Ewing, of course, had worked there, and so would presumably have had a reasonable (at least) grasp of Arabic, enabling him to render names more accurately than happened in the 1895 volume.

Aside from the depictions of the work carried out, there are also brief descriptions of the localities that the mission work is carried out in. Chapters give geographical and population information, as well as describing the mission work; titles include, 'Tiberias and the Sea of Galilee', 'The City Set on a Hill' and 'Kirjath-Arba' – these latter two referring to Safad and Hebron. Safad had been viewed by the Scots in 1839 as the 'city on a hill' referred to by Jesus,[68] though there is no evidence that this was the case. The title of the chapter on Hebron is explained in the first lines in terms of Biblical origins, and then the more usual name is used throughout the remainder of the book.[69] The medical work in Hebron, for example, is connected to the evangelising aim of the Committee: 'evangelism is kept steadily in view in all the work as the great end to be achieved ... the door is open and opportunities for the evangelist are many'.[70] The only thing that prevents more being done, similarly to the message of the 1895 volume, is the lack of financial support and personnel, explaining the request for donations at the end of the section on Palestine.

These books represented an attempt by the Committee to further their work: although others may have written about the missions as part of a travelogue, dedicated descriptions highlighting the aspects of the work that were most important to the JMC could most easily be produced under their own auspices. The relatively inexpensive volumes were advertised in the church's journals, but it is difficult to assess whether they had much effect in increasing income for the missions.

Missionary journals

Of course, whilst people might read a brief article or attend a missionary meeting in a church hall, they would not necessarily want to read a book about the Levant, presuming always that they could (considering financial, social, and educational factors).

The missionary journals therefore represent the most significant extant written source showing how the missionaries related to the wider church. With the wider interest in missions that developed from the mid-19th century onwards, and since the Tiberias mission represented the first major new engagement in the Levant in that period, the analysis below will focus attention primarily on the Free Church records from this period on: the *Free Church Monthly and Missionary Record* (MMR) and from the United Presbyterian/Free Church union, the *Missionary Record of the United Free Church* (MR).[71] Since the missionary journals were generally run by the FMC, the space allocation for the JMC needed to be renegotiated or confirmed at various intervals, particularly as circumstances changed, e.g. with the United Presbyterian/Free Church union.[72] Their purpose is clear: they were produced to inform the church constituency at large of work being carried out, and also to generate further prayer, donations and material support from those already convinced of the need for this work. Critical articles will not, therefore, have been considered for publication.

In the context of Jewish missions, one can assume readers to have had a certain – very minimal and probably hazy – knowledge of Jewish traditions, but given the general inability of the missionaries and their supporters to see their target audience of Jews as actional persons rather than as constructs of their own theology, any change in views as a result of missionary communications would be shaped accordingly. Furthermore, the missionaries, who generally spent several years overseas at a stretch, sometimes lost touch with the interests and perceptions of their sending communities, or tried too hard to tailor their writing to their imaginary readership, who had perhaps changed without the missionaries noticing it. For example, Macdonald highlights Annie Small's idealising of Scotland and her disappointment with the churches on her return,[73] whilst Ross shows how Livingstone presented his *Missionary Travels and Researches in South Africa* so as to appeal to a wider readership, but thereby increased 'the distance between what he believed and what his audience understood him to mean',[74] leading to misinterpretations of his position.

The MMR and MR carried certain regular features on an annual basis, most notably brief reports from the General Assembly (usually in the June edition), and a report/appeal in time for the 'Jewish Sunday' (usually in December). Travel accounts, whether copied from books (especially in the early years, when few accounts existed by Scots[75]) or written by missionaries or travellers (often ministers) also featured regularly, alongside more general tales of missionary endeavour written by the missionaries themselves.

With the initiation of the mission in Tiberias, the geopiety of the Scottish churches was given free rein: in response to an appeal for funds, a donor is recorded as having written that there 'is no spot on earth I feel so deeply interested in, and I am glad to have the opportunity ... of furthering ... this most interesting mission'.[76] Although there is an article on the same page repeating (and explaining) the assumption that Jesus probably never went to Tiberias, the connection with the Christ narrative is played on in numerous appeals for further support from that time onwards. In connection with the annual December collection, it is noted on more than one occasion that the mission reflects 'the prayers of many who have longed for the salvation of Israel in all lands, and especially their own, from which they have been exiled since their rejection of their own Messiah'.[77] The annual collection provided an opportunity, as did in briefer form, the journal's General Assembly report, for a summary of all that had happened in the course of the year, and here, as in the reports to the Assembly noted below (p207), the hope was always expressed that large numbers of Jews were about to convert, even if there had been none in any of the mission fields operated by the church in the past year:

There are many and striking indications that that "day of visitation" has at length begun to dawn ... [our work is] preparatory work, but we believe in *sowing*, and can wait for the *harvest*. Already some of the first fruits are being gathered in, some of them rich and beautiful ... [a request for funds is made, and] we earnestly ask each family ... to make frequent mention at the throne of grace of Israel, and of our Jewish agents and work, especially on Friday evenings and Saturday mornings.[78]

The use of Biblical and theological language here is striking – 'day of visitation', dawn, sowing and harvest, fruits gathered in, the quality of the fruits, throne, grace, Israel – and would have been designed to evoke strong emotions and reactions with a church membership that would have recognised much of this terminology, bringing the missions closer to the people whose money and support was so desperately needed. The request for prayers on Friday evenings and Saturday mornings to link with the Jewish Sabbath would have had a similar purpose, as do the regular requests that readers should mark the Jewish Day of Atonement 'with special mention of Israel' in the course of intercessory prayer.[79] Even if no converts could be reported, near-conversions were, as in the December 1893 appeal written by the Convener, James Wells:

A young ex-rabbi ... feeling keenly the incompleteness of Judaism, he was haunted with the question, "What if, after all, Jesus is the Messias?" ... He saw that his own faith required him to leave the Old for the New Covenant. Such a progress as his seems well-nigh inevitable for a devout Jew.[80]

Although converts are few in number, hope for future converts was, as has been shown, a constant. Additionally, reference was regularly made to unnamed other missionaries who supported the Scots' work: 'several leaders in other Churches have declared that no other [Jewish] mission ... has a better record than our own, in respect both of the number and quality of the converts, and the "converts' converts'".[81] Resorting to the reported support of other societies who were, in general, facing similarly poor numbers of converts can hardly be seen as a recommendation, but this perspective would not have been available to most of the journal's readership, and perhaps not even to most of the comments' authors. Instead, the failure to gain converts was sometimes seen as a 'serious trial of faith' that should induce 'self-examination and humiliation, and [lead] to more earnest prayer and supplication that God would give guidance and crown his own work with blessing.'[82]

Mostly, however, missions were regarded as failing because of Jewish 'loss of spiritual insight', Jewish and Christian self-righteousness which prevented the gospel message being understood properly, and the difficulties for converts in terms of social and material consequences. However, the first reason dominated, revealing a deep undercurrent of anti-Jewishness: Jews were blamed for their unwillingness to convert, often being described as 'stubborn', 'obstinate', 'blind' etc. in relation to the gospel message, rather than simply acknowledging that most Jews were actional persons who had decided not to convert. Brutal language could be employed: in wishing for Jews' 'stubbornness' to be overcome, the JMC Convener in 1884 yearned for 'the outstretched arm of the Lord in saving mercy, to "bend or break the iron sinew of their neck"'[83] – note the 'saving mercy' in the bending or breaking. Anti-Judaism/anti-Jewishness is widely reflected, even when it is condemned, for example, the MMR editor noted that 'the race is hated [in Germany] because it increases so fast and is so aggressive. Its money-making power is extraordinary ... the notion ... is that they are a sharp, grasping, close-fisted, narrow-hearted, selfish people'.[84] That German attitudes might be important is not addressed, rather German Jews are blamed for non-Jewish Germans 'hating' them – for contemporary readers, deeply disturbing imagery given events in Germany a few decades later.[85] Theologically too, 'the curse that they invoked on themselves at the crucifixion'[86] is clearly Jews' responsibility – but this did not prevent their evangelisation. The origins for this anti-Judaism can be interpreted as the dark side of the imperial-style 'concern' for Jews: since they refused the offer of salvation made to them (which would further their well-being), they could be blamed and condemned. From being the victims of oppression and hatred, they became the villains of ingratitude.[87]

Material support was elicited not only in monetary terms to the Jewish or women's committees. Notices requesting donations of 'clothing for the poor Jews in and around Tiberias'[88] appeared regularly, coordinated by a few Edinburgh women, who sustained this action for many years. A few months later a note of thanks from Torrance's wife would usually appear – one of the very few occasions on which an active and public role is accorded to the wife of any of the missionaries (they are often included in photographs and occasionally mentioned in terms of social contact, but only very rarely in any official capacity to do with the mission's work).

Travel accounts, often written in the present tense, perhaps with the intention of involving the reader more, formed a major part of reports from the field. As tourism to the Levant gained in popularity and ease at the end of the 19th century, increasing numbers of clergy (in particular) found the time for extended tours of the region. In part these were connected to the JMC (e.g. June 1891 recorded Wells' visit), and generally always included the mission stations as well as more usual tourist sites. The message communicated, whether the individual was connected with the mission or not, was universally one of praise for the dedication and achievements of the mission. These latter are often put in terms of social benefit, since conversions were thin on the ground. The Free and United Free Churches devoted substantial space to travel accounts, in 1895 even giving over several pages in every issue dedicated to a series entitled 'Free Church Travellers in the Holy Land' (though not all of these were 'genuine' travellers, since Torrance wrote one article, and at least two others were by prominent JMC members). This series may well have been one of the first fuller introductions to the geography of Palestine and Damascus (December issue) that church members in Scotland would have had – Smith's *Historical Geography* had only been published the previous year – and whilst the accounts are replete with geopious references and images, details about the condition of roads, building materials, relative wealth and poverty, agricultural usage, archaeological significance (not just related to Biblical materials) etc. abound. Since Smith's volume was already in its fourth edition within two years of publication, the MMR editor was probably simply being astute in tapping into a general interest caused by this book. Further travel accounts appeared at regular intervals, generally always including news of the mission stations, as did general information articles, e.g. Soutar's 1904 series of four articles on 'Jewish Life in Palestine'. Extensive histories of the missions were also offered, as in 1902 when a history of the Jewish missions spread over all 12 issues appeared.

Missionaries' accounts often included details of a recent operation or some incident in one of the schools, and examples of contact with patients, pupils or parents over a discussion of a Biblical text or theological principle. These latter were presumably included as evidence of the missionaries' attempts at conversion, and served to show how 'difficult' it was to bring 'the Jews' to Protestantism. These accounts were written by a variety of people; whilst most official communications were from the male staff of the mission, this was a space that was also occasionally open to females.[89]

Other missionary work in the region, such as that of the Anglican Church and its agencies, was seldom mentioned until the onset of the First World War, although many of the methods and aims of the competing missions in the region were similar. During the war, the Scottish churches' JMCs co-operated with emergency relief work that involved Anglicans: it has already been noted that both Torrance and Paterson, as well as others, worked for the Syria and Palestine Relief Fund (c.f. Chapter 3). Before the war, Anglican and other missions were barely discussed beyond pointing to occasional co-operation or assistance (such as medical treatment by or of other medical missionaries), perhaps in part because the Scots were facing such difficulties in raising sufficient funds for their work[90] that they would not wish to offer any distraction to their donating public. This would be particularly important if it appeared that other missions were perhaps experiencing more 'success' than the Scots' missions: awkward questions regarding methods, purpose and achievements might result, followed by diminished givings. There were occasional exceptions to this, but these were often connected to the purposes of the church: for example, Jane Walker-Arnott's school work was widely praised upon her death, but this was, of course, because the church had an interest in taking on the work (c.f. Chapter 3). However, if missions by other Protestants were only occasionally mentioned, engagement by non-Protestants was almost completely ignored. That there might have been comparable aspects to e.g. English and Russian involvement in Palestine[91] was not acknowledged. Instead, such minimal references as there are to the involvement of non-Protestants in Palestine generally point to the link between e.g. Russian imperial ambition in the context of the Ottoman Empire and the activity of the Russian Orthodox Church. Whilst there is truth in this portrayal, given that the Russian Ecclesiastical Mission in Jerusalem was founded by the Tsar to shore up Orthodox influence in Palestine under the guise of supporting Russian pilgrims to the Holy Land, such connections between the Scots' church and British imperial power were not recognised.[92] To all intents and purposes, other missions were largely invisible to the readership of the church journals.

In contrast, a topic that featured regularly in the context of the later missionary journals was 'the condition of the Jews', and, increasingly as the First World War approached, Zionism and immigration issues. Zionism was initially dismissed because Christ did not feature in it:

> While this idea of "the Zionists," as they call themselves, is out of the question, there is no reason why the colonization of Palestine should not be encouraged ... But ... we have no belief in the good time coming to which the Jews are looking forward, until they are brought to mourn for Him whom their fathers pierced.[93]

However, by the following year, the MMR ran a half page article on the Second Zionist Congress in Basle, quoting Theodor Herzl at length, and citing a rabbi who argued for the inclusion of religion in the Zionist project. The article conveys enthusiasm, excitement and conviction: it is not clear whether the author, Andrew Moody of the JMC's Budapest mission, had been in Basle; it is certainly possible. The following year, Soutar wrote a piece entitled 'An Appreciation of the Jewish Problem', which addressed the 'problem' of converting Jews, arguing that 'the young men in the Jewish colonies'[94] may offer the best hope for conversion, since they were secular and not bound by the religious commandments of the rabbis; this is also one of the reasons given for finding it easier to get along with the colonisers than the indigenous Jews,[95] although it seems likely that their European cultural background was more of a factor in this. Further comment on Zionism and the more general situation of Jews in Europe continued to take up occasional space, mostly, as with Soutar's article, reflecting concern about the conversion of Jews. The position of the indigenous Palestinian population in this context is never addressed; it is doubtful, at this stage, that many of the missionaries could envisage the scale of

Jewish immigration that was beginning to take shape, and they could therefore also not have imagined the conflict that would divide the communities they had targeted.

The purchase of land by 'Western Jews' is commented on: 'very many ... [have] come to build upon the land which is now being bought up everywhere':[96] 'at the present rate ten years will see practically the whole soil of Palestine in Jewish hands'.[97] The new Jewish colonies represented an abiding topic of interest, one of Soutar's articles mentioned above addressing the topic in detail. He generally finds only praise for their work and organisation, having probably visited a number of them. Rishon le Zion, Zikron Ya'akob, Rosh Pinah and others are described in some detail as to their history and present production. He notes the help of Baron Rothschild in much of this, but also argues that if the colonists will 'honestly' do the work themselves (rather than hiring locals to do it for them 'while they take their ease') then success is guaranteed.[98] He does not follow the (future) Zionist myth of the 'desert being turned green', stating that the 'land is rich, and ... there is scarcely any crop which could not be cultivated with success'[99] – he would also have seen plenty of agricultural work over the years, even if he felt the Jewish immigrants were using more 'efficient' (i.e. European) methods. The colonies' growth and the increasing immigration is observed regularly – and placed, as so often, in a familiar Biblical context:

> Twenty years ago there were not more than 12,000 Jews in Jerusalem, and not more than 30,000 in all the Holy Land. Now there are 45,000 in Jerusalem alone, and over 100,000 in the country. Between 70,000 and 80,000 have gone there in the last few years – nearly double the number that returned with Zerubbabel.[100]

The 1908 constitution enacted because of the Young Turk revolution was widely welcomed by the missionaries, who saw advantages in the provisions regarding religious freedom, and hoped that this would be the first step towards a diminution of Sultan Abdülhamid II's power.[101] This, of course, was seen largely in terms of their own interest in pursuing mission work, though the new situation Jews were expected to find themselves in was also looked at more generally, concluding that Jews 'will be less afraid of persecution' but might have difficulty earning a living.[102] Paterson wrote about 'the first meeting of the Ottoman Parliament – a true House of Commons, I imagine',[103] categorising, in classic orientalist manner, something in western terms and denying it an identity of its own. He felt that the 'new environment' was a positive one, and whilst recognising that 'the jealousies of races and sects are immemorial' and set-backs inevitable, nonetheless, 'the mere fact that the sense of nationality, and pride therein, have been awakened, is an incalculable factor for good in the long-run' (having a few sentences before denied the individuality of national identity in relation to the parliament). Christie, formerly employed at the Sea of Galilee mission but in 1908 in Aleppo working for the English Presbyterian Church, wrote for the MMR in apocalyptic terms, predicting a Jewish Palestine, with immense opportunities for missions:

The leopard has actually changed his spots [referring to the newly 'polite' behaviour of Ottoman officials], and if things go on as they have begun, you may expect the millennium any day.

Now the Jews are free too, and Palestine will be wholly theirs in ten years, probably under Turkish suzerainty ...

Lengthen your cords and strengthen your stakes in Palestine: the future of Judaism, and of Jewish Missions too, is in the Holy Land; and in the Hebrew tongue.[104]

Imbuing the political changes with eschatological significance fits into the pattern already described, of converting (Said, p29 above) the reality on the ground in order to accommodate it within the Scots' understanding of the divine economy – similar statements are made in the context of the annual appeal of 1908.[105] It is notable that for the Scots involved in Jewish missions work, the predicted Jewish success for Palestine was at this stage not necessarily seen as deriving from Zionism, but was more of a religious matter, as the Secretary to the JMC made clear in an article on 'A New Israel' published that year. Acknowledging the significance of political pressures and events, Rae nonetheless argued that 'every nucleus of regenerate Jewish life [i.e. converted] is prophetic of a community of such life co-extensive with the House of Israel, and that what Ezekiel (xxxvii. 1-10) saw in vision shall yet be realised in fact, namely, A NEW ISRAEL'.[106] This symbolic language, equating the 'House of Israel' (i.e. Jews) with the 'New Israel' (i.e. Christians), is clearly derived from New Testament texts and theology.[107]

With the British military advances during World War I the political context changed rapidly,[108] this being accentuated still further by the Balfour Declaration. With most staff being back in Scotland, time to reflect on the issues was available, and a notable event in this context was a one-day conference reported on in April 1917. Tracing the progress of Zionism, it was noted that 'we [the church] had little interest in the setting up of a secular state', and that in any case Zionism 'would not help to solve the problem' of Jews' mistreatment and discrimination beyond Palestine (blamed 'as much on the unhumbled, exclusive and proud Jew as on the unforgiving Christian', however, it was the former that was criticised here to the exclusion of the latter: confronting anti-Jewishness with further anti-Jewishness has already been commented on).[109] The war had resulted in a state of considerable flux in Jewish thought and new possibilities for mission work would emerge, for which the church should be preparing itself. The Balfour Declaration was generally welcomed for the possibilities it offered Jews, though more cautiously than was the Russian revolution (which liberated Jews from the 'barbarous oppression ... of the Muscovite'[110]). There was a wariness of 'our lads ... sacrificing their lives to replace a Turkish by a Jewish tyranny', since the Declaration 'limits toleration to "existing" non-Jewish communities and ignored the possibility of the formation, *e.g.*, of a Jewish Christian Church'.[111] Ensuring 'religious liberty' – i.e. the possibility for missionary work – was a priority for the churches in general so that new communities might be created, and this had been brought to the attention of the British government after Allenby invaded, and appropriate assurances had been received prior to the Balfour Declaration. When it was released, some perceived a retreat on these assurances, hence the cautious welcome.[112] It is only in connection with a note about a new volume by George Adam Smith that mention is made of the (Declaration's) 'non-Jewish' inhabitants, though this is followed by a generally positive assessment of the situation based on Jewish development of the country:

> The Turk is an alien with no root in the land. Who is to succeed him? It is clear that Jews are ready, and must be allowed, to settle; but what is to be the area of their occupation, and what of the other inhabitants? "It is not true," Sir George remarks, "that Palestine is the national home of the Jewish people and of no other people." For instance, there are the fellahin, – the native peasantry, – with a deep stake in the country, to be considered.[113]

It has been noted that all topics considered so far in the missionary journals that related in some way to the missions have been seen in a positive vein, with virtually no criticism of technique, method, investment or area of interest apparent. There was, however, one area of the work that was graphically described as failing in the missionary journals: the inability of the JMC to raise sufficient funds to meet its obligations. For example, the December 1891 collection article noted that

> Last year's collection brought in only £2,584 ... £136 less than ... the previous year. For some years the ... collection averaged £3,280. The Committee appeal ... [this year for] not less than £3,500. The growth of our missions, especially in Palestine, is increasing our expenditure.
> St. Kilda has lately sent 17s. 3d. ... Were the rest of the Church to aid in like proportion to their ability ... [the JMC] could support this mission till the centenary of the Disruption.[114]

The appeal – firstly on the basis of the reduced giving and the increased need, and secondly on the basis of comparison with the donation of the congregation of the tiny, remote island of St Kilda – was ineffective in raising the desired amount, which was put down to the poor weather in the subsequent year's appeal.[115] This kind of article was found year after year, with ever more inventive ways of appealing to the generosity of the JMC constituencies. The missionaries were also involved in raising funds via the missionary journals – e.g. Torrance urging donations for Safad in 1894.[116]

Perhaps the reason that this was so publicly admitted and help was so desperately appealed for was that this was the one area of the missions' failure that ordinary church members and ministers could do something about – the vast majority of congregational members would have been hard-pressed to consider ways of increasing the number of converts the mission was generating, for example, but additional financial support could more easily be arranged.[117]

In thinking about this failure, one might consider David Cannadine's suggestion that 'many metropolitan Britons saw their settlement Empire, not as a great white hope, but as a sociological dumping ground ... of the dross and detritus of the ... metropolis ... [for, amongst others,] failed professionals in the law and the church and the military'.[118] Whilst he is careful not to make this into too much of a generality, with regard to the Scottish missionaries in the Levant it can hardly suffice as an adequate explanation for the lack of popular support that is indicated by the desperate pleas for financial aid by the JMC. Scottish attachment to church representatives overseas was generally strong, with missionaries being highly regarded, and often honoured when in Scotland again, both formally and informally. Gikandi, in noting the Scottish attachment to the imperial narrative and the connection between imperial possessions, thereby points to the disconnection felt between Scottish and British (minus the Empire) identities: the overlap occurs with the imperial element of British identity more than the notion of Britain as a union of four nations – something that Colley likewise points to.[119] So even if Cannadine's statement holds true for some 'Britons' (English?[120]), the image of the Scottish missionaries with the population at home cannot be taken as a reason for the poor level of financial support given to the missions. Rather this can be ascribed to two main factors, firstly, the obvious failure to achieve notable successes – time and again the pleas for money are accompanied by assurances that conversions are imminent and/or far more numerous than can be shown, but actual figures really are, of course, minimal, not just for Jewish missions in the Levant, but for Jewish missions as a whole. Certainly when compared to the apparent successes of foreign missions, churches and members might be forgiven for thinking that on a 'converts per pound' basis, the foreign missions were far more worthy of support, as the income table in the Appendix amply demonstrates. Secondly, there was the limited basis of support that the missions had, as shown above, which meant that although missionaries were respected and honoured, no matter how successful they were perceived to be (leaving open the question of how this can be measured), they were nonetheless seen as marginal figures, whether in 'successful' missions, or the 'unsuccessful' missions described here. This marginalisation is emphatically not to be equated with 'dross and detritus' since the missions and their representatives were not cast out in the sense that Cannadine describes, but simply ignored as an irrelevance, or at best treated with benign neglect.

Conclusion

The missionaries generally came from a relatively exclusive middle-class oriented background that determined how they understood the environment they were going to, as well as their image of their sending communities and country. This substantially determined the way they interacted with their committee and church constituency. The inability of the JMCs and their agents to reach out to people beyond this middle-class church-going background resulted in ever decreasing levels of financial support and increasingly desperate attempts to develop interest in the work. Particularly as the work expanded, the committees appear to have become less responsive to new challenges, arising partly from the lack of financial manoeuvrability that meant new projects or extensions of existing work often needed to be postponed until sufficient funds had been raised, or abandoned altogether: there was virtually no contingency funding that would allow suitable projects to proceed quickly.

The communications with the sending constituency show a wide range of topics was covered, connecting with contemporary events and offering a range of authors. However, many of the political predictions, infused with religious meaning, were hopelessly inaccurate, indicative more of wishful thinking than relation to reality. Little was done to move beyond the middle-class context and allow greater participation and ownership of the Jewish missionary effort. Increases in income required a Herculean effort that was seldom rewarded to the extent desired, and the extra publications did not seem to help in this regard. Consistent support that did not increase substantially over the course of many years meant that a certain minimum of work could be continued at all times, but the great expansion in opportunities that the missionaries saw could not be realised. Most notable amongst these was the idea of the 'Industrial Mission', which would have opened a whole new field of missionary endeavour, and might even have succeeded in bringing some of Scotland's artisan or working-class into contact with missionary work, thereby also increasing the constituency of support for the missions in Scotland. That this was not possible left the churches with traditional models of missionary activity. Of these, confrontation, education, medicine, examined in more detail in the next chapter, certainly the latter two, at least, were mostly the preserve of the middle-classes, restricting the promotion of the work being done in Palestine largely to this same class. Although I am not suggesting that the working-classes would only have been interested in supporting missions that involved working-class missionaries, the lack of such meant that there was a failure to appreciate (in the context of a church that was increasingly failing to appreciate) how to make their work appear relevant and worthy of support, since the middle-class oriented missionaries had little idea of how to relate to the working-classes.

5
MISSIONARY METHODS AND INTERACTION WITH THE LOCAL POPULATION

Introduction

Imperial historians have at times described the work of 19th century missionaries in monolithic terms, portraying an aloofness, distance, an unwillingness to become integrated with the local community, and a prominent role in the western powers' imperial and colonial efforts. For example, the Comaroffs' memorable description of early 19th century missionaries in South Africa as 'the agent, scribe and moral alibi'[1] for the imperial power or Said's (self-confessed) gross outline that describes missions that 'abetted' imperial expansion[2] epitomise such perspectives. Whilst such descriptions do reflect a valid perspective of reality, and altruistic or 'good' intentions cannot be taken as an excuse for destructive behaviour in a context of power relationships, the picture is far more complex than this.

The previous chapter having examined the relationship the missionaries had with their church constituency in Scotland, attention in this chapter is given to the interaction of the missionaries with local actors in the Levant. Elements of this have already been described, here the interaction will be examined more closely by firstly analysing the missionary methods used and their impact on the target population, before portraying what this meant for the missionaries' dealing with the dialectic of identity and difference. This will be done using models of reculturation and missionary identification.

As this book relies mostly on Scottish sources, the analysis of impact will of necessity be indirect, but local actors were, of course, not silent in these sources.[3] Whilst overt descriptions addressing people in Scotland (Committees, church members) were mostly monolithic – '*the* Jews' or '*the* eastern Churches' (usually – not often as 'the eastern Christians') or '*the* Muslims/Muhammedans' – the missionaries did make some occasional differentiations, for example in relation to Ashkenazi and Sephardic Jews, Latin or Greek Orthodox Christians, and Muslims or Druze (this latter usually seen as an aberration of Islam).[4] But in general, the indigenous Christian Churches were generally seen as 'eastern', and scant attention was paid to individual church beliefs, histories or practices. These churches were seen as failures because they were not actively engaging in missionary work to their non-Christian neighbours.[5] Usually being described as 'churches', not

'Christians', allowed individual members to undergo conversion at the hands of the Scots so that they might 'become' (Protestant) Christians.

Changes in methods

The missionaries' aim was simple: the conversion of Jews to Protestant Christianity. The missions created to achieve this that are described here are the short-lived missions in Aleppo and Damascus, the schools in Jaffa, Tiberias and Safad; in the latter two, and in Hebron, medicine played a prominent role.

An analysis of the methods of missionary practice needs to take into consideration the context of the work. There are three significant aspects to this: the situation of Jews in the Levant, Victorian society's ideals of philanthropy, and the missionary movement as a whole.

Regarding the situation of Jews in the Levant from the missionaries' perspective: Jews were seen as poor, ill-educated, and above all, utterly removed from the true Jewish faith (as the missionaries understood it to be): the contrast was often put in language such as this: there is 'a root-difference, not between us and the Israelites of the Psalms and the prophets, but between the true Christian and the modern Jews, and is one of the good reasons why we so earnestly desire their conversion to the truth as it is in Jesus'[6] – the Scots appropriated for themselves the right to define a (far from monolithic) group and the standards its religious observance and commitment should be striving towards. That this group might have or form its own narrative and myth of truth and redemption which would give meaning to its existence is not something that could be accommodated within the missionaries' narrative (c.f. Chapter 1). The missionaries were clear that Jews who converted to Protestantism would likely have been ostracised from their family and community, which without a doubt reflected the reality of the situation.[7]

Secondly, the 19th century was also a time when social and philanthropic concerns dominated the agenda, particularly in Scotland.[8] This concern to help others would have been a factor in missionary work, but it was always meant to be subservient to conversion – what was being changed was the process by which the target population could be reached.[9]

The third contextual element is the wider context of the missionary movement as a whole, for none of the Scottish missionaries operated in a 'missionary vacuum', and all would have had some contact with other missionaries to the Jews and missionaries to other peoples. It is notable in this regard that some of the missionaries were called to their positions from other missionary fields, for example, Paterson worked in Aden and Cairo and visited South Africa before going to Hebron. They would already have experienced being in a context that was not dominated by (Evangelical) Christianity.[10]

The Scots employed three main strategies: confrontation, education, and medicine. These were standard methods of missionary enterprise and were being developed in different forms around the globe by western missionaries from all ecclesiastical and national backgrounds, including in the Near East by Scots and others. In this context, the missionaries, of course, thought they were using the best tools and resources available to them.[11]

Considering the wider context of the global missionary movement and the Near East does not, however, preclude individual developments (including the perceived failure of existing practice) on the ground for the Scottish missionaries. Although described separately here, their usage, of course, often overlapped.

Confrontation

The first Scots who went on an exploratory trip to Palestine in 1839 argued for 'controversial' skills, in other words, direct confrontation.[12] Recent experience of Jewish missions was not available to them, this being, for the Scots at least, a new field. Joseph Wolff's expeditions on behalf of the LJS provided for many a basis on which to work: the Scots knew about his travels, and it is reasonable to assume that they would have read his journals, published between 1827 and 1829. Wolff, by his own account,[13] had converted to Protestant Christianity having been born into a German Jewish family with a rabbi as a father. To himself and to others, he would have served as an example of what Jews could become. The Scots met with John Nicolayson, effectively Wolff's successor, and were advised by him – or, depending on one's perspective, had their previously-held views confirmed by him – that disputation would prove to be the most effective tool in seeking conversion: they wrote that a 'Missionary ought to be well grounded in prophecy, and he should be one who fully and thoroughly adopts the principles of literal interpretation ... in order to fit him for reasoning with Jews' – 'controversial' skills were required.[14] However, 'Talmudical logic'[15] – whatever that might be – was required. Interestingly, they do not clarify exactly how this 'Talmudical logic' actually functioned, though one can note in passing that one of the main problems they saw for Jews they encountered was 'Talmudism',[16] which they interpreted to mean an excessively strict adherence to Jewish law. If 'Talmudical logic' perhaps entailed argument based on Jewish law, the missionaries would appear to be wanting to prosecute their cause against a pattern of behaviour with principles established from the origins of this behaviour.

One of the practical implements for effecting change that the Scots recommended, based on discussions with those already working in the field, was the use of evangelical tracts, although this had to be done carefully, since, as they put it,

> [t]he most useful tract for a Jew is a plain Christian tract, such as one would give to a careless professing Christian, setting before him the simple truth of his lost condition, and the death and atonement of Christ. This is much better than a deficient controversial tract. If it is controversial, it ought to be complete, for otherwise a Jew, accustomed as he is ... to acute reasoning, will soon see its deficiency and throw it aside.[17]

In its early workings, this was clearly one of the approaches that the JMCs encouraged: there were efforts to procure tracts for the short-lived mission in Damascus in the 1840s and the proposed library indicates an acceptance that straightforward argument was seen to be a suitable method to win Jewish converts to Protestantism. The medical facilities proposed for Damascus in order to reach Jews more effectively were not agreed upon and the idea of medicine being a tool in this way in the Levant did not arise until the Tiberias mission was initiated.

Confrontation represented a direct but exclusivist approach avoiding any compromise with the missionaries' truth: wholehearted conversion and true salvation were offered in and for themselves without the complicating trappings of education or medicine (the Scots, of course, held that only their Protestant Evangelical understanding of the gospel offered the possibility of true salvation).[18] Compromise, such as perhaps allowing for the possibility of elements of religious truth in Judaism or Islam that could be retained whilst adopting Protestant beliefs, was not regarded as a viable possibility.[19]

Because compromise was impossible, when missionaries argued (correctly) that e.g. for a Jew to convert would result in ostracisation from their family and community, the missionaries were also arguing, in effect, for self-ostracisation, in the form of a rejection of a former way of life. This, unsurprisingly, was never openly acknowledged by the missionaries, although they regularly referred to potential converts worried about ostracisation.

Throughout the period under consideration in this book, confrontational methods of missionary endeavour formed the backbone of all missionary work in the Levant. Regardless of how else the missionaries tried to communicate their message (for example, through education or medicine, examined below), it was always cloaked in the mantle of verisimilitude based on their understanding of the gospel message. Only through a clear rejection of past beliefs and acceptance of the gospel that the missionaries proclaimed was there to be any hope of redemption from sin – all these terms being defined, of course, only by the missionaries, as for example, this exchange between the Tiberias mission's Biblewoman[20] and a Bedouin woman shows:

> "Are you a sinner?" – "No," indignantly, "I am not a sinner."
> "Do you tell lies?" – "Sometimes."
> "Do you curse?" – "Yes, many times."
> "Swear?" – "Very often."
> "Steal?" – "Well, sometimes – olives."
> "Hate? quarrel?" – "Oh yes, very often."
> "Well, all that is sin." – "That is sin?"
> "Yes; now are you not a sinner?" – "God knows!"[21]

No context to this conversation is given beyond the role of the Biblewoman, but one might wonder what this Bedouin woman was to make of the knowledge that she should henceforth regard herself as a sinner. Although the missionary described the woman's actions as 'sin', the closing exclamation appears to indicate that the Evangelical thinking behind this meant little if anything to her. To understand this more fully, a broader context is needed: pre-millenarian Evangelical theology was essentially pessimistic in its world-view,[22] in apparent (strange) contrast to the general feeling of the age, particularly in Britain, which, with the empire at its height around the turn of the century, seemed to many to have reached a point of ever-increasing dynamism, progress and development[23] with no end in sight.[24] However, this contrast can be explained not by reference to progress, but to pilgrimage as a *Leitmotiv* of Victorian Evangelical theology, reflected most obviously, perhaps, in some of its hymnody: 'Strangers and pilgrims here below,/We seek a home above'.[25] In this context, the discussion about the Bedouin woman's 'sin' would represent – in the missionaries' understanding – the first stage of a pilgrimage to overcome such sin: a need for an understanding of personal sin, followed by a recognition of the attendant negative implications for an individual's relationship with God, closing with a resolution of this situation in the form of acceptance of the (Evangelical) gospel – and rejection of past behaviour, including religious practices. Whether this particular conversation was part of such an ongoing 'pilgrimage' is not clear, but regardless of whether it actually took place in this form or not, it can be taken as representing a typal interaction, implied, not least, by the wider context of the chapter.

Although confrontation and the appeal to the missionaries' understanding of reason dominated the initial approach to Jews, its ineffectiveness meant it could not be the only method used to approach the target populations.

Education

Education was the first of the additional methods employed by the churches in their missionary activity.[26] Scottish education was highly regarded and the JMCs, in seeking to expand their influence, sought to use education from an early stage: Daniel was sent to Damascus as a teacher, though the Free Kirk withdrawal from Damascus prevented further development by the Scots. The United Presbyterians in Aleppo pursued education, including with the British Consul, this being described as 'religious', though basic literacy skills would undoubtedly have formed part of this project, had it been implemented. The Tiberias and Safad missions had educational and medical facilities (in Safad, medicine was later dropped), but one of the most important forays into education by Jewish missions was Tabeetha, bequeathed to the churches in 1911. The Scots did not operate schools as part of the Hebron mission.

Ottoman policy as pursued by Sultan Abdülhamid II emphasised the Islamic nature of his position in order to encourage the loyalty of his Arab notables, thereby seeking to ensure the power of western states was kept within limited confines in the core regions of his empire. Through the various aspects of *tanzimat* reform, he encouraged, amongst other things, the creation of new professional schools and teacher training facilities. Although the later years of his reign saw ever-increasing censorship emerge, which to a certain extent impinged on education,[27] it was understood that a populace able to compete with western states was needed, and that both Ottoman and foreign schools could contribute to this. Concessions granted to western powers for trade by the Ottoman empire included the necessary freedom for religious activity that gave missionary bodies the space within which to operate. Documented and described in various ways,[28] the influx of foreign capital in the latter part of the 19th century of necessity reduced

Ottoman control of some areas of public life; religious practice and education were among the areas where influence was most strongly contested.

The missionaries' educational services can therefore be understood as part of the trend within the Empire towards enabling greater participation in an international context dominated by western European language and culture. For example, although Arabic was specified as the language of instruction to Gwladys Jones she was told that 'Hebrew and English shall both be taught as languages'[29] – the latter the language of the dominant imperial power and the former the language of the hoped-for-converts and putative self-governing individuals – the educators also extended their reach beyond the confines of the school curriculum into the private sphere: Stockdale cites Walker-Arnott, writing in 1880, before her school became part of the Scottish churches' missions, describing a pupil 'actively altering her home environment as a result of her mission education'.[30] The children, it was hoped, would become an active influence on the parents, ultimately leading them to Christian belief,[31] and in that sense the prohibitions that were regularly reported back to Scotland by the missionaries were seen as a mark of success in reaching the families of the children.

Education was seen by the missionaries as offering not only an opportunity to encourage belief in (their version of) Christianity, but was also perceived to be a way of improving the culture and general environment of the people they found themselves amongst. Like the Americans in Syria, Scottish missionaries in Palestine, when pressed, would argue that their purpose was not explicitly the conversion of Ottoman subjects.[32] On the other hand, their educational programmes were not explicitly meant to Anglicise the indigenous population ('A gospel neither German nor British but Jewish must be preached to the Jew'[33]) in the way that Macaulay on a governmental level sought to turn children in India into English people 'in taste, in opinion, in morals and in intellect'[34] even if he could do nothing about their colour and blood (a 'mental miscegenation', to use Benedict Anderson's language, Macaulay not seeking to convert the 'idolaters' to Christianity, but to Englishness). The missionaries were, of course, convinced of the superiority of their offering: as they saw it, their education was not just responsible for reading and writing,[35] but included science (a new subject for most schools in Palestine at the time)[36], 'cleanliness'[37] and 'hygiene',[38] aspects of domesticity (for girls: housework, knitting and embroidery, for example)[39] and industrial and agricultural training (for boys: although some fishing took place, further plans were frustrated, c.f. Chapter 3 above),[40] good behaviour (in the widest sense[41]): in other words, a holistic and rounded education as an ideal of the best education Scotland could offer:

> It should be our aim to set a good example to the people in the art of training the young, and to establish model schools where mental improvement is energetically cultivated, where physical training is not neglected, and where spiritual nurture is sympathetically imparted.[42]

The representative function ('a good example') was clearly part of the missionary purpose: offering an education that was superior in quality to anything offered by the local communities[43] would not only to encourage attendance at the Scots' institutions rather than any others (e.g. the LJS or AIU), but would also send a clear signal of the benevolent intentions of the mission station as a whole, and be a model for an emerging and developing people.[44] The export of western-style education was seen as a way of equipping the children of Palestine for integration into the world at large, a way of developing and building a nation, and whilst not propagated as explicitly as in the Mandate era Anglican schools,[45] there was a clear sense that the schools, teaching Arabic, Hebrew and English, were able to bridge the divides between the communities in a way that Jewish (e.g. AIU) or state/Muslim schools,[46] regardless of the quality or otherwise of their teaching, could not do. This, then, is where Macaulayism,[47] the conflation of Christianity and civilisation in education with 'civilising' as its aim, becomes most apparent. This is perhaps especially so in that the Scots brought about very few converts to Protestantism, but a considerable number of talented and well-educated Ottoman subjects, who were able to play a full part in the important debates that helped shape the future of their region at the turn of the century and beyond.[48]

This points to a link between the method of education and the theme of confrontation. Whilst confrontation has been described above as a missionary method, it is, in a different sense, the most appropriate term to use in relation to the understanding of missionary educational systems in the Ottoman context. Although the Scottish missions were smaller than the American missions in Anatolia and Syria, for example, the Scots, especially in the north of Palestine, formed a significant part of the foreign missionary educational contingent. In some places the Scots represented the only western missionary educational offering,[49] meaning that if parents wished to give their children a western-based education, the Scottish schools were their only option (it is worth pointing out that as AIU schools[50] spread throughout Palestine, many missionary schools – not just those of the Scots – suffered the loss of Jewish children). But in no other matter, as Deringil has coherently argued,[51] did the Ottoman state feel so threatened as in the area of education, which offered children, the subjects and decision-makers of the future Ottoman empire, an alternative ideology to that of the Ottoman state: 'when we speak of the struggle between the missionaries and the Ottoman government, [we are] dealing with nothing less than ideological war, a war that challenged the very basis of Ottoman legitimacy among Christian and Muslim'.[52] Although Deringil bases much of his argument on American missionaries working mainly with Armenian and other minorities, the argument can equally be seen in relation to smaller Protestant missionary organisations.[53]

Ottoman legislation on religious freedom, introduced partly as a result of pressure from the western powers, was understood differently by the missionaries/western governmental authorities and the Ottomans. Whilst the westerners saw the rulings as granting the freedom for Ottoman subjects to *change* their religion, the Ottomans saw in them the freedom to *defend* their existing religion. Deringil cites a question of the Ottoman ambassador to London:

Can it be supposed that whilst condemning religious persecutions, the Sublime Porte has consented to permit offence and insult to any creed whatever? That at the same time as she was proclaiming liberty to all non-Mussulman creeds, she had given them arms against Islamism? That she had, in fine, destroyed at the same stroke the guarantees with which she surrounded the liberty of religious conviction?[54]

Indeed, the missionaries were always aware that direct proselytising to Muslims would be severely dealt with; they did not openly pursue it, hoping Jews and especially Oriental Christians (once they had become Protestants) would convert them in due course. However, the Ottomans (correctly) perceived there to be a close relationship between the missionaries and their home countries' imperial ambitions and representatives,[55] and this insidious intrusion of western thought into Ottoman territories threatened, in the Sultan's view, the future of the existing order far more even than threats of an economic and military nature,[56] which could be dealt with there and then, given sufficient planning and resources. This explains in part, at least, the problems around obtaining permission for school buildings, with the conversion of ordinary houses, something that was regularly done until such time as more appropriate premises could be obtained or built, coming in for particularly strong criticism because it was seen as a more covert means of opening schools. The governor of the *vilayet* of Syria recorded the extent of missionary teaching, in the absence of comparable educational establishments of the Ottoman state, and urged counter-measures: 'Jesuit and Protestant schools therefore accept non-Muslim children free of charge, clothe and feed them and even pay subsidies to their parents'.[57] As has been shown above, this is indeed a reasonably accurate picture of the Scots' activities, though it would tend usually to include Muslims, and the 'subsidies to ... parents' would not have existed in any structured way, but be at most occasional relief to the poor.[58] Ottoman concern at the missionaries' impact was undoubtedly justified, but the unwillingness to engage in large-scale conflict with the European powers over this issue meant that although occasional harassment took place, the missionaries were relatively free to pursue their aims.[59]

However, although it is easy when examining missions to assume that large numbers of (Jewish, Christian and Muslim) children passed through their schools and were therefore given a western education that stood in competition to Ottoman establishments, Ottoman educational efforts under the aegis of the *tanzimat* reforms were undoubtedly more effective at reaching the majority of children – the missionaries, after all, could only afford to work in a limited number of localities, and central though these may often have been (major cities such as Jerusalem, Beirut and Cairo, or important towns such as Aleppo, Tiberias or Jaffa), there were far more Ottoman than missionary schools in the empire, and their influence was correspondingly greater.[60] Where Ottoman and missionary schools competed, the hostility could be intense, with both sides using war-like language.[61] Viewed from a historical perspective at least, the Ottoman aim of creating an educated middle-class that could later take the empire forward as the global context developed was fulfilled, whether they attended Ottoman or missionary schools, with those attending the latter mostly remaining within their existing communities and continuing to be loyal subjects.

In summary then, missionary educational efforts, although meeting resistance from the Ottoman state, were seen by the Scots as a way for the missionaries to improve their relationship to the local population and gain inroads, via the children, to the families and communities of the area, particularly as the confrontational model was generally so unsuccessful in this regard. The other tool to compensate for the confrontational model's inadequacy was medicine.

Medicine

Although a medical missionary was suggested for Damascus, it was in Tiberias and Safad in the 1880s, and several years later in Hebron, that the Scots fully exploited medicine as a method for missionary work.

This fits a worldwide pattern: generally, medical missions are seen as coming into their own only in the last 25 years of the nineteenth century, though they had originated much earlier, with Rev Peter Parker's mission in China. Parker, a medical and theology graduate from Yale, worked there in the 1820s and 1830s. The creation of the EMMS in 1841 was a direct result of Parker's address to a group of medical and ministerial practitioners in Edinburgh, part of a tour he made having had to leave China because of the First Opium War. Groups supporting his work and exploring their own place in the new field of medical missions were created in various British and American cities. By the latter part of the 19th century, an unprecedented expansion in medical missions had taken place around the globe, 'fostered by the Victorian period's stability, medical capabilities, and personal availability' as well as a social concern for the poor arising out of a deep sense of personal piety which led to a desire to help those in need regardless of personal cost.[62] With the development of 'scientific medicine, especially surgery, epidemiology, and pharmacology' and the manifest ability to cure once-fatal diseases, the medical profession gained in acceptability not only with mission boards, but also with their supporting public – medical missions grew alongside the growth and establishment of the medical profession itself.[63] It was easy to define and describe what a medical missionary might achieve, which was not always the case with an ordained missionary. From the perspective of missionary organisations, medical missions therefore served (at least) two clear purposes: (a) they were a way of straightforwardly assisting people in need; (b) they resonated with the donating public who could easily witness the direct benefit to the target population of the funds they were giving. A further explanation for the growth of medical missions is that they provided a 'lever' with which to gain access to a target population that might otherwise be reticent to allow access to missionaries – Walls quotes Herbert Lankaster of the CMS: 'It was as heavy artillery that medical missions were used above all: in the less responsive fields, in Islamic societies, and above all in China'.[64] Walls' analysis of the development of medical missions highlights four distinct factors: the imitative (obediency to Jesus, who healed people and commanded his disciples to do likewise), the humanitarian/philanthropic, the utilitarian (preserving the health of the missionaries themselves), and the strategic ('the acceptability of medical missions when no other form of mission could gain a hearing').[65]

By the time the missions in Tiberias/Safad and later in Hebron were being developed, health care in Britain had come on a long way from the 1840s, when a medical mission had first been suggested for Damascus: the shocking state of Britain's inner cities (which had undergone a huge population explosion with the advent of industrialisation) and the high death rate from infectious diseases such as cholera had spurred great advances in public health, and coupled with technical advances in medical practice and the regulation of the profession with the 1858 Medical Act, medicine became a much more obvious missionary tool. It is easy to understand the place of Tiberias in such a model: healing the sick, particularly in the very region that Jesus is supposed to have carried out most of his healing ministry, would have great geopious attractions. Secondly, providing a service to those in need: the Jews of Tiberias and Safad, regularly described as poor and without significant material support, would have been an obvious target for social concern.[66] Thirdly, concern for the health of the missionaries was felt to be a real issue,[67] with numerous descriptions of the 'unhealthiness of the place':[68] the missionary doctors regularly treated each other.[69] Finally, the strategic concern was repeatedly referred to as a demonstration of the success of the mission in reaching people. Torrance provided an example of the strategic benefits of a medical missionary:

> for a time the mission was boycotted by the Jews ... [but] gradually the opposition was overcome ... One of the rabbis had been specially bitter and stubborn in his opposition ... [but he] fell ill ... [and] would not ... send for me; but one morning ... his son ... frantically besought me to come to his father. I was able to give him immediate relief, for which he has never ceased to be grateful, and, as far as I know, he has never since opposed the medical mission.[70]

Even at the very beginning of his career in Tiberias, Torrance wrote about his need for quality medicines, stating that, amongst other things, he was 'anxious to make a good impression from the beginning, so as to gain the confidence of my patients at least'.[71]

However, occasional concern was also expressed about the amount of medical work, and that this might create problems to the detriment of mission's work as a whole.[72] Seen in this way, the strategic angle became self-defeating, as the means (medical care) took up so much time that the ends (preaching the gospel and creating converts) became impossible to implement, or were in some way restricted, as this summary of speeches by Gustav Dalman of Leipzig held in Glasgow and Edinburgh indicates:

> The value of medical missions is unquestionable, but perhaps their methods might be improved. The multitudes in the dispensary, to be seen and prescribed for by the doctor within certain hours, make spiritual work for him practically impossible. This is left, therefore, mainly to assistants ... [which] is not quite satisfactory. A Christian physician dwelling among the Jews, visiting their sick, the friend of their homes, the

help of their poor, would find many doors open to him, and splendid openings for individual spiritual work. The annual number of cases might be less, but numbers here are of little importance. It would surely be a good principle for medical missions – fewer cases, more visiting of the sick, more individual work, not only by assistants, but by the medical missionary himself.[73]

However, the Scottish missionaries saw this differently. Whilst Torrance might have complained of overwork in the hospital (Ewing records 2, 000 patients being treated each month),[74] there are no records of him turning patients away (quite the contrary, he appears to have attempted to resolve every medical case he came across),[75] and whilst he was unhappy about the lack of opportunity afforded him to engage more with the population, he argued this highlighted the need for additional staff to share the medical cases and make more time for teaching and preaching.[76] In addition, this argument, notable for its division between the 'spiritual' and the 'material', would not have been persuasive for Torrance and the like, who argued that missionary work consisted of a way of life as well as what was taught: i.e. by caring unreservedly for the sick, they saw themselves as living witnesses to their faith, exactly as the instructions to Torrance had stated when he first went to Palestine: 'It should ever be kept in view that these results ['the enlightenment of their minds, the salvation of their souls' etc.] will be most effectively secured when, to the religious instruction communicated, is added the example of a holy and consistent life'.[77] This kind of holistic approach was typical of 19th century Scottish Evangelicalism, which laid great stress on living a 'godly life'.

Grundmann emphasises the educational nature of medical missionary work, making it clear that medical education, both formally and informally, played a significant role beyond the confines of medical practice. The Scottish missions fit elements of his description of the role of such work. These are firstly, the search for 'scientific truth' which emerged as a by-product of the practice of scientific medicine; secondly, a moral position on the sanctity of life which Grundmann contrasts with the cultures the missionaries were in;[78] and thirdly, the faith position that motivated such work:

In addition to transferring medical skill and know-how they wanted to impart to their students a consciousness of the values implied in the exercise of the art, values of intercultural validity: the authentic commitment of those missions' doctors to help others, even at the expense of tremendous personal, career, and financial gain. They themselves were telling examples who showed that the power to do this work lay in a strong personal faith and commitment.[79]

Peter Williams argues that particularly in Scottish Presbyterianism, the desire to educate was as much a part of the medical mission as the physical healing itself, and that this confluence of Christianity and civilisation was an element of evangelisation: in other words, the desire 'for the erection of a christian civilization'.[80] Towards the end of the 19th century, in which Grundmann sees 'Victorian stability' (p153 above), Williams sees clear links to imperialism and the communication of Western cultural models: an 'impetus to benevolence ... came from the puritan, and often Scottish, concern to relate christianity and civilization and it became more convincing as an imperialistic cast of mind became dominant'.[81]

The communication of 'standards and values' (to borrow from the title of Grundmann's article) clearly played a role in the Scots' work, as the description of the hospital as a 'real Bethel' (p79 above) shows. Bethel (i.e. בֵּית־אֵל) refers to e.g. Gen 35:15, meaning 'house of God'[82] – in itself a powerful claim of divine involvement – and the comparison between the 'squalid huts and tents' and the 'sweetness', 'cleanness' and 'abundance' of the hospital represented not only the 'civilised European' to the 'semi-demi-semi-European and civilised' Palestinians (Torrance, Chapter 5, note 136 below), but was a metaphor for personal redemption suggested by Old and New Testament texts: the imagery of uncleanliness as a mark of evil and sin, and cleanliness as a mark of redemption and forgiveness, would have been known to many who used the hospital.[83]

Assessing the extent to which the missionaries were successful in communicating their 'standards and values' can be a difficult task, though one measure would be the acceptance into institutions with western-style entrance criteria, such as the Syrian Protestant College in Beirut or institutions in Europe, and in this limited way, a measure of success can be identified. One of the most famous examples of such acceptance would be Leon Levison, who left Tiberias for Edinburgh after conversion to Christianity and became involved in the International Hebrew Christian Alliance as well as being the superintendent of the Edinburgh Jewish Medical Mission for many decades; he was eventually knighted, achieving a level of civil recognition that perhaps even exceeded his impact on the Scottish and international ecclesiastical scene.[84] This is a pointer to the influence that missionary efforts had, which the next section examines.

The influence of the missions on the target population

In terms of measuring the influence the missionaries had on the target population, an obvious place to begin is to examine the known conversions that took place: this was the missions' primary and clearest objective.

Conversions as a measure of influence and success

However, in terms of conversions, the conclusion has to be that the numbers were negligible, as fits Hobsbawm's general description of missions.[85] Whilst calculating an exact number of conversions is difficult, the fact the JMCs appear to note (and celebrate) each one in their minutes, and this happens only rarely, means it can be safely assumed that there were few conversions.

Potential conversions were sometimes also recorded (e.g. p76 above). Cohen, referred to above, was one of the very few converts to find gainful employment with the mission. However, this was generally not viewed as a favourable option:

Mr Soutar ... [wrote] that a young Jew had been ... coming to him for instruction with a view to baptism, and that it would be "absolutely impossible for him to make his confession and then stay in Safed," and asking if it would be advisable "to send him to some of our other Jewish Mission Stations." The Committee greatly sympathise with their Missionaries in connection with such cases, but are unable to advise the removal of inquirers to other station to facilitate baptism.[86]

Soutar would have been aware of the ease with which *dhimmis* could travel in the Ottoman empire, and so the decision to appoint this Jew – and secure the conversion – would have been dependent only upon the JMC. However, whilst employment of converts in the mission stations was discouraged, sending converts to Scotland was almost positively forbidden. Missionaries were warned several times that their employers did not wish to find Jewish enquirers or converts from Palestine turning up in Edinburgh seeking support, particularly material support, as this note (addressed to all Free Kirk JMC mission stations) shows:

The Convener having called attention to the inconvenient practice of young men being sent home from Mission Stations, as Students or otherwise, it was agreed to address a circular to the Missionaries to the effect that in no case should anyone be encouraged to come to this country, until the case has been reported to the Committee, and their sanction gained.[87]

It is almost superfluous to note that on the few occasions when a case was brought to the JMC's attention, sanction was generally withheld. Similar messages reappear at various times, presumably because the Committee perceived a need for them: the missionaries appear to have at times, at least, ignored previous such orders. Baptism represented a very public acceptance of the missionaries' theology, which for most Jews would have resulted in severe social consequences, and so few took this public step, even though they perhaps continued sending their children to the missionary schools, or themselves attended services, evening classes, or used the missionary hospital.[88] It can be concluded, then, that the level of success and influence in terms of conversion was minimal, particularly when bearing in mind that this was after all the primary objective of the missions.[89]

However, this lack of converts did not serve to disillusion the missionary committees, even if individual missionaries became disheartened (Brown, Wortabet). John Hall, reviewing Jewish missions for the United Free Kirk in 1914, wrote that

Doubt is frequently ... cast upon the value of ... [Jewish missions], judged especially as to their results. These mission efforts are popularly supposed to be practically a failure. Nothing could be further from the truth, as a little careful inquiry speedily shows. The Jew is becoming Christian at a much quicker rate than is the heathen, and the future is great with expectancy.[90]

Although he outlines some statistics that purport to show that 'the converts [from Judaism] are eight times more numerous than those coming in from heathenism'[91] the vague notion of 'expectancy' is in fact all that he can offer, since

> no statistical tables can set forth the true figures relating to the progress of the Gospel amongst the Jews. Many are secret believers and delay a public profession until circumstances ... [of] residence or otherwise ... involve less difficulty and persecution. Also in the missionary schools are many young people who have received Christian teaching and training, yet are compelled to postpone an open adherence to Christianity ... [in addition] the effects of itineracy work are very inadequately reflected in the returns reported upon by the missionary societies: the missionary never knows how Christ has revealed Himself to those who sought not after Him.[92]

In these two paragraphs lie the defence of all the Jewish mission workers throughout the years covered by this book: the conversions may be few in number, but the effect on the hearts of those addressed cannot be known, and the prospect of large-scale conversions is always imminent, if only the Christian churches would exercise more patience and continue to support the work. This reflects the eschatological hope found in Davidson's theological exposition[93] and is repeated year after year in JMC reports to the church. For example, in the presentation of the JMC Report to the General Assembly of 1897, the following comment was made:

> When [critics] spoke of absence of results ... they were confining themselves to a numerical estimate. There were results ... which could not be tabulated, yet they were not the least valuable fruit of mission work. Prejudices were being removed; Christianity was being understood; Christ Himself was being recognised in the excellence of His character; and thus a leavening process was at work throughout Judaism. One great encouragement was to be found in the opposition of the Rabbis. Whenever ecclesiastics bitterly hated a movement, and fiercely persecuted its followers, one might be pretty certain it was of God. (Applause.)[94]

These views – the difficulty in quantifying success, the diminution of 'prejudice', rabbinical opposition as a mark of success – dominated the rationale for further expenditure on Jewish missions.[95] Indeed, a century later, Mary Torrance,[96] a colleague of Herbert Torrance in Tiberias in the early 1950s, argued in an interview that one could never know how many Jewish people subjected to missionary activity might hold Christian beliefs, even if not evidenced by baptism:

> **Michael Marten**: In terms of comparison with missions in other parts of the world, relatively few people actually were converted. There were a number of notable Hebrew Christians from Tiberias as a result of the mission work, but it was relatively few ...
> **Mary Torrance**: ... you see you don't know that ...

MM: ... well, who were baptised ... clearly, you can't know whether people don't want to be baptised because of the social consequences but the actual numbers were relatively small when compared to missions that they [the missionaries] would know about in other parts of the world, in Africa or ...

MT: ... do you know, I don't know, because people worked in very tough Jewish situations, and you didn't see the results, perhaps ... you know, what Dr [Herbert] Torrance would say about this, 'we don't know about the possibilities of change' ... [of one person MT described:] she may well have been baptised years later and produced many converts herself.

MM: The reason that I ask is that ... in terms of the church's records, the church committees, in order to seek funds, needed to show statistics ... what they want to know is how can they ... compete with other demands within the wider church if they can't show a single convert for the previous year ... so what I'm trying to get to is ... [that] people ... [who converted] were fairly rare, and I was wondering in how far ... the difficulty in producing statistics [for Herbert Torrance]...

MT: ... I'm sure that he found that difficult ... but I have no doubt things were effective, I really don't have any doubts ... [later on] they might go to the Church of England to get baptised ... it wouldn't happen the way it happened here [in Scotland] ... so you never knew.[97]

The Jewish missionary movement in Scotland came from the Evangelical wing of the church, and, as Jongeneel points out, it is generally Roman Catholic and Evangelical missions that show most interest in statistical evidence of missionary activity and success, whilst what he describes as their 'Ecumenical companions' tended to have a greater interest in the more general notion of the

> kingdom of God rather than for the size of the churches, and its struggling with the presence of Christ outside the 'gate' (Hebr. 13:12) of the churches rather than with the 'unreached people' who will be lost if they will not accept Christ as their personal Lord and Saviour.[98]

Jongeneel, in his analysis of Christian mission statistics,[99] does not address what is apparent from the evidence here: that although Jewish missions clearly emanated from the Evangelical wing of the churches, the circumstances which led to the lack of converts meant it was impossible for these missions to measure their achievements in traditional 'Evangelical' ways, since these measurements could only lead to the conclusion that the work was failing dismally. Instead, the propagators of the mission work adopted a more 'Ecumenical' approach (Jongeneel's terminology, though its use in this context is problematic[100]), utilising subjective instead of objective means of measurement. The former are more difficult to quantify, but perhaps point to more meaningful measures of influence than do the latter;[101] and so, given the failure in 'Evangelical' terms (Jongeneel), historical assessments of the missions' influence, like those of the missionaries, need to look beyond the formal sacrament of baptism to other measures.

Other measures of influence and success

One measure of influence and success has been hinted at on p156: Grundmann's communication of 'standards and values', measured, perhaps, by Palestinians (of any religion) joining institutions with western-style entrance criteria such as the Syrian Protestant College. This is an indication of a level of appropriation by local actors of elements of the missionaries' offerings: conversion was not a part of this, whereas the utilisation of the missionaries' education and medicine was. Hobsbawm argues that this is the defining characteristic of 19th century missionary endeavour in general, applying mostly to the élites, and when it did not,

> to the chagrin of the more unbending missionaries, what indigenous peoples adopted was not so much the faith imported from the west as those elements in it which made sense to them in terms of their own system of beliefs and institutions, or demands ... This was so even where the faithful nominally followed the orthodoxies of their denomination. But they were also apt to develop their own versions of the faith ... What imperialism brought to the elites or potential elites of the dependent world was therefore essentially 'westernization'.[102]

Hobsbawm's 'westernization' took place in a context of contesting world-views: here, in the Scottish/Levant context, the missionaries' perceived their world-view to be based most significantly on a particular theological position and they offered education and medicine to try, as they saw it, to gain access to Jews and others in order to offer them a way of adopting this world-view.[103] However, whilst the evidence shows that the local population could obviously see the benefits of the Scots' education and medicine for themselves in their own environment (Scottish accounts of ever-increasing demand and usage indicate this), they did not use it as a path to appropriation of the new world-view.

It is in this that local agency, generally not explicitly acknowledged in the missionaries' communications, can be seen to have wrought change: had the missionaries persisted solely with the confrontational methodology, as Joseph Wolff did to little lasting effect, then the anger and offence Bonar and McCheyne at times described would have done little to reassure the missionaries that their message was being well-received. On the other hand, the regular references to the 'access' education and medicine provided (e.g. the daily teaching at the clinics before surgery began) show that the missionaries' facilities indeed enabled greater contact to local people. That local people appear to have been willing to tolerate, but mostly no more than that, these attempts at conversion in order to gain access to the Scots' education and medicine, does not seem to have occurred to the missionaries. Local actors' accommodation, even embrace of the missionaries' services shows that despite missionary claims to continually decreasing 'prejudice' against the Christian gospel etc. on the part of Jews, claims of increased access aiding conversion were therefore a misinterpretation of local actors' behaviour.

These claims are most readily observed in the field of education. For example, a travel account published in 1883 by Andrew Thomson, a minister from Edinburgh, described a visit to a Damascus educational establishment run by 'Irish and American Protestant missionaries' (almost certainly the successor to the Scots' Damascus mission): they saw

> a large class for young men ... conducted by one of the missionary brethren. They read along with him in Arabic, and were examined on ... Romans [chapter 9]. The intelligence and promptitude of their answers surprised us. The name of God was never mentioned by them without some adoring epithet, – such as "God, Most High." We were struck with the look of elation and awakened thought which Christian education always gives to the countenance of a convert, as compared with those who continue slumbering in their old darkness and error.[104]

The supposed contrast between 'darkness and error' and 'elation and awakened thought' was a common missionary claim: experience in India, for example, which was widely seen as having a 'civilisation not dissimilar to that of ancient Egypt, Babylonia, Greece or Rome',[105] sought to 'raise ... [the lower caste pupil] mentally, morally, socially, spiritually, so that in his lowly labour he will yet rise to the level of a man, and never sink below it',[106] whilst for the upper-classes the aim was to develop 'an intimacy of touch with the West hitherto impossible'.[107] With the recognition of Levantine (Jewish, Christian and to a lesser extent Muslim[108]) culture as having a value and complexity on a par with civilisations such as were found in India and China, the missionaries had a similar sense that bringing western-style education to the region was bringing, beyond Macaulayism (since they wanted religious conversion too), the 'benefits' of the west to the east. Indeed – and here is the move from missionary claims to missionary practice – that e.g. the school in Jaffa employed girls that had completed their schooling to help teach the younger pupils is a mark of the accommodation of these girls to Walker-Arnott's expectations: she employed them since they fitted her vision of what school teachers should be. Equally, in the Sea of Galilee mission, some of the staff at the schools were former pupils, and this (re-)integration into local western-dominated institutions indicates an appropriation of what the schools represented by at least some of their pupils. Occasional records of pupils moving on to e.g. the Syrian Protestant College also point to this assessment.[109] Those who later taught, either at the school they had attended or elsewhere, and those who pursued further study became part of the élite that Hobsbawm describes. Since very few converted to Protestantism, his statement that indigenous people adopted only what they wanted from missionaries' offerings can be seen to apply here to almost everyone the missionaries tried to convert, whether part of the educated élite or those who made use of other services offered.[110]

Of course, the missionaries' understanding of the changes they effected and the impact their work had depended to a great extent on their perception of the situation in the Levant prior to their arrival. Chapter 1 has already gone some way to presenting

Scottish views of the Levant, using the three categories of the image of the local churches, biblical understandings in relation to the land, and Jews' place in the divine economy. Given that the missionaries' image of the local churches was a predominantly negative one, that their understanding of the land as a theological concept was not connected in a meaningful way to the reality they encountered, and that the Jews that they had contact with were only seen as a part of their own model of the divine economy, what they saw, heard, experienced and related to their constituencies in Scotland was clearly an image that mostly suited their own purposes. From this position, any influence they might have which would make the context they encountered 'better' would be an improvement in their eyes (this would mean more like their own image of what it should be – e.g. raising people 'mentally, morally, socially, spiritually ... to the level of a man'). Had they been able to imagine and then describe to supporters in Scotland the local population utilising their services with no intention of converting, the implications for a mission basing its financial security on prospective conversions would have been disastrous – and this in itself would be a factor in their denying this interpretation of the situation.

Reculturation: the influence of the missionary encounter on the missionaries

The missionaries generally started their work with a clear understanding of their purpose, and, confident in their assumed superiority of culture and civilisation, were clear that personal changes (e.g. religious conversion) would occur primarily within the context of their target population, rather than with themselves and their own attitudes. However, understanding the missionaries necessitates more than their own representation of their (ideal?) self-identity: it must be self-identity qualified by their encounter with people of other cultures. This process has been defined by Susan McAllister as 'reculturation':

> It is in the changes resulting from communications and interaction between different people where *culture* both occurs and exists as a differentiating process. *Reculturation* results when two or more cultures keep close contact and the effects of such contact resonates in the writing of both the imposed on and the imposing cultures. These points of change occur as cultures come into the evaluative process of redefinition when they encounter other cultures. In this evaluative process of redefinition, the members of one culture must reconsider not only the members of another culture, but they must also reconsider themselves in relation to and perhaps as part of that other culture.[111]

Although 'both the imposed on and the imposing cultures' will interpret reculturation in different ways, here, in keeping with the basis of this book, the missionaries' perspectives of their own reculturation will be examined in terms of their self-identity as Scottish Christian missionaries, and how they perceived that to change in encounter. Following McAllister's portrayal, culture in this context exists primarily in relation to the Other: in that sense it is a differentiating process.

The missionaries went to the Levant as examples of British imperial culture, with lifestyles, habits and attitudes that generally reflected their origins, which in terms of ecclesiastical, class and educational background have been examined in Chapter 4. Whilst confidence drove most of the missionaries in their work, lingering self-doubt, or doubts about the value of the work that was being carried out, manifested itself quite clearly in Aleppo, where first Brown, and then Wortabet departed. Brown explicitly explained his departure in terms of the failure of the mission to attract converts to Protestantism and his doubts that this situation would change, no matter what he tried to do. His role in the conversion process of local Jews was clearly the *raison d'être* of the Scottish mission, and once he no longer believed that he could be a successful agent of conversion, he could no longer function there. In the time that he had been in Aleppo, he had obviously undergone a dramatic change in his views and perspectives on the possibility of successful work.

Expressing their national identity as Scots, both an 'oppositional-marginal and dominant-central'[112] people in the context of the British Empire whose self-identity depended in substantial measure on the existence of Britain itself as a construct in which 'imperialism ... [became] the raison d'être of Britishness',[113] the missionaries can be clearly placed in relation to this construction of British identity dependent on imperial possession.[114] Whilst the Levant was not a formal imperial possession of Britain in the way that e.g. India was, the missionaries saw themselves in a role akin to that of an imperial power.[115] Their use of military and imperial language in this regard is illustrative: talk of 'occupying' or 'possessing' territories and the delineation of territory in connection with the LJS and Safad are clear markers of imperial modes of thought.[116] In terms of the missionaries' identity as Scottish and British, Gikandi has argued that the nations peripheral to England had a greater emotional investment (and, I would argue, need) for an invented British nationalism than the English aristocratic class had. He notes that,

> the invention of a British identity did not obliterate older loyalties ... but proffered a conduit through which such loyalties could be synthesized and, indeed, legitimated, by the civilizing mission embedded in doctrines of conquest and rule ... to be Scottish in the service of colonialism, was to belong to a larger, more compelling and authoritative narrative, one made possible by the imperial mission.[117]

The notion of overlapping identities[118] can be seen in that the missionaries referred almost exclusively to Scotland as 'home' and whilst English visitors were regarded as 'countrymen', the attachment to the construct 'Britain' manifested itself primarily in the missionaries' use of the imperial political might behind this idea, such as in relation to the British Consul's proposed activities in Aleppo or the LJS conflict in Safad. It becomes clear that the missionaries' primary national identification was to Scotland, and secondly to the British *Empire*, rather than to Britain (as the unified nation state of Scotland, Wales, Ireland and England). This element of their identity cannot be said to have undergone substantial change in a process of reculturation, rather, if anything, as the development of the imperial idea approached its zenith,[119] it was strengthened. This is a point illustrated not least by their general adherence to western dress, a powerful symbol of national and cultural identity. Rejecting local dress symbolised rejecting the local lifestyle, from both the male and the female perspectives. The importance of Victorian dress in symbolising moral rectitude and spiritual willingness to self-sacrifice is reflected in literature and imagery of the time (c.f. the representational function of clothing particularly for the female characters in novels such as *Jane Eyre* and *Tess of the D'Urbervilles*), and would have had meaning for the missionaries. There is no mention of it in official records, but Livingstone's biography of Torrance does show one image of him as a relatively young man 'in Arab Dress' (c.f. Figure 3-5 on p93); but this was almost certainly not his usual attire, with all other known pictures of him either in Western clothes, e.g. suit and hat (e.g. Figure 3-4 on p90), or, during the First World War, in military uniform (e.g. Figure 3-6 on p96). Similarly for other missionaries: there are virtually no images of missionaries wearing local dress during their working day. On the contrary, images of medical staff, for example, show traditional western-style nurses' and doctors' clothing, as illustrated in Figure 5-1 on p167, taken in 1906 (note Torrance sitting on the steps).[120]

Appearance offered a clear example of the possibility of reculturation: McAllister points to Chinese missionaries' adoption of local clothing as a marker of this, having unsuccessfully attempted to engage in mission work wearing western clothes. Chinese clothes changed this radically, according to the missionaries, and is an example of the missionaries reconsidering their position in relation to, and in, Chinese culture. For instance, Hudson Taylor 'believed the best way [for missionaries] to navigate around the inevitable "foreignness" of their appearance was to adopt Chinese dress and manners', despite their feelings of discomfort.[121] Conceding that Chinese dress was more appropriate to the climate of the country, Taylor crossed '[cultural] boundaries and challenge[d] the dogma of strict Victorian codes of dress and etiquette for the sake of making Jesus Christ's message of eternal salvation clear to the Chinese' and found benefits in terms of the ability to enter the domestic realm of the Chinese more readily, giving greater opportunities for preaching.[122] This was not an avenue that the Scots in the Levant seemed to have chosen to try and relate more appropriately to their target audience: even though one must take into account that photography in the 19th century was generally not a matter of 'snapshots' but of meticulously planned arrangements and settings which would have included a careful choice of suitable clothing designed to relate most clearly to the prospective viewer, had the Scots' adopted oriental dress for everyday purposes, it is reasonable to assume that it would have been commented upon – as Taylor did in China – or even photographed for the interest of supporters in Scotland. Clearly, the missionaries in the Levant hoped to achieve the inward conversion of Levantines without themselves undergoing outward conversion, to use (and distort) McAllister's analogy.[123]

However, the missionaries' purpose by definition required a level of both identification and reculturation with the local people they encountered, and most obviously this happened in terms of language: all the Jewish missionaries learnt at least Arabic and most a form of Hebrew or Yiddish, some of this before going to the Levant, much of it whilst there. This was widely seen as necessary from the first exploratory trip in 1839.[124] But language usage for the Scots had its limits, since schooling relied in part also on English language knowledge (compounding the paradox that although their religion – Protestantism – was to be integrated and adopted by the local people, this was to happen by means of a western-style education taught in part in a western language).[125] If, in the context of the confrontational model, one understands the (proposed) adoption of 'Talmudical' disputation as an attempt (however plausible it may or may not have been) to engage with local Jews, then this can perhaps be seen as the closest way in which Scottish modes of communication might have undergone reculturation – all of this consciously noted in a conditional form as there is no evidence to show that this suggestion was acted upon in any meaningful way; that the confrontational model as such failed to win substantial converts has been shown.

If the use of vernacular languages was a relatively clear issue, other areas were less so. Medical and educational practice was clearly westernised, and making use of these services required adoption of western/Scottish standards (e.g. school uniforms), with perhaps the only indication that the schools were not in Scotland being the alternative languages and the need to take religious holidays as determined by several faiths. Medicines were often procured from Scotland and resources for the schools were generally western (witness, for example, a minute regarding the acquisition of maps: 'Miss Gwladys Jones ... [applied] for a map of Europe and one of Palestine; also a Terrestrial Globe. Resolved to authorise the Secretary to procure and send these'[126] – even a map of the children's own country had to come from Europe!); though the scriptural texts sold and given away by the mission were in local languages (part of the funding for this came from the National Bible Society in Scotland).

Mention has been made of the attitudes to other missions in the region as represented in the journal accounts.[127] In relation to Palestine's communities beyond just the Jewish community that they were primarily targeting, further examples of the failure to engage in reculturation can be identified. Muslim and Christian children and patients utilised the services that the missionaries offered, but understandings of the communities these people were part of was extremely limited. Given prohibitions on the evangelisation of Muslims, there was perhaps felt to be little that could be offered this community. Correspondingly, there appears to have been no significant attempt to understand Islam or the practices of its Ottoman adherents: existing records do not even indicate that the missionaries differentiated between communities at the most basic Sunni/Shi'i level. Equally the Christian communities: as already noted briefly,[128] little attempt was made to differentiate the various Christian traditions in the Ottoman Empire. Although Wortabet's book[129] described the various religious traditions of the region, no records exist from any of the missionaries of Scottish origin that would indicate an appreciation of the manifold religious traditions in Palestine (or the Ottoman Empire as a whole). Such knowledge as there was of existing Christian communities came partly through the filter of other missions: for example, American missions in Lebanon and Anatolia directed to Armenians were known of (and it was known that Armenians could be found in Palestine), but understanding the differences between the Armenian and, for example, the Greek Orthodox community was not something the Scots ever seemed to feel the need to do, at least in their extant communications.[130] Only rarely are the differences even acknowledged,[131] but this alone cannot be taken as evidence of the Scottish missionaries understanding Palestinian Christians as anything more than part of a generic body of 'Eastern Churches'. It is worth noting that the term 'churches', not 'Christians' was usually used – members of these churches could therefore 'become' (Presbyterian/Protestant) Christians. In summary, not only was the understanding of the Jewish communities minimal, but little attempt was made to understand any of the other existing religious complexities of the region.

An area that some form of adoption to local practice took place in is the principle of *bakshish*. Generally condemned, the missionaries found they often had to comply with *bakshish* requests in order to progress matters, especially the more important transactions of land purchase and building work.[132] At times subverted and avoided,[133] this was not always possible,[134] and in this grudging adoption of a practice that their moral values ('fair' price etc.) resisted, one can perhaps see a form of (reluctant) reculturation.

A clear picture of resistance to local contexts, customs and attitudes emerges from the subjects outlined above. In reflecting on why this was the case, and reculturation was so limited, there are several factors that can be considered. Firstly, the geographical context the missionaries were in was populated by far more westerners than e.g. Taylor's Chinese context. Aside from other missionaries, whether Scottish (the Shweir and Beirut missions), American (in Beirut and its hinterland) or English (the LJS in Safad and elsewhere, or the Anglican church in Jerusalem), there would also have been regular and frequent contact with consular officials, entrepreneurs, Jewish immigrants from Europe, tourists etc. – many of these did not adopt oriental dress or other patterns of behaviour, and so the motivation for the Scots to do so would have been reduced. The presence of a large number of westerners would have helped to reaffirm and cement attitudes to western lifestyles, habits, and manners. Connected with this was the intrinsic racism that has already been mentioned, which led the missionaries to assume their culture and background to be superior to that of the Orient (regardless of religious adherence) and would have mitigated against any move to adopt or accept aspects of the culture that could possibly be avoided. A further factor connected to this relates to their theological and philosophical position: bringing, as they saw it, the truth of the Christian gospel to a benighted land[135] (as Lebanon was described by a Scot; the epithet could equally have been applied to Palestine by the Scots[136]) there could be little room for compromise with 'truth', an absolute concept which entailed salvation or damnation, with nothing in between. Given that 'westernization' (Hobsbawm) was being communicated together with the Christian gospel, where could the room for compromise on such issues be found? Although it is perhaps merely idle speculation, one might in this context wonder at the depression Brown found himself in: the failure to procure converts might even be connected to a fundamental questioning of his own presuppositions and western values, though a definitive understanding on this is impossible on the basis of the historical record, and with no closer knowledge of his psychological state.

Figure 5-1 Tiberias Hospital staff 1906[137]

There is, however, one example of reculturation that can be indirectly deducted. This centres on the issue of infant circumcision, which the following section outlines briefly.

Reculturation in medical practice: the circumcison of infant boys

Torrance and Paterson were the two leading Scottish medics in the Levant, and although over the decades they will have formed opinions, learnt skills, and developed methods that were new or different to medical practice as they would have learnt or experienced it in Britain, few records of these exist. However, an interesting example that can illustrate reculturation in their professional sphere as medics in the Levant is the case of circumcision of infant boys, albeit that this can only be shown indirectly.

Ronald Hyam describes the introduction of circumcision into British society:[138] circumcision on infant boys was not practised until the end of the 19th and beginning of the 20th century, though it was known that it took place in other countries: he cites a British traveller seeing a circumcised penis when in Egypt in about 1870.[139] The British public had not encountered circumcision in any meaningful way: for example, images in

European art of Mary and a naked Christ-child with Jesus much older than the statutory eight days prescribed in the Jewish tradition, never show a circumcised penis, though the genitals are often visible.[140] However, much of the debate about circumcision in the early years of the 20th century centred on Jewish and Indian-imperial arguments: firstly, Jewish family life and methods of child care, including circumcision, were idealised and held up as models for British families generally, and secondly, Hyam notes that 'Hot, humid climates are not good for sensitive foreskins, any more than sandy ones are (as the Jews and Muslims of the Middle East had always known)'.[141] In order to ease potential medical problems in later life, circumcision was viewed favourably for the upper and professional middle-classes, i.e. the future servants of the British empire who would be working in climates such as those found in India or the Middle East: a reason some medics gave for circumcision was that men would be more likely to clean their penis properly, thereby avoiding infections and reducing the demands on colonial medics.[142] Doctors who had some connection to the colonial enterprise were amongst the most vociferous in arguing for general wholesale circumcision of infant boys.[143]

However, this author has not come across any mention of circumcision in the writings of Torrance and Paterson. This is of particular relevance with this first generation of Scottish medical missionaries in Palestine.[144] Neither David Torrance nor Paterson appear to have participated in the public debate in Britain about circumcision, though they would both have had many years of experience of the practice, new to them on arrival in Palestine, and would probably have formed an opinion as to its benevolent (or otherwise) effects on male genital health. It may therefore appear surprising that there seems to have been no overt interest on their part in participating in the argument taking place in Britain, particularly in the early years of the 20th century when numerous articles appeared and debates on the subject were prominent. It would be a mistake to attribute this to some vague notion of 'Victorian prudery' or 'church morality' since there is evidence of them writing about medical issues relating to sexual organs (though these writings tend only to be alluded to and this author has not seen any such records; no records exist or are referred to that would show they wrote about sexual matters in anything other than a strictly medical context, and certainly nothing describing sexual practice analogous to e.g. Burton's work on homosexual and pederast practices[145]). Their silence on the British debate on infant circumcision is probably due to the fact that although they would have been aware of the debate taking place in Britain – purchases of medical publications and subscriptions to journals were seen as an important way of staying in touch with medical progress and debates – they were not, as some of the ex-colonial doctors were when the debate was in full swing, practising medics in Britain: for them, circumcision was simply a daily occurrence in relation to all Jewish and Muslim male patients, and not a topic worth discussing. In this sense, one can perceive an obvious change in their professional medical attitudes and understandings arising from their work in the Levant: they had needed to reflect on and be clear about their attitude to infant circumcision at least 15 years before it became a topic in British public debate; by the time that debate took place, they seem to have felt it was not an issue that overly concerned them. Reculturation had occurred in this area of their professional lives, at least.

Missionary identification on the material-social level

> For though I am free with respect to all, I have made myself a slave to all, so that I might win more of them [to faith]. To the Jews I became as a Jew, in order to win Jews ... To the weak I became weak, so that I might win the weak. I have become all things to all people, that I might by all means save some.[146]

Identification as a part of what missionary activity is about is rooted in these verses from one of the first great Christian missionaries, Paul, writing here to the Corinthians. Positing Paul's statement as an ideal for a Christian missionary and examining the extent of the Scottish missionaries' identification with their target populations becomes an interesting task, useful as another way of highlighting the extent of their connection to European colonial and civilisation norms.[147] In particular, I wish to focus attention briefly on what Jonathon Bonk describes as the 'material-social level' of missionary identification[148] as offering one of the clearest indicators of this influence.

Torrance may have worn Arab clothes at times and identification in terms of language and contexts for communication took place to varying degrees in the course of the missionaries' work,[149] but identification with the local population was minimal on the material-social level. Bonk notes that in general the four major western missionary conferences of the 19th and early 20th centuries

> reveal missionaries to have been convinced of the practical importance of material-social identification ... to the degree that it was vigorously encouraged, if not insisted upon, in their native agents. Like football fans observing a match, missionaries knew what was likely to produce effective results on the field; and like most armchair strategists, they remained spectators themselves, lacking the will or the capacity to become anything more.[150]

This damning summary applies not only to the LMS in Africa and China, as Bonk shows, but also to the Scots in the Levant. This can be illustrated by examining the issue of salaries and payments to staff.

An important factor in reflecting on missionary identification is the inherent racism already referred to, which convinced the missionaries that their culture was superior to cultures found in other parts of the world. Stated simply, socially as well as materially, this manifested itself in a context of 19th century thinking of ever-developing 'progress': since the West was (from most westerners' perspectives) clearly superior to other cultures, and westerners were generally 'white', 'whites' were obviously superior to people of other 'races'.[151] Furthermore, since religion lay at the heart of culture, it was also clear that Christianity, the religion of the 'white' Europeans, was superior to any other religion which had not led its people to a similarly elevated position, quite aside from theological claims of exclusivity.[152] The role of women in society was also a factor in this thinking: Christian women were perceived as being liberated, whilst the subordination of women that westerners saw in other cultures was a clear indication of their inferior nature.[153] Given this perceived reality, parity between westerners and indigenous targets of missionary endeavour seemed an impossibility to most westerners.

Employees of the Scottish churches in the Levant were categorised into one of two groups: staff appointed in Scotland, and locals appointed by these staff. The salaries and conditions of the staff in Scotland were fixed by the JMCs (or their equivalent) and staff were paid directly from Scotland. Only other westerners could be in a position of authority over any of these figures, and ultimately their accountability was to their sending Committee, which expected regular reports and communications back to Scotland (either for publication, or simply for the Committee to be aware of what was happening). Local staff, on the other hand, were appointed by the Scottish staff, were paid by them out of the budget allowed for that particular part of the mission station, and were answerable to them. On the very rare occasions that local staff contacted the Scottish committee with problems, they tended to be referred back to the western mission staff on the ground, with the Scottish committees unwilling to become involved in any kind of dispute between local and western staff.

Salary levels show a great disparity between different categories of staff. Male and female staff from Europe were treated differently, as were local male and female staff. Scottish/western males in high positions such as doctors or teachers were at the end of the 19th century receiving around £300 a year, with occasional extra allowances for certain individuals; regular return trips to Scotland were paid for, and additional allowances were made for a wife and family. Women were paid less, usually around £100-£130, with board included. Eventually pension arrangements were put into place, and payments were generally made in sterling, converted into local currency as required by the missionary. Local staff, on the other hand, received considerably less than this: the initial staff complement of seven planned for Safad was budgeted at £320. They were paid a rate negotiated by the Scottish missionary staff with each individual, and only rudimentary salary scales existed, with most changes in rates being at the discretion of the missionary concerned, or, in Tiberias and Safad to some extent, the Sea of Galilee Mission Council. There was a sharp disparity between male and female staff, with local women earning less than half their local male colleagues, who themselves earned only a fraction of the western missionaries. Figure 5-2 on p171 shows salary levels for the Sea of Galilee mission, this mission being chosen here because it offered the widest range of salaries and the most positions.[154] It is notable that even when local staff were employed to carry out the work of one of the western missionaries, salaries and responsibilities were much lower. For example, when Torrance returned to Scotland on furlough, Arab doctors were employed in his stead, receiving a much lower salary and answerable to western staff based at the mission station, not to the JMC.

Position	Salary £	Gender	Appointment by
David Torrance	300	male	JMC
John Soutar	300	male	JMC
George Wilson	300	male	JMC
Doctor's Assistant	120	male	local
Schoolmaster	54	male	local
Jewish teacher/colporter	36	male	local
Scripture reader	29	male?	local
Nurse	50	male?	local?
Dispenser	48	male	local
Attendant in dispensary	24	male	local
Schoolmaster	48	male	local
Jewish teacher	29	male	local
Evangelist	50	male	local
Miss Jones	30	female	WAJM*
Miss Bender	48	female	local (almost certainly)
M. Zareefy	24	female	local
Jewish teacher	10	female	local
M. Rogena Nasser	36	female	local
M. Zuleika	20	female	local
Third teacher	15	female	local
Pupil teacher	9	female	local
TOTAL SALARY COST	1580	male/female	

Male JMC salary cost: £900, average male JMC salary: £300
Male local salary cost: £488, average male local salary: £49
Average male local salary as a % of average male JMC salary: 16%

Female local salary cost: £162, average female local salary: £23
Average female local salary as a % of average male local salary: 47%
* NB: allowance, not salary (volunteer)

Figure 5-2 Sea of Galilee salaries – budget for 1901[155]

Although not explicitly stated, it is reasonable to assume that local staff were paid a salary commensurate with what they might expect to earn from other employers. It is most unlikely that they were paid substantially less, as the incentive to remain with the Scottish missions would then have diminished considerably. On this basis, local staff could in theory, at least, never attain a level of income equivalent to that of their Scottish counterparts, no matter what their qualifications might be (Wortabet represents the one exception to this pattern, and his case is examined below).

Bonk identifies this behaviour as 'vicarious' identification,[156] noting that since 'Western civilization was an inevitable by-product of Christianity, it behooved natives to identify with missionaries – up to a point – and not vice versa.'[157] Westerners were there 'to transform material and social elements of society, not identify with it'.[158] Clearly, as representatives of the superior culture (the role of racism is mentioned above) the Scots felt they could hardly be expected to 'lower' themselves to this level – and indeed they ensured they did not.

There is of course a wider financial and social context to these attitudes: whilst the missionaries earned far more than any of the local staff, their salaries were unchanged over many years, and generally the missionaries were not as well paid as if they had remained in Scotland and pursued their professional interests there. Whether as ministers, teachers or doctors, the professional males could have expected at least an equivalent salary, if not more, had they stayed in Scotland; this is particularly the case with medics from the second half of the 19th century onwards as recognition of the medical profession in Britain became increasingly formalised. Women too, had they remained in Scotland, would perhaps have earned more. One can therefore argue that *by western standards*[159] the missionary staff lived simply, as well as perhaps putting themselves at greater personal risk than if they had stayed in Scotland. It has already been made clear that women, however, particularly those who wished to devote themselves in some way to work of the church,[160] had a great deal to gain from missionary work aside from relative salary levels: economic independence and the freedom to develop talents and skills in a way that was not open to them in Scotland made missionary work in general an attractive career choice for some.[161] Whether in the low-wage economy (where women's salaries in 19th century Scotland were about 42% of men's salaries[162] – the parallel to the 47% noted in Figure 5-2 on p171 for Sea of Galilee local women is striking) or in the middle-classes, working overseas could appear to be a very attractive option, and beyond working for the church, there were relatively few openings for women abroad. That women of both the working and the middle-classes found fulfilment in mission work is amply demonstrated by the social and class 'extremes' of Mary Slessor and Elizabeth Hewat (who became a professor at Wilson College, Bombay and an elder in the Church of South India long before either was possible in Scotland[163]) others such as Gwladys Jones and her colleagues in the Levantine missions would have found their roles somewhere between these two. That the likes of Slessor appeared to achieve a measure of identification that Torrance, Paterson and the like did not, can perhaps even be attributed to issues of class, as has been suggested above.

An interesting exception to the difference between western and indigenous identification can be found in the example of John Wortabet of the United Presbyterian mission in Aleppo. Wortabet, a Syrian who had studied at the Syrian Protestant College and had already been employed by the American mission, demanded to be treated as an equal to the Scottish incumbent in terms of salary and conditions. He had left his American employers over the inferior position he felt they had given him and the church, having considered his references, acceded to his demands and employed him as Brown's equal. That this was a very unusual step can be seen by the fact that the Americans, once they had heard about this situation, complained about it to the Scots, worried that their native agents would demand similar treatment. Wortabet clearly felt of himself that, to use Bonk's language, he had identified with the missionaries to the extent that he felt of himself that his ability, manner, and attitude warranted equal treatment. The LMS that Bonk examines was representative of all western missionary agencies in maintaining that it was 'unthinkable that there should *not* be a clear material-social differentiation between Western missionaries and natives – even favoured natives'.[164] In this context, the adverse American reaction to finding out about the United Presbyterian Church's decision can be more readily understood.

Wortabet's level of identification with the west is symbolised yet further in his decisions regarding the income levels of local staff, Syrians like himself. One of the most notable instances occurs when he, at a salary of £250 a year, makes clear that one of his catechists and teachers, Denour Abdie, should not be paid more than £27 a year. As far as can be established, Wortabet appears to have had no more demands on his income than any other Syrian such as Denour Abdie might have done, but seeing himself on a par with western colleagues, he also adopted their attitude to salaries. This was missionary identification on the material-social level characterised by its western/native divide carried to its ultimate logical conclusion: here was a convert to Protestantism who identified with the *missionaries* he was working with, and then did not identify with the *people* he, as a missionary, was supposed to be converting.[165]

Why did the United Presbyterian Church appoint Wortabet on these conditions and treat him as a western/Scottish missionary, probably the only native agent to be appointed on this basis amongst any of the Scottish churches at the time? There is no direct explanation for this, but the simplest one also appears to be the most obvious: Brown, as the only 'Evangelical Christian Teacher' in Aleppo, had indicated his despair at the lack of converts (and therefore lack of success) his work had generated up until this point and although he had not specifically asked for a colleague, Wortabet proactively offering himself to the service of the United Presbyterians at this time (obviously highly qualified and with references from individuals that the Committee knew and trusted) might have seemed an opportune way of extending the work and providing support to Brown. Wortabet's obvious skills in presenting himself as equal to a Scottish missionary in ability, learning, and worth in financial terms appear to have induced the Committee to treat him as he desired, and with that a native agent had achieved identification not only on a religious level (he joined the United Presbyterians in order to be appointed) but also on a material-social level. Putting Wortabet into a wider context, Hobsbawm notes that if missionary

Christianity insisted on the equality of souls, it underlined the inequality of bodies – even of clerical bodies. It was something done by whites for natives, and paid for by whites. And though it multiplied native believers, at least half the clergy remained white. As for a coloured bishop, it would take a powerful microscope to detect one anywhere between 1880 and 1914.[166]

Since Presbyterians had no bishops, one might be tempted to argue that their equivalent in the mission field were their western missionaries as the most senior representatives of their religious tradition in the field; on that score Wortabet clearly occupies an unusual place in the history of mid-19th century world missions.

In summary then, the conflation of Christianity and culture that the missionaries represented can be shown by reference to the material-social level of missionary identification to have been very difficult to overcome to the extent of real and meaningful identification with the local population: not intending to engage in missionary identification out of a concern for the preservation of their superior cultural background, actual identification largely eluded them. This, and the theme of reculturation, will be returned to in the concluding chapter assessing the missions.

Conclusion

Clearly, and understandably, Jews of the Levant were not attracted to conversion and its attendant dire social consequences. Offering educational and medical services went some way to making the presence and evangelistic activity of the missionaries more palatable to the local population. That they were only able to achieve this by offering something more than a message of conversion is a measure of the compromise the missionaries found they had to engage in,[167] though their ability to engage in missionary identification with the local population was severely limited.

Educational services reflected Ottoman moves towards enabling greater participation for the indigenous population in an international context, whilst medical facilities served not only to provide health care, but also indirectly communicated further aspects of European practice. Beyond this, that as Hobsbawm argues for missions in general, many of the target population (Jews, Arabs, and Eastern Christians) remained unpersuaded of the foreigners' belief system but appropriated their educational and medical services regardless, can perhaps be interpreted as a kind of mutual accommodation. In this schema, the target population made use of those elements of the mission's offering that they perceived to be valuable and useful, whilst the missionaries – unable to imagine that local people might perceive the Scots' mission in terms other than their own – could feel they were offering not only social services, but, given the framework within which they interpreted the use of education and medicine, could allow themselves to think they were also being given opportunities to communicate the message that formed the basis and impetus for their own engagement in the region.

This helps to explain why the methods employed were largely useless when viewed alongside their ultimate aim of securing Jewish converts. In this, they were spectacularly *un*successful, producing only a handful of converts from Judaism despite a number of highly committed people working in the region, years of engagement, large amounts of money, and considerable resources. Whilst the Scots also failed to garner significant numbers of converts from non-Jewish communities, as part of the overall western missionary effort during the 19th and early 20th centuries they contributed to the losses suffered by the Orthodox communities: most Levantine adherents to the Protestant churches came from the Orthodox tradition.[168] Although in most cases, and certainly for the Scots, this was not the missionaries' explicit aim, the overall tactics employed for achieving their aims helped to bring about this situation, rather than the one they had hoped, planned and prayed for.

PART 3
CONCLUSIONS

6

USING RECULTURATION AND MISSIONARY IDENTIFICATION TO ASSESS THE MISSIONS

The end of the Introduction cited Courbage and Fargues' statement that the 'colonial and expansionist West had established its hegemony while proclaiming its Christianity. Economic and missionary victory went hand in hand'.[1] How is the Scottish missionary effort in Palestine to be understood and assessed in the context of this claim for 'economic and missionary victory', a narrative that is not primarily a theological one, but one based on administrative structures, finances, material concerns and human personalities? One might concur with Valognes that 'Le bilan des interventions britanniques n'est pas simple à dresser',[2] but there are clear pointers to an assessment.

It has been amply demonstrated that the stated purpose of the Scots' engagement in the Levant – the conversion of Jews to the Protestant gospel – was a dismal failure. Even extending the purpose to include converts from the indigenous churches – no records of Muslim conversions exist – does not change this, as only a tiny number were converted, despite the investment of enormous financial, personal and material resources by the Scots. Here, at least, one looks in vain for the 'missionary victory'.

But does it exist, and if so, can it be found in other areas?

Scottish missionaries' attitudes have been shown to be complex, dominated by a reluctance to recognise the agency of others, particularly their targets. Chapter 1 introduced the Scottish missionaries' difficulties, given their ecclesiastical and theological background, in seeing Jews as actional persons, rather than as participants in some pre-defined notion of the divine economy. This represented but one part of the imperial discourse that framed the missionaries' experience of the Levant in which – whether in terms of understanding Zionists 'as they call themselves' (the Scots unwilling to allow this self-descriptor to go uncommented), the 'Eastern' Churches (little attempt being made to acknowledge self-portrayal and internal differences), general negativity about all things Muslim (arising from medieval images of Islam[3]), the equating of local political institutions and systems with those in Britain (e.g. Paterson's comments about the 'Ottoman Parliament'), conversion (which could happen only on the Scots' terms, an ultimate tool of religious power), and the geopious associations with the land of Palestine – the subjectivity of the colonised was consistently ignored and overridden. Denial of the voice of the subjected is an inherent part of the imperialist discourse: negation, subjugation and the ability to transform the agency of others into subsidiary roles that serve one's own world-view in turn remove one ever further from the subject itself.[4] Self-identification relies in these circumstances on non-identification with the Other. In this context, one can understand the Scottish activity in the Levant as an ongoing struggle to seek out a meaningful role for themselves in the region: being agents of conversion was clearly not a successful role and so what was? – or, to formulate it differently, how, if their self-identity as agents of religious conversion was not being validated, could they affirm and validate their identity?[5] Although the Scots as nationals – 'both oppositional-marginal and dominant-central'[6] – and as church members[7] were largely peripheral in the British context when in Britain, their behaviour and thinking in relation to the Other when they were overseas in the service of colonialism resorted to imperial models. This made them part of 'a larger, more compelling and authoritative narrative, one made possible by the imperial mission'[8] – the regular recourse to the imperial political power of Britain in furthering the missionaries' aims indicates something of the diffusion of the boundaries between Scottish and English identity in dealing with the colonised beyond these boundaries.

Questioning the missionaries' efficacy as agents of conversion was only addressed head on in Aleppo: the mission was judged to be a failure by Brown and Wortabet, and their sending committee concurred, noting that 'eight Years trial [had] completely failed'. However, this represents the only recorded instance of missionaries or a JMC engaging in self-reflection regarding success in terms of the number of converts. At all the other stations, local factors, insufficient resources, the subjects themselves, or all three and more were blamed for the absence of converts. The eternal hope for large-scale conversion (that was regularly cited in an attempt to bolster the ever-volatile support in Scotland for the missions) obscured any sense that local people had made a decision for themselves about how to react to the incomers, appropriating the elements of the missionary offerings they could see as useful, whilst ignoring or rejecting the element that did not appeal – this latter being, of course, the rationale for the missionaries' engagement in the first place. Although it was only in Aleppo that this was clearly recognised, not all the missionaries pursued the work in the same way. Of Jaffa, the period under consideration here between the adoption of the mission and the war is too short to be able to make any useful assessments, and likewise with Damascus – the half-hearted engagement affords few insights into missionary activity, never mind assessments of activity. However, Hebron and the Sea of Galilee are different: Paterson seems to have expressed few views on his effectiveness or otherwise in converting Jews, of whom there were relatively few in Hebron to start with, and the JMC, faced with losing Martineau's donation without Paterson, did not appear to question the validity of their work there once they had taken him and his mission station on; beyond this also, lies the arrangement with the German mission which moved most of the responsibility for direct evangelisation and all the responsibility for education onto another body. Under these circumstances, it is not a great surprise to find no comments on this theme from Paterson, especially in the ten years during which the German-Scottish partnership appeared to be functioning. The Sea of Galilee has its origins in common with Aleppo: initiated by a JMC on its own and not ventured into with other partners, gifted, or inherited. But unlike with Aleppo, an occasion to engage in self-reflection on the validity of the work never arose, at least none has been recorded. Torrance considered leaving, but he did not record doubts about his mandate and so the JMC was not encouraged to do so either.

So if the missionaries – with the exception of Aleppo, which closed – did not significantly question their work, how did they understand and give meaning to their self-identity as agents of Protestant conversion? The Scottish missionaries (more so perhaps than Wortabet who was working in his own country) were faced with dealing with the dialectic of identity and difference[9] in relating to the alterity they encountered in the Levant, and assessing the way they dealt with this using the themes of reculturation and identity offers pointers to further understanding, enabling a conclusion to be reached on the question of the 'missionary victory'.

The missionaries' reculturation has been shown to have been characterised by reluctance (e.g. *bakshish*), minimal acquiescence (e.g. language), and unplanned changes to perceptions (the circumcision issue comes to mind – the changes in professional terms were directly related to their experience of the practice of those who represented the Other to them). Accepting McAllister's definition, reculturation necessitates (amongst other things) that actors 'must ... reconsider themselves in relation to and perhaps as part of ... [the] other culture'[10] – in other words, an element of identity and a willingness to allow personal change is required. In how far the missionaries did this beyond a few areas, some mentioned above, is doubtful. Clear differentiation was a constant feature, and if the Pauline example of missionary identification represented an ideal, the missionaries were clearly not wanting to identify on this level with the local population. The rejection of local practices symbolised by the adherence to western clothing and the high differential in salary and responsibility between Scots and local Palestinians meant that the difference was always present. This adherence to difference was derived in part from nineteenth century racism, but also had a theological basis: first and foremost their gospel message most fundamentally required *metanoia* – a 'change of mind' and repentance, entailing rejection of a previously held world-view and the adoption of a new belief system. Beyond this, whether reflecting on the 'sweetness and cleanness' of the hospital ('To them it is a real Bethel'), or the establishing of 'model schools where mental improvement is energetically cultivated, where physical training is not neglected, and where spiritual nurture is sympathetically imparted', the contrast is always made with the environment the missionaries found themselves in; one might speculate that this in some way perhaps helped to affirm them in the usefulness of their presence since their usefulness as agents of conversion increasingly lacked meaning. In this context it is irrelevant to reflect on the accuracy of these contrasts, what matters here is that they highlight the perspective of the missionaries and show that on an ideological level they tended towards *avoiding* relation to the Palestinian environment, and had difficulty seeing themselves as *part* of it. This is further supported by assessing the role of local people in the missionary narrative: only Wortabet appears as a native agent equal to a Scot (and this has been explained above), whilst the agency of local people in general is minimised (e.g. there were only Scots on the Sea of Galilee Mission Council) or set within strict parameters (e.g. the medics who replaced Torrance when he was in Scotland). This is most obviously apparent in the process of change in method: the confrontational model offering nothing that local people wanted, it was augmented by education and medicine, which in the missionaries' eyes represented a way to overcome e.g. the 'stubbornness' of local Jews, but was actually utilised by indigenous actors as a public service. The missionaries recognised no local agency in these changes, interpreting the increase in contact to their Scottish constituency as a positive sign of interest in their gospel message.

As will be clear, the emphasis on difference manifested itself in numerous ways. In some cases this happened with a surprising degree of tenacity. For example, the land and its inhabitants remained a constant Other for most of the Scots involved in the missions. Stockdale refers to English women in Palestine who

> worked hard to make the land of Palestine and its inhabitants fit their notions of what the "Holy Land" was meant to be, colonizing the Bible itself through their interpretation of the land of its genesis as timeless and peopled with Biblical characters rather than contemporary actors.[11]

Whether despairing at the state of Shiloh in 1839, writing about the romance of church travellers in 1895 Palestine, or in the 20th century describing the 'new Israel' that was coming into being in Palestine, the land is almost always seen as the missionaries would like to see it: mostly in a Biblical context (as they understood it) – leading to a level of equivocity that colours all reading of these materials. The link to the foundational incarnation myth of Christianity determined the missionaries' perspective on the land, so that even contemporary events were seen in a context that had to relate in some way to the Biblical canon (e.g. Jewish immigration was compared to the return from the Babylonian exile). Geopiety, referring to 'reverence' and 'devotion' of a space, does not go far enough in this context. Reverence and devotion are major constituent elements, but what the Scots were actually doing is similar to their approach to Jews in general, who were viewed as participants in the Scots' understanding of the divine economy: all events, characters, movements and political changes they encountered in Palestine were as if viewed through a prism, the elements of which included geopiety, but also incorporated a vision of the place of the land linked to the Biblical so-called 'promise' to and 'return' of Jews, as well as a need for a validation of their theological assumptions about divine action in the material world. Transforming the land into something that served their purposes symbolised difference on a wide scale: unwilling to allow themselves to identify with the land as they encountered it, they needed the difference in order to validate their model of the divine economy. And even when their encounters did allow for change, this happened within a pre-determined context that only served to support the missionaries' existing world-view. They were, as Stockdale has it, 'colonizing the Bible itself'. Another example relates to this, and is to be found in relation to attitudes to Zionism.

Initially averse to the Zionist movement and giving it little chance of success, a gradual development of sympathy, coloured with self-interest, is identifiable in e.g. Soutar's views: it was hoped that the newcomers would be more readily converted than their co-religionists in Palestine. Whilst these targets of the missionaries' work, Palestinian Jews, were in a political context that was undergoing a process of tremendous change, this was always seen as part of a divine involvement towards the fulfilment of Old Testament prophecies.[12] Imperial subjects of the Porte, western, particularly British interference was beginning to enable, via, as it transpired, imperial subjugation by the British during the Mandate period, the independence of Palestinian Jews. Perceiving Jews in Palestine to be on the cusp of change,[13] the missionaries saw a role for themselves in filling what they observed to be the spiritual gap that the secular Zionists 'suffered' from. Having had virtually no success in converting Palestinian Jews until that time, hopes were that European Jews newly arrived in Palestine would be more amenable to missionary endeavour. In the context of the gradual disintegration of the Ottoman Empire, and at a time when the demographic pattern of Palestine was undergoing radical change with large-scale Jewish *aliya* and the foundations for the Jewish-Arab conflict being laid as a result (compounded by the mixed messages of the British government to both sides), the missionaries' attempts to transform European Jews (who were coming to Palestine in ultimate search of political independence) into colonial subjects in their own divine economy can perhaps be seen as more than just another connection to the imperial discourse. Missionary protest at the imperial subjugation of Palestine was not about empire as such, but the perceived iniquities of Ottoman rule. They were keen supporters of British imperialism, agitating for freedom to operate in a Palestine under British rule. Indeed, one might even say that their objections to Balfour's 'interesting experiment' were that British intentions appeared to herald the possible independence of Jews in Palestine, which they expected to result in restrictions on their work (replacing the 'Turkish by a Jewish tyranny'). Seeking to avoid this, British imperial 'protection' as offered by the Capitulations, or British rule which would grant the missionaries space to operate freely, represented far more amenable environments to the Scots than what they expected Jewish independence would bring. The Comaroff's image of the missionary as the 'agent, scribe and moral alibi' of the imperial power is strikingly apt here: the Scottish missionaries might have had a marginal role in Britain, but this was irrelevant beyond the boundaries of Britain, in a space where the British *Empire* played a role, even if British imperial control over Palestine was not (yet) a formal reality.

In conclusion, what is to be made of Courbage and Fargues' 'missionary victory'? Given the picture painted above, it is difficult to see how it can be argued that the Scottish missions represented a 'victory'. Aside from the almost total failure to garner converts, the missionaries' general approach to the inhabitants of the Levant was based not primarily on identity and therefore (attempts at) integration, but on difference. The theory of missionary identification deriving from Paul did not lead to actual identification by the missionaries: instead, identity was understood to mean that the local population should identify with the incoming missionaries, rather than the missionaries with the local population: a form of mental miscegenation was demanded. Trying to make others identify with themselves, and only reluctantly allowing themselves to change in response to their encounter with the alterity in the Levant (reculturation) represented a comprehensive failure in their aims: the local population identified not with the imperialistic ideology of religious conversion that the missionaries brought, but with the services they offered. Ironically, perhaps, these (later) enabled in part an articulation of resistance to western interference in the form of Arab nationalism. Whilst Ernest Dawn cautions against overstating the role of western missionaries in the development of Arab nationalism,[14] it appears that the same must be said of at least the Scottish missions in terms of their missionary influence in pre-World War I Palestine: ultimately, the missionaries found themselves unable to bring about large-scale conversions to their world-view, finding instead that they had to adapt and change their methods in order to offer services that were useful to the local population in order to have any kind of meaningful interaction with this population. Palestinians, as subjects of imperial domination first by the Ottomans and then by Britain, had therefore succeeded in shaping the offerings from an imperial centre to something that they, on the periphery of empire, could use and benefit from. Seen in this light, the 'missionary victory' belongs not to the Scots, but to the Jews, Christians and Muslims in Palestine who resisted, appropriated and embraced the varying models of interaction offered them by the representatives of an imperial centre.

APPENDIX AND BIBLIOGRAPHY

APPENDIX

Divisions and reunions of the Scottish churches, 1840-1930

All traditions noted here originate with the (Established) Church of Scotland at the time of the Scottish Reformation.[1]

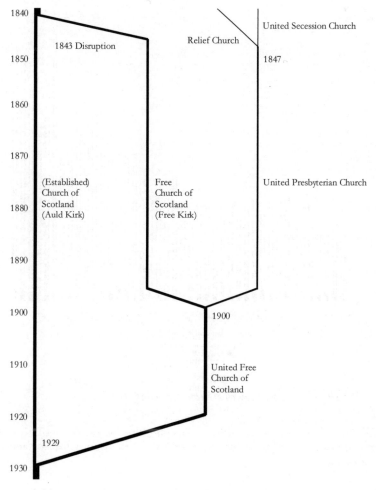

Figure 7-1 Divisions and unions – Scottish Presbyterian churches 1840-1930

Free Church of Scotland income 1844-1885

Any attempt at compiling income statistics for the churches is complicated by the absence of complete records, different forms in which records were kept, the different purposes of the records, and so on. Rather than attempt to produce a coherent impression for the entire period covered by this book from these varied sources, I have based the following chart on a table created by the Free Kirk in a pamphlet of 1885.[2] This shows Jewish, Foreign, and total missionary income for the financial years ending 1844-1885, i.e. up until the founding of the Tiberias mission by David Torrance.

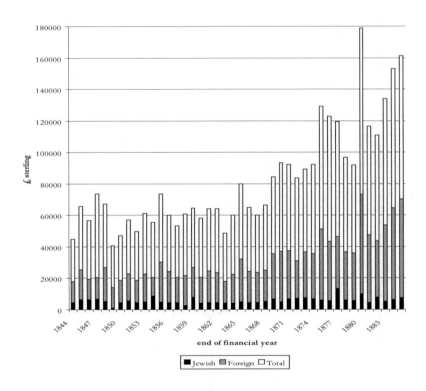

Figure 7-2 Free Church of Scotland, 1844-1885 income

The JMC was clearly failing to maintain its proportion of the overall missionary income, in contrast to the FMC. This sets a context for the regular funding appeals; c.f. Chapter 4 above.

Torrance family tree

This family tree shows only selected family members. Abbreviations used are as follows: * birth, b baptism, m marriage, † death; dotted lines point to children, solid lines to marriage partners. Details are taken from JMC records, biographies, and photographs made by the author of gravestones in the Tiberias mission graveyard, as well as from information generously given by two of David Torrance's descendants, Lydia Dorward and David Byrne, whose help is hereby gratefully acknowledged.

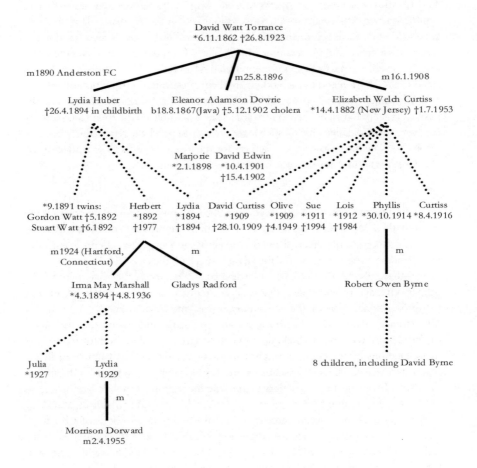

Figure 7-3 David Watt Torrance family tree

Free Church of Scotland Jewish Mission Committee instructions for Amsterdam missionaries

Extracted from the minutes of a meeting on 17.10.1871:[3]

The Committee appointed ... to prepare instructions for the guidance of the Mission at Amsterdam gave in a Report ... of proposed Instructions. The Committee approved of these Instructions, ordered them to be printed, and sent to their Missionary at Amsterdam. The Committee also ordered a copy of these Instructions to be sent to all their Missionaries, as embodying in general the views of the Committee on the work of Mission to the Jews, and as applicable mutatis mutandis to all other Stations.

> The Committee, taking into account the large experience they have had in superintending Missionary operations among the Jews in Amsterdam, and the knowledge they have acquired of the many practical difficulties which stand in the way of their successful prosecution, arising partly from the special requirements of the place itself, and partly from the complicated relations in which various local parties stand to the Mission and to each other, and being desirous, on the appointment of a new Missionary, that full advantage be taken both of the lessons and labours of the past, and that the work be carried forward as far as possible on the foundation already laid, with the avoidance only of such errors as may in part have retarded its progress; resolve to issue the following instructions for the guidance of Mr Van Andel, or any Missionary who may for the time being occupy that Station.

(1)   As a first and most essential requisite, the Committee desire to impress on the mind of their Missionary the necessity of keeping the primary end of the Mission, viz, the conversion of Israel, distinctly and always in view. They do not regard this as precluding various activity for the advancement of the cause of Christ generally, provided always that it be strictly subordinated as a means to the attainment of the primary end, and provided also, that though conducive to this end, it do not occupy a disproportionate part of the time and energy of the Missionary.

(2)   In accordance with the above, it must be clearly understood that the object of the Committee is not to build up a Dutch congregation detached from the other denominations of the country, and in communion with the Free Church; or in any manner to relieve Dutch Christians of the responsibility of supporting their own ministry. In giving their sanction to the administration of public ordinances as hitherto in the Mission Church, their aim is to reach the mind of the Jews, and along with this, as a means to its attainment, to organise and train up a body of Christians, whatever be their denominational connexion, who shall take a special interest in the welfare and destiny of God's ancient people, and, through the Divine blessing, thus become, in the hands of the Missionary, channels of influence and effort with a view to their conversion.

It might not be expedient to conduct the services as if exclusively intended for Jews, yet neither on the other hand, should the presence of such Jews as may attend them be ignored, and in any case both the truths presented and the manner of presenting them should make it manifest to all that the ingathering of Israel is specially aimed at.

(3)   In order to the attainment of these ends, the Committee deem it indispensable that the proclamation of the great truths of the gospel be based not on the foundation of the Apostles only, but of the Apostles and <u>Prophets</u>, Jesus Christ himself being always the chief corner-stone; in other words, they regard it as of first importance that the preaching be mainly expository, and especially that it present the truth in its historical and prophetic aspects, connecting the New Testament with the Old, and the past history with the future hope of Israel. The ministration in the Mission Church hitherto has possessed this distinctive character. The Committee are assured that this has been a chief ground of the appreciation it has met with, and that a large number of the most pious people in Amsterdam are prepared to welcome its continuance, and to give it their countenance and support on this footing. On the other hand, they are informed that, considering the increase in the number of earnest and eloquent Evangelical Ministers of late years in Amsterdam, there is little prospect, apart from this specialty, of these services being either successful or permanent.

(4)   In the present circumstances of Holland, it is not the wish of the Committee to place themselves, or the Free Church which they represent, either in antagonism or in special relationship to any of the existing Churches. They desire however, that their Missionary cultivate the closest and most friendly relations with good men of all denominations, and that he make his position and aims so manifest, as if possible to disarm all ecclesiastical jealousies, and make the Mission as far as may be a neutral territory, on which those who are otherwise opposed to each other may meet in harmony, and co-operate with the Missionary and with each other in the work which ought to have a common interest for all, the salvation of God's ancient people.

(5)   As the starting point of all his future labours, the Committee commend the special care of their Mission the proselytes, who have already been gathered into the fold of Christ. They have regarded with deep interest the successful efforts made by Mr Meyer to promote their spiritual growth, to bind them together by common interests and sympathies, and to foster in their minds the idea of a common vocation to commend the truth of Christ by word and deed to their yet unconverted brethren. They also consider the weekly social meetings, established by Mr Meyer for expositions of Scripture, conversation and prayer, as eminently suited to secure these ends, and they would strongly urge their continuance, as one of the most important and hopeful parts of the work of the Mission.

(6)   In the distribution of temporal relief, which has hitherto been made from the Church collections or seat-rents, the Committee recommend the exercise of great caution, lest in ministering to the wants of Christ's poor, encouragement be given to idleness or a false profession of the truth. They are not unmindful that undue hardness and severity would detract from the Christian character of the Mission, and impair its

moral influence both among Jews and Gentiles, but they cannot forget that the same evil effects will follow, unless the spirit of independence and self-reliance be cultivated among the converts. In this most delicate department of duty, in which equal harm may be done by an error on either side, they can only commit their Missionary to the guidance of Him alone who can impart the requisite tact, prudence, tenderness and firmness.

(7)   The Committee welcome with no ordinary satisfaction the earnest desire expressed by the several societies which owe their origin to the Scottish Mission, still to continue in friendly connexion with it, and to yield to it all available encouragement and help. In order, as far as possible, to avoid every cause of jealousy and mutual collision, they recommend on the one hand the fullest recognition by their Missionary of the independent position claimed by them, and on the other, the establishment of such carefully considered and well-understood relations as will form the basis of the most cordial and active co-operation. The Committee would regard as highly advantageous any arrangement by which all the agencies concerned, without prejudice to their individual freedom of action, might work together, less as separate bodies each complete in itself, than as mutually dependent parts, each bringing its special contributions to the common cause.

(8)   They deem it desirable that their Missionary associate with himself two or three gentlemen, in whom he has confidence, for the management of the property, and generally for consultation and aid in the affairs of the Mission. This instruction, however, is not intended to supersede his sole personal responsibility, but rather to enable him to exercise it with better effect.

(9)   In granting the use of the Church or Committee Rooms to other societies for stated or occasional meetings, special care must be taken to retain the entire control over the buildings, and to prevent any moral or quasi-legal right to spring up by prescription. They recommend that in all cases of stated use, permission be asked and given in writing, either for limited periods or during pleasure. All proposals by other parties to make alterations or improvements in any part of the buildings at their own hand, and for their own convenience, ought to be at once rejected.

(10)   Having in view the customary practice in all similar cases, and especially the large outlay required in Amsterdam to maintain house property in a state of thorough repair, the Committee deem it only reasonable that the several Societies, or other parties, who are permitted to hold meetings in the Mission premises, should pay a moderate sum to the funds of the Mission for the accommodation received. The precise amount may be determined at the discretion of the Missionary, after consulting with the Managers, care being taken that the estimate in no case exceed the cost of similar accommodation elsewhere, lest the position of these premises as a centre of Missionary operations in Amsterdam be endangered.

From the above rule those Societies might be accepted which have for their object the Conversion of Israel, in recognition of their brotherly co-operation in the same work, and in return for the pecuniary aid which they may see right in various forms to extend to the resources of the Mission.

The Committee have drawn up these instructions specifically for the Station of Amsterdam, which is at present unoccupied, but they direct a copy of them to be sent to each of their Missionaries in all their Stations, as expressing generally their mind on the whole work of the Mission to the Jews, and as applicable mutatis mutandis to all Stations.

Free Church of Scotland Jewish Mission Committee instructions for Torrance leaving for Tiberias
Extracted from the minutes of a meeting on 16.12.1884:[A]

The Sub-Committee appointed to prepare instructions for Dr Torrance submitted them as follows:-

The Committee of the Free Church of Scotland for the Conversion of the Jews, taking into consideration the many hindrances and difficulties in the way of successful prosecution of their work in such a new and untried field as that embraced in the Sea of Galilee Mission, resolve to furnish Dr Torrance with the following instructions for his guidance:-

I.   That he should regard it as one chief part of his work to gather patients together to hear the Scriptures read and expounded, so that, while obtaining healing for their bodies, they may be led, by the blessing of God on his own Word, to seek the removal of their soul's maladies – such religious service to be begun as soon as circumstances admit, and to be held daily before entering on the examination of the cases of those who are in attendance.

II.   So far as interpreters can be trusted, no time should be lost in making known with prudence to the people the grand leading object of the Mission, which is the enlightenment of their minds, the salvation of their souls, and as a result of this, the elevation of their character, and the improvement of their general condition, individual and social. It should ever be kept in view that these results will be most effectively secured when, to the religious instruction communicated, is added the example of a holy and consistent life.

III.   It being of the utmost importance that he should be in a position, with the least possible delay, to conduct services without the aid of an interpreter, the Committee will expect him to apply himself with all diligence to the acquisition of the native language.

IV.   That he should heartily cooperate with the various labourers in the same field, as well as with any other agents who may hereafter be employed in connection with the Mission, identifying himself with the interests and efforts of such agents, and endeavouring as far as possible to imbue them with a missionary spirit, so that they may become a real addition to the spiritual power of the Mission.

V.   That in regard to any fees which may be paid to him on account of Medical advice or attendance, he should keep an exact account of them and have them placed to the credit of the Mission. It is understood that the Medical Instruments +c. be provided by the Committee remain the property of the Mission.

VI.   As being new to the country, and unexperienced as regards the native people, he should remember that much explanation will be required in all his dealings with them; and that patience and simple acts of kindness and courtesy are never thrown away. He is further counselled to promote, to the utmost, peace and goodwill between families and neighbours; to avoid, if possible, taking any side in the event of disputes arising; and never to believe the first reports that may reach his ears, until by further enquiry the truth is made plain.

VII.   He should keep a daily journal, according all matters of general interest relating to weather, climate, health, work, +c., – facts only being stated at first, and inferences after a time when there appear to be sufficient data in explanation of them.

VIII.   That, with a view to the successful prosecution of the work of the Mission, he should use every precaution for the preservation of his health, removing temporarily, on the approach of the hot season, to the most convenient and suitable sanatorium and carrying on his medical and evangelistic labours there as God in his providence may open up the way.

IX.   That he report from time to time to the Committee on all matters affecting the wellbeing and progress of the Mission.

X.   In conclusion, it should not be forgotten that the success of the Mission is to be judged of in the light of ultimate and permanent results, and not with reference to any incidents in connection with its origin and progress. He is urged to look to God in all his difficulties, to put his trust in Him, in the assured confidence that His Word will not return unto him void – and to be much in prayer for the outpouring of the Holy Spirit, – while at the same time no effort should be spared which wisdom or experience may suggest.

The Committee approve and adopt them and record their thanks for the Sub-Committee especially Colonel Young and also to the Clerk.
They direct that a copy be sent to Dr Torrance.

Free Church of Scotland Jewish Mission Committee creation of Sea of Galilee Mission Council

Extracted from the minutes of a special meeting of members of the committee on 9.4.1890:[5]

Letters from Dr Torrance, Mr Ewing, and Mr Christie were read, containing the suggestions referred to in Telegram of March 12th, as recorded in Minute of 18th March. After careful consideration the following Minute was adopted, copy of which was to be sent to each of the three missionaries by the first post:–

I.   The Committee welcome and derive comfort from the letters now received, as showing a revival of brotherly feeling and mutual confidence, and their prayer and hope is that the issue may, by the blessing of God, be a settled concord.

II.   The Committee approve of the suggestion that there should be a Mission Council, this Council to be composed of the European brethren and to be entrusted with the general interests of the mission, with the management of everything affecting the relationship of the Mission to the Turkish Government, with all matters connected with the buying of land and building thereon, as also the renting and repairing of buildings used for missionary purposes, and the use and care of the boats. Further, while there are significant departments of work in the mission, - Medical, Educational (male & female), and Pastoral & Evangelistic, - all its departments must necessarily be under the general control and joint responsibility of the Council, subject to the Committee at home. The unity of the work will thus be secured, and at the same time the overlapping of one department by another will be prevented.

III.   As to the question of Chairman of the Mission Council, there certainly ought to be no head of the mission, but full and equal responsibility among its members. In the Mission Council at Constantinople the three missionaries preside in rotation, and one of their number acts as Secretary, taking minutes of the proceedings, and transmitting these to the Secretary of the Committee at home. This has been found to work well, and seems to form a good precedent for the Sea of Galilee Mission.

IV.   The Female Teacher, who is the Agent of the Ladies' Committee and is responsible to them, shall receive notice and have a seat in the Council when the work of her department is being considered, but shall not have a vote in the general affairs of the mission. This is the rule and practice in our Indian missions. Of course the arrangement now proposed must be regarded as tentative, and is open to modification as circumstances may seem to require. It forms, meanwhile, a basis, on which the affairs of the mission may be conducted with efficiency and comfort.

V.   The Committee in their last telegram:– "No censures to withdraw", intended to intimate the fact that in the several minutes no censures were either conveyed or designed. This they abide by. What they "deplored" had reference, as the minute bears, to Mr Ewing's resignation, which they are happy to think he is now prepared to withdraw.

[Approved by the Committee on 22.4.1890. Some corrections were made shortly after this Minute was approved and other amendments were made over subsequent years, but these are not detailed here.]

Endnotes

1. This diagram is a simplified version of the fold-out at the end of Burleigh (1960).
2. Free Church of Scotland, (1885) *Tabular Abstracts of the Sums Contributed Yearly to the Various Funds and Schemes of the Church During the Forty-Two Years from the Disruption to 1884-85 Inclusive, With Remarks Thereon by the Convener of the Finance Committee*, Edinburgh: 22-23. All figures have been rounded down to the nearest pound, e.g. £350 15s 4d becomes simply £350.
3. FC-JMC 17.10.1871
4. FC-JMC 16.12.1884
5. FC-JMC 9.4.1890

NOTES

Chapter 1

1. For details of the Free Church's involvement in the Levant in the only non-Jewish Scottish mission, see Michael Marten, (2001) 'Representation and misrepresentation in 19th century Lebanon – Scottish and American missionaries in conflict', in *Orientalische Christen zwischen Repression und Migration. Beiträge zur jüngeren Geschichte und Gegenwartslage*, ed. Martin Tamcke, series, *Studien zur Orientalischen Kirchengeschichte*, vol. 13, Hamburg, and, (2002) 'The Free Church of Scotland in 19th-century Lebanon', *Chronos. Revue d'Histoire de l'Université Balamand*, No. 5, 51-106. The former focuses on the beginnings of the mission in relation to the existing American mission in Lebanon, whilst the latter offers a more general overview of the origins, practices, and end of the mission.

2. c.f. Bibliography below

3. Charles R Taber, (1990-1) 'The Missionary Movement and the Anthropologists', in *Bulletin of the Scottish Institute of Missionary Studies*, No 6-7, 16-32: 16

4. Examining local responses to missionaries has been carried out by, amongst others, anthropologists, e.g. Willy Jansen, who describes a community in Jordan. She notes the significant role of social factors such as kinship, marriage and divorce needs in determining religious/ecclesiastical allegiance; (2000) 'Fragmentation of the Christian minority in Jordan. Conversion, marriage and gender' in, *Anthropologists and the Missionary Endeavour. Experiences and Reflections*, eds. Ad Borsboom, Jean Kommers, series, *Nijmegen Studies in Development and Cultural Change*, Saarbrücken

5. An essay that falls into this category is Colin Morton, (1999) 'Motives for the Scottish Mission in Palestine. 19th and 20th Centuries', in, *Patterns of the Past, Prospects for the Future. The Christian Heritage in the Holy Land*, eds. Thomas Hummel, Kevork Hintlian, Ulf Carmesund, London, which must unfortunately be disregarded when trying to present a historical account. Although general surveys of mission such as Stephen Neill, (1964) *A History of Christian Missions*, Harmondsworth, revised edition 1986, or Elizabeth G K Hewat, (1960) *Vision and Achievement 1796-1956. A History of the Foreign Missions of the Churches united in the Church of Scotland*, Edinburgh, accord missions in the Middle East a very small role, more geographically specific surveys such as Julius Richter, (1910) *A History of Protestant Missions in the Near East*, Edinburgh, or Naomi Shepherd, (1987) *The Zealous Intruders. The Western Rediscovery of Palestine*, London, pay little attention to the Scots. J H Proctor, (1997) 'Scottish Missionaries and the Struggle for Palestine, 1917-48', in *Middle Eastern Studies*, vol. 33, no. 3, July, 613-629, offers a useful and well-founded analysis of Scottish missionaries' opinions on Zionism and the political situation in Mandate Palestine, but that is beyond the time frame covered by this book.

6. Abdul Latif Tibawi, (1961) *British Interests in Palestine 1800-1901. A Study of Religious and Educational Enterprise*, Oxford, for many years represented the most authoritative account of Anglican work, but recent years have seen more material forthcoming, e.g. Nancy L Stockdale, (2000) *Gender and Colonialism in Palestine 1800-1948: Encounters among English, Arab and Jewish Women*, unpublished PhD thesis, University of California Santa Barbara, Rafiq A Farah, (2002) *In troubled waters: A History of the Anglican Church in Jerusalem, 1841-1998*, Leicester, 2002, and Inger Marie Okkenhaug, (2002) *The Quality of Heroic Living, of High Endeavour and Adventure. Anglican Mission, Women and Education in Palestine, 1888-1948*, series: *Studies in Christian Mission*, ed. Marc R Spindler, Leiden. Many less useful works have also appeared, often from a 'Western Fundamentalist Christian Zionist' perspective (c.f. MECC, (1988) *What is Western Fundamentalist Christian Zionism?*, Limassol), including Kelvin Crombie, (1991) *For the Love of*

Zion. Christian witness and the restoration of Israel, London.

7.   Note, however, the Anglican Communion's difficulties with this issue at the 1988 Lambeth Conference: Braybrooke, (1990) *Time to Meet. Towards a deeper relationship between Jews and Christians*, London: 31; 36 details the Union of Evangelical Churches in Switzerland's position.

8.   The Leuenberg Church Fellowship, a grouping of Lutheran, Reformed and United churches based in Berlin to which the modern-day Church of Scotland belongs, has recently been engaged in trying to improve its understanding of the relationship between Jews and Christians. Páraic Réamonn laconically notes that '[o]nly the end of time will tell' if the study on *The Church and Israel*, presented to the Leuenberg Assembly in Belfast, Ireland, in June 2001, represents 'Socratic wisdom or eschatological copout' in postulating that '[u]ntil the final goal of "all of God's history with the world" has been reached ... Christian theology "will not be able to solve the mystery" of the relation between the church and Israel. Only then will the people of God appear visibly "in the way God has predetermined for it"'. Réamonn notes that although the study '[r]ightly ... says that Christians are "united in solidarity" with Jews ... it fails to ask how Christians may speak a word of critical solidarity in the face of the current murderous policies of the state of Israel'; (2001) 'Christians and Jews, Catholics and Protestants', in *WARC Update*, September, vol. 11, no. 3, 11-12. Réamonn, a Church of Scotland minister, is the Communications Secretary of the World Alliance of Reformed Churches, to which the Church of Scotland also belongs. This wariness of criticism of 'Jews', 'Israel', 'Israeli policies' etc. is an ongoing issue for those engaged in dialogue with Jews or in politics related to the Palestine-Israel conflict. This issue cannot be discussed here in more detail, though the following address different aspects of the problem: Hans Küng, (1992) *Judaism. The Religious Situation of our Time*, London, see especially Part 2 Section B ('The Dispute between Jews and Christians') and Part 3 Section C ('Jews, Muslims and the Future State of Israel'); 632-3 outline what he sees as the (religious) pre-conditions for peace in the Near East; see also the last chapter of his book. Marcus Braybrooke, (2000) *Christian-Jewish Dialogue: The Next Steps*, London, examines theological issues, clearly outlining the problems with contemporary missionary activity (96-108); Tony Bayfield provides a helpful (Reform) Jewish response (113-126). Saperstein, (1989) *Moments of Crisis in Jewish-Christian Relations*, London, describes key problems in Jewish-Christian relations; see especially 61-3 on the issue of mission. In terms of Christian theology, contemporary Palestinian theologians such as Naim Stifan Ateek, (1989) *Justice, and only Justice. A Palestinian Theology of Liberation*, New York, have wrestled with 'Jewish' texts (e.g. on issues such as 'chosenness' and 'land') whilst attempting to reject anti-Jewish sentiment, despite the perceived oppression by a 'Jewish state'. Uwe Gräbe, (1999) *Kontextuelle palästinensische Theologie. Streitbare und umstrittene Beiträge zum ökumenischen und interreligiösen Gespräch*, series: *Missionswissenschaftliche Forschungen*, Neue Folge, vol. 9, Erlangen), gives a definitive analysis of contemporary Palestinian theology, examining biblical exegesis in this context (230-274), as well as theological responsibility 'after Auschwitz' (286-290). His reflections on the potential antagonism between contextual Palestinian theology and what he describes as 'North Atlantic' theological models 'after Auschwitz' deserve a wide audience, particularly his criticism of theologians such as Paul van Buren and Friedrich-Wilhelm Marquardt (299-319) and his suggestions for alternative models (see especially 315-319). Gräbe's work has the potential to move Jewish-Christian dialogue on in helpful ways that have been felt to be lacking by many, including Braybrooke, 2000, above. See also the collection of essays by Palestinian theologians in the volume edited by Harald Suermann, (2001) *Zwischen Halbmond und Davidstern: Christliche Theologie in Palästina heute*, Freiburg i. Br. Michael Hilton, (1994) *The Christian Effect on Jewish Life*, London, takes a perspective that has often been overlooked; chapters 6 and 7 examine Christian influence on Jewish readings of key biblical passages (87-89 address the subject of mission).

9.   Andreas Feldtkeller, (2000) 'Sieben Thesen zur Missionsgeschichte', series: *Berliner Beiträge*

zur Missionsgeschichte, Berlin, Heft 1, September: 3. Feldtkeller's seven theses on mission history are presented as the common history of mission-oriented religions, the aim being to enable community between people of different cultures, implying the crossing of cultural and religious boundaries. His outline leads him to describe the relation of mission history to religious freedom and the need for mission history in order to understand pluralistic societies.

10. Neill (1964): 207-208

11. The references to 'ages' are, of course, to Eric J Hobsbawm, (1962) *The Age of Revolution 1789-1848*, London, (1975) *The Age of Capital 1848-1875*, London, and (1987) *The Age of Empire 1875-1914*, London.

12. Eric J Hobsbawm, (1968) *Industry and Empire*, Harmondsworth, 1999: 13

13. ibid.: chapter 2

14. Neill (1964): 212. Of course, the commercial value of the missionaries was also often recognised by those seeking financial rewards from their efforts in the colonial enterprise (though this was not always the case, particularly in the early years, as the East India Company's general dislike of missionaries shows).

15. Jongeneel, (1995) *Philosophy, science, and theology of mission in the 19th and 20th centuries: a missiological encyclopedia. Part I: The philosophy and science of mission*, series: *Studies in the Intercultural History of Christianity*, vol. 92, Frankfurt am Main: 228

16. The Roman Catholic tradition also experienced increased missionary interest.

17. Neill (1964): 213-215; for a general overview of Western missionary motivation, c.f. esp. 187-204 for pre-19th century inclinations to missionary work from the West, and 222-272 for a summary of missions in the first half of the 19th century.

18. Gavin White, (1977) "Highly Preposterous': Origins of Scottish Missions', in *Records of the Scottish Church History Society*, vol. XIX, 111-124, records the early stages of missions from Scotland.

19. Hewat (1960): 1-7

20. It was the first statement of Reformed Scottish belief; by the nineteenth century the Westminster Confession (1647), a considerably less harsh interpretation of Calvinistic orthodoxy than the Scots Confession, was pre-eminent; Jan Rohls, (1987) *Theologie reformierter Bekenntnisschriften: von Zürich bis Barmen*, Göttingen: 31

21. Alasdair I C Heron, (1980a) *Das schottische Bekenntnis (1560)*, revised typescript of a lecture given at the Protestant Faculty of Theology, Munich, on 30.6.1980: 2-3; the Confession was widely read and gained widespread acceptance, so was not just a hierarchically imposed statement; William Stacy Johnson/John H Leith, (1993) *Reformed Reader: a Sourcebook in Christian Theology. Volume 1: Classical Beginnings, 1519-1799*, Louisville: xx

22. Cited in Karl Barth, (1938) *The Knowledge of God and the Service of God. The Gifford Lectures, 1938*, London: 148 (Barth's emphases); Barth's exposition is one of the most thorough modern theological treatments of the Confession.

23. Rohls (1987): 22; Roman Catholic teaching, which the Scots Confession was seeking to defend against, took a similar line (*extra ecclesiam nulla salus*), initially against Christian heresies, though by 1442 (Council of Florence) it was also directed against Islam and the westward expansion of the Turks; David Kerr (2000) 'Muhammad: Prophet of Liberation – a Christian Perspective from Political Theology', in *Studies in World Christianity*, vol. 6, no. 2, 139-174: 151.

24. The churches were as poor as the people: 'Dark, damp, dirty hovels' is the memorable description by a minister of many churches at the end of the 18th century; James Mackinnon, (1921) *The Social and Industrial History of Scotland From the Union to the Present Time*, London: 45.

25. Hugh McLeod, (1981) *Religion and the People of Western Europe 1789-1970*, Oxford: 75

26. Although Michael Lynch warns against excessive simplification of the outcome of the 1707 Union, particularly referring to the immediate economic benefits, the longer-term benefits

are clear; (1991) *Scotland. A New History*, London: 323-324.

27. Olive and Sydney Checkland, (1984) *Industry and Ethos. Scotland 1832-1914*, Edinburgh, 2nd ed. 1989: 12

28. Callum Brown, (1997) *Religion and Society in Scotland since 1707*, Edinburgh: 18

29. J H S Burleigh, (1960) *A Church History of Scotland*, Oxford: 328

30. I have omitted to describe the various secessions and divisions that took place in the Scottish ecclesiastical landscape of this period, focusing instead on tendencies and movements in the thinking and life of the church; Burleigh (1960) Part IV has more details; the last page of the volume is a detailed fold-out page showing in time-line form the major denominations and the different branches of the church; a simplified version of this is in Appendix below.

31. Jon Roxborogh, (1999) *Thomas Chalmers: Enthusiast for Mission. The Christian Good of Scotland and the Rise of the Missionary Movement*, Carlisle/Edinburgh: 238

32. Mt 28:19

33. Hewat cites this as the response to William Carey, the founder of the Baptist Society, when he argued for missions at a Baptist Conference in 1786; (1960): 5

34. ibid.: 36

35. Lynch (1991): 401; although the extent to which the Disruption shook Scottish society is now perhaps difficult to imagine, the increasing irrelevance of the later 19th and early 20th century churches in Scotland became ever more apparent.

36. Roxborogh (1999): c.f. esp. the first part.

37. ibid.: 153 explores the early background to this development.

38. Lynch (1991): 402; society's increasingly liberal attitudes were not welcomed by either church: 'The dawn of liberality in the House of Commons alarmed both the Scottish Churches and undoubtedly the spirit of the Church as a whole was intolerant, more intolerant than was Parliament'; Elizabeth S Haldane, (1933) *The Scotland of our Fathers: A Study of Scottish Life in the Nineteenth Century*, London: 141-2

39. Brown (1997): 103; Susan Thorne explores the links between class and missionary activity (this is returned to below): (1997) '"The Conversion of Englishmen and the Conversion of the World Inseparable": Missionary Imperialism and the Language of Class in Early Industrial Britain', in *Tensions of Empire. Colonial Cultures in a Bourgeois World*, eds. Frederick Cooper, Ann Laura Stoler, Berkeley, Los Angeles, London, 238-262.

40. Brown (1997): 107

41. Andrew C Ross, (1972) 'Scottish missionary concern 1874-1914. A golden era?', in *Scottish Historical Review*, vol. LI/I, no. 151, April, 52-72; c.f. also Chapter 4 below.

42. Brown (1997): 189; in the wider British context the Scottish churches were diminishing in importance. Although the Church of England 'would not ... be the only Church of the nation, but could instead be no more than a large and privileged denomination, one among a number', Presbyterianism in England was seen largely 'as an extension of Scotland', so that although there was a presence in Northumberland, Liverpool and London, 'elsewhere [it was] very weak' and Presbyterianism as an element of the so-called Free Churches of England remained a marginal force, particularly compared to the Methodists, Congregationalists and Baptists; Adrian Hastings, (2001) *A History of English Christianity 1920-2000*, London, (4th ed. 2001: first published 1986 as *A History of English Christianity 1920-1985*): 103.

43. Brown (1997): 190

44. Linda Colley, (1992) *Britons: Forging the Nation. 1707-1837*, London: 388

45. ibid.: 394

46. ibid.: 35; her chapter on 'Protestantism' makes for useful reading on these issues. In summary, myth is here understood as a narrative or foundational story (symbolic or real) that provides a cultural group with its origins and destiny. Robert Eric Frykenberg ((1996) *History and Belief: The Foundations of Historical Understanding*, Grand Rapids) has a useful chapter on 'History as Destiny: An Interpretative Quest'.

47. Lynch notes that more than half the British army's officer corps was Scottish or Irish, with Scots dominating the administration of India; (1991): 386.

48. Colley (1992): 37

49. Checkland (1984): 118

50. ibid.: 118

51. This is somewhat simplistically stated, implying a level of automaticity on the part of the deity's actions that was not necessarily perceived to function in quite this way.

52. Anne Michaels, (1997) *Fugitive Pieces*, London: 193

53. Hans-Ulrich Wehler refers to a mental map in constructing national identity: what is outlined here is not so much the subjects creating the map (Jews), but Christians who needed it for their own self-understanding. This creation borrowed from multiple sources: Christian-influenced images of Jews, of the Biblical narrative, of the place of Christians and Jews in the divine economy and so on; (2001) *Nationalismus: Geschichte, Formen, Folgen*, München: 38.

54. For a later example of similar sentiments c.f. A J Sherman, (1997) *Mandate Days. British Lives in Palestine 1918-1948*, London: 16. Such thinking permeates all aspects of a culture and is reflected not just in an overtly religious context: Bryan Cheyette, (1993) *Constructions of 'the Jew' in English literature and society: racial representations, 1875-1945*, Cambridge, examines the literary links to Judaism in the context of 'race'.

55. Staying overnight in Rosetta, the 1839 delegation noted: 'All was now truly oriental, and the scenery of the Arabian Nights occurred vividly to our mind'; Andrew A Bonar/Robert Murray McCheyne, (1843) *Narrative of a Visit to the Holy Land and Mission of Inquiry to the Jews*, Edinburgh: 55. On the confusion of 'the real East with the East of the stories' (Rana Kabbani, (1986) *Imperial Fictions. Europe's Myths of Orient*, Pandora, London, 1994: 29), including an examination of the ألف ليلة و ليلة and Galland's text, see Kabbani's section on the 'Arabian Nights', 23-36.

56. Clyde Binfield, (1994) 'Jews in Evangelical Dissent: The British Society, The Herschell Connection and the Pre-Millenarian Thread', in *Prophecy and Eschatology*, series: *Subsidia 10*, ed. Michael Wilks, Oxford, 225-270: 226

57. Checkland (1984): 118-119

58. Binfield (1994): 226; the title of a publication from 1890, printed in Beirut, indicates general Evangelical thought at this time: *The Everlasting Nation: An International Monthly Journal of History, Biography, Prophecy, Literature, Exegesis, and Passing Events Relating to the Jewish People*. Scottish attitudes to Jews and Palestine reflected this sentiment closely.

59. Northern 'Europe received little ... attention ... [from] most medieval Arab historians and geographers ... These regions were generally considered savage and barbaric with little to offer and, as al-Muqaddasi put it, it was not "worthwhile to describe them"'; Thabit Abdullah, (1997) 'Arab views of northern Europeans in medieval history and geography', in *Images of the Other: Europe and the Muslim World Before 1700*, ed. David R Blanks, series: *Cairo Papers in Social Science*, vol. 19, monograph 2, summer 1996, Cairo, 73-80: 74

60. Alan Macquarrie, (1997) *Scotland and the Crusades 1095-1560*, Edinburgh: 21-22

61. Sylvia Schein, (1991) *Fideles Crucis. The Papacy, the West, and the Recovery of the Holy Land 1274-1314*, Oxford: 47, 152 indicate a certain reluctance to pay the tithe for financing the Crusades, with Scottish bishops being requested to excommunicate those who had not paid.

62. Macquarrie (1997): 3-7

63. ibid.: 128

64. ibid.: 133-4

65. Carole Hillenbrand, (1999) *The Crusades: Islamic Perspectives*, Edinburgh

66. Amin Maalouf, (1983) *Les croisades vues par les Arabes*, Paris: 279

67. ibid.: 283

68. Wehler (2001): 36

69. Bonar/McCheyne (1843): 2

70. Lionel Alexander Ritchie, (2005?) entry for Keith in the forthcoming *New Dictionary of National Biography*. I would like to record my thanks to Alexander Ritchie for providing me with a number of his entries to the NDNB prior to publication.

71. Email correspondence from Alexander Ritchie, 30.4.02, describes inconclusive allegations regarding plagiarism.

72. Bonar's brother, Horatius, was also a pre-millennialist, and particularly in the 1840s the three of them, along with Edward Irving of the Regent Square Scottish Church in London, did much to further this tendency in Scotland; David Bebbington, (1989) *Evangelicalism in modern Britain. A history from the 1730s to the 1980s*, London: 78-80. Although not necessarily the case (and certainly not with the individuals mentioned here), the 'pre-millennialist was world-denying save in a general fascination with such current events as might confirm prophecy'; Binfield (1994): 234 (see also 235-7). Indeed, one of Horatius Bonar's hymns still included in the 1973 edition of the Church of Scotland hymnary (CH3 483) directly links purposeful missionary engagement with the return of Christ and the end times (the 'world's highway' is clearly derived from Lk 14:23):

> Toil on, faint not, keep watch, and pray;
> Be wise, the erring soul to win;
> Go forth into the world's highway,
> Compel the wanderer to come in
>
> Toil on, and in thy toil rejoice;
> For toil comes rest, for exile home;
> Soon shalt thou hear the Bridegroom's voice,
> The midnight peal, 'Behold, I come!'

Bebbington describes millenarianism, pre-millenarianism and post-millenarianism, linking these to pessimism and optimism in viewing world affairs: 81-86, 60-63, 102-104 respectively; c.f. 191-194 for the period around WWI; see also Binfield, (1994): 233-237. In the latter half of the 19th century, many prominent Scots were convinced pre-millennialists, and though the likes of John Cumming of London's Covent Garden Crown Court Scottish Church did not pursue the increasing eccentricities of Irving, this perspective came to dominate 19th century Evangelical thought, preceding J N Darby's dispensationalism of the 20th century; Bebbington (1989): 85-6. On the influential role played by Scots in London on theology in Scotland and England, c.f. George C Cameron, (1979) *The Scots Kirk in London*, Oxford: particularly 107-110 (Irving) and more generally chapters 8-10. Stephen Sizer elaborates on the wider topic of Dispensational Christian Zionism; on Irving; (2003) *Christian Zionism: Fueling the Arab-Israeli Conflict. Historical Roots, Theological Basis and Political Consequences*, unpublished PhD thesis, Middlesex University (CD version, available via http://www.sizers.org (accessed 20.6.03)): 36-45. Eugen Weber, (1999) *Apocalypses: Prophecies, Cults and Millennial Beliefs through the Ages*, London, provides a more general overview of these themes in 19th century Europe (though sometimes somewhat flippantly expressed, which unfortunately undermines his desire to retrieve millennial study from the 'lunatic fringe': 3) c.f. 129-146. He places the apocalypse in the context of 19th century Romanticism (122-125): 'rejuvenation and revival ... [is] also about the twilight and trials that precede them' (123) – although this cannot be addressed in more detail here, millenarian beliefs were, of course, intrinsically connected to beliefs about the meaning of the apocalypse (147-165).

73. Andrew A Bonar, (1865) *Palestine for the Young*, London; there is no date in the volume but his diary gives this as the date of publication: c.f. entry for 20.9.1865 in (1960) *Diary and Life*, (no place of publication). The British Library has also recorded this as the date of publication.

74. Bonar (1865): 10
75. Lester I Vogel, (1993) *To See a Promised Land: Americans and the Holy Land in the Nineteenth Century*, Pennsylvania: 10
76. ibid.: 11
77. Bonar (1865): 343-4 (Bonar's emphasis); c.f. Deut 9:2, Josh 11:22-23.
78. F F Bruce, (1977) 'The History of New Testament Study', in *New Testament Interpretation. Essays in Principles and Methods*, ed. I Howard Marshall, Exeter: 21-59, offers a Western-dominated outline of New Testament studies (38-46 focus on the 19th century): other essays in this volume describe the various critical methods used; Andrew L Drummond/James Bulloch, (1978) *The Church in Late Victorian Scotland 1874-1900*, Edinburgh, examine the advent of biblical criticism in Scotland; In *The Bible in Scottish Life and Literature*, ed. David F Wright, Edinburgh, Alex Cheyne, (1988) 'The Bible and Change in the Nineteenth Century': 192-207, outlines the changes in biblical interpretative methods in 19th century Scotland whilst Donald Meek, (1988) 'The Bible and Social Change in the nineteenth Century Highlands': 179-191, portrays the interpretative use of Biblical texts in specific social circumstances. The translation of the Bible into vernacular languages was of limited effect in Scotland: although there were translations into Scots, English versions tending to dominate: Graham Tulloch, (1989) *A History of the Scots Bible with selected texts*, Aberdeen.
79. The volume containing this article was published on 7.12.1875. Subsequent articles furthered the tensions. An acrimonious and bitter public dispute arose that went through the media and the highest courts of the church as Smith was prosecuted for heresy. A detailed and reasonably readable account is in Drummond/Bulloch (1978): 40-78; for a briefer summary, c.f. Bebbington (1989): 184-186.
80. Contemporary political/feminist theology bases much of its need for new biblical scholarship on this basis, e.g. Marla J Selvidge, (1996) *Notorious Voices: Feminist Biblical Interpretation, 1500-1920*, London: 3, 14-18, but also *passim*.
81. Drummond/Bulloch (1978): 75
82. ibid.: 78
83. Checkland (1984): 124
84. Results were mostly in the lower middle-classes, and even there, the widening of the political franchise and the rise of spectator sports meant that political movements and football were strong rivals for the emotions of the people. Other reasons for reduced working-class church attendance between ca. 1864 and 1914 are described by Bebbington (1989): 141-143. Increased urbanisation and the corresponding 'breakdown of religious unity in the cities' was also a factor in change; McLeod (1981): 89; the chapter this quotation comes from describes the effects of urbanisation on religious behaviour throughout Europe.
85. A literal understanding of Biblical texts was seen as necessary for Jewish missionary work for many years. Adolph Saphir, whose family was converted in Budapest by "Rabbi" Duncan of the Free Kirk, states that Jewish missionaries 'thoroughly ... and without any reservation believed in the divine authority of Scripture from Genesis down to the book of the Apocalypse' (from a lecture given on 1.10.1889); (1950s) *Christ and Israel. Lectures and Addresses*, collected and edited by David Baron, Jerusalem, nd (the edition used here – 'Printed in Israel' – is possibly from the 1950s; it was originally published in ca. 1911 or 1912: c.f. UFC-CCJ 27.2.1912): 88-9.
86. Davidson was 'Rabbi' John Duncan's successor in this post; Israel Finestein, (1991) 'British Opinion and the Holy Land in the Nineteenth Century: Personalities and Further Themes' in, *With Eyes Toward Zion III – Western Societies and the Holy Land*, eds. Moshe Davis, Yehoshua Ben-Arieh, New York, 227-238: 228. These two, along with George Adam Smith (who taught at Glasgow and Aberdeen) had a profound influence on how the Old Testament, the land of Palestine, and the place of the Jews in the world and the divine economy was

perceived in Scotland throughout the period covered by this book. See also Graeme Auld, (1996) 'Hebrew and Old Testament', in *Disruption to Diversity: Edinburgh Divinity 1846-1996*, eds. David F Wright, Gary B Badcock, Edinburgh, 53-71: 57-59.

87. Alexander Paterson (Hebron) attended his services (William Ewing, (1925) *Paterson of Hebron: "The Hakim" Missionary Life in the Mountain of Judah*, London, nd – 1925, 1930, 1931?: 27); he was also one of Robertson Smith's teachers (Bebbington (1989): 185). UFC-MR, 5.1917: 110 offers a review of a biography which points to the importance of Davidson's work and influence long after his death. He 'sought to present ... the actors in the Hebrew Bible as participants in a live historical process ... [the Hebrew Bible influencing] private practice and public policy'; Finestein (1991): 229.

88. Andrew Bruce Davidson, (1903) *Old Testament Prophecy*, ed. J A Paterson, Edinburgh; the work was edited by James Alexander Paterson, Davidson's colleague and successor at New College, on the basis of lectures by Davidson (Davidson died in January 1902). Davidson's (1904) *The Theology of the Old Testament*, ed. S D F Salmond, Edinburgh, was also published posthumously, based on notes.

89. Davidson (1903): 469

90. Davidson does not address practicalities such as present-day ownership and title deeds – Jewish 'ownership' was not necessarily understood in these terms; in some ways, this is what the remainder of the chapter attempts to address.

91. ibid.: 469

92. ibid.: 470

93. ibid.: 470

94. ibid.: 471

95. ibid.: 472

96. ibid.: 474

97. ibid.: 478-9

98. ibid.: 483

99. ibid.: 485

100. This is a familiar view in the broader context of missionary activity, e.g. Dolores Clavero cites concerns about 'the often unchristian behaviour of the Spanish laymen' in 17th century Peru: (1998) 'The Discourse of the Newly-Converted Christian in the Work of the Andean Chronicler Guaman Poma de Ayala', in, *Christian Encounters with the Other*, ed. John C Hawley, New York, 44-55: 51.

101. Davidson (1903): 491

102. ibid.: 492; c.f. Rom 1:16, 10:12, Gal 3:28 etc.; the Pauline term 'Greek' describes non-Jews.

103. ibid.: 500

104. John Hall, (1914) *Israel in Europe*, series: *Our Jewish Missions II*, Edinburgh: cover page; Hall was a member of the JMC.

105. ibid.: 103

106. ibid.: 103

107. ibid.: 105

108. ibid.: 106-9

109. ibid.: 109-113, this quotation from 113 reflects the ever-present understanding that numerous conversions were always imminent, an understanding referred to constantly by the missionaries, who had only few converts to show for their labours. On 115, having offered various statistics on the conversion of Jews (which cannot now be treated as having any degree of reliability), Hall explains the various reasons many Jews would not openly profess Christian faith but would nonetheless be believers – another theme that the missionaries often returned to. The JMC, who issued this book, clearly had a financial interest in this: promises of imminent conversion would generate further support for their work.

110. ibid.: 115-117; he means the intellectual ability and/or involvement in missions by the converts, giving selected examples.

111. ibid.: 118; this ambitious aim of converting 'the whole world' has distinct origins in the nineteenth century: Thorne (1997): 245.

112. Robert P Carroll, (1991) *Wolf in the Sheepfold. The Bible as Problematic for Theology*, London, 2nd ed. 1997: 97 (Carroll's emphasis)

113. ibid.: 150 provides pointers to research on this topic.

114. ibid.: 102 (Carroll's emphasis); the most recent examination of this kind, confirming Carroll's point, can be found in Michael Prior, (2003) 'The State of the Art: Biblical Scholarship and the Holy Land', in *Holy Land Studies*, vol. 1, no. 2, March, 192-218: esp. 207-214. Historically, of course, Jews have often suffered at the hands of ruling powers for reasons other than Christian persecution. The Scots perceived this to be the case, reflecting particularly in later years on the persecution of Jews in Russian and Eastern Europe, not seeing this necessarily as linked to religion. For many Scots, this fitted Feldman's description of the 'lachrymose theory of Jewish history, highlighting the weakness and suffering of the Jews', though as he has shown, this did not apply to the ancient period. Whilst wishing to avoid the dangers of ignoring or downplaying the very real persecution of Jews through the ages, particularly in spheres of Christian dominance, I think there is an urgent need for reassessments of the place of Jews in different periods and locations in the manner of Feldman's work on the ancient world; Louis H Feldman, (1993) *Jew and Gentile in the Ancient World: Attitudes and Interactions from Alexander to Justinian*, Princeton: 445.

115. Carroll (1991): 101 (Carroll's emphasis)

116. Examples of this abound: c.f. e.g. p26 below.

117. Victor G Kiernan, (1995) *Imperialism and its contradictions*, edited and introduced by Harvey J Kaye, London: 146

118. Edward W Said, (1978) *Orientalism: Western Conceptions of the Orient*, London, 1978, 1995: 252

119. ibid.: 251

120. ibid.: 67; (Said's emphasis)

121. ibid.: 92

122. Tibawi (1961): 31

123. Simon Gikandi, (1996) *Maps of Englishness: Writing Identity in the Culture of Colonialism*, Columbia, New York: 86

124. c.f. p29 below.

125. i.e. about the force of passionate conviction the defence of which is personal, and not dictated by preference; that involves a way of being, and not simply an ontological or cognitive commitment.

126. c.f. p16 above – offering the best they had.

127. As will be seen, all the churches made free use of the power and authority of their government, gratefully accepting letters of support from the Foreign Office and seeking the support of local government representatives whenever they felt it appropriate.

128. Proctor (1997)

129. e.g. William L Cleveland, (1994) *A History of the Modern Middle East*, Boulder/Oxford; Albert Hourani, (1991) *A History of the Arab Peoples*, London; Malcolm E Yapp, (1987) *The Making of the Modern Near East 1792-1923*, London.

130. Philippe Fargues, (1998) 'The Arab Christians of the Middle East: A Demographic Perspective', in, *Christian Communities in the Arab Middle East: the challenge of the future*, ed. Andrea Pacini, Oxford, 48-66: 52

131. Special taxes and lack of military service opportunities characterised *dhimmi* status.

132. Anthony O'Mahony, (1999) 'Palestinian Christians: Religion, Politics and Society, c. 1800-1948',

in *Palestinian Christians: Religion, Politics and Society in the Holy Land*, ed. Anthony O'Mahony, London, 9-55: 19-20

133. ibid.: 21-22

134. Children of a Christian/Muslim marriage would automatically be Muslim. More generally, 'The legally tolerated status of *dhimma* ... established a 'default' position which amounted to gentle but relentless pressure in smaller internal communities to become Muslim and legitimised a generally hostile attitude to Christians outside the Muslim realms'; Jørgen S Nielsen, (2003) 'Is there an escape from the history of Christian-Muslim Relations?', in *A Faithful Presence: essays for Kenneth Cragg*, ed. David Thomas with Clare Amos, London, 350-361, 352. This was part of a more general condemnation of Christianity, Nielsen argues on the previous page.

135. Fargues (1998): 53

136. ibid.: 54-57; of course, Jewish immigration played a significant role in the change in population of this particular *millet*; Courbage/Fargues (1997): 154. Donald Quataert, (1994b) 'Part IV: The Age of Reforms, 1812-1914', in *An Economic and Social History of the Ottoman Empire. Volume Two: 1600-1914*, ed. Halil İnalcik with Donald Quataert, Cambridge, 1994, 1997, pp759-943: 790, points out that birth-control methods can be presumed to have been known in the 19th century (primarily through jurisprudence and erotica), similarly abortions, though he does not differentiate between population groupings in their knowledge and application of these methods.

137. Fargues (1998): 56-57

138. Courbage/Fargues (1997): 74

139. c.f. e.g. Yapp (1987): 47-96

140. Catholic missions in Palestine are generally under-researched; this has only recently begun to change.

141. O'Mahony (1999): 23-25

142. ibid.: 26-27; although the Greek Orthodox patriarchate had existed since Roman times, newer positions can be seen as primarily religio-political creations; e.g. the new Latin patriarchate was clearly designed to further 'ambitions de latinisation'; Jean-Pierre Valognes, (1994) *Vie et mort des chrétiens d'Orient. Des origines à nos jours*, Paris: 81; see also 505-512.

143. Roger Owen, (1982) 'Introduction', *Studies in the Economic and Social History of Palestine in the Nineteenth and Twentieth Centuries*, ed. Roger Owen, London, 1-9: 2

144. Courbage/Fargues (1997): 75

145. ibid.: 75-76

146. ibid.: 79; Courbage/Fargues attribute the 1860 Lebanese war almost exclusively to economic factors, though this is somewhat simplistic: demography, patronage etc. all played a role: Leila Tarazi Fawaz, (1994) *An Occasion for War – Civil Conflict in Lebanon and Damascus in 1860*, London: 222-223. Ussama Makdisi has highlighted the role of sectarianism in the context of modernity, c.f. e.g. (2000) *The Culture of Sectarianism: Community, History, and Violence in Nineteenth Century Ottoman Lebanon*, Berkeley, Los Angeles, London, 166-172.

147. Courbage/Fargues (1997): 79

148. Stanford J Shaw, (1991) *The Jews of the Ottoman Empire and the Turkish Republic*, London: 175, 177

149. Justin McCarthy describes them as 'either dependent on the charity of the world's Jews (*Halukka*) or [they] earned a precarious existence as craftsmen or merchants ... they were peripheral to the economic and political life of the region'; (1990) *The Population of Palestine – Population History and Statistics of the Late Ottoman Period and the Mandate*, New York: 13

150. Shaw (1991): 179-181 outlines the background to this, with the following pages detailing newspapers in more detail.

151. Jonathan Frankel has given a detailed account of this saga: (1997) *The Damascus Affair. "Ritual Murder," Politics, and the Jews in 1840*, Cambridge.

152. Shaw (1991): 210

153. Shaw (1991): 214
154. McCarthy (1990): 13
155. Shaw (1991): 215; 211-217 outlines the Porte's reaction to Jewish immigration and Zionism. The parallels to similar minorities, such as Slavs and Armenians, would also have been noted by the Sultan, keen to avoid nationalist tendencies.
156. McCarthy (1990): 10, 223 – note that the Zionist statistics describe the Jewish urban population of Palestine, and so agricultural settlers would need to be added to these figures; Shaw (1991): 216; Courbage/Fargues (1997): 82 – note that Courbage and Fargues cover Syria, Palestine and Lebanon.
157. The Scottish missionaries were to write about the settlements: c.f. p140 below.
158. McCarthy (1990): 7, 8
159. This topic is further examined on p165 below.
160. ibid.: 80

Chapter 2

1. Bonar/McCheyne (1843): 1
2. Except for Black, the other three members of the deputation had all been appointed as members of the committee. CS-GA 1838, 21-22
3. Keith convened the JMC from 1841; Shepherd describes an interesting dispute about Palestine in Biblical times that Keith was involved in; (1987): 94-95
4. Born in 1810, Bonar became General Assembly Moderator in 1878.
5. It went into well over 40 editions (at least) in Britain, as well as being published in the USA by the Presbyterian Board of Publications in Philadelphia (the first edition probably being published in 1842 but further editions would have ensured a wide readership), and in European countries such as France (in 1843) and the Netherlands (in 1851). Most recently, it has been republished in an edition edited by Allan Harman: (1996) *Mission of Discovery: The Beginnings of Modern Jewish Evangelism. The journal of Bonar and McCheyne's Mission of Inquiry*, Fearn (Ross-shire). Unfortunately, this is suited more for personal enrichment of today's believers than academic study: appendices have been removed, the original page layout has been changed making page references to the original edition meaningless, some footnotes have been incorporated into the text and others have been added. Consequently, it is not used at all in this study, all references being to one of the original editions.
6. N L Walker, (1895) *Chapters from the History of the Free Church of Scotland*, Edinburgh: 168
7. Bonar played an on-going role in Jewish missions, being an active member of the JMC for many years.
8. Bonar/McCheyne (1843): 108; c.f. 1 Kgs 4:20.
9. ibid.: 109
10. ibid.: 122
11. ibid.: 207; c.f. Jer 7, 12; this thinking is found in travel accounts at the end of the century and beyond, e.g. viewing ruined buildings, Rev A C Fullarton, a Glasgow Free Kirk minister, wrote: 'The woes denounced by Christ on these cities, as recorded in Matt. xi. 20-24, took fearful effect'; FC-MMR, 2.1.1898, 9.
12. Bonar/McCheyne (1843): 207
13. ibid.: 127, 198
14. Friedrich Heyer describes Nicolayson's methods; (2000) *2000 Jahre Kirchengeschichte des Heiligen Landes. Märtyrer, Mönche, Kirchenväter, Kreuzfahrer, Patriarchen, Ausgräber und Pilger*, series: *Studien zur Orientalischen Kirchengeschichte*, vol. 11, Hamburg: 230-232
15. Tibawi (1961): 13

16. ibid.: 40
17. Although Bonar & McCheyne note that there were five converts in Jerusalem when they visited; they do not say how they were converted or by whom; Bonar/McCheyne (1843): 149.
18. Tibawi (1961): 16, 66-67. This problem faced all the incoming western churches.
19. Bonar/McCheyne (1843): 148
20. Courbage/Fargues indicate higher numbers: in 1580 13, 140 Jews, in 1882 27, 382; (1997): 82. Abdul Latif Tibawi refers to 1 Chr 21 to argue that Jews were reluctant to provide numbers: I have come across no evidence that would support this; (1969) *Jerusalem. Its Place in Islam and Arab History*, Beirut: 27.
21. Bonar/McCheyne (1843): 149
22. ibid.: 149; note the Biblical reference to the twelve tribes.
23. ibid.: 156f
24. ibid.: 254-5
25. ibid.: 264
26. ibid.: 277
27. ibid.: 163ff
28. ibid.: 163f; they note that this is the largest estimate they had received.
29. ibid.: 164f
30. ibid.: 171
31. ibid.: 171
32. ibid.: 172; c.f. also Chapter 5 below.
33. Referring to the eastern Churches, which most western missionaries regarded as corrupt and not in the least representative of Christianity as they saw it. For examples of Bonar and McCheyne's attitude to e.g. the Church of the Nativity in Bethlehem, ibid.: 186, or monks in Acre, 312.
34. Protestant missionaries (and perhaps even more so Presbyterians) often assumed that Jews, like the Roman Catholics so many of them despised (and knew so little of), accorded non-Scriptural texts more importance than the Scriptures themselves. Bonar and McCheyne print an appendix showing the 'striking similarities in the main features of Judaism and Popery, proving ... one author'; ibid.: 531. Of course, equating Jews they knew relatively little of with Catholics they thought they knew a great deal of made it easy to criticise aspects of Judaism as they encountered it; e.g. after lengthy and convoluted arguments with Jews they met in Moldavia/Wallachia, they noted that 'Jesuitical casuistry is as much a feature of Judaism as of Popery!'; ibid.: 424.
35. ibid.: 172
36. ibid.: 172
37. ibid.: 168
38. ibid.: 166, notes that the largest contributions come from Amsterdam, with little coming from Britain.
39. ibid.: 193f
40. It is noteworthy that they emphasised Hebrew, though at the time, Yiddish was the dominant language of the Ashkenazim. On the language issue, c.f. e.g. Eric J Hobsbawm, (1990) *Nations and Nationalisms since 1870. Programme, Myth, Reality*, Cambridge, ²1992: 110-114.
41. Later missions would be open to all, but the primary targets would still be Jews.
42. c.f. the Smith case, p12 above. Echoes of Homi Bhabha's '"partial" diffusion of Christianity ... [to] construct a particularly appropriate form of colonial subjectivity' come to mind here; (1997), 'Of Mimicry and Man: The Ambivalence of Colonial Discourse', in *Tensions of Empire. Colonial Cultures in a Bourgeois World*, eds. Frederick Cooper, Ann Laura Stoler, Berkeley, 152-160: 154.
43. In India, for example, this was also recognised as a problem, but for other reasons; c.f. Neill

(1964): 234 – the missionaries were bound to maintain their converts, who were wholly rejected by their families, until such time as suitable employment could be found for them.

44. The following year Pieritz became very involved in the 'Damascus Affair' regarding ritual-murder charges brought against a group of Jews. He produced a full and highly regarded report on the matter as well as encouraging Muhammad Ali into relieving the pressure on the Syrian Jews; Frankel (1997): 166-7; see also chapter 7.

45. Gerstmann was later to treat McCheyne when he fell ill: Bonar/McCheyne (1843): 320.

46. ibid.: 248; Joseph Wolff, a converted Jew (firstly to Roman Catholicism and then to Anglicanism), had travelled widely along the north African coast and the eastern Mediterranean in the earlier years of the century, working as a missionary to Jews, sponsored by the banker Henry Drummond. He recorded his travels in a three volume missionary journal. This tediously written document records one dispute after another, triumphalism at the superiority of his own arguments obscuring any real understanding of the arguments of his opponents – which included Jews, Maronites, Muslims as well as other Protestants (e.g. 1827, 121). The members of the Deputation will almost certainly have read Wolff's accounts: (1827) *Missionary Journal and Memoir of the Rev. Joseph Wolff, Missionary to the Jews: comprising his first visit to Palestine in the years 1821 & 1822 (Vol I)*, London; (1828) *Missionary Journal of the Rev. Joseph Wolff, Missionary to the Jews: comprising his second visit to Palestine & Syria in the years 1823 & 1824 (Vol II)*, London; (1829) *Missionary Journal of the Rev. Joseph Wolff, Missionary to the Jews (Vol III)*, London. Also: Heyer (2000): 228-230.

47. He also discusses the usefulness of different types of tracts, the understanding of prophecy a missionary should have (like Nicolayson, he believed literal interpretation of prophecy to be superior to analogies) etc. Bonar/McCheyne (1843) 242ff.

48. ibid.: 246; 8,000 in total.

49. ibid.: 246; no Sephardic/Ashkenazi breakdown is provided.

50. ibid.: 247

51. ibid.: 248

52. Earlier the Scots had reflected on the value of Jewish converts as missionaries, arguing that although they would initially encounter greater opposition than non-Jewish missionaries, over a longer time span the change in the missionary's life would make a greater impact, and that although Jews listen more readily to non-Jewish missionaries, they listened more carelessly, and that once confidence in Jewish converts had been established, they would be more 'efficient' than non-Jews. They conclude these thoughts with the statement that 'perhaps the true principle in mission to the Jews, is to unite both Jewish and Gentile labourers in the same field.' ibid.: 131. Davidson's references to 'jealousy' come to mind here.

53. It was clear to them that Palestine in general was a suitable location for a Jewish mission, and this for a number of reasons: for example, 'that Palestine is the stronghold of Rabbinism appears ... a sufficient reason why Christians should direct their most vigorous efforts to ... this land' ibid.: 132; Palestine and Jerusalem form the centre of the Jewish world, 'the heart of the nation' (321) and news of conversions taking place there travelled to other parts of the Jewish world; 'in Palestine, the Jews look upon the English as friends' which made it easier to gain their confidence, (321f); Palestine was close to the heart of every Christian, (322): 'On these grounds, we rest our conviction that the Holy Land presents not only the most attractive, but the most important field for missionary operation among the Jews'; (322).

54. ibid.: 284f, 320-323

55. Of course, this happened when the Sea of Galilee mission was founded.

56. ibid.: 284

57. ibid.: 284

58. Note that according to John J Rousseau/Rami Arav, (1996) *Jesus and his world. An archaeological and cultural dictionary*, London, (Augsburg Fortress, 1995): 317, of the other cities (Tiberias, Hebron and Jerusalem), there were particular issues around Tiberias and its suitability for

Jews, an issue that even today has relevance for Orthodox Jews. Although Tiberias 'became an important centre of Judaism' the discovery of a necropolis when the city was first being built around 18 or 19 C.E. meant that it was regarded as unclean by Jews, and initially appears to have been more of a non-Jewish city, though from ca. 150 C.E. it became the seat of the Sanhedrin and its fame developed through until the Middle Ages. It is barely mentioned in the gospels, references being John 6:1, 23; 21:1. This is of interest given that this became the primary Palestinian mission station for Jewish work in later years.

59. Bonar/McCheyne (1843): 285

60. Mt 5:14

61. Bonar/McCheyne (1843): 285

62. ibid.: 322. There is an interesting footnote on their understanding of the ecclesiastical situation: 'Of course, as a Presbyterian Church, claiming equal apostolic authority with the Church of England, the Church of Scotland will not consider the appointment of a Bishop, which has taken place during this year (1842), as in any way debaring her from coming into the field.' Dividing territories by denomination is known as comity: although not explicitly described as such until the 1880s, it had been practised for 60 years previously. Comity, as defined by R Pierce Beaver ((1962) *Ecumenical Beginnings in Protestant World Mission: A History of Comity*, New York) is 'the division of territory and assignment of spheres of occupation including delimitation of boundaries, on the one hand, and non-interference in one another's affairs, on the other': 15. Comity was generally seen positively, serving to preserve resources and delineate responsibility: 'Comity, then, was the creation of denominationalism by geography. Yet its fundamental purpose was not that by any means. Comity through delimitation of territory and assignment of spheres of occupation sought to assure the responsibility to specific missionary agencies for the speedy evanglization of every region of the earth and every district in each region, to the end that the Kingdom of God might spread through the whole world and that a great Church of Christ might arise in every land through the combined efforts of the separate societies': 16. Beaver describes the Jerusalem bishopric as one of the first major examples of comity agreements: 228. The principle of comity meant that western Protestant missionary organisations tried not to 'intrude' on the geographical territory in which another society was already active. The imperial attitude behind this idea, based on the obvious parallels to imperial map-drawing and territorial delineation of foreign lands, need not be elaborated on further here.

63. Bonar/McCheyne (1843): 285. Their account was being written in 1842; c.f. the 1840 General Assembly calling for the protection of Jews, note 65 below.

64. ibid.: 320

65. The Committee noted 'the accounts which have recently reached this country respecting the persecution of the Jews in Syria ... details of the cruel barbarities inflicted on that people, on the most wanton pretences, are in the last degree revolting'. The General Assembly accepted the proposal that 'it would be a highly proper and becoming act on the part of the Assembly, to interfere on their behalf, by addressing a Memorial to the British Government, and praying that its influence may be used to arrest this grievous wrong' – the use of the word 'interfere' is interesting to note; CS-GA-JMC 1840: 6.

66. Bonar/McCheyne (1843): 519f

67. Lionel Alexander Ritchie describes Edward's work: (2002) 'Daniel Edward (1815-1896) and the Free Church of Scotland mission to the Jews in Central Europe', in *Records of the Scottish Church History Society*, vol. XXXI, 173-187.

68. FC-GA 1846: 65

69. William Garden Blaikie, for example, in his brief overview of the Church's Jewish missions, writes that 'there has been a certain measure of success ... but no community of Hebrew Christians has been formed able to stand on its own feet'; (1893) *After Fifty Years*, London/Edinburgh: 111

70. FC-JMC 21.2.1893
71. CS-JMC April or May 1839 (nd)
72. CS-JMC April or May 1839 (nd)
73. CS-JMC 12.8.1839
74. CS-JMC 17.6.1840
75. CS-JMC 3.8.1840
76. CS-JMC 13.10.1840
77. CS-JMC 2.6.1841
78. CS-JMC 10.6.1841 & 14.6.1841
79. CS-JMC 4.7.1841
80. CS-JMC 26.7.1841, 11.8.1841; this was understandable: Keith had spent time in Pesth on his way back to Scotland as Black convalesced.
81. CS-JMC 11.8.1841; it has not proved possible to locate the original letter.
82. These minute books later went to the Free Kirk; see pp38-40.
83. CS-JMC 17.11.1841
84. CS-JMC 20.12.1841
85. CS-JMC 23.3.1842
86. CS-JMC 18.4.1842, 31.5.1842
87. CS-JMC 18.4.1842
88. CS-JMC 5.7.1842, 9.8.1842 and 5.10.1842; he perished in the 1860 war; Fawaz (1994): 91; Andrew Thomson, (1883) *In the Holy Land*, Edinburgh: 313.
89. CS-JMC 5.7.1842; the LJS came into dispute with the Scots in Safad too; p68 below.
90. CS-JMC 10.8.1842, 5.10.1842 & 28.10.1842
91. Hans-Jürgen & Jutta Kornrumpf, (1998) *Fremde im Osmanischen Reich 1826-1912/13: Bio-bibliographisches Register*, Stutensee, (publ. by authors): 335
92. CS-JMC 16.11.1842; the Committee also recognised the need for an interpreter, and was prepared to pay for this; CS-JMC 28.10.1842
93. M S Anderson, (1970) *The Great Powers and the Near East. 1774-1923*, London: 60
94. Hourani (1991): 272; Rashid Pasha, the prominent reformer at the height of the *tanzimat* period, was behind the Hatt-i Sharif: Cleveland (1994): 80.
95. Cleveland (1994): 72-73; Hourani (1991): 272-3
96. Cleveland (1994): 73
97. Kamal Salibi, (1988) *A House of Many Mansions. The History of Lebanon Reconsidered*, Berkeley, Los Angeles, London: 15
98. Fawaz (1994): 20-2
99. ibid.: 22, 25
100. CS-JMC 12.12.1842, 2.2.1843
101. FC-JMC 12.10.1843
102. FC-GA 1843, 84; Schwartz was later sent to the new Free Kirk Berlin mission, FC-GA 1845, 117.
103. CS-JMC 5.4.1843
104. The Appendix contains a diagram illustrating church divisions and reunions.
105. Lynch (1991): 397
106. Roxborogh (1999): 152
107. Haldane (1933): 142
108. Brown (1997): 101-2; Brown notes that Thomas Chalmers, the minister who led the Disruption, had 'ideals [which] were grounded in a rural society of landed interest and paternalism... [he was] a high Tory paternalist and a rural romantic...'; 101. He did, however, capture the mood of the time.
109. Lynch (1991): 391
110. Warren (1967) explores the issue of social and economic background of missionaries in his

second chapter. Scottish education was generally better (and perceived to be so) than that in England and this resulted in a proportionally higher number of graduates from Scotland going overseas than from England. However, the second half of the 19th century saw an increasing number of English graduates offer themselves for missionary service as well.

111. Lynch (1991): 398

112. Ironically, perhaps, the division of the church can be regarded as a motivator of, amongst other things, missionary activity: John Wolffe, (1996) 'Unity in Diversity? North Atlantic Evangelical Thought in the Mid-Nineteenth Century', in *Unity and Diversity in the Church (Papers read at the 1994 summer meeting and the 1995 winter meeting of the Ecclesiastical Historical Society)*, ed. R N Swanson, Oxford, 363-375: 366.

113. FC-JMC 31.5.1843, 23.6.1843; Keith wrote to the missionaries encouraging them and informing them that they expected to be able to continue the work.

114. House of Commons, (1847) *Third Report from the Select Committee on Sites for Churches (Scotland); together with the Minutes of Evidence, Appendix and Index*, London, minutes 6366, 6367. Maurice Grant covers further, albeit in a somewhat tendentious manner, the strict adherence to anti-Establishment principles and other confessional issues: (1993) 'The Heirs of the Disruption in Crisis and Recovery 1893-1920', in, *Crown Him Lord of All: Essays on the Life and Witness of the Free Church of Scotland*, ed. Clement Graham, Edinburgh, 1-36.

115. FC-JMC 5.9.1843; Edwards and Allan were the last to respond; all but one of the Church of Scotland overseas missionaries went over to the Free Kirk in the aftermath of the Disruption. In the 1900 United Presbyterian/Free Church union, all the Free Church missionaries moved went over to the new church, leaving the tiny rump that refused participation in the union with no missionaries whatsoever; W D Graham, (1993) 'Beyond the Borders of Scotland: The Church's Missionary Enterprise', in, *Crown Him Lord of All: Essays on the Life and Witness of the Free Church of Scotland*, ed. Clement Graham, Edinburgh, 91-105: 101.

116. J R Fleming, (1927) *A History of the Church in Scotland 1843-1874*, Edinburgh: 65

117. Robert W Weir, (1900) *A History of the Foreign Missions of the Church of Scotland*, Edinburgh: 51-53, indicates that the correspondence showed courtesy, but it is not clear what he bases this on.

118. CS-GA 1843: 55

119. CS-Accounts, 1843: 13 and 1844: 12

120. Robert Kernohan, (1979) *Scotland's 'Life and Work'. A Scottish view of God's world through 'Life and Work': 1879-1979*, Edinburgh: 32; Weir (1900): 51-6, outlines the need to start afresh and subsequent difficulties in maintaining a secure mission base.

121. FC-JMC 26.7.1843 Hamilton expressed a desire to send an Irish missionary to work alongside the Free Kirk missionary already in Constantinople. It is unclear whether he is perhaps referring to Schwartz.

122. FC-JMC 5.9.1843

123. FC-JMC 12.10.1843

124. FC-GA 1843: 96

125. FC-JMC 23.6.1843

126. FC-JMC 24.1.1844; the meeting of 28.2.1844 notes that the Irish were also giving £100 worth of books.

127. c.f. Chapter 5 for discussion of methods.

128. Chapter 5 contains a fuller analysis of the role of medicine.

129. C Peter Williams, (1982) 'Healing and evangelism: the place of medicine in later Victorian missionary thinking', in *The Church and Healing (Papers read at the twentieth summer meeting and the twenty-first winter meeting of the Ecclesiastical Historical Society)*, ed. W J Shiels Oxford, 271-285: 281

130. ibid.: 281

131. ibid.: 273

132. ibid.: 277

133. Andrew F Walls, (1982) "The heavy artillery of the missionary army': the domestic importance of the nineteenth-century medical missionary', in *The Church and Healing (Papers read at the twentieth summer meeting and the twenty-first winter meeting of the Ecclesiastical Historical Society)*, ed. W J Shiels, Oxford, 287-297: 290; c.f. Chapter 5 below.

134. FC-JMC 15.7.1844

135. FC-JMC 28.2.1844

136. FC-JMC 9.4.1844

137. FC-JMC 17.4.1844

138. FC-GA 1845: 115; Robson spent many years in Damascus and was involved in aiding refugees from the 1860 war; Fawaz (1994): 79.

139. FC-JMC 15.7.1844; reiterated 26.8.1844

140. FC-JMC 16.5.1845 & 31.12.1845

141. FC-GA 1844: 50

142. FC-GA 1845: 115

143. FC-GA 1845: 117, 119

144. FC-JMC 29.4.1846

145. FC-JMC 30.9.1846

146. FC-GA 1846: 63

147. FC-JMC 13.7.1847

148. FC-JMC 28.9.1847, 30.11.1847 & 8.2.1848; this latter minute indicates a reluctance on Daniel's part to explain his behaviour: his letter 'stated that there were various circumstances which if mentioned, would explain his conduct; and the Convener was requested to ... [ask him] what these circumstances were.'

149. The 'Secretary of the American Society for ameliorating the condition of the Jews' had written in mid-April; Duncan was instructed to reply 'and state what was the reason of the Committee discontinuing their connection with Mr Newhaus'; FC-JMC 6.5.1848.

150. FC-JMC 1.6.1848

151. FC-JMC 20.6.1848

152. FC-JMC 24.4.1849; the reference had originally been written 9.11.1848.

153. Richter (1910): 211

154. c.f. Appendix 7

155. Transferring work from other organisations was not unusual: for example, the United Presbyterians took on work in Jamaica from the Scottish Mission Society 1847. UPC-GMBM, 11.5.1847.

156. UPC-Synod 1857: 12

157. UPC-Synod 1857: 29

158. David McDougall, (1941) *In Search of Israel. A Chronicle of the Jewish Mission of the Church of Scotland*, London, Edinburgh, etc.: 74

159. Interestingly, all these locations except the first were at one time or another in the course of the 19th or 20th century Jewish mission stations of at least one Scottish denomination.

160. UPC-GMBM 4.8.1857; the identity of the medical missionary is unclear.

161. UPC-GMBM 4.8.1857; he later clarifies that these are 'nominal Christians' c.f. p48 below.

162. Courbage/Fargues (1997): 82

163. ibid.: 86; Fawaz locates 17, 000 Christians among a Muslim population of 100, 000: (1994): 77.

164. All figures are, of course, subject to the usual limitations, c.f. p*ix* above.

165. UPC-GMBM 4.8.1857

166. UPC-GMBM 1.9.1857

167. UPC-GMBM 1.9.1857 states that he would be ready to leave Britain from 16.9.1857, but there is no record of when he actually did leave.

168. UPC-GMBM 13.6.1859
169. UPC-GMBM 13.6.1859
170. Roger Owen, (1981) *The Middle East in the World Economy 1800-1914*, London, New York, 1993: 168
171. ibid.: 168
172. UPC-GMBM 13.6.1859
173. Jonathon Bonk examines missionary identification in what he describes as 'the material-social sphere'; further reference to his methods will be found in Chapter 5; (1989) *The Theory and Practice of Missionary Identification, 1860-1920*, series: *Studies in the History of Missions*, vol. 2, New York.
174. UPC-GMBM 1.11.1859, 6.12.1859
175. Skene, who had travelled through Wallachia and Bosnia in 1850/51 (publishing two volumes of his travels), was the British Consul in Damascus and Aleppo from 1860/61. Kornrumpf and Richter note that Skene tried to settle Bedouin, encourage them to farm and to send their children to Christian schools and record this work as being carried out with a doctor, Arnold Mühleisen (who had at one time been employed by the CMS as a missionary in Abyssinia); they also note that these attempts failed. It is not clear if Brown was being asked to become involved in this project, but this seems likely; Kornrumpf, (1998): 352, 258; Richter (1910): 210.
176. UPC-GMBM 6.12.1859
177. UPC-GMBM 7.2.1860
178. Issawi (1988) 430-431 indicates a substantial increase in the cost of living from 1820-1840 in Lebanon using the personal accounts of Tannus al-Shidyaq (1794?-1861) as an example. Shidyaq came from a prominent Lebanese family who had 'provided leaders in the Maronite districts of the north [of Lebanon] for 300 years, and officials for the nobility of the centre and south'; Albert Hourani, (1962) *Arabic Thought in the Liberal Age 1798-1939*, Cambridge, 2nd ed. 1983: 97. However, Tannus' brother was the famous 'Martyr of Lebanon', Asad al-Shidyaq, who died in unclear circumstances having turned to Protestantism; his brother Faris did likewise, but left Lebanon after his brother's death; ibid.: 98. The most recent treatment of the Asad al-Shidyaq story is David Kerr, (2003) 'Maronites and Missionaries: A critical appraisal of the affair of As'ad al-Shidyâq (1825-1829)', in *A faithful presence: essays for Kenneth Cragg*, ed. David Thomas with Clare Amos, London, 219-236.
179. no mention is made of the medical missionary, p68 above.
180. UPC-GMBM 7.2.1860
181. Henry Harris Jessup, (1910a) *Fifty-Three Years in Syria, Vol. 1*, New York: 48-49
182. UPC-GMBM 3.4.1860
183. UPC-GMBM 1.5.1860
184. Bonk (1989): 38. Bonk does point out that this did not seem to apply to western missionaries.
185. c.f. p48 above.
186. UPC-GMBM 3.7.1860, 2.10.1860
187. UPC-GMBM 26.6.1866; the Presbytery of Edinburgh ordained him on 31.5. and he appears to have left immediately afterwards – UPC-GMBM 6.6.1860
188. UPC-Synod 1860: 298; note: Jews are not mentioned.
189. UPC-GMBM 6.6.1860
190. Fawaz (1994): 78
191. ibid.: 66-68
192. ibid.: 78-81
193. ibid.: 77
194. Donald Quataert, (1994a) 'Ottoman Manufacturing in the Nineteenth Century', in *Manufacturing in the Ottoman Empire and Turkey, 1500-1950*, ed. Donald Quataert, New York, 87-121: 101

195. UPC-GMBM 2.10.1860; Biliss appears to be modern-day Maskaneh, located further inland on the Euphrates; Leradia is not immediately identifiable.
196. UPC-GMBM 2.10.1860
197. UPC-GMBM 7.1.1861
198. Fawaz (1994): 62
199. Wortabet later claimed his losses from the government – it is not known whether this was successful; UPC-GMBM 27.1.1863; on the compensation c.f. Issawi (1988): 45-47.
200. UPC-GMBM 7.1.1861
201. UPC-GMBM 7.1.1861
202. UPC-GMBM 30.8.1862
203. The items had been addressed by the Jewish sub-committee which brought them to the main Committee for a decision. The Committee had been reorganised the year before, when four sub-committees had been created to deal with the work: '1. Jamaica, Trinidad and Canadian Missions 2. Old Calabar and Caffrarian Missions 3. India and China Missions and 4. Jewish Mission, Australia and the Continent of Europe': UPC-GMBM 25.3.1862. One cannot but get the impression that Jewish missions were lumped together with the missions that were left after the major fields had been subdivided.
204. UPC-GMBM 27.1.1863
205. Killis is about 55km north and Idlib a similar distance south-west of Aleppo.
206. UPC-GMBM 27.1.1863
207. On the basis of the material to hand, this cannot be established with any certainty – post could take several weeks, and if the Secretary had not written immediately after the meeting, he, Brown, may not have known that permission to visit Britain had been denied him. He clearly did know this by May.
208. Perhaps this was the Brown's medical missionary? p46 above.
209. UPC-GMBM 30.6.1863
210. UPC-GMBM 30.6.1863
211. c.f. also Chapter 5
212. UPC-GMBM 30.6.1863
213. UPC-GMBM 29.9.1863
214. UPC-GMBM 29.9.1863
215. Hogg directed a boys' school in Alexandria (later taken over by the Americans), and established an educational centre in Asyut; Richter (1910): 345, 352. He was written to by the Committee, but no further details are recorded. See also Marten, (2002): 65.
216. UPC-GMBM 27.10.1863
217. c.f. p60 below
218. Richter (1910): 215
219. UPC-GMBM 28.6.1864
220. UPC-GMBM 25.10.1864
221. UPC-GMBM 27.9.1864
222. UPC-GMBM 25.4.1865; the letter was written 26.12.1864
223. c.f. p49 above
224. UPC-GMBM 27.9.1864; the exact spelling in the minutes is not entirely clear.
225. UPC-GMBM 26.9.1865
226. Bonk (1989): 38; this is analysed further on p172 below.
227. Quataert (1994b): 788 describes it thus, stating it came originally via Russia; Hourani locates the origin as India; (1991): 268.
228. UPC-GMBM 27.3.1866
229. Quataert (1994b): 788
230. Yapp (1987): 14-15
231. UPC-GMBM 27.3.1866; presumably he is referring to the region between Latakia and

Suweydiyah.

232. UPC-GMBM 27.3.1866
233. UPC-GMBM 27.3.1866
234. UPC-GMBM 27.3.1866
235. UPC-GMBM 26.6.1866
236. UPC-GMBM 26.6.1866
237. UPC-GMBM 26.6.1866
238. The initial enthusiasm for Jewish mission work indeed appeared to be waning: even the Anglo-Prussian bishopric had turned from exclusively Jewish missions with Samuel Gobat's appointment in 1846; Farah (2002): 32.
239. UPC-GMBM 25.9.1866
240. The Americans later passed it to the Presbyterian Church of England, and the Scottish United Presbyterian Church then made financial contributions to help the English maintain the mission station, which lasted well into the 20th century. Christie, initially employed by the Sea of Galilee Mission, later worked in Aleppo; c.f. p84 below.
241. Hermann Philip had also worked with Edward in Jassy as a licensed preacher – a stage prior to full ordination – and later went on to Galatz before going to Algiers; Ritchie (2002): 176-177. Philip wrote to his daughter, Mrs R C Henderson, from Rome on 10.6.1881, reviewing his understanding of the reason for the poor results of mission work amongst the Jews: 'after all my experience no great work will be seen among the Jews, except that such missions are put upon an equal footing with other missions, or amalgamated with them ... No church can be formed from a Jewish element alone, there must be a Christian Church to bring them into. Fancy 50 Evangelists, Teachers, colporteurs in Rome among the Catholics, and myself alone among the Jews. 360 in Italy, and myself the only one to the Jews in the Kingdom, without help or means'; NLS Acc 10139(i).
242. Weiss had been a convert of the Free Kirk mission run by Edward; Ritchie (2002): 176. Substantial financial irregularities also appeared to have played a role in Weiss' demise. See also UFC-MR, 10.1902: 462.
243. Hall (1914): 96-9
244. e.g. John Wortabet, (1860) *Researches into the Religions of Syria: or, Sketches, Historical and Doctrinal, of its Religious Sects*, London. The frontispiece describes him as a 'Missionary of the United Presbyterian Church of Scotland to Aleppo, Syria'. Interestingly, when describing the missions in Syria, he failed to mention the United Presbyterian Church at all – perhaps an indication of Wortabet's estimation of its significance. According to the preface, which is dated Beirut, 15.8.1860, the book was written in Hasbeiya 'where the author laboured for several years as a minister of the gospel' – this would have been for the American mission – but it is unlikely he would not have known of the United Presbyterians, and this could not be the case if my assumption that he had had contact with Brown prior to his application were to be true (c.f. p49).
245. CS-JMC 3.8.1840

Chapter 3

1. e.g. FC-JMC 4.12.1849, 19.3.1850, 7.5.1850 reducing salaries was discussed, ostensibly because they were too high in relation to Scottish stipends, but the item immediately preceding the first discussion focussed on 'retrenchment' – due to the protest of missionaries, the salaries were not reduced. Further financial problems were addressed in subsequent years, e.g. 19.4.1853 etc. Converts were rare, a reasonable assumption since every convert is noted by the JMC, e.g. 13.8.1861. See also Chapter 5 below.
2. FC-JMC 8.8.1851
3. FC-JMC 21.12.1875
4. FC-JMC 18.1.1876; Marten (2001), (2002)
5. FC-JMC 22.2.1876
6. FC-JMC 20.4.1880, 22.11.1881
7. FC-JMC 19.12.1882
8. FC-JMC 22.2.1882
9. FC-JMC 16.1.1883
10. FC-JMC 20.2.1883
11. John Wilkinson, (1991) *The Coogate Doctors: The History of the Edinburgh Medical Missionary Society 1841 to 1991*, Edinburgh: 43-4
12. FC-JMC 16.10.1883
13. FC-JMC 18.12.1883
14. FC-JMC 22.1.1884
15. This was known as 'comity': c.f. Chapter 2, note 62 above.
16. FC-JMC 19.2.1884
17. James H Wilson/James Wells, (1895) *The Sea of Galilee Mission of the Free Church of Scotland*, Edinburgh; this book contains chapters by the editors, Torrance, George Wilson, A Moody Stuart (a convener of the JMC) and a hymn text by McCheyne. The book is discussed in Chapter 4. Unless it is significant or useful to know who wrote citations used in this book, referencing will be solely by the editors' names.
18. Wilson/Wells (1895): 30-32
19. ibid.: 32
20. ibid.: 34
21. FC-JMC 22.4.1884
22. FC-JMC 17.6.1844 incl. sub-committee meeting, 22.7.1884, 16.9.1884
23. FC-JMC 16.12.1884, 21.4.1885
24. The late Dr Emrys Thomas, who worked for the EMMS from about 1929 in Nazareth and Damascus, recalled that although he attended a language school in order to learn Arabic, medical terminology was gleaned from fellow medics and a volume of Arabic-English medical terms produced by medical missionaries to help new-comers. Torrance, of course, would initially have learnt his medical Arabic only from Vartan and his colleagues. Interview with Emrys Thomas, Edinburgh, 15.6.2001.
25. FC-JMC 21.4.1885
26. Courbage/Fargues (1997): 154
27. ibid.: 167
28. ibid.: 154
29. W P Livingstone, (1923) *A Galilee Doctor. Being a Sketch of the Career of Dr. D. W. Torrance of Tiberias*, London, nd (probably 1923): 40; Wilson/Wells (1895): 40.
30. FC-JMC 22.9.1885, 17.11.1885, 22.12.1885, 19.1.1886, 16.2.1886, 16.3.1886
31. FC-JMC 16.2.1886
32. The Association consisted of women living in Glasgow: it did not carry out mission work

in Glasgow.

33. Lesley Orr Macdonald's excellent summary (chapter 3) of the role of church women in foreign missions excludes the work of the Jewish mission committees and their women's associations; (2000) *A Unique and Glorious Mission. Women and Presbyterianism in Scotland, 1830-1930*, Edinburgh. The origins of the Foreign Missions Ladies' Associations are examined on 113-115, and whilst she does not mention Jewish Associations, they followed a similar pattern.

34. FC-WJMA 22. & 25.5.1895

35. FC-MMR 1.5.1886: 105

36. FC-JMC 20.4.1886; c.f. also FC-MMR 1.5.1886: 146

37. FC-JMC 11.5.1886

38. Fenton had previously worked with Jewish girls at 'Kouskoundjouk, by the Bosphorus'; FC-MMR 1.10.1886: 303

39. FC-JMC 2.6.1886 & 21.9.1886

40. Livingstone (1923): 73

41. ibid.: 73

42. She is hardly mentioned in the minutes of the JMC beyond this brief note. Wives or sisters were often brought along; Macdonald (2000): 112.

43. FC-JMC 19.10.1886

44. FC-JMC 19.10.1886, 21.12.1886, 18.1.1887 & 22.2.1887

45. FC-JMC 18.1.1887, 22.2.1887, 22.3.1887, 28.6.1887, 19.7.1887, 18.10.1887, 20.12.1887 and 17.1.1888. He was licensed by the Presbytery of Kirkcudbright shortly after the 20.9.1887, a strange anomaly in that he is recorded as having been in Leipzig until the winter; FC-JMC 20.9.1887

46. Although he translated the New Testament into Hebrew and devoted much of his energy to the study of Judaism and Jewish traditions, his interests extended well beyond this; Friedrich Mildenberger, (1981) *Geschichte der deutschen evangelischen Theologie im 19. und 20. Jahrhundert*, series: *Theologische Wissenschaft*, vol. 10, Stuttgart: 257.

47. Karin Haufler-Musiol, (1998) '125 Jahre Zentralverein: Ein historischer Überblick', in *Auf dem Wege zum christlich-jüdischen Gespräch: 125 Jahre Evangelisch-lutherischer Zentralverein für Zeugnis und Dienst unter Juden und Christen*, ed. Arnulf H Baumann, Münster, 11-46: 20.

48. Christopher Clark, (1995) *The Politics of Conversion: Missionary Protestantism and the Jews in Prussia 1728-1941*, Oxford: 2-3, 244-5. Clark's is one of the few English descriptions of the Institutum Judaicum, though he concentrates more on its antecedents. Haufler-Musiol (1998) has written more fully on the Leipzig Institutum. The volume her essay appears in also contains a theological biography of Franz Delitzsch (Arnulf H Baumann, (1998a) 'Franz Delitzsch (1813-1890)', in *Auf dem Wege zum christlich-jüdischen Gespräch: 125 Jahre Evangelisch-lutherischer Zentralverein für Zeugnis und Dienst unter Juden und Christen*, ed. Arnulf H Baumann, Münster, 48-59), as well as similar pieces on subsequent directors. Manfred Unger describes the role of the Institute from its very early days in countering anti-Jewish tendencies; (1998) 'Das vergessene Institutum Judaicum', *Leipziger Blätter*, 33, 58-59. With the Nazi assumption of power in Germany in 1933, such an institution found itself in an invidious position, closing with the permanent loss of its archives and library, re-opening in quite a different form in Münster after the war under Karl Heinrich Rengstorff. Many theologians, especially before the war, had connections to the Institutum, including Adolf Schlatter and Joachim Jeremias; some maintained connections with the new body after the war, including Jeremias; c.f. his 1953 Franz Delitzsch lectures which address mission to Jews in particular: (1958) *Jesus' Promise to the Nations*, London. I would like to record my gratitude to S Perthus of the Israelitische Gemeinde zu Leipzig for supplying me with Unger's article, to Dr Ina Lorenz of the Institut für die Geschichte der deutschen Juden, and the Zentralrat der Juden in Deutschland for help in detailing parts of the Institutum's history.

49. e.g. FC-JMC 22.9.1885, 22.2.1887
50. FC-JMC 20.12.1887
51. FC-JMC 17.7.1888; the use of military language points to imperial thinking, c.f. p163 below.
52. FC-JMC 16.11.1886
53. FC-JMC 17.7.1888
54. FC-JMC 16.10.1888
55. c.f. Chapter 2, note 62 above
56. FC-JMC 18.12.1888; c.f. also FC-JMC 20.11.1888
57. Ewing's post was meanwhile sponsored by an Australian donor in memory of his late son; the position became known as the 'Charles Russell Missionary'; FC-JMC 22.1.1889; 16.4.1889.
58. FC-JMC 19.2.1889
59. The frequent contact the missionaries had with Beirut (rather than Jerusalem) confirms the assertion that northern Palestine was more influenced by the provincial capital than by Jerusalem; Owen (1982): 2.
60. FC-JMC 19.2.1889
61. Livingstone (1923): 78, Livingstone's transliteration. Females were often described as 'Eastern girls', 'Oriental women' etc. and not by their faith, unlike most males, who were far more likely to be accorded religious agency; c.f. also Okkenhaug (2002): 33.
62. FC-JMC 16.10.1888, 20.11.1888, 19.3.1889
63. FC-MMR 1.10.1889: 312-313 records full details.
64. FC-JMC 18.6.1889, 16.7.1889, 17.9.1889, 22.10.1889
65. FC-JMC 17.9.1889
66. FC-JMC 17.12.1889
67. FC-JMC 17.12.1889
68. FC-JMC 21.1.1890
69. FC-JMC 18.2.1890
70. FC-JMC 9.4.1890
71. William Ewing, (1914) *The Holy Land and Glasgow*, series: *Our Jewish Missions I*, Edinburgh
72. FC-JMC 9.4.1890
73. c.f. Chapter 4 below for an examination of how this structure operated.
74. FC-JMC 21.1.1890: Fenton had intimated her resignation.
75. FC-JMC 22.7.1890
76. FC-JMC 9.4.1890
77. FC-JMC 17.6.1890
78. FC-JMC 22.7.1890, 16.9.1890
79. FC-JMC 16.9.1890; organised through resorting to the British imperial authorities, c.f. p106 below.
80. FC-JMC 20.1.1891
81. FC-JMC 20.1.1891
82. FC-JMC 21.4.1891
83. FC-JMC 22.9.1892; see also the discussion of committee functions in Chapter 484.
FC-JMC 21.4.1891, 7.5.1891, 16.2.1892, 22.3.1892, 1.6.1892
85. c.f. Chapter 5 below
86. FC-JMC 16.6.1891
87. FC-JMC 21.7.1891
88. FC-JMC 16.6.1891
89. Ewing (1914): 21
90. Ewing is entirely accurate in noting that the 'purchase of the land and securing of proper titles was a tedious and intricate business, calling for infinite tact and patience'; ibid.: 20.
91. FC-JMC 22.9.1891

92. e.g. FC-JMC 20.3.1894 and *passim*.
93. FC-JMC 22.3.1892
94. FC-JMC 21.6.1892, 18.10.1892
95. FC-JMC 20.9.1892
96. FC-JMC 19.4.1892
97. FC-JMC 15.11.1892, 20.12.1892, 21.2.1893
98. FC-JMC 14.11.1893
99. FC-JMC 20.12.1893
100. Ewing (1914): 28
101. Livingstone (1923): 176
102. FC-JMC 22.9.1891
103. FC-JMC 21.7.1891
104. FC-JMC 20.6.1893
105. FC-JMC 20.9.1892
106. FC-JMC 19.1.1892
107. FC-JMC 16.2.1892; perhaps with good reason: the Committee discussed whether to replace Ewing with a second medical missionary, rather than a cleric. It did not, though no clear decision to appoint a clerical missionary is in fact recorded, although the post was then advertised in such terms: FC-JMC 22.3.1892, 21.6.1892, 18.10.1892, 15.11.1892.; 31.5.1893.
108. e.g. FC-JMC 19.4.1892, 17.1.1893 – in the latter instance, the candidate had also been offered a post by the FMC for India, which he had accepted.
109. FC-JMC 17.1.1893
110. FC-JMC 21.3.1893; Dalman was Delitzsch's successor in Leipzig, though it would appear this application was shortly before his re-appointment to the post (he had left the Institutum Judaicum a few years earlier); Arnulf H Baumann, (1998b) 'Gustav Dalman (1855-1941)', in *Auf dem Wege zum christlich-jüdischen Gespräch: 125 Jahre Evangelisch-lutherischer Zentralverein für Zeugnis und Dienst unter Juden und Christen*, ed. Arnulf H Baumann, Münster, 60-69: 63. Dalman felt a deep connection to Palestine, spending 18 months there in 1899-90, and working there from 1902 (Frank Foerster, (1991) *Mission im Heiligen Land. Der Jerusalems-Verein zu Berlin 1852-1945*, series: *Missionswissenschaftliche Forschungen*, vol. 25, Gütersloh: 106); it is almost certain that he had met Ewing and discussed working for the Scots. Although convinced of the need for Jewish missions, he became better known for his work on Palestine. However, he remained convinced of the deep theological connection Christians had to the land (geopiety) e.g. Gustaf Dalman, (1900) *'Nicht sei doch Streit!' Eine Osteransprache an Juden*, Leipzig: 4.
111. FC-JMC 21.2.1893
112. FC-JMC 31.5.1893
113. FC-JMC 9.8.1893
114. FC-JMC 18.7.1893; perhaps Zerbeck came from the Institutum Judaicum, but no details are given.
115. FC-JMC 20.6.1893, 21.3.1893
116. FC-JMC 19.9.1893
117. FC-JMC 17.10.1893
118. Ewing (1914)
119. ibid.: 25, 27
120. FC-JMC 17.11.1891
121. The JMC sent him a silver watch 'as a token of the Committee's sympathy with him in his recent imprisonment'; FC-JMC 5.5.1892
122. FC-JMC 22.12.1891; it has not proved possible to identify this newspaper.
123. FC-JMC 16.2.1892
124. Founded in Paris in 1860, it ran numerous schools around the Mediterranean including in

Palestine. French was the teaching medium, and the educational system was French-based – it was 'universal' in name only; David Vital, (1999) *A People Apart. A political history of the Jews in Europe 1789-1939*, Oxford: 477-482. 'The principle aim ... was to "regenerate" and transform Eastern Jewries into the image of their emancipated Western, especially French, co-religionists'; Shaw (1991): 163.

125. FC-JMC 19.7.1892, 18.10.1892, 17.1.1893
126. Wilson/Wells (1895): 63; Livingstone (1923): 145
127. FC-JMC 14.11.1893
128. FC-JMC 19.12.1893
129. Brown (1997): 154
130. Lynch (1991): 403
131. Macdonald (2000): 63
132. ibid.: 403
133. FC-JMC 16.1.1894
134. FC-JMC 16.1.1894, 20.2.1894, 20.3.1894
135. FC-JMC 18.12.1894; i.e. in Constantinople and the Sea of Galilee
136. FC-GA 1894: p23
137. The first Jewish baptism was on 10.2.1895.
138. FC-GA 1894: 23
139. FC-GA-JMC 1894: 26-7
140. FC-GA-JMC 1894: 27-8
141. Wilson/Wells (1895): 38; c.f. p205 below on this important text.
142. FC-GA-JMC 1894: 28
143. FC-GA-JMC 1894: 27-8 (FC's emphasis)
144. Livingstone (1923): 112
145. FC-JMC 8.5.1894
146. The Torrance family tree in Appendix provides more details.
147. FC-JMC 17.9.1895
148. FC-JMC 30.5.1895; Lydia Dorward, Herbert Torrance's daughter and granddaughter of David Torrance, is sure that her father was also asked to be ordained, but resisted this strongly at the time, and indeed, Herbert was never ordained. This, of course, would have been much later, since Herbert Torrance only began work in Tiberias during the last few years of his father's life, continuing to work there, interrupted by World War II, until the 1950s. Interview with Lydia Dorward, 8.3.2001.
149. Saadeh attended a Free Kirk school in Shweir; FC-MMR 6.1891, 173.
150. FC-WJMA 22 & 25.5.1895
151. Macdonald outlines, in the context of foreign missions, the origins of Scottish women's missionary work, and the justification for separate women's work, portraying the social forces at work in the increasing prominence of women in Scotland and its churches; (2000): 111-115, 128-133.
152. FC-WJMA 10.2.1897
153. The contribution of women to the JMC's work in all its mission stations would form a very interesting study in and for itself; women's roles are mentioned by some of the texts about the missions, but there is nothing that addresses the influence of women as actors in the mission field. The only text that this author has located that even has a chapter on women's mission to the Jews is Annie S Swan (1937) *Seed Time and Harvest. The Story of the hundred years' work of the Women's Foreign Mission of the Church of Scotland*, London. However, this consists largely of wistful ramblings about the opportunities for conversion amongst the Jews, with precious little in the way of meaningful information.
154. Wilson/Wells (1895): 90
155. FC-JMC 20.9.1892, 8.5.1894

156. FC-JMC 17.4.1894; the minute did not indicate what these 'certain matters' might be.
157. FC-JMC 8.5.1894
158. FC-JMC 17.7.1894 indicates that he and his wife (with their children) had travelled to Scotland separately at various times: they had been to Scotland without him, and had remained in Safad when he had gone to Scotland. However, it is extremely problematic to infer marital difficulties on this basis.
159. FC-JMC 20.11.1894; he was buried in the Tiberias graveyard, as the church had no graveyard in Safad.
160. FC-JMC 19.6.1894
161. FC-JMC 18.9.1894, 16.3.1895
162. FC-JMC 22.1.1895, 19.2.1895, 19.3.1895
163. FC-JMC 9.5.1895
164. FC-JMC 5.6.1895, 18.6.1895
165. FC-JMC 16.7.1895
166. FC-JMC 17.12.1895
167. FC-JMC 19.2.1895; Christie was later re-recruited to serve the JMC in Glasgow: UFC-CCJ 27.6.1911.
168. FC-JMC 22.1.1895, 19.2.1895
169. FC-JMC 16.7.1895
170. FC-JMC 17.9.1895
171. FC-JMC 22.12.1896
172. FC-JMC 26.1.1896
173. FC-JMC 18.2.1896; the marriage took place on 25.8.1896; c.f. Appendix
174. Macdonald (2000): 114; Dowrie was not expected to repay her travel and expenses since she would have been granted these had she gone to Tiberias as Torrance's wife.
175. FC-JMC 21.4.1896, 20.10.1896
176. Livingstone (1923): 241
177. FC-JMC 16.3.1897, 20.4.1897
178. FC-JMC 19.5.1897, 15.6.1897
179. FC-JMC 18.1.1898
180. In the year ending 30.11.1901, the Bible Depot in Tiberias is recorded as having distributed 842 Bibles or Bible portions; in Safad the number was 171. The NBS had paid £20 towards a colporteur in Tiberias, but not yet in Safad – this would help to explain the large differential; UFC-JMC 24.12.1901.
181. FC-GA-JMC 1899: 13-14
182. FC-GA-WJMA 1899: 8-9
183. FC-GA-WJMA 1899: 8; (FC's emphasis)
184. FC-GA-WJMA 1899: 9
185. FC-GA-WJMA 1899: 9
186. FC-JMC 15.6.1897
187. c.f. e.g. FC-JMC 21.4.1896: 'Read letters from Mr Thomson, to the effect that, owing to the issue of a *cherem* by the Rabbis, the schools had been practically deserted, though at the date of the last letter the *cherem* seemed to be losing its force, and the pupils were beginning to return.'
188. A small number of other baptisms had been recorded, but not of Jews: the first, a Greek Catholic, is recorded in FC-MMR 1.2.1889: 54.
189. FC-JMC 16.4.1895
190. Ewing (1914): 27-8; UFC-CCJC 26.3.1912
191. Schools offered limited 'industrial and agricultural' training, but this faltered once pupils left school; Ewing (1925): 109-110.
192. Livingstone (1923): 143

193. c.f. p156 below

194. The African Lakes Company was cited as a precedent: Wilson/Wells (1895): 90. Whilst this cannot be described here in further detail, industrial mission played a role in various places where it was clearly perceived to be a 'civilising' influence, c.f. J N Ogilvie, (1924) *Our Empire's Debt to Missions: The Duff Missionary Lecture, 1923*, London, (preface dated): 68-73. For example, in South Africa, Scottish missionaries thought it encouraged 'civilisation': '[Stewart's] chief end ... was to make men. He was dealing with a race as unprogressive as any known to us ... Industrial training was essential to their uplifting'; James Wells, (1909) *Stewart of Lovedale: The Life of James Stewart*, London: 218.

195. That 'civilising' was not the main purpose since the Middle East was already perceived to be relatively 'civilised' (at least in comparison to, e.g., Africa) is analysed further in Chapter 5. below, particularly in examining the parallels between Africa, China and the Middle East with reference to Bonk (1989). Although the medical work was pursued partly in order to educate (Chapter 5 below), the Middle East was not perceived to be as 'backward' as Africa was supposed to be, though the missionaries thought some measure of 'civilising' was still required.

196. FC-JMC 15.11.1898

197. FC-JMC 19.6.1900

198. e.g. FC-JMC 18.12.1900

199. UFC-JMC 25.3.1902

200. UFC-JMC 28.10.1902

201. UFC-JMC 24.2.1903

202. UFC-JMC 22.12.1903; note that these are all traditionally male trades: females were obviously not being considered.

203. Livingstone (1923): 204

204. UFC-JMC 26.1.1904

205. UFC-JMC 23.2.1904

206. The Plain is described as fertile and open to extensive cultivation in George Ernest Wright/ Floyd Vivian Filson (eds.), (1946) *The Westminster Historical Atlas to the Bible*, London: 20, 55.

207. UFC-JMC 26.7.1904; the language used is interesting: what did they want to conserve? With virtually no conversions so far, future hope of conversions is again apparent, presumably to come about as soon as the conditions were 'right'.

208. UFC-JMC 24.5.1905

209. This concerned the ownership of ecclesiastical property following the United Presbyterian/ Free Church union – a remnant of the Free Church refused to unite and claimed all church property etc. for themselves; eventually the House of Lords settled in favour of the United Free Church.

210. Bebbington shows that anti-Catholicism pervaded the Evangelical churches, but was particularly strong in pre-millenarian circles; (1989) 101-102.

211. Livingstone (1923): 204

212. UFC-JMC 26.7.1904

213. Medical facilities in particular were a constant drain on resources, resulting in much discussion, c.f. e.g. UFC-CCJ 20.12.1910 and subsequent minutes which addressed the Tiberias hospital's finances. Torrance eventually even took on private patients, the funds raised going to the upkeep of the hospital, though this was initially resisted (p90 below). On the costs of medical work, c.f. Walls (1982): 291-295.

214. Livingstone (1923): 161; caption from Livingstone.

215. UFC-JMC 25.10.1904

216. UFC-JMC 20.12.1904

217. UFC-JMC 28.2.1905, 28.11.1905; it has been impossible to locate a copy of the pamphlet.

218. UFC-JMC 28.3.1905, 26.9.1905, 19.11.1907, 17.12.1907

219. UFC-JMC 22.11.1904, 27.6.1905, 26.9.1905
220. UFC-JMC 24.7.1906
221. UFC-JMC 23.2.1904
222. UFC-JMC 28.3.1905
223. UFC-JMC 28.11.1905, 19.12.1905
224. UFC-JMC 19.12.1905
225. UFC-JMC 19.12.1905
226. UFC-JMC 23.1.1906
227. UFC-JMC 24.7.1906, 3.10.1906
228. UFC-JMC 27.2.1906
229. UFC-JMC 3.10.1906, 22.1.1907
230. Dr Runa Mackay notes that there was a reluctance to use the term 'TB' since doctors felt it simply generated fear, and more 'medical' terminology was often preferred. Conversation with Runa Mackay, 12.2.2003.
231. UFC-JMC 17.12.1907; the second opinion is almost certainly from the Dr Scrimgeour of the Nazareth EMMS. Two certifying doctors were generally preferred for certificates, particularly for something as serious as sending a missionary back to Europe.
232. UFC-CCJ 17.11.1908, 23.1.1912
233. UFC-JMC 17.11.1908, 22.12.1908
234. UFC-JMC 23.2.1909; it was read to the Committee, and the full qualifications of the certifying doctor along with his conclusions – that Semple was 'in sound health and physically fit in every way to undertake work in Palestine' – were included in the minute.
235. UFC-JMC 27.4.1909, 16.11.1909, Livingstone (1923): 218
236. Livingstone (1923): 49; caption is Livingstone's.
237. UFC-JMC 28.9.1909
238. Livingstone (1923): 221; note how, in this positive context, clear denominational and religious differentiations occur in order to show how widespread support for Torrance was.
239. ibid.: 223; it is interesting to note that tourists would not be expected to share a ward with locals.
240. recorded as a friend of the Patersons: Ewing (1925): 110.
241. The JMC did not do that either, e.g. although Torrance founded the medical mission in Tiberias, the JMC clearly recognised the leading role Vartan had played, describing him as the 'father' of medical missions in Palestine in the obituary recorded in the Committee's minutes; UFC-JMC 22.12.1908
242. Livingstone frequently records the doctor being on the verge of 'breaking down' though this is not, of course, made quite so clear in the minutes, where such things were barely alluded to: see for example, (1923): 222. One occasion on which this topic is addressed very explicitly in the minutes also shows the Committee trying to do something about it: 'it appeared that he was still without an assistant and had no prospect of getting one till December, that the work was suffering, and that he himself and the staff were being overwrought. Resolved to endeavour to secure at once a temporary assistant on an engagement of two or three years; and ... to seek for a suitable medical man'; UFC-CCJ 25.2.1913
243. Alasdair I C Heron, (1980b) *A Century of Protestant Theology*, Cambridge: 169.
244. UFC-JMC 26.3.1907, 16.11.1909
245. Hebron offers another example in its links to the German mission; c.f. p102 below
246. UFC-CCJ 24.1.1911, 25.7.1911, 27.2.1912
247. UFC-JMC 28.11.1905
248. UFC-JMC 19.12.1905
249. UFC-JMC 21.3.1916; there are echoes here of how Jewish 'affliction' makes it easier than 'carnal ease' to approach Jews, p31 above. See also 16.5.1916, 20.6.1916.

250. Livingstone (1923): frontispiece; a similar photograph was hanging in the Tiberias offices in May 2001.

251. UFC-JMC 16.10.1917; Paul Charles Merkley describes the impact of Chaim Weizmann on British Christian politicians in the months and years leading up to the Balfour Declaration: the concerns of the missionary bodies did not appear to feature strongly in the politicians' assessments, based as they were on *realpolitik* and a mystical sense of Jewish restorationism, not religious conversion; (1998) *The Politics of Christian Zionism 1891-1948*, London/Portland: 40-53

252. UFC-JMC 20.11.1917

253. UFC-JMC 18.12.1917; 'Holy City ... infidel' – there is no recognition that Jerusalem might have religious significance for Muslims, nor that British occupation might be seen in exactly this way by others.

254. UFC-JMC 18.12.1917

255. UFC-JMC 15.1.1918

256. Proctor, 1997, provides an analysis of this.

257. The JMC received an account of the First Zionist Congress from one of their missionaries: FC-JMC 19.10.1897 and p138 below.

258. Livingstone (1923): 167-168

259. UFC-JMC 15.9.1914, 20.10.1914

260. UFC-JMC 25.6.1907 records her appointment.

261. Livingstone (1923): 244-245

262. UFC-JMC 15.12.1914, 19.1.1915

263. Livingstone (1923): 244-247

264. ibid.: 247-248, UFC-MR 10.1918: 140

265. UFC-WJMA 15.10.1915

266. Livingstone (1923): 251

267. CS-LW 8.1915: 256

268. Livingstone (1923): 252

269. Okkenhaug (2002), 251-253 outlines Anna Irvine's moves from Tiberias (1911-1914) via the Syria and Palestine Relief Fund (war years) to the Jerusalem Girls' College.

270. c.f. e.g. Proctor (1997): 617

271. Richter (1910): 211

272. Ewing (1925): 37; at Barclay Church, which had a long association with Jewish missions.

273. W Idris Jones, (1935) *The Arab*, series: *The Races Beyond*, The Committee on Publications for the Foreign Mission Committee, Church of Scotland, np (probably Edinburgh), nd (probably 1935): 59

274. NLS Acc 4499(8): 27.12.1892

275. Ewing met Paterson in 1894, when accompanying two friends through Palestine, and by his own account, 'a friendship was formed that has weathered all the buffetings of the intervening years' – his biography of Paterson needs to be seen from this perspective.

276. Ewing (1925): 68-71

277. ibid.: 72; note the generalisation about 'eastern peoples', (magically?) brought nearer by the magical opening of doors found in the *Arabian Nights*.

278. U O Schmelz, (1990) 'Population characteristics of Jerusalem and Hebron regions according to Ottoman census of 1905', in *Ottoman Palestine 1800-1914. Studies in Economic and Social History*, ed. Gad G Gilbar, Leiden, 15-67: 22 – see his accompanying notes for explanations of how these figures were arrived at. Figures for the town itself are harder to come by.

279. Ewing (1925): 117; see also Michael Marten, (2005) 'Anglican and Presbyterian Presence and Theology in the Holy Land', in *International Journal for the Study of the Christian Church*, vol 5, no.2, July 2005, 182-199: 194

280. ibid.: 116

281. NLS Acc 4499(9): Paterson diary 22.10.1900
282. NLS Acc 4499(9): Paterson diary 20.10.1900; noted the Mildmay discussion document on the future of the mission was surprising, 'not so much ... as to its conclusions, as to the rapidity with wh[ich] they had been formed'.
283. Ewing (1925): 119
284. Ewing offers higher figures; what is clear is that there certainly was substantial support for the work.
285. UFC-JMC 23.4.1901
286. UFC-GA 1901: 49
287. UFC-GA 1901: 49; c.f. Num 35:6-34 regarding the 'cities of refuge'.
288. UFC-GA 1901: 50
289. UFC-JMC 24.9.1901, 16.5.1901, 22.10.1901, 25.2.1902; it was noted that agreement with the Germans was required. The connection with the Berlin Society eventually became a formal division of responsibilities.
290. see p31 above
291. Schmelz (1990): 22; Ewing (1925): 119 – whichever is more accurate is irrelevant here, either way, the numbers were small.
292. UFC-MR 8.1901: 375
293. UFC-GA 1901: 43; interestingly, Jews are here described as being in Hebron in 'large [though unspecified] numbers' – one cannot help but wonder if this is simply propaganda to encourage the church membership to support the mission.
294. UFC-JMC 22.7.1902, 30.9.1902
295. See Foerster (1991) on the 'Jerusalemsverein zu Berlin'.
296. It was renewed for a further five years: UFC-JMC 23.7.1907, 22.10.1907, 19.11.1907.
297. UFC-JMC 28.10.1902; the mission was on the verge of closure until the agreement with the Scots, but even so, it was never a great success; Abdel-Raouf Sinno, (1982) *Deutsche Interessen in Syrien und Palästina 1841-1898: Aktivitäten religiöser Institutionen, wirtschaftliche und politische Einflüsse,* Berlin: 130.
298. Ewing (1925): 238; no year is given
299. UFC-JMC 24.2.1903
300. UFC-JMC 24.3.1903; 27.10.1903
301. She eventually left in 1906 to care for her sick mother; later Vartan worked in Tiberias for Torrance.
302. Ewing (1925): 125
303. ibid.: 127-130
304. UFC-JMC 26.1.1904, 28.11.1905
305. UFC-WJMA 13.10.1903
306. UFC-JMC 22.9.1903, 27.10.1903, 22.12.1903
307. UFC-JMC 23.11.1904
308. UFC-JMC 27.3.1906
309. UFC-JMC 18.9.1906
310. UFC-JMC 17.12.1907
311. UFC-JMC 26.10.1909, UFC-CCJ 20.12.1910, Ewing (1925): 137-140
312. UFC-JMC 27.7.1909; the ordinary work of the mission had of course continued, including several departures and new appointments.
313. UFC-JMC 28.9.1909
314. UFC-JMC 28.12.1909
315. Ewing (1925): 133. John James Moscrop gives some details of Dickie's background: born in Dundee in 1868, he became an architect for the Palestine Exploration Fund in Jerusalem in 1895, working on excavations until June 1897. He left the country that year after being attacked by a gang of Arabs who stabbed him and broke his arm. However, he maintained an

involvement with the PEF in subsequent years. He practised as an architect in London until 1912, before being appointed Professor of Architecture at the University of Manchester in 1913. He retired in 1933 to become Emeritus Professor and died in 1942; (2000) *Measuring Jerusalem. The Palestine Exploration Fund and British Interests in the Holy Land*, London, New York: 168. Ewing describes Dickie as being Professor of Architecture at Manchester, implying he was this at the time the hospital plans were drawn up – though Moscrop records this appointment as taking place several years later. It is likely that Moscrop's record of Dickie's appointment to Manchester in 1913 is accurate, and that Ewing, writing in the 1920s, recalled Dickie's position at the time of the hospital design incorrectly.

316. UFC-JMC 25.1.1910
317. UFC-JMC 22.2.1910
318. Ewing (1925): 133
319. UFC-JMC 22.3.1910
320. ibid.: 141-142, UFC-CCJ 27.9.1910; she arrived 23.1.1911: UFC-CCJ 28.2.1911.
321. Ewing (1925): 238
322. UFC-CCJ 20.12.1910, UFC-JMC 21.10.1913
323. Ewing (1925): 142
324. UFC-CCJ 28.2.1911
325. Ewing (1925): 143
326. UFC-CCJ 24.10.1911
327. UFC-CCJ 23.7.1912; Ewing (1925): chapter 12 gives a succinct overview of the situation.
328. UFC-CCJ 28.6.1910
329. UFC-JMC 20.10.1914
330. Ewing (1925): 149
331. UFC-JMC 15.12.1914
332. UFC-JMC 19.1.1915
333. UFC-JMC 16.2.1915; NLS Acc 4499 (2)
334. UFC-JMC 16.3.1915; Ewing (1925): 155-161
335. ibid.: chapters 19 and 20, and appendices
336. Ewing (1925): 238, c.f. the notes to Figure 3-10 below.
337. My thanks to Dr Peter Green for allowing the use of his photograph here. Note the contrast to Figure 3-9, where the hospital appears to be half-completed (or half-destroyed?). Here, it becomes clear that Dickie's original plans were never completed under the CMS. The wards are on either side of the central entrance, along with some staff living quarters. The building had been slightly extended from Paterson's time: to the right, just visible in this picture, is an extension constructed in the 1930s, whilst the white balconies at the front of the building (centre/right) were added, Dr Green thinks, in the late 1940s.
338. Proctor (1997); Paterson does not appear to have discussed Zionism and its implications publicly to any great extent prior to the war.
339. ibid.: 615
340. ibid.: 615
341. ibid.: 618
342. The brief account given here is based on salient details taken from chapters 2-10 of Isobel Goodwin, (2000) *May you live to be 120! The Story of Tabeetha School, Jaffa. 1863-1983*, Edinburgh.
343. The name derives from Acts 9:36-43.
344. The land was purchased by Thomas Cook for £500 on 17.9.1874, the seller, George Henderson Gibb, had paid £100 for it in 1856; document at Tabeetha School: the head teacher at Tabeetha School, Chris Mottershead, located a number of files for my perusal when I visited the school in May 2001. They were not archived or registered systematically; it is unclear whether copies exist elsewhere, though Mr Mottershead presumed not. I here wish to record my thanks to

Mr Mottershead for his time and for granting access to the documents in the course of a busy school day.

345. Kernohan (1979): 33
346. Goodwin (2000): 32, see also Stockdale's reference to Walker-Arnott p150 below.
347. CS-LW 5.1912: 159
348. Goodwin (2000): 38; Walker-Arnott wrote that 'All my teachers have been brought up and educated in my school – they live with me and are like my children'; CS-LW 5.1912: 159. Displaced from their own families, they were to be taught domesticity for their futures in the Scotswoman's school.
349. ibid.: 1
350. ibid.: 55; note the apparent absence of Hebrew (which the Sea of Galilee mission included in its curriculum), and the Friday evening activity for children of all faiths.
351. ibid.: 56, Foerster (1991): 118
352. Goodwin (2000): 56
353. CS-JMC 14.11.1911
354. CS-GA-JMC 1912: 447
355. They were enthusiastic not least in terms of the effect it might have on other work: 'were the Church to have a Mission in the Holy Land it might prove a most stimulating influence upon the [JM] Committee's work' – the next page reported a deficit of £1,300; CS-GA-JMC 1913: 372.
356. CS-JMC 5.3.1912
357. CS-LW 5.1912: 160; (emphases: LW)
358. CS-LW 5.1912: 160
359. CS-LW 5.1912: 160
360. CS-LW 5.1912: 160, 7.1912: 223
361. In fact, the United Free Church JMC recorded the proposal in such as way as to imply that the Home Committee itself had asked both the Church of Scotland and United Free Church to become involved; UFC-JMC 29.5.1912.
362. CS-LW 7.1912: 223; an equally open mandate was given to the equivalent United Free Church body, which in addition suggested that a boys school should be considered – this was not pursued; UFC-JMC 25.6.1912.
363. CS-JMC 19.11.1912
364. CS-JMC 3.3.1914
365. the final version was agreed on 26.2.1914: CS-GA-JMC 1914: 432-434.
366. UFC-JMC 24.6.1913; c.f. also e.g. CS-WAJM 24.6.1913
367. CS-LW 9.1912: 288, 12.1912: 384, 1.1913: 31-32, 2.1913: 64; it has not been possible to locate the pamphlet.
368. CS-LW 11.1914: 352, also: CS-LW 7.1912: 223
369. CS-LW 11.1914: 352
370. CS-LW 3.1915: 96
371. CS-LW 3.1915: 96
372. CS-LW 11.1915: 351
373. Goodwin (2000): 60-61
374. CS-GA-JMC 1914: 406
375. Bernhard Porter, (1975) *The Lion's Share: A Short History of British Imperialism 1850-1995*, Harlow, 3rd ed. 1996: 141-145

Chapter 4

1. Andrew Porter, (1997) "'Cultural Imperialism' and Protestant Missionary Enterprise, 1780-1914', in *Journal of Imperial and Commonwealth History* vol. 25, no. 3, September, 367-391: 369

2. Williams describes 'evangelical philanthropy' (1982): 277; see also Bebbington (1989): 120-123.

3. Ross (1972): 57

4. ibid.: 64-66

5. ibid.: 66

6. ibid.: 68

7. ibid.: 69-71

8. Edward W Said, (1993) *Culture and Imperialism*, London: 76: 'empire was a universal concern'.

9. Ross (1972): 71

10. ibid.: 52-3, 67-71

11. Kernohan (1979): 35; only the second quotation is taken from the original article.

12. UFC-JMC 23.6.1908

13. Kernohan is typical of those who wax lyrical of 'The Very Special Mission ... in some ways senior in prestige [to the foreign missions]' without recognising the small overall role played by Jewish missions in Scottish church life; Kernohan (1979): 32.

14. See e.g. the minute regarding John Soutar, appointed whilst still a probationer: FC-JMC 19.9.1893

15. For example, Torrance 'never experienced any difficulty with his lessons' (Livingstone (1923): 17), and Paterson also apparently thrived, particularly in his teens (Ewing (1925): 22-23). This pattern is repeated elsewhere – a random assessment of missionary biographies around the turn of the century leads one to the conclusion that the schooling of the subject is always a matter of praise, and that even if a pupil's behaviour was not always exemplary, then a reason for this was found that still made them a model for others to follow.

16. Bebbington (1989): 138

17. Bonar's diary, for example, refers to numerous materials that he read over the years.

18. Joanna Trollope, (1983) *Britannia's Daughters. Women of the British Empire*, London: 186

19. Kwok Pui-lan, (1996) 'The Image of the "White Lady": Gender and Race in Christian Mission', in, *The Power of Naming: A Concilium Reader in Feminist Liberation Theology*, ed. Elisabeth Schüssler-Fiorenza, Maryknoll/London, 250-258: 251

20. Myrtle Hill, (2000) 'Women in the Irish Protestant Foreign Missions c. 1873-1914: Representations and Motivations', in, *Missions and Missionaries*, eds. Pieter N Holtrup, Hugh McLeod, Woodbridge/Rochester, 170-185: 185

21. Macdonald (2000): 114

22. Bonk (1989): 28-9

23. Other Westerners thought similarly: Heleen L Murre-van den Berg analyses attitudes among American Presbyterians in Lebanon and elsewhere in the Middle East; (2000) 'Why Protestant Churches? The American Board and the Eastern Churches: Mission Among 'Nominal' Christians (1820-1870)' in *Missions and Missionaries*, eds. Pieter N Holtrup, Hugh McLeod, Woodbridge/Rochester, 98-111: 99-104.

24. This was particularly apparent in Lebanon, e.g. Marten (2002): 54. Models of 'race' and 'development' such as Gobineau's 'Aryan', 'Mongolian' and 'Savage' categories were prominent in the 19th century, c.f. Bonk (1989): 240-242. In the context of this kind of thinking, Torrance saw his surroundings as 'semi-civilised': see Chapter 5, note 136 below.

25. Livingstone (1923): 12-13, 16-17

26. Livingstone (1923): 21, 23

27. For a romanticised account of her life and work, c.f. W P Livingstone, (1915) *Mary Slessor of Calabar: Pioneer Missionary*, London, 21st ed. 1924. See also Macdonald (2000): 140-142 and Trollope (1983): 194-199.

28. Macdonald (2000): 142

29. Paterson is an obvious examples of this: he demonstrated a broad knowledge of many and varied subjects, his lucubration filling numerous notebooks on medical issues, Greek New Testament vocabulary, political analyses, theological essays, as well as liturgical material and poetry; some of this was also published; c.f. NLS Acc 4499.

30. See also the Checklands' analysis of education in Scotland at this time: (1984): 111-115. Their examination of the universities and medical training is also helpful: 147-151. Certain assumptions about background can be made on the basis of education, but this is not always a straightforward task.

31. ibid.: 66; the first election in which this applied was in 1868.

32. ibid.: 75-6; Thorne (1997): esp. 246-248 shows how 'home missions' suffered in attention as foreign missions dominated the mission agenda of the evangelical churches. Attempts to link enthusiasm for work with the working-classes to foreign missions were generally unsuccessful, with one Scot complaining that many in his own country were 'living in the ignorance of heathens' (quoted by Thorne, 247). This failure to engage with the lower-classes had serious consequences for the support base for overseas mission. Thorne draws useful lessons for understanding 'race' and 'class' as axes of identity from this scenario, pointing to their similarities and the symmetry here.

33. Gikandi (1996): 32

34. The poor tended to lower attendance anyway; Bebbington (1989): 112-114.

35. UFC-JMC 5.4.1917

36. When it was agreed Wells should be asked to be Convener of the Free Kirk JMC, two reasons were given why he might not have been a suitable candidate: he 'is also the minister of a large congregation, and he has the disadvantage of living in Glasgow. But Glasgow is no great distance from Edinburgh, and we all know that Mr Wells is equal to any amount of labour'; FC-JMC 18.2.1890. Glasgow and Edinburgh, although about 60km apart, were well-connected by rail at this time.

37. FC-JMC 17.10.1871

38. FC-JMC 16.12.1884

39. Torrance, for example, attended 10 of 13 meetings that took place between 16.10.1894 and 17.9.1895.

40. FC-JMC 16.10.1894 notes that Torrance spoke about the work in northern Palestine, focusing specifically on 'the importance of Safed'.

41. FC-JMC 16.9.1890 and 16.6.1891; the meeting of 14.11.1893 noted a final estimated cost for the hospital of £3,241.

42. FC-JMC 17.9.1889

43. See the Constitution adopted by the FC-JMC on 18.1.1894 for details.

44. FC-JMC 16.12.1890

45. FC-JMC 19.4.1892, 19.7.1892

46. e.g. FC-JMC 21.7.1891

47. Benjamin Weiss, c.f. p60 above.

48. NLS Acc 4499 (9): Paterson's diary 9.9.1900, states that although he says 'being tired' was 'ample excuse' for refusing his instructions, the fact that he himself took on work despite this would appear to indicate that he actually thought otherwise: 'Found Miss Bellamy rather sulky after yesterday's incident when she practically set my authority at defiance. I had asked her to go to town and dress 'A. Alttalin [spelling not clear], A Sumaineh's [spelling not clear] leg and she declined to go on the score of being tired – which was ample excuse, but immediately added "Besides the work closed yesterday (Friday) and you have no right to ask

me to do it" or words to that effect. I got warm & said that if I gave an order I expected it to be done... [she left], with a gesture of defiance. I added, If you ask to be excused on the score of tiredness that is a matter of humanity but you have no case or right to take up the position you have done, and reminded her how many times I had gone to town to do her dressing cases simply to relieve her, ... sometimes because Miss Macpherson point blank refused to go for her. With this I left her.' As with Torrance, Paterson was also ill at times, attributed, for example, to 'overwork and anxiety as to immediate developments'; UFC-MR 11.1909: 490.

49. e.g. FC-JMC 19.11.1895 and 17.3.1896, addressing property issues and expanding work into the villages of Galilee.

50. Unfortunately, there are no surviving records of Mission Council meetings.

51. FC-JMC 18.1.1894

52. FC-JMC 20.7.1897

53. Susan Fleming McAllister, (1998) 'Cross-Cultural Dress in Victorian British Missionary Narratives: Dressing for Eternity', in *Christian Encounters with the Other*, ed. John C Hawley, New York, 122-134: 122

54. c.f. also Thorne (1997): 239: 'The attractions of foreign missionary intelligence were considerable in an age before alternative means of enlightenment, entertainment, and even assembly were widely available. This was particularly true of public missionary meetings at which audiences were treated to a foreign missionary's eyewitness account of travels and battles among the heathen or the testimony of a convert from the colonies resplendent in exotic "native" dress.'

55. George Adam Smith, (1894) *The Historical Geography of the Holy Land*, London, 25th ed. 1931; Smith claims Allenby used it in planning his campaign during World War I.

56. Alexander Andrew, (1891) *My Visit to Palestine*, Paisley, nd (but journey began February 1891, publication probably that year or soon after); it describes a trip the Free Kirk minister from Paisley made.

57. c.f. also Bonar (1865)

58. Smith (1894): xvii

59. Andrew (1891): 137-159

60. The 1914 volumes were also advertised in the Church of Scotland magazine, which pointed out that Hall's last chapter was also available as a separate booklet; CS-LW 6.1914: 192

61. Wilson/Wells (1895): 22-24

62. ibid.: 38

63. ibid.: 76

64. Ewing (1914): 14

65. ibid.: 26

66. ibid.: 25

67. ibid.: 54

68. Mt 5:14

69. There is no link to the present-day illegal Israeli settlement of Kiryat Arba near Hebron.

70. Ewing (1914): 69

71. At varying times, there were publications catering to a more specific audience, most notably to women.

72. FC-WJMA 29.10.1900

73. Macdonald (2000): 220-222

74. Andrew C Ross, (2002) *David Livingstone. Mission and Empire*, London/New York, 2002: 116; McAllister, (1998): 122 notes that Livingstone's book was widely used by missionaries preparing to go overseas.

75. e.g. FC-MMR 1.1.1885: 16

76. FC-MMR 1.7.1884: 207; Shepherd (1987) outlines, though somewhat unreflectively, more general western 'rediscovery' of Palestine, see particularly chapter 3.

77. FC-MMR 1.12.1884: 364; the JMC Convener penned this, c.f. p136 below for the anti-Jewish tendencies apparent here.

78. FC-MMR 2.12.1889: 357; (FC's emphases)

79. UFC-MR 9.1907: 410

80. FC-MMR 1.12.1893: 271; echoes of Davidson's 'jealousy' are apparent here, Chapter 1

81. FC-MMR 1.12.1891: 358. The 'quality' of the converts is regularly mentioned; c.f. also p27 above.

82. FC-MMR 1.12.1897: 282; c.f. p8 above on the topic of further prayer.

83. FC-MMR 1.12.1884: 364

84. FC-MMR 1.6.1899: 139

85. Werner Jochmann portrays anti-Jewishness as in part a protest movement for all who felt threatened by modernisation in the state and social realm; these Scots would have been sympathetic to this feeling; (1985) 'Struktur und Funktion des deutschen Antisemitismus 1878-1914' in *Antisemitismus. Von der Judenfeindschaft zum Holocaust*, eds. Herbert A Strauss, Norbert Kampe, Bonn, 99-142: 134.

86. FC-MMR 1.6.1899: 139

87. Damascus, Russia and Germany all featured in JMC concern about treatment of Jews at different times. Thorne's examination of anti-slavery attitudes informs this imagery: (1997): 249.

88. e.g. FC-MMR 1.11.1890: 120

89. e.g. UFC-MR 6.1909: 266: 'an account of a day's work in the Hospital at Tiberias, written from the nurse's point of view'.

90. c.f. p141 below

91. c.f. e.g. Ruth and Thomas Hummel, (1995) *Patterns of the sacred: English Protestant and Russian Orthodox pilgrims of the Nineteenth Century*, London

92. Eileen Kane (2005) elaborates on the founding of the Russian mission in considerable detail; 'Pilgrims, Piety and Politics: The Founding of the First Russian Ecclesiastical Mission in Jerusalem', in *Christian witness between continuity and new beginnings: modern historical missions in the Middle East*, ed. Michael Marten, series: *Studien zur Orientalischen Kirchengeschichte*, Hamburg, (forthcoming)

93. FC-MMR 1.9.1897: 216

94. FC-MMR 1.4.1899: 90; women were not mentioned in such contexts: females were seen as religious actors, as evidenced by the women who were employed to relate to girls and women, but generally in much diminished roles: the unspoken expectation was that men would lead conversion processes.

95. UFC-MR 4.1909: 169

96. UFC-MR 6.1909: 267

97. UFC-MR 7.1909: 296

98. FC-MMR 7.1904: 297 – the Protestant work ethic makes its appearance; c.f. also Chapter 4, note 48 above.

99. FC-MMR 7.1904: 297

100. UFC-MR 11.1905: 514; the reference is to Ez 2.

101. Ilan Pappe describes the wider context of the reforms; (2004) *A Modern History of Palestine. One Land, Two Peoples*, Cambridge, see especially the first pages of chapter 2.

102. UFC-MR 10.1908: 460

103. UFC-MR 3.1909: 121

104. UFC-MR 4.1908: 461

105. UFC-MR 11.1908: 504

106. UFC-MR 12.1908: 534-544
107. e.g. 2 Cor 5:17, Gal 6:15, Eph 2:15-16
108. The impact of the war on the missions has been outlined in Chapter 3.
109. UFC-MR 4.1917: 86
110. FC-MR 1.1918: 7; Russian treatment of Jews had been condemned in the past, c.f. p95 above.
111. FC-MR 1.1918: 7
112. Proctor, (1997), 613; the essay examines the Scots' reaction to events between 1917 and 1948.
113. UFC-MR 6.1918: 100
114. FC-MMR 1.12.1891: 358
115. FC-MMR 1.12.1892: 286
116. FC-MMR 1.12.1894: 274-275
117. The role of additional and more sincere prayer in averting the poor outcomes of human action – c.f. p8 above – should not be ignored, but prayer and its efficacy or otherwise is not measurable in this context.
118. David Cannadine, (2001) *Ornamentalism: how the British saw their Empire*, London: 125
119. Gikandi (1996): 29, 31; c.f. p8 above
120. William Dalrymple, fastidious in his attributions of national background throughout his work, mentions the 'long tradition of dubious English clergymen exported to India after failing to find a living at home'; (2002), *White Mughals. Love and Betrayal in Eighteenth-Century India*, London: 412.

Chapter 5

1. Jean and John Comaroff, (1991) *Of Revelation and Revolution. Christianity, Colonialism, and Consciousness in South Africa. Volume I*, Chicago/London: 88
2. Said (1978): 100
3. However, there is clearly also a substantial work needing to be done describing reactions to the missions using local actors' responses.
4. Mostly, the interest in such differences was minimal, though sometimes used to show the putative favour that the missions found amongst the local population, c.f. e.g. p94 above.
5. In 1937 a Seventh-Day Adventist journal records one of the very few western analyses of the work of western missionaries in the eyes of oriental Christians. Here the lack of Muslim converts is ascribed to survival, western missionaries being welcomed in order to revive the oriental churches and help convert Muslims. Here again, the oriental churches 'need' 'reviving', a process aided by the westerners; F Bäcker, (1937) 'Die Arbeit der Missionare im Urteil orientalischer Christen', in *Der Adventbote: Gemeindeblatt der Siebentags-Adventisten*, Hamburg, vol. 43, part 12, 189-190.
6. FC-MMR 2.12.1888: 357
7. Vital (1999): 17-24. He notes that when rebellion 'occurred, it could, often as not, even in the face of countervailing support for the rebel, be made to collapse': 22.
8. Williams provides some analysis of this: (1982): 278-281
9. c.f. on this topic Bonk, (1989): 263
10. Those coming directly from Scotland, even if they had attended the Leipzig Institutum Judaicum, would probably have encountered significant numbers of people of other faiths in a non-Christian majority context for the first time on their arrival in the Levant.
11. Taber (1990-1): 22; c.f. p16 above

12. Bonar/McCheyne (1843): 193
13. Wolff (1827): 1-63 explains his background and the origins of his first trip.
14. Bonar/McCheyne (1843): 193; c.f. p29 above
15. ibid.: 248; c.f. p53 above
16. e.g. FC-MMR 1.6.1891: 173
17. Bonar/McCheyne (1843): 243
18. This applied equally to their encounters with Muslims, though Muslims were not, of course, their main target. Jan Slomp analyses Calvin's attitudes to Muslims, which partly determined what thinking there was on this issue in Scotland; (2002) 'Calvin and the Turks', in *Encounters: Documents for Muslim Christian Understanding (Pontificio Istituto di Studi Arabi e d'Islamistica)*, October, No. 288, 3-15. Jane I Smith examines a selection of Protestant attitudes to Islam: (1997) 'Some Contemporary Protestant Theological Reflections on Pluralism: implications for Christian-Muslim Understanding', in *Islam and Christian-Muslim Relations*, vol. 8, no. 1, 67-83.
19. e.g. FC-JMC 17.10.1871: '... the proclamation of the great truths of the gospel [should] be based ... on the foundation of ... the Apostles and <u>Prophets</u>, Jesus Christ himself being always the chief corner-stone' – from the Amsterdam instructions (see above). The prophets are emphasised since it was held the prophets foretold Jesus as the Messiah, which Jews would understand.
20. A diffuse term, almost certainly based on roles established in Scotland: Macdonald elaborates on this: mainly working-class women (often widows) who 'tended to combine, in their visits and meetings, practical sewing, cooking and nursing work, with simple scriptural instruction and encouragement ... [to] women and families of their own class', (2000): 85.
21. Livingstone (1923): 230-231
22. c.f. Chapter 1, note 72 above.
23. Ian Bradley, (1997) *Abide with Me: The World of Victorian Hymns*, London: 119-120
24. This perspective was challenged especially with the devastation wrought by World War I, which so clearly mitigated against a belief in the ongoing progress of humankind as a whole.
25. Bradley (1997): 120
26. Warren (1967): chapter 5 examines education in mission.
27. Cleveland (1994): 115-6
28. e.g. Quataert (1994b): 770-775 examines the effect of trends in the world economy on the Ottoman empire and includes analysis of the state of Ottoman finances; Owen (1981): chapter 6, looks particularly at the effects on Greater Syria. Using world-systems analysis, Peter J Taylor shows how this influence works in his section on "Informal imperialism: dominance without empire" and his discussion of Friedrich List in the 19th century; (1993) *Political Geography. World-Economy, Nation-State and Locality*, Harlow, 1985, 3rd ed. 1993: especially 135-136. Suraiya Faroqhi presents an assessment based on continuity and gradual change, prompted from within and not just from without; (1992) 'In Search of Ottoman History', *New Approaches to State and Peasant in Ottoman History*, eds. Halil Berktay, Suraiya Faroqhi, London, 211-241: 216-221.
29. UFC-WJMA 11.10.1912
30. Stockdale (2000): 187
31. In connection with Anglican schools, 'education work tended to foster a desire to join the church of the teachers [and this] led to complications later in relations with the Orthodox Church'; Anthony O'Mahony, (1994) 'Church, State and the Christian Communities and the Holy Places of Palestine', in *Christians in the Holy Land*, eds. Michael Prior, William Taylor, London, 11-27: 17.
32. Selim Deringil, (1998) *The Well-Protected Domains: Ideology and the Legitimation of Power in the Ottoman Empire, 1876-1909*, London: 132
33. UFC-MR 1902: 125

34. Macaulay argued for English education in order that in 30 years time 'there will not be a single idolater among the respectable classes in Bengal'; Benedict Anderson, (1983) *Imagined Communities*, London, 2nd ed. 1991: 91. Gikandi highlights the term 'mimic men' (1996): 40.

35. 'The children seem quite as sharp as our own. Five years ago not one girl in Tiberias could read, or distinguish between the bottom and the top of a page. Only one native woman in Tiberias knows the alphabet'; this is from a report of a visit to Fenton's school, FC-MMR 6.1891: 172.

36. Livingstone (1923): 230

37. From Jane Hope Grierson's impressions of the school in 1889, cited by Goodwin (2000): 42

38. These were introduced in Tabeetha in 1913 as a course of study, Goodwin (2000): 60

39. Goodwin (2000): 54; Okkenhaug (2002) elaborates on domesticity vs. academic achievement in Mandate era Anglican schools in her fourth chapter, a development of what had happened in a variety of mission schools in the Ottoman era.

40. Livingstone (1923): 109

41. Livingstone cites a Greek Orthodox priest trying to prevent children from his community attending: 'It is better ... that the girls should grow up ignorant and bad than that they should come under the influence of the Protestant women.' Whether or not this was actually said is irrelevant in this context: it communicates the Scots' perception of the Greek priest's feelings about the effects their work would have on 'his' girls; ibid.: 107. On the subsequent page he contrasts the 'cheerful, well-ordered activity' of the girls in Fenton's school with their 'wild and untrained condition' before their enrolment.

42. UFC-MR 1902: 555

43. Livingstone (1923): 108

44. Victorian ideals of progress being the key thought pattern here.

45. Okkenhaug (2002): 153, but see also the whole of that chapter.

46. That competition was rife, is not in doubt; Deringil (1998): 131. As Deringil points out (130), the primary Ottoman concern was that the Protestant schools undermined the state's legitimacy. Of course, this was but one of many factors that played a role in the decline and undermining of Ottoman authority, c.f. Michael Ursinus, (1993) '"Nicht die Türken siegten über Byzanz, sondern Byzanz über die Türken." Zur Vergangenheitsbewältigung im Osmanischen Reich am Vorabend des Ersten Weltkrieges', in *Periplus: Jahrbuch für aussereuropäische Geschichte*, vol. 3, 47-60. But in the light of military and diplomatic defeats and economic disadvantage on the global market, the prominence of western missionary organisations in the life of certain Ottoman subjects can easily be understood to have received more attention from the political authorities than they perhaps warranted.

47. Anderson (1983): 91

48. C Ernest Dawn, (1993) 'From Ottomanism to Arabism: The Origin of an Ideology', in *The Modern Middle East: A Reader*, eds. Albert Hourani, Philip S Khoury, Mary C Wilson, London, 375-393: 379, 381; regardless of whether one sees the role of the mission-educated Arabs as central to the creation of Arab nationalism or not, the fact that they participated prominently in the debate is undisputed; c.f. e.g. C Ernest Dawn, (1991) 'The Origins of Arab Nationalism', in *The Origins of Arab Nationalism*, eds. Rashid Khalidi, Lisa Anderson, Muhammad Muslih, Reeva S Simon, New York, 3-30: 3-4; Albert Hourani (1962): 67, 95-98, 259 and Okkenhaug (2002): 41, 46-50. It should be noted, however, that a level of disconnection with both their home environment and Europe marked many of the participants. This cannot be explored further here, but basic secondary literature can be referred to: e.g. Anderson (1983): 92-93, Hourani (1962): 96-97. Butrus al-Bustani, a prominent Maronite convert to Protestantism in Lebanon, founded his 'National School' (*al-madrasa al-waṭaniyya*) as an attempt to bridge the Europe he had come to know with the Syria of his birth; for an examination of this issue,

see Hourani, 1962: 99-102, Ussama Makdisi, (2002) 'After 1860: Debating Religion, Reform, and Nationalism in the Ottoman Empire', in *International Journal of Middle East Studies*, vol. 34, 601-617: esp. 614.

49. The result of comity: c.f. Chapter 2, note 62 above. Few Palestinians would have been aware of the reputed high quality of Scottish education and chosen a Scottish school for this reason.

50. The AIU eventually operated schools in both Tiberias and Safad; Shaw (1991): 164.

51. Deringil devotes an entire chapter to Ottoman and missionary education in his analysis of late Ottoman legitimacy (1998).

52. ibid.: 115

53. Catholic missions, though not viewed with great favour by the Porte, were not perceived in quite the negative light that Protestant missions were.

54. ibid.: 115; see also Jeremy Salt, (1993) *Imperialism, Evangelism and the Ottoman Armenians 1878-1896*, London: 30-39.

55. Even if this relationship was sometimes rather strained: 'Missionary effort was by no means an agency of imperialist politics. Often it was opposed to the colonial authorities; pretty well always it put the interests of its converts first. Yet the success of the Lord was a function of imperialist advance.' Hobsbawm (1987): 71. A necessary correction, reflecting imperialistic patterns of thought, would be that the missionaries always put *their perception* of 'the interests of ... [the] converts first'. This contrast with e.g. the Comaroffs' position, is returned to in Chapter 6 below.

56. Deringil (1998): 112; also: 'by the 1890s the missionaries had come to be regarded by the sultan as 'the most dangerous enemies to social order', among all the foreigners living in his domains' (114) because not 'only did the missionaries undermine the efforts the Ottomans were making to legitimize the basis of their rule at home, they also proved influential in creating adverse conditions abroad by feeding the Western press with anti-Turkish sentiment'; 113.

57. ibid.: 116; this is dated 1892.

58. This was, of course, strictly circumscribed: the missionaries, and even more so the Edinburgh committees, were wary of giving handouts, thereby perhaps creating dependency and interest in the mission for monetary reasons, quite aside from the unwillingness to use their limited funds in this way.

59. ibid.: 117-119

60. ibid.: 132-133

61. ibid.: 133-134 cites the war-like language of Ottoman officials. The language used by Scottish missionaries in many contexts resembled that of a military campaign – the frequent references to 'occupying territory' and such like come to mind here (this use of language was typical of most western missionaries); c.f. p212 below on this topic.

62. Christoffer H Grundmann, (1991) 'The Contribution of Medical Missions: The Intercultural Transfer of Standards and Values', in *Academic Medicine*, December, vol. 66, no. 12, 731-733: 731.

63. Walls (1982): 287

64. ibid.: 290

65. ibid.: 288

66. The Christian and Muslim population barely registered in the planning stages (these were *Jewish* Mission Committees), though they did form a substantial number of the patients.

67. This became less of a concern in the later years of the 19th century; the short life of Ion Keith-Falconer in Aden and many similar examples made it a very real issue earlier in the 19th century or when regions were not so well known. Keith-Falconer's death led to a great upsurge in volunteers for overseas mission, including to Aden: his immediate successor was Alexander Paterson; Nick R P Houghton (1997) *Pioneering with the Gospel in South-West*

Arabia: The Keith-Falconer Mission between 1885 and 1906, unpublished MTh thesis, University of Edinburgh: 37-41.

68. Wilson/Wells (Torrance) (1895): 40
69. For example Vartan of the EMMS in Nazareth treated Torrance; ibid.: 42; Livingstone (1923): 74; Torrance treated a 'London Mission' (LJS) colleague in Safad shortly after he arrived in Palestine: FC-MMR 1.3.1885: 77
70. Wilson/Wells (Torrance) (1895): 42-43
71. FC-MMR 1.4.1886: 105
72. Walls (1982): 292-4 expounds on the ever-expanding investment required once a medical facility or mission had been initiated. Even though in the 1840s the Committee may have known of only few examples on which to base such an assumption, it would have been obvious to them that the ongoing cost of medicines and equipment would be a financial burden.
73. UFC-MR 1902: 125. Dalman had, of course, once applied to work in the Free Kirk Galilee mission.
74. Ewing writing in Livingstone (1923): 208
75. ibid.: 217: "'If the work is worth doing, it is worth doing well. No quack work in medical work." But when faced with the tragedy of suffering in the mass ... what course could he adopt? He either had to ... turn away, or do what he could ... to ease their pain. He was too sympathetic to take the sterner course.' – the quotation is from an address Torrance gave.
76. Overwhelmed by patients from both sides of the Jordan, he also (in 1908/9) suggested opening an additional mission station elsewhere, but the funds for this were not available; ibid.: 218.
77. FC-JMC 16.12.1884
78. Grundmann displays a level of prejudice on this issue that is somewhat problematic. His orientalist perspective fails to allow for other cultures' understanding of the sanctity of life; (1991): 733.
79. ibid.: 733
80. Williams (1982): 281
81. ibid.: 277
82. Similarly, Torrance refers to his hospital (the rented premises) as 'a very Bethesda to many a poor sufferer' – using Biblical place names to signify a purpose or a state of mind was a useful way of relating to the church membership in Scotland, the people who ultimately were needed in order to support the mission; FC-MMR 1.9.1892: 212.
83. e.g. Is 1:16, Jer 2:22, 4:14, Heb 10:22
84. Frederick Levison, (1989) *Christian and Jew: The Life of Leon Levison, 1881-1936*, Edinburgh; that acceptance into the western Christian fold could be tenuous is clear from the account of Levison's supposed recanting of his Christian faith when visiting Safad, in which Thomas Steele, one of the Galilee missionaries, played a significant, and apparently, somewhat malevolent role, with adverse consequences for Levison (52-54). Steele, recently arrived, had not known Levison personally, and reported the 'recantation' on the basis of hearsay. The biographer, especially considering he is writing about his own family, generously notes (53): 'That Mr Steele was a sick man who had to come home after only a year at Tiberias may have affected his attitude.'
85. Hobsbawm (1987): 76
86. FC-JMC 19.6.1894
87. FC-JMC 22.3.1892
88. FC-JMC 14.11.1893 records: 'Read letter from Mr Christie ... giving interesting accounts of the number of Jews that attend the evening classes, and stating certain difficulties he had ... the Secretary was instructed to make a suitable reply.' From this, and there is no other information to go on, it is not clear what the 'difficulties' were, but Christie was clearly interesting some Jews in his message.

89. The social consequences for Muslims would perhaps have been even more severe: western missionaries saw this as the primary explanation for the lack of Muslim converts. Jessup claims to have taken an undisclosed number overseas to prevent adverse repercussions; Abdul Latif Tibawi, (1966) *American Interests in Syria 1800-1901. A Study of Educational, Literary and Religious work*, Oxford: 239. Zwemer notes that in general, 'fear of death' would face any Muslim who converted to Christianity; Samuel M Zwemer, (1924) *The Law of Apostasy in Islam. Answering the Question why there are so few Moslem Converts, and giving examples of their Moral Courage and Martyrdom*, London, Edinburgh, New York, (preface dated): 24.

90. Hall (1914): 112-3

91. ibid.: 114

92. ibid.: 115

93. c.f. page 13 above

94. FC-GA 1897: 21; in 1896 James Wells gave an eloquent five-point address pleading for the support of the JMC: FC-GA 1896: 21-23. Such sentiments were repeated year on year, and any number of examples of this kind of argument can be identified.

95. Binfield quotes an address in connection with Jewish missions from 1892: 'We are probably on the eve of a conflict ... [to achieve conversion of the Jews].' He then notes acerbically that the 'weasel word was 'probably'. For all its brave certainty, pre-millennialism 1890s- ... style was carefully imprecise'; (1994): 238.

96. Mary Torrance is not directly related to the Torrance family of Tiberias: her surname derives from her husband, a descendant of a 19th century missionary to China and a distant relation of David Torrance.

97. Interview with Mary Torrance, Edinburgh, 19.4.2001.

98. Jongeneel (1995): 273

99. ibid.: 272-284

100. In this context, it is problematic since the whole concept of 'ecumenical' that he refers to only took the form (and the term) recognised today from the early 20th century onwards. Therefore, in describing the pattern being examined here, 'Ecumenical' can only be used by reference to Jongeneel's description in contrast to the Roman Catholic and Evangelical movements, and not in a more general sense. On the other hand, in the specific context of the Scottish church, the use of the term 'Evangelical' is perhaps slightly less problematic than it might be in other circumstances, since the term was used by segments of Scottish ecclesial tradition as a self-descriptor.

101. ibid.: 273

102. Hobsbawm (1987): 76-77

103. Even though they rarely acknowledge it explicitly, national and cultural backgrounds, of course, influenced the missionaries as well: Presbyterianism itself was (is) after all a Scottish appropriation of a religion that had originated in the Levant many centuries earlier.

104. Thomson (1883): 312-313

105. Ogilvie (1924): 103-4; note that these four were seen to have contributed to the development of western culture. Nineteenth century archaeological work in all four regions was a significant factor in this.

106. ibid.: 111; the implication that Indians might not be fully human fits the racist imagery of the time; various theories existed, but Europeans were always at the top of the scale, and others somewhere below that in terms of progress, achievement, and ability.

107. ibid.: 121

108. c.f. the note that 'the Jewesses are the most apt to learn' – ability to learn and adopt western attitudes was often seen as a sign of progress; FC-MMR 2.4.1888: 105

109. e.g., in 1903-1904 there were at least two students from Safad at the Syrian Protestant College; whether they came from the Scottish schools is not known; Syrian Protestant College, (1904) *Catalogue of the Syrian Protestant College, Beirût, Syria, 38th Year, 1903-1904*, Beirut: 73.

110. Of course, the AIU, the LJS, and other institutions also played a role in the creation of a western-educated segment of the Palestinian Jewish, Muslim and Christian population; clearly the Scots were not necessarily very different to them in their impact.
111. McAllister (1998): 124; (McAllister's emphases)
112. Gikandi (1996): 41; using Radhakrishnan's term
113. ibid.: 31
114. ibid.: 29
115. Kabbani has shown how the reduction of real threat, followed by hegemony, enabled 'the East [to be studied] calmly and carefully', reshaping 'the Orient in order to comprehend it; there was a sustained effort to devise in order to rule'; (1986): 138.
116. This denial of the (existence, validity, right of the) voice of the subjected is an inherent part of the imperialist discourse: comity represents a self-willed domination by the western missionaries, c.f. on this theme Andrew Fleck, (1998) 'Crusoe's Shadow: Christianity, Colonization and the Other', in *Christian Encounters with the Other*, ed. John C Hawley, New York, 74-89: 79-80; 'missionary aggression' was found in other Jewish missions: Ritchie (2002): 179.
117. Gikandi (1996): 33
118. c.f. Colley, p8 above.
119. This can be placed at the turn of the century: the 'scramble for Africa' between 1885 and 1895 representing its peak, with the first effective criticism of the imperialist narrative coming in 1902 with the publication of J A Hobson's *Imperialism*; see e.g. Ross (2002): 240-241, Gikandi (1996): 21.
120. Dundee Archives, MS 38/2/1(36); this image is also used in UFC-MR 10.1906, 468. For a similar image taken two years earlier, see http://www.dundee.ac.uk/archives/p-torrnc.htm (accessed 2.6.03).
121. McAllister (1998): 127
122. Taylor and his China Inland Mission was an exception: e.g. Bonk notes that only one of the LMS missionaries to China attempted to adapt to a Chinese way of life; Bonk (1989): 62. This, of course, in noted contrast to Jesuit missionaries, who attempted to live much more as Chinese amongst the Chinese. See also Jonathon Bonk, (1991) *Missions and Money: Affluence as a Western Missionary Problem*, series: *American Society of Missiology Series, No. 15*, Maryknoll: 67.
123. McAllister (1998): 133: 'In the end they hoped that their outward conversion would result in the inward conversion of Chinese souls for eternity.'
124. With regard to worship, Torrance noted that his 'servant' might soon make an excellent precentor (importing this position from Scotland marks simply one more element of western culture that was confused with Christian religion), and comments on the singing at his prayer-meeting of 'What a friend we have in Jesus' and other hymns – in Arabic; FC-MMR 1.3.1887: 74. On another occasion, 'I need thee every hour' was 'rendered into Arabic, and set to the same tune to which it is set in Sankey's collection' – Moody and Sankey in Arabic on the shore of Lake Galilee is an intriguing thought; FC-MMR 2.1.1898: 9.
125. on this topic, c.f. Bonk (1989): 157-166.
126. UFC-WJMA 17.5.1909
127. c.f. p137 above
128. c.f. pp33 and 145 above
129. Wortabet (1860)
130. These are mostly limited, of course, to official or semi-official records, c.f. Appendix.
131. Such as when noting the variety of people honouring Torrance's 25 years labour in the Galilee; c.f. p94 above.
132. Although probably not meant to be seen in this way, a hilarious encounter between Torrance

and the customs officers relayed in Livingstone (1923): 59-65, serves as an example of the way in which Torrance, Paterson and others had to deal with the issue.

133. e.g. ibid.: 95

134. e.g. FC-MMR 1.2.1890: 49

135. FC-GA 1871: 76

136. c.f. Torrance on Palestine: 'semi-demi-semi-European and civilised'; FR-MMR 1.3.1887: 75

137. Dundee University Archives, MS38-2-1(36)

138. Ronald Hyam, (1990) *Empire and Sexuality: The British Experience*, series, *Studies in Imperialism*, ed. John M MacKenzie, Manchester/New York: 75-79

139. ibid.: 75

140. ibid.: 75; see also his footnote 77; for some of the reasons for this, see David M Friedman, (2001) *A Mind of Its Own. A Cultural History of the Penis*, Harmondsworth: 52.

141. Hyam (1990): 77

142. ibid.: 76

143. Hyam also notes less directly pragmatic reasons to do with notions of masculinity and related themes; (1990): 77-8. This period also saw the rise of so-called 'muscular Christianity' and the cult of 'Christian manliness', and if circumcision could increase a man's general well-being, then in this context it would have been welcomed. For an examination of some of the issues around muscular Christianity, see Sean Gill, (1998) 'How Muscular was Victorian Christianity? Thomas Hughes and the Cult of Christian Manliness Reconsidered', in *Gender and Christian Religion*, ed. R N Swanson, series: *Studies in Church History*, vol. 34, Woodbridge/Rochester, 421-430. This was also a factor in Palestine, coming to particular prominence in the Mandate era, c.f. Inger Marie Okkenhaug, (2005) '"To give the boys energy, manliness, and self-command in temper": the Anglican Male Ideal and St. George's College in Jerusalem, ca. 1890-1940', in *Gender, Religion and Change in the Middle East: Two Hundred Years of History*, eds. Inger Marie Okkenhaug, Ingvild Flaskerud, Oxford, 47-66.

144. Later records such as the letters from William Fyffe Dorward, writing to his parents from Palestine about his experience in 1923-4 of working alongside Herbert Torrance, David's son and successor at Tiberias, are less relevant to this issue: although Dorward's letters also fail to mention circumcision, by the 1920s it was normal practice for the upper and middle-classes in Britain, generally carried out by GPs, and Dorward would probably not have thought it anything unusual. I here wish to record my grateful thanks to Morrison Dorward for lending me his father's letters.

145. Stephen O Murray discusses Burton's 'sotadic zone', arguing that although Burton's survey was organised geographically, the 'sotadic zone' is essentially non-Christian rather than geographic or climatic; (1997) 'Some Nineteenth-Century Reports of Islamic Homosexualities', in *Islamic Homosexualities*, eds. Stephen O Murray, Will Roscoe, New York, 204-221: 211-217.

146. Cor 9: 19-20a, 22

147. Note that it is not being suggested that this is an ideal that is achievable: total transcendence of cultural history is an impossibility, but it does represent a goal.

148. Bonk (1989): esp. 37-90; Bonk also examines identification on the linguistic, political-economic, and religious-education levels in relation to the LMS and its missionaries, but notably does not discuss gender identification. Pui-lan highlights the connections between race and gender when dealing with the 'white lady' missionary: that male converts might achieve positions with the church, such as ordination, which a 'white lady' could not, potentially led to ambivalence – gender awareness did not necessarily lead to racial awareness; Pui-lan, 1996: 254.

149. It can be coherently argued that the employment of women to convert girls and women was a form of identification, though the Scots did not identify this as such at the time. For many years the lack of a female doctor was not perceived as an issue, though the appointment of Wilson was warmly welcomed by Paterson. Whilst in the early years of the Tiberias mission it would have been almost impossible to identify a suitable individual to work as a doctor,

by the early 20th century, this was not the case. On this topic, c.f. e.g. Sinno (1982): 215, Okkenhaug (2002): 37.

150. Bonk (1989): 45

151. ibid.: 240-242 outlines some of the nuances behind this thinking; many other accounts exist.

152. ibid.: 248-252

153. Pui-lan (1996): 255. Of course, the subordination of precisely these western Christian women within their own western church, whether Protestant or Catholic, was not seen as a problem. Pui-lan develops this theme briefly in the remainder of her essay.

154. UFC-WJMA 12.12.1909; note that Lizzie Jones' position was unusual in that she did not draw a full salary – Gwladys Jones, several years later, was paid £130, most other salaries having remained at much the same level.

155. This, the year of the United Presbyterian and Free Church union, was a typical year in terms of expenditure. The information is based on budgets for 1901 in UFC-JMC 18.12.1900 and UFC-WJMA 22.2.1901; all figures are rounded down to nearest £. Gender and appointment basis is not always clear – where these are doubtful, they are indicated as appropriate.

156. Bonk (1989): 38

157. ibid.: 40

158. ibid.: 43

159. Bonk (1989): 44-45

160. Although the role of the women's movement led to decreasing church involvement by many women, c.f. p78 above.

161. Macdonald (2000): 111-115, 128-133

162. ibid.: 49

163. ibid.: 93

164. Bonk (1989): 40; (Bonk's emphasis)

165. Beyond the issue of identification that is the main focus here, control over others' pay, particularly if one's own salary is relatively high, ensures a substantial degree of power.

166. Hobsbawm (1987): 71

167. Porter makes it clear that missionaries' belief systems were adopted in circumstances where they 'addressed important aspects of everyday life inadequately dealt with by traditional religions' – this strengthens the argument here, that Palestinians were happy with their own belief system, and so appropriated the other two elements of the missionaries' offering whilst declining to adopt the missionaries' religion. Palestinian societal structures are therefore shown to be less 'fragile to any external touch' than is sometimes implied by scholars describing western involvement in Ottoman Palestine; Porter (1997): 384, 374.

168. Stefan Durst, (1993) *Jerusalem als ökumenisches Problem im 20. Jahrhundert*, Pfaffenweiler: 119 states that in 1830 90% of Arab Christians were Orthodox, but by 1900, this had dropped to 30%. His footnote acknowledges that this is perhaps too low: McCarthy (1990): 12,

Chapter 6

1. Courbage/Fargues (1997): 80
2. Valognes (1994): 86
3. Nielsen (2003): 351 details this more generally.
4. Fleck (1998): 78-80
5. Gikandi's use of the term 'valorization' is relevant here; (1996): 18.
6. Gikandi (1996): 41
7. Hastings (2001): 108-109
8. Gikandi (1996): 33; p163 above
9. Gikandi (1996): 2
10. McAllister (1998), 124; (McAllister's emphases)
11. Stockdale (2000): 351
12. Contrary to Davidson's statement that migrations 'are part of the providence of God ... but find no place in prophecy'; p14 above
13. The terrible consequences of this change for the Christian and Muslim victims of Jewish emancipation were not envisioned by the missionaries at this stage.
14. Dawn, (1991): 3-4 and (1993): 379, 381.

BIBLIOGRAPHY

Primary sources

Official church records

Church of Scotland
General Assembly minutes, generally titled: Proceedings and Minutes of the General Assembly of [date]
General Assembly accounts, generally titled: Abstract of the Public Accounts of the Church of Scotland for the year ending [date]
Jewish Mission Committee minutes (exact title varies)
Jewish Mission Committee General Assembly report: title generally based on usage of Committee name
Women's Association for Jewish Mission minutes
Life and Work (magazine)

Free Church of Scotland
General Assembly minutes, generally titled: Proceedings and Minutes of the General Assembly of [date]
Jewish Mission Committee minutes (exact title varies)
Jewish Mission Committee General Assembly report: title generally based on usage of Committee name
Women's Jewish Missionary Association minutes
Women's Jewish Missionary Association General Assembly report
Monthly and Missionary Record (magazine)

United Free Church of Scotland
General Assembly minutes, generally titled: Proceedings and Minutes of the General Assembly of [date]
Colonial, Continental and Jewish Committee minutes
Jewish Mission Committee minutes
Women's Jewish Missionary Association minutes
Missionary Record (magazine)

United Presbyterian Church
Synod minutes, generally titled: Proceedings of the Synod of the United Presbyterian Church [date]
General Minute Book – Missions

Other primary sources

National Library of Scotland, Edinburgh
Missionary manuscripts are catalogued in volume 6 of the NLS Catalogue of Manuscripts; documents are also to be found in Accession records and in Deposit 298. These contain most committee minutes, the remainder of Alexander Paterson's unpublished materials, as well as a number of (mainly outgoing) letters, reports and miscellaneous items.

I am grateful to Dr Gavin White, formerly of Trinity College, University of Glasgow, for explaining, in a telephone conversation on 24.2.1999 and in a meeting in St Andrews on 26.4.2000, the lack of communications from missionaries back to their churches in Scotland: the NLS catalogue simply notes that many documents were lost during the war (see page vii in National Library of Scotland, (1984) Catalogue of Manuscripts acquired since 1925 Volume VI Manuscripts 7530–8022 (Scottish Foreign Mission Records 1827-1929), Edinburgh). During World War II, when European cities were being bombed for the first time and most people had little idea about the efficacy or otherwise of such bombing, panic ensued amongst those responsible for the Church of Scotland offices at 121 George Street, Edinburgh. At that time, much of the material that would be required for this book (and the work of many others) was kept in boxes in the attic of the building, although not, it appears, in any organised fashion. There was a worry that a bomb landing on the roof would ignite the dry paper in the attic and the building would be destroyed. The attic was therefore emptied and most of the contents destroyed instead. Amongst the few things that escaped the devastation were so-called 'flimsies' – the duplicate records of out-going letters – because the leather bindings were regarded as too valuable to destroy (the minutes of some of the Committees were unaffected by these events as copies were held elsewhere). Thankfully, these are now safely archived in the NLS; given that today's Church of Scotland appears to be treating much of its material in a similarly cavalier manner as in the past, one can only hope for the sake of future historians that as much as possible is passed on to the NLS or another archive. In conclusion, it must be noted that incredible though it may now seem, it apparently took two weeks for office staff to realise the enormity of what they had done. Dr. White was told of these events by a Mr Hamilton, a staff member at the Church of Scotland offices. Although Hamilton was not responsible for these acts, his account is regarded as reliable by Dr White and others, and although these events have yet to be documented, Dr White has elaborated on them in public several times without contradiction or denial being offered.

New College Library and CSCNWW, University of Edinburgh
New College Library contains copies of most of the public General Assembly documents, e.g. Reports, Proceedings etc. The Centre for the Study of Christianity in the Non Western World holds a large collection of missionary pamphlets and other documents. At the time of writing, cataloguing was still in progress.

Dundee University Archives

The collection, reference MS38, consists primarily of Herbert Torrance's photographs, and some text items. The photographs depict the town, hospital and staff, but also reflect his interest in flora and fauna. The collection was deposited by members of the Torrance family. Much of it dates from the inter-war years; the looting of the hospital during World War I resulted in the loss of most of David Torrance's material. Details can be located at: http://www.dundee.ac.uk/archives/ms038.htm (accessed 4.10.2004).

Secondary sources

Unpublished sources

Heron, Alasdair I C, (1980a) *Das schottische Bekenntnis (1560)*, revised typescript of a lecture given at the Protestant Faculty of Theology, Munich, on 30.6.1980

Houghton, Nick R P, (1997), *Pioneering with the Gospel in South-West Arabia: The Keith-Falconer Mission between 1885 and 1906*, unpublished MTh thesis, University of Edinburgh

Ritchie, Lionel Alexander, (2005?) entry for Keith in the forthcoming *New Dictionary of National Biography*

Sizer, Stephen, (2003), *Christian Zionism: Fueling the Arab-Israeli Conflict. Historical Roots, Theological Basis and Political Consequences*, unpublished PhD thesis, Middlesex University, (CD version, via http://www.sizers.org (accessed 20.6.03))

Stockdale, Nancy L, (2000) *Gender and Colonialism in Palestine 1800-1948: Encounters among English, Arab and Jewish Women*, unpublished PhD thesis, University of California Santa Barbara

Published sources

Abdullah, Thabit, (1997) 'Arab views of northern Europeans in medieval history and geography', in *Images of the Other: Europe and the Muslim World Before 1700*, ed. David R Blanks, series: Cairo Papers in Social Science, vol. 19, monograph 2, summer 1996, Cairo, 73-80

Anderson, Benedict, (1983) *Imagined Communities, London*, 2nd ed. 1991

Anderson, M S, (1970) *The Great Powers and the Near East. 1774-1923*, London

Andrew, Alexander, (1891) *My Visit to Palestine*, Paisley, nd (but journey began February 1891, publication probably that year or soon after)

Ateek, Naim Stifan, (1989) *Justice, and only Justice. A Palestinian Theology of Liberation*, New York

Auld, Graeme, (1996) 'Hebrew and Old Testament', in *Disruption to Diversity: Edinburgh Divinity 1846-1996*, eds. David F Wright, Gary B Badcock, Edinburgh, 53-71

Bäcker, F, (1937) 'Die Arbeit der Missionare im Urteil orientalischer Christen', in *Der Adventbote: Gemeindeblatt der Siebentags-Adventisten*, Hamburg, vol. 43, part 12, 189-190

Barth, Karl, (1938) *The Knowledge of God and the Service of God. The Gifford Lectures, 1938*, London

Baumann, Arnulf H, (1998a) 'Franz Delitzsch (1813-1890)', in *Auf dem Wege zum christlich-jüdischen Gespräch: 125 Jahre Evangelisch-lutherischer Zentralverein für Zeugnis und Dienst unter Juden und Christen*, ed. Arnulf H Baumann, Münster, 48-59

Baumann, Arnulf H, (1998b) 'Gustav Dalman (1855-1941)', in *Auf dem Wege zum christlich-jüdischen Gespräch: 125 Jahre Evangelisch-lutherischer Zentralverein für Zeugnis und Dienst unter Juden und Christen*, ed. Arnulf H Baumann, Münster, 60-69

Beaver, R Pierce, (1962) *Ecumenical Beginnings in Protestant World Mission: A History of Comity*, New York

Bebbington, David W, (1989) *Evangelicalism in modern Britain. A history from the 1730s to the 1980s*, London

Bhabha, Homi, (1997) 'Of Mimicry and Man: The Ambivalence of Colonial Discourse', in *Tensions of Empire. Colonial Cultures in a Bourgeois World*, eds. Frederick Cooper, Ann Laura Stoler, Berkeley, 152-160

Binfield, Clyde, (1994) 'Jews in Evangelical Dissent: The British Society, The Herschell Connection and the Pre-Millenarian Thread', in *Prophecy and Eschatology*, series: Subsidia 10, ed. Michael Wilks, Oxford, 225-270

Blaikie, William Garden, (1893) *After Fifty Years*, London/Edinburgh

Bonar, Andrew A, (1865) *Palestine for the Young*, London

Bonar, Andrew A, (1960) *Diary and Life,* (no place of publication)

Bonar, Andrew A & McCheyne, Robert Murray, (1843) *Narrative of a Visit to the Holy Land and Mission of Inquiry to the Jews*, Edinburgh

Bonar, Andrew A & McCheyne, Robert Murray, (1996) *Mission of Discovery: The Beginnings of Modern Jewish Evangelism. The journal of Bonar and McCheyne's Mission of Inquiry*, ed. Allan Harman, Fearn (Ross-shire)

Bonk, Jonathon, (1989) *The Theory and Practice of Missionary Identification, 1860-1920*, series: Studies in the History of Missions, vol. 2, New York

Bonk, Jonathon, (1991) *Missions and Money: Affluence as a Western Missionary Problem*, series: American Society of Missiology Series, No. 15, Maryknoll

Bradley, Ian, (1997) *Abide with Me: The World of Victorian Hymns*, London

Braybrooke, Marcus, (1990) *Time to Meet. Towards a deeper relationship between Jews and Christians*, London

Braybrooke, Marcus, (2000) *Christian-Jewish Dialogue: The Next Steps,* London

Brown, Callum, (1997) *Religion and Society in Scotland since 1707*, Edinburgh

Bruce, F F, (1977) 'The History of New Testament Study', in *New Testament Interpretation. Essays in Principles and Methods*, ed. I Howard Marshall, Exeter, 21-59

Burleigh, J H S, (1960) *A Church History of Scotland*, Oxford

Cameron, George C, (1979) *The Scots Kirk in London*, Oxford

Cannadine, David, (2001) *Ornamentalism: how the British saw their Empire*, London

Carroll, Robert P, (1991) *Wolf in the Sheepfold. The Bible as Problematic for Theology*, London, 2nd ed. 1997

Checkland, Olive and Sydney, (1984) *Industry and Ethos. Scotland 1832-1914*, Edinburgh, 2nd ed. 1989

Cheyette, Bryan, (1993) *Constructions of 'the Jew' in English literature and society: racial representations, 1875-1945*, Cambridge

Cheyne, Alex, (1988) 'The Bible and Change in the Nineteenth Century', in *The Bible in Scottish Life and Literature*, ed. David F Wright, Edinburgh, 192-207

Clark, Christopher, (1995), *The Politics of Conversion: Missionary Protestantism and the Jews in Prussia 1728-1941*, Oxford

Clavero, Dolores, (1998) 'The Discourse of the Newly-Converted Christian in the Work of the Andean Chronicler Guaman Poma de Ayala', in *Christian Encounters with the Other*, ed. John C Hawley, New York, 44-55

Cleveland, William L, (1994) *A History of the Modern Middle East,* Boulder/Oxford

Colley, Linda, (1992) *Britons: Forging the Nation. 1707-1837*, London

Comaroff, Jean and John, (1991) *Of Revelation and Revolution. Christianity, Colonialism, and Consciousness in South Africa.* Volume I, Chicago/London

Courbage, Youssef/Fargues, Philippe, (1997) *Christians and Jews under Islam*, London

Crombie, Kelvin, (1991) *For the Love of Zion. Christian witness and the restoration of Israel*, London

Dalman, Gustaf, (1900) *'Nicht sei doch Streit!' Eine Osteransprache an Juden*, Leipzig

Dalrymple, William, (2002) *White Mughals. Love and Betrayal in Eighteenth-Century India*, London

Davidson, Andrew Bruce, (1903) *Old Testament Prophecy*, ed. J A Paterson, Edinburgh

Davidson, Andrew Bruce, (1904) *The Theology of the Old Testament*, ed. S D F Salmond, Edinburgh

Dawn, C Ernest, (1991) 'The Origins of Arab Nationalism', in *The Origins of Arab Nationalism*, eds. Rashid Khalidi, Lisa Anderson, Muhammad Muslih, Reeva S Simon, New York, 3-30

Dawn, C Ernest, (1993) 'From Ottomanism to Arabism: The Origin of an Ideology', in *The Modern Middle East: A Reader*, eds. Albert Hourani, Philip S Khoury, Mary C Wilson, London, 375-393

Deringil, Selim, (1998) *The Well-Protected Domains: Ideology and the Legitimation of Power in the Ottoman Empire, 1876-1909*, London

Drummond, Andrew L/Bulloch, James, (1978) *The Church in Late Victorian Scotland 1874-1900*, Edinburgh

Durst, Stefan, (1993) *Jerusalem als ökumenisches Problem im 20. Jahrhundert,* Pfaffenweiler

Ewing, William, (1914) *The Holy Land and Glasgow*, series: Our Jewish Missions I, Edinburgh

Ewing, William, (1925) *Paterson of Hebron: "The Hakim" Missionary Life in the Mountain of Judah*, London, (nd – 1925, 1930, 1931?)

Farah, Rafiq A, (2002) *In troubled waters: A History of the Anglican Church in Jerusalem, 1841-1998*, Leicester

Fargues, Philippe, (1998) 'The Arab Christians of the Middle East: A Demographic Perspective', in *Christian Communities in the Arab Middle East: the challenge of the future*, ed. Andrea Pacini, Oxford, 48-66

Faroqhi, Suraiya, (1992) 'In Search of Ottoman History', in *New Approaches to State and Peasant in Ottoman History*, eds. Halil Berktay, Suraiya Faroqhi, London, 211-241

Fawaz, Leila Tarazi, (1994) *An Occasion for War – Civil Conflict in Lebanon and Damascus in 1860*, London

Feldman, Louis H, (1993) *Jew and Gentile in the Ancient World: Attitudes and Interactions from Alexander to Justinian*, Princeton

Feldtkeller, Andreas, (2000) *Sieben Thesen zur Missionsgeschichte*, series: Berliner Beiträge zur Missionsgeschichte, Berlin, Heft 1, September

Finestein, Israel, (1991) 'British Opinion and the Holy Land in the Nineteenth Century: Personalities and Further Themes', in *With Eyes Toward Zion III – Western Societies and the Holy Land*, eds. Moshe Davis, Yehoshua Ben-Arieh, New York, 227-238

Fleck, Andrew, (1998) 'Crusoe's Shadow: Christianity, Colonization and the Other', in *Christian Encounters with the Other*, ed. John C Hawley, New York, 74-89

Fleming, J R, (1927) *A History of the Church in Scotland 1843-1874*, Edinburgh

Foerster, Frank, (1991) *Mission im Heiligen Land. Der Jerusalems-Verein zu Berlin 1852-1945*, series: Missionswissenschaftliche Forschungen, vol. 25, Gütersloh

Frankel, Jonathan, (1997) *The Damascus Affair. "Ritual Murder," Politics, and the Jews in 1840*, Cambridge

Free Church of Scotland, (1885) *Tabular Abstracts of the Sums Contributed Yearly to the Various Funds and Schemes of the Church During the Forty-Two Years from the Disruption to 1884-85 Inclusive, With Remarks Thereon by the Convener of the Finance Committee*, Edinburgh

Friedman, David M, (2001) *A Mind of Its Own. A Cultural History of the Penis*, Harmondsworth

Frykenberg, Robert Eric, (1996) *History and Belief: The Foundations of Historical Understanding*, Grand Rapids

Gikandi, Simon, (1996) *Maps of Englishness: Writing Identity in the Culture of Colonialism*, Columbia, New York

Gill, Sean, (1998) 'How Muscular was Victorian Christianity? Thomas Hughes and the Cult of Christian Manliness Reconsidered', in *Gender and Christian Religion*, ed. R N Swanson, series: Studies in Church History, vol. 34, Woodbridge/Rochester, 421-430

Goodwin, Isobel, (2000) *May you live to be 120! The Story of Tabeetha School, Jaffa. 1863-1983*, Edinburgh

Gräbe, Uwe, (1999) *Kontextuelle palästinensische Theologie. Streitbare und umstrittene Beiträge zum ökumenischen und interreligiösen Gespräch*, series: Missionswissenschaftliche Forschungen, Neue Folge, vol. 9, Erlangen

Graham, W D, (1993) 'Beyond the Borders of Scotland: The Church's Missionary Enterprise', in *Crown Him Lord of All: Essays on the Life and Witness of the Free Church of Scotland*, ed. Clement Graham, Edinburgh, 91-105

Grant, Maurice, (1993) 'The Heirs of the Disruption in Crisis and Recovery 1893-1920', in *Crown Him Lord of All: Essays on the Life and Witness of the Free Church of Scotland*, ed. Clement Graham, Edinburgh, 1-36

Grundmann, Christoffer H, (1991) 'The Contribution of Medical Missions: The Intercultural Transfer of Standards and Values', in *Academic Medicine*, December, vol. 66, no. 12, 731-733

Haldane, Elizabeth S, (1933) *The Scotland of our Fathers: A Study of Scottish Life in the Nineteenth Century*, London

Hall, John, (1914) *Israel in Europe*, series: Our Jewish Missions II, Edinburgh

Hastings, Adrian, (2001) *A History of English Christianity 1920-2000*, London, (4th ed. 2001: first published 1986 as *A History of English Christianity 1920-1985*)

Haufler-Musiol, Karin, (1998) '125 Jahre Zentralverein: Ein historischer Überblick', in *Auf dem Wege zum christlich-jüdischen Gespräch: 125 Jahre Evangelisch-lutherischer Zentralverein für Zeugnis und Dienst unter Juden und Christen*, ed. Arnulf H Baumann, Münster, 11-46

Heron, Alasdair I C, (1980b) *A Century of Protestant Theology*, Cambridge

Hewat, Elizabeth G K, (1960) *Vision and Achievement 1796-1956. A History of the Foreign Missions of the Churches united in the Church of Scotland*, Edinburgh

Heyer, Friedrich, (2000) *2000 Jahre Kirchengeschichte des Heiligen Landes. Märtyrer, Mönche, Kirchenväter, Kreuzfahrer, Patriarchen, Ausgräber und Pilger*, series: Studien zur Orientalischen Kirchengeschichte, vol. 11, Hamburg

Hill, Myrtle, (2000) 'Women in the Irish Protestant Foreign Missions c. 1873-1914: Representations and Motivations', in *Missions and Missionaries*, eds. Pieter N Holtrup, Hugh McLeod, Woodbridge/Rochester, 170-185

Hillenbrand, Carole, (1999) *The Crusades: Islamic Perspectives*, Edinburgh

Hilton, Michael, (1994) *The Christian Effect on Jewish Life*, London

Hobsbawm, Eric J, (1962) *The Age of Revolution 1789-1848*, London

Hobsbawm, Eric J, (1968) *Industry and Empire*, Harmondsworth, 1999

Hobsbawm, Eric J, (1975) *The Age of Capital 1848-1875*, London

Hobsbawm, Eric J, (1987) *The Age of Empire 1875-1914*, London

Hobsbawm, Eric J, (1990) *Nations and Nationalisms since 1870. Programme, Myth, Reality*, Cambridge, 2nd ed. 1992

Hourani, Albert, (1962) *Arabic Thought in the Liberal Age 1798-1939*, Cambridge, 2nd ed. 1983

Hourani, Albert, (1991) *A History of the Arab Peoples*, London

House of Commons, (1847) *Third Report from the Select Committee on Sites for Churches (Scotland); together with the Minutes of Evidence, Appendix and Index*, London, minutes 6366, 6367

Hummel, Ruth and Thomas, (1995) *Patterns of the sacred: English Protestant and Russian Orthodox pilgrims of the Nineteenth Century*, London

Hyam, Ronald, (1990) *Empire and Sexuality: The British Experience*, series, Studies in Imperialism, ed. John M MacKenzie, Manchester/New York

Issawi, Charles, (1988) *The Fertile Crescent 1800-1914: A Documentary Economic History*, New York, Oxford

Jansen, Willy, (2000) 'Fragmentation of the Christian minority in Jordan. Conversion, marriage and gender', in *Anthropologists and the Missionary Endeavour. Experiences and*

Reflections, eds. Ad Borsboom, Jean Kommers, series, Nijmegen Studies in Development and Cultural Change, Saarbrücken

Jeremias, Joachim, (1958) *Jesus' Promise to the Nations*, London

Jessup, Henry Harris, (1910) *Fifty-Three Years in Syria*, Vol. 1, New York

Jochmann, Werner, (1985) 'Struktur und Funktion des deutschen Antisemitismus 1878-1914', in *Antisemitismus. Von der Judenfeindschaft zum Holocaust*, eds. Herbert A Strauss, Norbert Kampe, Bonn, 99-142

Johnson, William Stacy & Leith, John H (ed.), (1993) *Reformed Reader: a Sourcebook in Christian Theology. Volume 1: Classical Beginnings, 1519-1799*, Louisville

Jones, W Idris, (1935) *The Arab*, series: The Races Beyond, The Committee on Publications for the Foreign Mission Committee, Church of Scotland, np (probably Edinburgh), nd (probably 1935)

Jongeneel, Jan A B, (1995) *Philosophy, science, and theology of mission in the 19th and 20th centuries: a missiological encyclopedia. Part I: The philosophy and science of mission*, series: Studies in the Intercultural History of Christianity, vol. 92, Frankfurt am Main

Kabbani, Rana, (1986) *Imperial Fictions. Europe's Myths of Orient*, London, 1994

Kane, Eileen, (2005) 'Pilgrims, Piety and Politics: The Founding of the First Russian Ecclesiastical Mission in Jerusalem', in *Christian witness between continuity and new beginnings: modern historical missions in the Middle East,* ed. Michael Marten, series: Studien zur Orientalischen Kirchengeschichte, Hamburg, (forthcoming)

Kernohan, Robert, (1979) S*cotland's 'Life and Work'. A Scottish view of God's world through 'Life and Work': 1879-1979*, Edinburgh

Kerr, David, (2000) 'Muhammad: Prophet of Liberation – a Christian Perspective from Political Theology', in *Studies in World Christianity*, vol. 6, no. 2, 139-174

Kerr, David, (2003) 'Maronites and Missionaries: A critical appraisal of the affair of As'ad al-Shidyāq (1825-1829)', in *A faithful presence: essays for Kenneth Cragg*, ed. David Thomas with Clare Amos, London, 219-236

Khalidi, Walid (ed.), (1992) *All That Remains: The Palestinian Villages Occupied and Depopulated by Israel in 1948*, Washington

Kiernan, Victor G, (1995) *Imperialism and its contradictions*, edited and introduced by Harvey J Kaye, London

Kornrumpf, Hans-Jürgen & Jutta, (1998) *Fremde im Osmanischen Reich 1826-1912/13: Bio-bibliographisches Register*, Stutensee, (publ. by authors)

Küng, Hans, (1992) *Judaism. The Religious Situation of our Time*, London

Levison, Frederick, (1989) *Christian and Jew: The Life of Leon Levison, 1881-1936*, Edinburgh

Livingstone, W P, (1915) *Mary Slessor of Calabar: Pioneer Missionary,* London, 21st ed. 1924

Livingstone, W P, (1923) *A Galilee Doctor. Being a Sketch of the Career of Dr. D. W. Torrance of Tiberias*, London, nd (probably 1923)

Lynch, Michael, (1991) *Scotland. A New History*, London

Maalouf, Amin, (1983) *Les croisades vues par les Arabes*, Paris

Macdonald, Lesley Orr, (2000) *A Unique and Glorious Mission. Women and Presbyterianism in Scotland, 1830-1930*, Edinburgh

Mackinnon, James, (1921) *The Social and Industrial History of Scotland From the Union to the Present Time*, London

Macquarrie, Alan, (1997) *Scotland and the Crusades 1095-1560*, Edinburgh

Makdisi, Ussama, (2000) *The Culture of Sectarianism: Community, History, and Violence in Nineteenth Century Ottoman Lebanon*, Berkeley, Los Angeles, London

Makdisi, Ussama, (2002) 'After 1860: Debating Religion, Reform, and Nationalism in the Ottoman Empire', in *International Journal of Middle East Studies*, vol. 34, 601-617

Marten, Michael, (2001) 'Representation and misrepresentation in 19th century Lebanon – Scottish and American missionaries in conflict', in *Orientalische Christen zwischen Repression und Migration. Beiträge zur jüngeren Geschichte und Gegenwartslage*, ed. Martin Tamcke, series: Studien zur Orientalischen Kirchengeschichte, vol. 13, Hamburg

Marten, Michael, (2002) 'The Free Church of Scotland in 19th-century Lebanon', *Chronos. Revue d'Histoire de l'Université Balamand*, No. 5, 51-106

McAllister, Susan Fleming, (1998) 'Cross-Cultural Dress in Victorian British Missionary Narratives: Dressing for Eternity', in *Christian Encounters with the Other*, ed. John C Hawley, New York, 122-134

McCarthy, Justin, (1990) *The Population of Palestine – Population History and Statistics of the Late Ottoman Period and the Mandate*, New York

McDougall, David, (1941) *In Search of Israel. A Chronicle of the Jewish Mission of the Church of Scotland*, London, Edinburgh, etc.

McLeod, Hugh, (1981) *Religion and the People of Western Europe 1789-1970*, Oxford

MECC, (1988) *What is Western Fundamentalist Christian Zionism?*, Limassol

Meek, Donald, (1988) 'The Bible and Social Change in the nineteenth Century Highlands', in *The Bible in Scottish Life and Literature*, ed. David F Wright, Edinburgh, 179-191

Merkley, Paul Charles, (1998) *The Politics of Christian Zionism 1891-1948*, London/Portland

Michaels, Anne, (1997) *Fugitive Pieces*, London

Mildenberger, Friedrich, (1981) *Geschichte der deutschen evangelischen Theologie im 19. und 20. Jahrhundert*, series: Theologische Wissenschaft, vol. 10, Stuttgart

Morton, Colin, (1999) 'Motives for the Scottish Mission in Palestine. 19th and 20th Centuries', in *Patterns of the Past, Prospects for the Future. The Christian Heritage in the Holy Land*, eds. Thomas Hummel, Kevork Hintlian, Ulf Carmesund, London

Moscrop, John James, (2000) *Measuring Jerusalem. The Palestine Exploration Fund and British Interests in the Holy Land*, London, New York

Murray, Stephen O, (1997) 'Some Nineteenth-Century Reports of Islamic Homosexualities', in *Islamic Homosexualities*, eds. Stephen O Murray, Will Roscoe, New York, 204-221

Murre-van den Berg, Heleen L, (2000) 'Why Protestant Churches? The American Board and the Eastern Churches: Mission Among 'Nominal' Christians (1820-1870)', in *Missions and Missionaries*, eds. Pieter N Holtrup, Hugh McLeod, Woodbridge/Rochester, 98-111

National Library of Scotland, (1984) *Catalogue of Manuscripts acquired since 1925 Volume VI Manuscripts 7530–8022* (Scottish Foreign Mission Records 1827-1929), Edinburgh

Neill, Stephen, (1964) *A History of Christian Missions*, Harmondsworth, revised edition 1986

Nielsen, Jørgen S, (2003) 'Is there an escape from the history of Christian-Muslim Relations?', in *A Faithful Presence: essays for Kenneth Cragg*, ed. David Thomas with Clare Amos, London, 350-361

O'Mahony, Anthony, (1994) 'Church, State and the Christian Communities and the Holy Places of Palestine', in *Christians in the Holy Land*, eds. Michael Prior, William Taylor, London, 11-27

O'Mahony, Anthony, (1999) 'Palestinian Christians: Religion, Politics and Society, c. 1800-1948', in *Palestinian Christians: Religion, Politics and Society in the Holy Land*, ed. Anthony O'Mahony, London, 9-55

Ogilvie, J N, (1924) *Our Empire's Debt to Missions: The Duff Missionary Lecture, 1923*, London, (preface dated)

Okkenhaug, Inger Marie, (2002) *The Quality of Heroic Living, of High Endeavour and Adventure. Anglican Mission, Women and Education in Palestine, 1888-1948*, series: Studies in Christian Mission, ed. Marc R Spindler, Leiden

Okkenhaug, Inger Marie, (2005) '"To give the boys energy, manliness, and self-command in temper": the Anglican Male Ideal and St. George's College in Jerusalem, ca. 1890-1940', in *Gender, Religion and Change in the Middle East: Two Hundred Years of History*, eds. Inger Marie Okkenhaug, Ingvild Flaskerud, Oxford, 47-66

Owen, Roger, (1981) *The Middle East in the World Economy 1800-1914*, London, New York, 1993

Owen, Roger, (1982) 'Introduction', *Studies in the Economic and Social History of Palestine in the Nineteenth and Twentieth Centuries*, ed. Roger Owen, London, 1-9

Pamuk, Şevket, (1994) 'Money in the Ottoman Empire, 1326-1914', in *An Economic and Social History of the Ottoman Empire, Vol 2: 1600-1914* ed. Halil İnalcik with Donald Quataert, Cambridge, 945-985

Pappe, Ilan, (2004) *A History of Modern Palestine. One Land, Two Peoples*, Cambridge

Porter, Andrew, (1997) '"Cultural Imperialism" and Protestant Missionary Enterprise, 1780-1914', in *Journal of Imperial and Commonwealth History vol. 25, no. 3, September*, 367-391

Porter, Bernard, (1975) *The Lion's Share: A Short History of British Imperialism 1850-1995*, Harlow, 3rd ed. 1996

Prior, Michael, (2003) 'The State of the Art: Biblical Scholarship and the Holy Land', in *Holy Land Studies*, vol. 1, no. 2, March, 192-218

Proctor, J H, (1997) 'Scottish Missionaries and the Struggle for Palestine, 1917-48', in *Middle Eastern Studies*, vol. 33, no. 3, July, 613-629

Pui-lan, Kwok, (1996) 'The Image of the "White Lady": Gender and Race in Christian Mission', in *The Power of Naming: A Concilium Reader in Feminist Liberation Theology*, ed. Elisabeth Schüssler-Fiorenza, Maryknoll/London, 250-258

Quataert, Donald, (1994a) 'Ottoman Manufacturing in the Nineteenth Century', in *Manufacturing in the Ottoman Empire and Turkey, 1500-1950*, ed. Donald Quataert, New York, 87-121

Quataert, Donald, (1994b) 'Part IV: The Age of Reforms, 1812-1914', in *An Economic and Social History of the Ottoman Empire. Volume Two: 1600-1914*, ed. Halil İnalcik with Donald Quataert, Cambridge, 1994, 1997, pp759-943

Réamonn, Páraic, (2001) 'Christians and Jews, Catholics and Protestants', in *WARC Update*, September, vol. 11, no. 3, 11-12

Richter, Julius, (1910) *A History of Protestant Missions in the Near East*, Edinburgh

Ritchie, Lionel Alexander, (2002) 'Daniel Edward (1815-1896) and the Free Church of Scotland mission to the Jews in Central Europe', in *Records of the Scottish Church History Society, vol. XXXI*, 173-187

Rohls, Jan, (1987) *Theologie reformierter Bekenntnisschriften: von Zürich bis Barmen*, Göttingen

Ross, Andrew C, (1972) 'Scottish missionary concern 1874-1914. A golden era?', in *Scottish Historical Review*, vol. LI/I, no. 151, April, 52-72

Ross, Andrew C, (2002) *David Livingstone. Mission and Empire*, London/New York

Rousseau, John J/Arav, Rami, (1996) *Jesus and his world. An archaeological and cultural dictionary*, London

Roxborogh, John, (1999) *Thomas Chalmers: Enthusiast for Mission. The Christian Good of Scotland and the Rise of the Missionary Movement*, Carlisle/Edinburgh

Said, Edward W, (1978) *Orientalism: Western Conceptions of the Orient*, London, 1995

Said, Edward W, (1993) *Culture and Imperialism*, London

Salibi, Kamal, (1988) *A House of Many Mansions. The History of Lebanon Reconsidered*, Berkeley, Los Angeles, London

Salt, Jeremy, (1993) *Imperialism, Evangelism and the Ottoman Armenians 1878-1896*, London

Saperstein, Marc, (1989) *Moments of Crisis in Jewish-Christian Relations*, London

Saphir, Adolph, (1950s) *Christ and Israel. Lectures and Addresses*, collected and edited by David Baron, Jerusalem, nd (the edition used here – 'Printed in Israel' – is possibly from the 1950s; it was originally published in ca. 1911 or 1912: c.f. UFC-CCJ 27.2.1912)

Schein, Sylvia, (1991) *Fideles Crucis. The Papacy, the West, and the Recovery of the Holy Land 1274-1314*, Oxford

Schmelz, U O, (1990) 'Population characteristics of Jerusalem and Hebron regions according to Ottoman census of 1905', in *Ottoman Palestine 1800-1914. Studies in Economic and Social History*, ed. Gad G Gilbar, Leiden, 15-67

Selvidge, Marla J, (1996) *Notorious Voices: Feminist Biblical Interpretation, 1500-1920*, London

Shaw, Stanford J, (1991) *The Jews of the Ottoman Empire and the Turkish Republic*, London

Shepherd, Naomi, (1987) *The Zealous Intruders. The Western Rediscovery of Palestine*, London

Sherman, A J, (1997) *Mandate Days. British Lives in Palestine 1918-1948*, London

Sinno, Abdel-Raouf, (1982) *Deutsche Interessen in Syrien und Palästina 1841-1898: Aktivitäten religiöser Institutionen, wirtschaftliche und politische Einflüsse*, Berlin

Slomp, Jan, (2002) 'Calvin and the Turks', in *Encounters: Documents for Muslim Christian Understanding* (Pontificio Istituto di Studi Arabi e d'Islamistica), October, No. 288, 3-15

Smith, George Adam, (1894) *The Historical Geography of the Holy Land*, London, 25th ed. 1931

Smith, Jane I, (1997) 'Some Contemporary Protestant Theological Reflections on Pluralism: implications for Christian-Muslim Understanding', in *Islam and Christian-Muslim Relations*, vol. 8, no. 1, 67-83

Suermann, Harald, (2001) *Zwischen Halbmond und Davidstern: Christliche Theologie in Palästina heute*, Freiburg i. Br.

Swan, Annie S, (1937) *Seed Time and Harvest. The Story of the hundred years' work of the Women's Foreign Mission of the Church of Scotland*, London

Syrian Protestant College, (1904) *Catalogue of the Syrian Protestant College, Beirût, Syria, 38th Year, 1903-1904*, Beirut

Taber, Charles R, (1990-1) 'The Missionary Movement and the Anthropologists', in *Bulletin of the Scottish Institute of Missionary Studies*, No 6-7, 16-32

Taylor, Peter J, (1993) *Political Geography. World-Economy, Nation-State and Locality*, Harlow, 1985, 3rd ed. 1993

Thomson, Andrew, (1883) *In the Holy Land*, Edinburgh

Thorne, Susan, (1997) '"The Conversion of Englishmen and the Conversion of the World Inseparable": Missionary Imperialism and the Language of Class in Early Industrial Britain', in *Tensions of Empire. Colonial Cultures in a Bourgeois World*, eds. Frederick Cooper, Ann Laura Stoler, Berkeley, Los Angeles, London, 238-262

Tibawi, Abdul Latif, (1961) *British Interests in Palestine 1800-1901. A Study of Religious and Educational Enterprise*, Oxford

Tibawi, Abdul Latif, (1966) *American Interests in Syria 1800-1901. A Study of Educational, Literary and Religious work*, Oxford

Tibawi, Abdul Latif, (1969) *Jerusalem. Its Place in Islam and Arab History*, Beirut

Trollope, Joanna, (1983) *Britannia's Daughters. Women of the British Empire*, London

Tulloch, Graham, (1989) *A History of the Scots Bible with selected texts*, Aberdeen

Unger, Manfred, (1998) 'Das vergessene Institutum Judaicum', *Leipziger Blätter*, 33, 58-59

Ursinus, Michael, (1993) '"Nicht die Türken siegten über Byzanz, sondern Byzanz über die Türken." Zur Vergangenheitsbewältigung im Osmanischen Reich am Vorabend des Ersten Weltkrieges', in *Periplus: Jahrbuch für aussereuropäische Geschichte*, vol. 3, 47-60

Valognes, Jean-Pierre, (1994) *Vie et mort des chrétiens d'Orient. Des origines à nos jours*, Paris

Verdeil, Chantal, (2001) 'Travailler à la Renaissance de l'orient Chrétien: les Missions Latines en Syrie (1830-1945)', in *Proche-Orient Chrétien*, 51, 267-316

Vital, David, (1999) *A People Apart. A political history of the Jews in Europe 1789-1939*, Oxford

Vogel, Lester I, (1993) *To See a Promised Land: Americans and the Holy Land in the Nineteenth Century,* Pennsylvania

Walker, N L, (1895) *Chapters from the History of the Free Church of Scotland,* Edinburgh

Walls, Andrew F, (1982) "The heavy artillery of the missionary army': the domestic importance of the nineteenth-century medical missionary', in *The Church and Healing* (Papers read at the twentieth summer meeting and the twenty-first winter meeting of the Ecclesiastical Historical Society), ed. W J Shiels, Oxford, 287-297

Ware, K T, (1972) 'Orthodox and Catholics in the Seventeenth Century: Schism or Intercommunion?', in *Schism, Heresy and Religious Protest* (Papers read at the tenth summer meeting and the eleventh winter meeting of the Ecclesiastical Historical Society), ed. Derek Baker, Cambridge, 259-276

Warren, Max, (1967) *Social History and Christian Mission,* London

Weber, Eugen, (1999) *Apocalypses: Prophecies, Cults and Millennial Beliefs through the Ages,* London

Wehler, Hans-Ulrich, (2001) *Nationalismus: Geschichte, Formen, Folgen,* München

Weir, Robert W, (1900) *A History of the Foreign Missions of the Church of Scotland,* Edinburgh

Wells, James, (1909) *Stewart of Lovedale: The Life of James Stewart,* London

White, Gavin, (1977) "Highly Preposterous': Origins of Scottish Missions', in *Records of the Scottish Church History Society,* vol. XIX, 111-124

Wilkinson, John, (1991) *The Coogate Doctors: The History of the Edinburgh Medical Missionary Society 1841 to 1991,* Edinburgh

Williams, C Peter, (1982) 'Healing and evangelism: the place of medicine in later Victorian missionary thinking', in *The Church and Healing* (Papers read at the twentieth summer meeting and the twenty-first winter meeting of the Ecclesiastical Historical Society), ed. W J Shiels, Oxford, 271-285

Wilson, James H/Wells, James, (eds.), (1895) *The Sea of Galilee Mission of the Free Church of Scotland,* Edinburgh

Wolff, Joseph, (1827) *Missionary Journal and Memoir of the Rev. Joseph Wolff, Missionary to the Jews: comprising his first visit to Palestine in the years 1821 & 1822 (Vol I),* London

Wolff, Joseph, (1828) *Missionary Journal of the Rev. Joseph Wolff, Missionary to the Jews: comprising his second visit to Palestine & Syria in the years 1823 & 1824 (Vol II),* London

Wolff, Joseph, (1829) *Missionary Journal of the Rev. Joseph Wolff, Missionary to the Jews (Vol III),* London

Wolffe, John, (1996) 'Unity in Diversity? North Atlantic Evangelical Thought in the Mid-Nineteenth Century', in *Unity and Diversity in the Church* (Papers read at the 1994 summer meeting and the 1995 winter meeting of the Ecclesiastical Historical Society), ed. R N Swanson, Oxford, 363-375

Wortabet, John, (1860) *Researches into the Religions of Syria: or, Sketches, Historical and Doctrinal, of its Religious Sects,* London

Wright, George Ernest/Filson, Floyd Vivian (eds.), (1946) *The Westminster Historical Atlas to the Bible,* London

Yapp, Malcolm E, (1987) *The Making of the Modern Near East 1792-1923*, London

Zwemer, Samuel M, (1924) *The Law of Apostasy in Islam. Answering the Question why there are so few Moslem Converts, and giving examples of their Moral Courage and Martyrdom*, London, Edinburgh, New York, (preface dated)

INDEX